BATTLE FOR BAQUBAH

Killing Our Way Out

1SG Robert S. Colella, Retired

Foreword by Major Pete Chapman

Edited by John David Kudrick & Stacy Shawiak

iUniverse, Inc.
Bloomington

Battle for Baqubah
Killing Our Way Out

iUniverse books may be ordered through booksellers or by contacting:

iUniverse
1663 Liberty Drive
Bloomington, IN 47403
www.iuniverse.com
1-800-Authors (1-800-288-4677)

ISBN: 978-1-4697-9106-7 (sc)
ISBN: 978-1-4697-9107-4 (e)
ISBN: 978-1-4697-9108-1 (dj)

Library of Congress Control Number: 2012904491

Printed in the United States of America

iUniverse rev. date: 4/6/2012

CREED OF THE NONCOMMISSIONED OFFICER

NO ONE IS MORE professional than I. I am a Noncommissioned Officer, a leader of soldiers. As a Noncommissioned Officer, I realize that I am a member of a time-honored corps, which is known as "The Backbone of the Army." I am proud of the Corps of Noncommissioned Officers and will at all times conduct myself so as to bring credit upon the Corps, the Military Service, and my country regardless of the situation in which I find myself. I will not use my grade or position to attain pleasure, profit, or personal safety.

Competence is my watchword. My two basic responsibilities will always be uppermost in my mind—accomplishment of my mission and the welfare of my soldiers. I will strive to remain tactically and technically proficient. I am aware of my role as a Noncommissioned Officer. I will fulfill my responsibilities inherent in that role. All soldiers are entitled to outstanding leadership; I will provide that leadership. I know my soldiers and I will always place their needs above my own. I will communicate consistently with my soldiers and never leave them uninformed. I will be fair and impartial when recommending both rewards and punishment.

Officers of my unit will have maximum time to accomplish their duties; they will not have to accomplish mine. I will earn their respect and confidence as well as that of my soldiers. I will be loyal to those with whom I serve; seniors, peers, and subordinates alike. I will exercise initiative by taking appropriate action in the absence of orders. I will not compromise my integrity, nor my moral courage. I will not forget, nor will I allow my comrades to forget that we are professionals, Noncommissioned Officers, leaders!

US SOLDIER'S CREED

I am an American Soldier.
I am a Warrior and a member of a team.
I serve the people of the United States, and live the Army Values.
I will always place the mission first.
I will never accept defeat.
I will never quit.
I will never leave a fallen comrade.
I am disciplined, physically and mentally tough,
trained and proficient
in my warrior tasks and drills.
I always maintain my arms, my equipment, and myself.
I am an expert and I am a professional.
I stand ready to deploy, engage, and destroy the enemies
of the United States of America in close combat.
I am a guardian of freedom and the American way of life.
I am an American Soldier.

On the Web

For a detailed look into the entire operational picture, including maps, operational graphics, reports, platoon pictures, and the 1-12 Cavalry's Executive Summary, please visit:

www.battleforbaqubah.com

FOREWORD

BEFORE OCTOBER 2006, it would be fair to say that the men of Bravo Company, 1-12 Cavalry, constituted an average and representative slice of America. They hailed from all corners of the United States, as well as Puerto Rico and the Dominican Republic. They had varying levels of formal education, family and financial issues, previous brushes with the law, etc. Each man had his own story and personal level of commitment to the US Army—and each man was at a different point in his life.

That notion of "average" evaporated in October 2006 when the company deployed in support of Operation Iraqi Freedom 06-08, the midway point of the Iraq war's fourth year. Upon deployment, "average" was replaced by "extraordinary" in terms of personal sacrifice, exposure to danger, level of accomplishments, and so much more. Upon deployment, each man gained a common point in life and, to a man, his contributions reflected an intense desire to do his absolute best.

In Baqubah and the surrounding areas, the men of Bravo Company rallied around a powerfully clear and unified twofold purpose: carry out any assigned mission and keep your buddy alive. What these men accomplished, and the conditions under which they operated, is the subject of this story. My personal thanks go to Bobby Colella, and all other contributors, for telling this story; it is truly the story of heroes, written by heroes.

As representatives of America, the soldiers in this story brought the American spirit to life. This spirit includes the courage to rise to the occasion and overcome adversity, no matter how insurmountable it may seem. I believe that most Army units—each as a cross-section of America—share this quality, and in that sense, this story may seem common to other veterans. I trust you will react favorably to its telling and see a bit of your unit inside the narrative.

To the family, friends, and acquaintances of those mentioned in this book: be proud of your soldier. His accomplishments are truly remarkable, and I count myself among the fortunate for having known and served with him. I loved each soldier as an individual and echo Bobby's mission objectives for this book. I hope you are able to gather a more complete understanding of your soldier's story.

So this is a story of ordinary men performing extraordinary feats under extremely difficult circumstances. I hope you enjoy the story and reflect positively upon it in good health.

Major Pete Chapman
United States Army

AUTHOR'S MISSION OBJECTIVES FOR THIS BOOK

What I want this book to accomplish:

- To tell the story of the soldiers, NCOs, and officers of B Company, 1-12 Cavalry, so that it does not get lost over time.
- To give family members and friends a way to catch a small glimpse of what their soldier, husband, father, son, brother, or friend went through—not for sympathy, but for a better understanding.
- For the soldiers who did not make it home, I hope that the families can get some closure and know that their loss and sorrow was shared by many—and to know that when their loved ones died, they were not alone and it was not in vain.
- Education, because this book has a lesson for everyone, no matter what their position is in life. I specifically would like to focus on the future leaders of the US Army and this country. I want young soldiers, noncommissioned officers, and officers to open this book and learn about what modern insurgency warfare is like and how many different challenges and struggles can be faced on the battlefield—and how one company met these challenges head on and persevered.

- Inspiration, because when people think they have it bad and things are getting tough, maybe they can look back and pull something out of this book that can remind them that no matter the odds, with the right people and the right intentions, and faith in God, you can do anything.

/////

What I don't want this book to accomplish:
- I do not want this book to be self-serving and sound like I'm saying, "Look at me and what a great guy I am!" If any part of this book comes off that way, it was not intended at all. This is about the soldiers and leaders of the company, and I just happened to be a leader, a soldier, and the one telling the story, so please bear with me.
- To be self-serving for B Co 1-12 Cavalry because our unit did not win the war by itself. There were many heroics and great battles fought by many different companies and units. This story just happens to be about B Co 1-12 Cavalry and the soldiers from the different units that fought side by side with us.
- To stir up a witch hunt, bad-mouthing, sniveling, and whining. I don't want it, and the only thing it would do is take away from the greatness that was accomplished by the war fighters on the ground. Though there are some leaders that did things I may have done differently or that I flat-out disagreed with, as I am sure people disagreed with certain things I did, I truly think that all the leaders had the best intentions of doing the job and taking care of the soldiers. We had plenty of opportunities to fail on multiple levels, and you can't always make everyone happy, accomplish the mission, and prevent soldiers and civilians from getting injured—that's why it is called WAR. Time, intelligence, troops,

weather, terrain, equipment, civilians, and the enemy all have a say-so in how the mission will unfold on the battlefield.

- Distort the truth in any way. What has been written is for the most part from my own memory and the details extracted from the combat outpost's log books of Bone X-Ray and COP Adam. I had a lot of help from many people to help fill in some of the blanks, and when possible, I had multiple people tell me their perspectives on a single event and I tried to "paint" the best picture possible from those stories. If there is a specific incident that I skipped, it is because I did not have enough information on it. If there is a story in the book that does not have the details exactly right, get over it. I did my best to tell the story of the company and its experiences.
- Be a "how to" guide for the insurgents. For the technical geeks and freaks, I did not talk about certain "gee-whiz" gadgetry, tactics, and capabilities because I thought it may help the enemy, so I left it out.

/////

Finally, just so you know going in, I was the first sergeant of Company B, 1st Battalion, 12th Cavalry Regiment, 3rd Heavy Brigade Combat Team, 1st Cavalry Division, out of Fort Hood, Texas. During our fourteen-month deployment to Iraq, I had the opportunity to witness the daily struggles and accomplishments, victories and defeats, heroics and moments less than heroic, compassion and brutality of war, and most of all the transformation of young, innocent soldiers into combat-hardened and seasoned war fighters who would eventually bring a determined enemy to its knees, and help rebuild a country and give its people hope for the future.

If you're ready to laugh, cry, yell, get frustrated, get mad, get scared, be proud, and be amazed, then go brew some coffee or grab a cool beverage, get into a comfortable chair in your happy place, and make sure you have plenty of time. My hope is that once you pick this book up and start reading, you're not going to be able to put it down.

Are you REDCON-1?

Follow me!

CHAPTER 1

ON NOTICE

August 2006

STANDING IN THE HOT Texas sun, squinting through my sunglasses, I observed the company guidon[1] frozen in place by the windless air. Standing behind it was a company of 19 kilos[2]—M1 tankers—all neatly aligned, all standing at parade rest. Their berets were fitted to their heads, and their ACUs[3] looked crisp. All of them wore a slight scowl on their faces because they had been told not to wear their sunglasses in formation. I knew without a doubt that each of those men were judging their new company commander standing in front of them, knowing he would be the one that was either going to make their imminent deployment successful or miserable.

In front of the guidon, my friend and previous S-3 coworker, CPT Matt Chitty, stood rigid at attention and called the company to

---

1   Flag that represents the specific unit and company with a letter and number combination. For the B 1-12, the color is red and white to represent cavalry.
2   19K is the designation for the military occupational specialty of M1 tank armor crewman.
3   Advance combat uniform (digital pattern).

1

attention for the very first time. The company snapped to attention with the dull sound of boot heels clapping together. CPT Chitty bellowed out, "First Sergeant!" The first sergeant (1SG) ran from behind the formation to the front of the company and stopped in front of his new commander and rendered a crisp salute. CPT Chitty returned his salute and said with a strong voice, "First Sergeant, take charge of the company," then turned away to be greeted by friends and family.

Not one to turn down free chow, CPT Marc Austin (Matt's replacement in the office) and I turned to walk away and head into the battalion conference room for the traditional lunch and refreshments, also known as a "grip and grin." The command sergeant major (CSM) of 1-12 Cavalry came over and told me to report to his office. With the, "Roger, Sergeant Major," still sitting on the tip of my tongue, he turned and walked away before I could respond. I thought, *That's odd.*

But not one to keep a CSM waiting, I told CPT Austin, "I'm off to the CSM's office, and I'll catch up with you back at the office."

I worked my way through the crowd to give Matt a quick word of congratulations and off I went. While walking to the CSM's office, a million things went through my mind. I didn't know much about the sergeant major and really kept my distance from the CSMs unless I absolutely had to interact with them.

But my mind wandered. *Could it be a 1SG job?* I was a sergeant first class promotable but knew there were no first sergeant openings within the battalions in our brigade, and I was already knee deep into the reception, staging, onward movement, and integration piece (RSO&I) for our upcoming deployment, so I really had no idea what he wanted to talk to me about. As I walked into the battalion headquarters, I gave myself a quick self-check and straightened the cuffing in my pant legs over the top of my boots, then headed toward his office. At his office door, I knocked without losing momentum and looked inside to find him sitting at his desk. I stopped the required amount of distance, three paces from the front, and stood at parade rest, clutching my beret behind my back in my right hand. He told me to relax.

"It appears that a 1SG in my battalion has gotten himself into a bit of a bind, and it looks as if he won't be able to recover from it," CSM Harris said. "We will need a replacement 1SG and you're it. You will continue to work for the brigade S-3 plans section as the brigade master gunner until the unit hits the ground in Kuwait and then they are yours. The company you will take over is Bravo Company. It has had a little bit of a discipline problem, and it will need to be addressed."

No worries, I thought. *I've dealt with this type of stuff before.*

The one thing I had found out throughout my career was that you never get a team, squad, platoon, company, or higher the way you want it. By the time you mold them into the way you want them, you move on to the next big challenge. Why would this be any different, right? The meeting was brief and to the point.

Shortly after, I walked back to brigade with my head spinning with thoughts of how exactly this situation came about. I knew MAJ Poznick, my old boss in the brigade S-3 plans section, was in 1-12 as the battalion S-3. We had a good working relationship and he had mentioned to me on several occasions that he was my spokesman down at battalion and he was going to get me down there eventually. Knowing he was talking to the CSM about me was the only logical explanation of how I had been selected for the position, not to mention that they were running out of time and had to get someone in that position sooner rather than later. I still had my doubts that it was really going to happen or if this was just part of a contingency plan.

Regardless, I went on as if I were now getting a company but took it with a grain of salt since replacements still trickled in. If there was an eligible master sergeant or sergeant first class (P) that came in while I was still in Kuwait on the advance party, they would slide him into that position since I was in the S-3 shop and already slotted in an important job for our deployment. Typically, a master gunner doesn't do a specific master gunner job while deployed, and instead finds himself doing tactical operations center work and or eventually getting slid over to a MTT[4] to help train and work with the Iraqi army. The 3rd Heavy Brigade Combat Team (HBCT) 1st Cavalry Division was going over to be the Theater Ready Brigade.[5] Based on that, we were supposed to stay in Kuwait for an untold amount of time, and if needed, we could be flexed into the troubled areas and quickly reinforce existing units. We were scheduled to replace the 1st Infantry Division brigade and they would stay in Kuwait for four months conducting training before they would receive the word to go north. So based on that assumption, we planned to do the same. We (Marc and I) had a major role in both the theater-specific mandatory training for the entire brigade and also had the task of planning and setting up the sustainment training for the battalions while they were in a hold status to go north.

The next few weeks were a blur of activity. We had meeting after meeting, PowerPoint slide after slide to get finished for the final deployment brief to the brigade commander, Colonel Sutherland. Once the big brief was over, we had a little bit of time to take care of our personal affairs, get our gear packed—including getting our new issue of ACUs and other Rapid Fielding Initiative (RFI) equipment—then try to spend time with the family before we left with the advance party to Kuwait to set things up for the main body. Little did we know that we would get the call with less than a twenty-four-hour notice of wheels up to leave. In typical Army fashion, we acknowledged last transmission, grabbed our gear, and prepared to leave.

I made one huge mistake in the final twenty-four hours at home: I left in the middle of the night without saying good-bye to my daughter, Abigail. I could not bear the heartbreak of saying good-bye to her—and my wife, Jennifer—one more time. I thought

---

4 Military Transition Team designed to train the Iraqi army.
5 A TRB is a brigade size element that had not yet been assigned a specific area of operations within Iraq and could be used as the commanding general of Multi-National Forces Iraq saw fit.

my daughter would not have really understood me leaving since she was only three years old. I had been gone most of her life, and she had no real idea who I was when I came home from my first deployment. I had been hesitant to establish that bond, knowing that I would be leaving again in less than a year. When I had left for Korea, she was only five months old, and I returned when she was two years, one month old. I was only home for twelve months and left again, two weeks before her third birthday. One out of three birthdays was not a good ratio, and I knew it would not get better for a few years.

On top of that, Jennifer's nerves were already shattered from the previous deployment. I just couldn't look them both in the eyes again and put us all through the drama of me leaving again for a twelve-month deployment. I figured it would be best to sneak into Abby's room, give her a kiss on her warm little head, tuck the sheets around her body, and leave for war in the middle of the night

So I shuttled my bags and rucksack out the front door to the ground behind my truck and went back to lock the door behind me. I clearly remember thinking, *Will this be the last time I ever walk through this doorway again?* I pulled the door tight and proceeded to throw my two duffle bags and rucksack into the back of the truck. I put the keys in the ignition and cranked the engine over. As the truck warmed up, I let my mind wonder about the "what if's." *What if I get killed? What if this is the last time I see my family? What if this is the last time I see the house? What if...?* I snapped out of the thoughts and turned off the mental switch that made me a husband and a dad—and I turned on the switch that made me a soldier. The switch was what got me through the last tour in Iraq: I had been able to think of the mission and my soldiers and block out the worries of family and household issues back in the States.

I soon linked up with Marc at the company to draw our weapons and other sensitive items from the arms room, and we shuttled our equipment over to the staging area, which was a gymnasium that had since been converted into a deployment staging area centrally located on the 1st Cavalry side of Fort Hood. We were piggybacking off of another brigade's flight that had deployed prior to us and had a few vacant slots. We were the only two guys flying out from our unit. As we were standing in the parking lot, we linked up with the point of contact from that unit and he informed us that we had to pack all our personal gear into our hull baggage (helmet, tactical vest, body armor). We were not told this prior to packing our equipment and now had to try and jam it into a bag in the middle of a parking lot. Recognizing this was not going to happen, Marc called his wife Katie and asked her to bring up an extra flight bag. Within thirty minutes, she showed up and we managed to get our equipment in the bag. I was glad he called Katie, but felt bad since he had to go through the good-byes one more time.

There is nothing like getting on or off of a civilian charter flight. Not wanting to waste space, the Army tends to pack the flight with overloaded soldiers carrying everything from their one personal bag to sensitive items (night vision, weapons, guidon, etc.). It never fails to have a bunch of people screaming at you to hurry up and sit down or hurry up and get off. I have never really seen the need to yell at people who want to sit down or get off the plane faster than anyone.

The plane was scheduled for one stop in the States and that was in Bangor, Maine. The stop in Bangor made a soldier feel proud. All the old-time veterans and their wives lined up at the arrival gate and shook each and every service member's hand. I had made that stop once before while I was taking my R&R from Iraq in 2005, and they did the same exact routine. This time I had a little extra time to wander around the terminal, and I went over toward the lead well-wisher's office to look around. In the office, I noticed a book that allowed service members to sign in and jot down a few notes. The book was opened to a random page and I quickly scanned it before turning to a blank page to sign in. As I scanned down the names, I noticed a name that stood out: "Don Eacho, SFC, HHC Scouts 1/9 IN Korea/Ramadi, Iraq." Seeing that name brought a flood of memories and emotions back that had been suppressed for over a year.

SFC Eacho was a fellow platoon sergeant in my last unit. He was the scout platoon sergeant, and we had talked often and found ourselves working together on many missions. In addition to his daily patrols, his platoon brought out the EOD[6] teams when we needed them. In March 2005 on our forward operating base (FOB), I ran into him in the latrines one early morning. He was just finishing shaving and packing up his hygiene kit as I was removing my toothpaste and toothbrush from mine.

"What you got going on today?" I asked.

"Same old same old," he said.

We both laughed halfheartedly as he wrapped up.

"See you later," he said and walked out.

But later never came. While on patrol, an IED blew up under his HMMWV and killed him; the medic, SPC McGowan; the driver, SPC Tymane; and the BN physician's assistant, CPT Sean Grimes.

So, standing there at the sign-in book, I asked myself, *Why was this page turned to that specific entry?* What were the chances of that? Was God sending me a message? I am a believer that things happen for a reason, and whether we figure it out or not is totally up to us.

After we left Bangor, we stopped in Ireland, but we did not get to see or do anything but grab a bite to eat, buy a quick souvenir, and stretch our legs for a minute. Then it was back on board for the final flight into Kuwait.

When we landed in Kuwait, we were quickly loaded onto a bus and shuttled to Camp Buehring an hour away, then unloaded in the dark with generator-powered lights shining down on the marshalling area, where we were to in-process and get herded around like a bunch of goats for the next few hours. Fortunately, we linked up with our brigade representative, CPT Parker, and he had our rooms squared away and a vehicle ready to transport us to our barracks.

---

6   Explosive ordnance disposal

The biggest challenge standing between us and our rooms was finding our green duffle bags in the mountain of hundreds just like them. It never failed that it would get stacked under a million other bags three rows deep, and you would end up passing by it a few times, getting your heart rate elevated because you'd start thinking, "Is it lost?" As you'd scan the mountain of bags, you'd feel a slight glimpse of excitement because you might spot something that resembled what you marked your bag with. You'd tear through the pile with much enthusiasm just to find out it was someone else that had tried doing the same thing you did to make your bag stand out. Finally, a small victory was won, and we found all our bags and could relax and go on to the next stage of our lives, complete with duffle bags and rucksacks. That day was September 11, 2006.

From that point on, Marc and I were pretty much together nonstop. We settled into our rooms and quickly set up a routine of exercising at the gym and running PT around the camp just to keep our edge and try to get acclimatized to the environment. We also started doing our range reconnaissance and setting the conditions for all the training that was about to happen. Fortunately, I ran into SFC Stanfield, an old Bradley master gunner friend I had known since 1996 in Korea. He was the brigade master gunner for the unit we were replacing, and was a wealth of knowledge and made our job easier for the time being. For about a week, we went about our daily routine of exercising, planning, attending meetings, and gathering outside our living areas to smoke our evening cigars and catch up on the latest information. As usual, we started hearing rumors of the brigade going straight into Iraq with only ten days on the ground in Kuwait to get the mandatory training completed. Rumors in this type of situation flew routinely, so Marc and I both took it as such and continued our planning.

A few days after hearing the initial rumors, we were sitting out in front of our rooms on a picnic table talking, smoking cigars, trying to relax, and taking in the coolness of the evening twilight. The brigade S-3, MAJ Tim Karcher, stopped by and pulled up a seat on top of the picnic table, pulled out his cigar and lighter, kicked his patrol cap back on his head, lit his cigar, took a big drag, and looked at the red hot cherry on the end.

"Gentleman, there has been a change of plans," he said. "Everything we have been planning for over the past few months is out the window. We will have minimal time on the ground as a brigade, and we are heading north."

Now, when you read things like this on the latrine walls or hear it from a friend that has a friend that works at the Pentagon that knows your aunt's sister, you don't pay any attention to it, but when it comes from a man like MAJ Karcher, it is as good as good will get. Talk about a bombshell being dropped. Marc was also informed that he would be going to a MTT team with MAJ Karcher to help get the Iraqi army (IA) stood up. The MTT team concept had been going on since the start of the US presence in Iraq. An MTT team was a group of non-commissioned officers (NCOs) and officers that get detailed out from other units and combined into an "advisor and trainer" role that helps mentor Iraqis into soldiers. The NCOs and officers live and fight side by side with the Iraqi army on a daily basis. Building the Iraqi army was the ticket out of Iraq for the United States, so the MTT teams had an important mission. Unfortunately, the importance of the mission required the brigade commander to give up some of his best officers and NCOs, including MAJ Karcher and CPT Austin.

From that point on, we had about a week and a half until the units started showing up. There wasn't much to do since all the major training was off the table, and we were only doing the mandatory training already scheduled. Our jobs just got simple so we occupied our time by working out and watching movies for the next couple of days until the brigade's equipment started to show up.

The brigade's Bradleys, M1s, connexes,[7] and advance parties started to trickle into camp and that got us fired up and ready to get back to business. I started wandering around the vehicle lines

---

7   Steel cargo container that is transported on truck and ships

checking on various things and seeing how the equipment looked. Marc had been a platoon leader in the 101st Airborne, which is a light infantry unit, and had zero experience with the Bradleys. He had asked me to take him down to the motor pool and give him some pointers on the Bradley. Naturally, I jumped at the chance to teach someone about the vehicle and also figured it would be a good chance to take a look at my soon-to-be company's equipment. While we walked down there, I went over the basic capabilities of the vehicle itself, the weapon systems, and the task organization of a platoon and company.

Once there, we crawled into the turret and I showed him some of the basics of the 25mm main gun. As we were going over it, I realized that the feed chutes that fed the ammo into the gun were missing. I thought that odd but figured maybe for some strange reason they were packed in a connex. After about thirty minutes in the turret, we transitioned to the outside of the vehicle, and I showed him some of the key maintenance points pertaining to the suspension. As I was pointing out some of the typical issues with the vehicles, I started to notice some serious and blatant maintenance issues. The more I looked, the more concerned I got. The track shoes were beyond their safe use, track sprockets were worn past the wear indicators, parts of the armored side skirts were missing, road wheels had massive chunks of rubber missing from them, shocks were daggling from their mounts, and numerous road wheel hubs were low and leaking oil. This was not the level of maintenance I expected for a unit that would be deployed, so naturally, I tried to reason why this equipment was in its current condition.

It was obvious that the operational tempo of the war was starting to take its toll on the vehicles. Units were only back for twelve to fifteen months, and during those months, the vehicles were gone for three to four months because they were in refit or being "modernized." In addition to not having their vehicles for three to four months, the men were in the middle of a complete makeover of leadership and trying to rebuild the company. Typically after a deployment comes a mass exodus of personnel. The main reason for the mass exodus is that soldiers had been stopped from leaving the service (aka, stop loss), retiring, or changing duty stations in order to fill the ranks and maintain continuity within the units, and once they returned from the deployment, they were authorized to depart the service.

With the mass exodus due to "stop loss" came the influx of new replacements, which caused the Bradleys to take a backseat, and to shift the focus to building the team and getting the basic individual and collective tasks trained. Once the vehicles got reissued to the units, they went into a high-tempo training cycle that would include a number of back-to-back crew, section, platoon, and company training exercises, to include gunnery live fires and at least one major battalion and brigade field training exercise—all capped off with a thirty-day Joint Readiness Training Center rotation at Fort Polk, Louisiana, where the vehicles not only got abused for a fourteen-day field-training exercise, but also got tied up on the railheads for a week before and after the exercises. Finally, once back at Fort Hood, the vehicles would be sent by truck and rail to the shipyard to be transported to Kuwait for the follow-on mission to Iraq. All of this didn't really leave much time for maintenance.

The time was getting short. I started to shift my attention from brigade tasks to my company. The company was a few days out, and I still had not heard anything different, so as far as I was concerned, I still had the job of 1SG. I did not ask too many questions prior to coming to Kuwait about B Co 1-12 and its history, including why the current 1SG was getting pulled from the unit. I figured I would know soon enough when I talked to the commander and other leaders within the company. I did not want to get a bunch of hearsay; I wanted facts, and I wanted them straight from the commander. I did, however, get some information on the company commander, and everything I heard was positive. He was a West Point graduate, Airborne qualified, Ranger qualified, and did a combat tour with the 101st Airborne as a lieutenant and executive officer, and a second tour with the 1st Cavalry as a young captain, and now this. I also knew he was under a microscope with the brigade commander with all the negative attention that had been brought to his company.

By the time Bravo Company's advanced party hit the ground, I had completed what I had to do for the brigade as the master gunner and was ready to join my company. It was now October 1st, and my promotion sequence number was effective. I was ready to be a 1SG, but there was no senior leadership on the ground to pin me, so I decided to take a gamble and promote myself. I did not want to show up to my company wearing the rank of sergeant first class; I wanted everyone to see me wearing first sergeant rank. The first thing I did was go over to the barber shop and get a real nice Army haircut: tight fade with a slight shadow of my sideburns, trimmed well within the regulations and then proceeded to my hooch.[8] Without any great ceremony or trumpets playing, I reached in my wall locker and pulled out the ACU hat on which I'd had the rank sewn on prior to leaving the States, then I grabbed the new first sergeant rank for my chest. I reached down, grabbed the corner of my old rank, and gave it a tug (with the sound of Velcro coming undone). When it was off, I carefully aligned the corners of the new rank and pressed it into position. I put on my new headgear, looked in the mirror to give myself a once-over, and off I went to find my new company.

I made it over to the battalion area and found the operations sergeant major. He did not say anything about the new rank (you never know with the cavalry when they will want to do a snap ceremony and bust out the Stetsons), so I figured I was good to go. The SGM gave me a quick rundown on the current status of the main body and a list of things I needed to make happen prior to the main body's arrival, then pointed me in the direction of my company's area. He told me my company executive officer (XO) was over there along with my supply NCO.

As I walked over to the company area, I passed a few soldiers.

---

8   Living quarters

They knew exactly who I was and were sure to say the day's greeting, "Good afternoon, First Sergeant"—and they kept their distance. I only knew two names: the commander's, CPT Pete Chapman, and SSG Lane the company master gunner—and the only reason I knew Lane's name was because our paths had crossed while working a few ranges together. I found the company XO in the cramped supply area trying to do inventories so he could get weapons hand-receipted for turn-in to be technically inspected (TI'd) and upgraded. He was a young-looking officer and introduced himself to me as "Lieutenant Moffitt." I gave him a quick once-over: he was physically fit with an athletic build, wore a Ranger tab, and had a good leadership presence about him. I had a good feeling about him and was happy to have him on the team.

I let him finish what he had going on, and I grabbed a few guys and a vehicle to shuttle all my kit over to my new living area. As I was walking out to the vehicle, I came across Specialist Aparicio—a slightly overweight soldier who had extremely long hair that was greased back. He was wearing a uniform that was wrinkled beyond explanation. I could not believe he was one of my guys! I totally lost it. I told that trooper that the next time I saw him, he would be un-F'd, starting with his haircut[9] and uniform. I had a hard time imagining how he could make it that long with no NCO taking the time to get him squared away, knowing good and well a new first sergeant was showing up any day. That incident really put my senses on high alert.

Once I got my living area squared away, I grabbed up the XO and started with the questions: how many soldiers, officers, NCOs … what about strengths, weaknesses, vehicle statuses, weapon stats, individual and crew served, night vision, drivers trained, combat life savers … and the questions went on nonstop for the next few days. I wanted to know everything I could since the commander was only going to be on the ground for a day or two. Then he was heading to Iraq to do the linkup with the unit we were relieving, get the

---

9   Anyone who knows me personally knows I am not a stickler for hair, so you know his hair had to be out of control for me to yell at him.

property books squared away, and start getting familiar with the ground we were to occupy. In between the regular line of questions pertaining to the unit's status, I would ask questions about the disciplinary issues within the company. The main question on my mind was, what happened that the first sergeant was getting pulled from the unit just prior to a deployment?

The XO told me that one of the guys within the company that was not really liked by his fellow soldiers had some sort of child porn on his computer. It had been found by another soldier who had skipped physical training that day and snuck into his room (also known as breaking and entering) to use his computer. He stumbled across the child porn link and reported it to his chain of command. The news made its way up to the first sergeant, and they brought the alleged perpetrator to the company area and put him under supervision of the CQ.[10] From that point, he reportedly was beaten by some soldiers and had to go to the hospital.

After CID[11] had finished their investigation of the so-called child porn case, it turned out that the link for the pornography was an imbedded link and it was something the soldier never directly went to. All this drama was based on one guy doing something he should not have been doing in the first place (skipping PT) and everyone else jumping to a conclusion. However, in the course of the investigation, a few other incidents of misconduct came up on the radar screen. The next thing you know, they had several other cases of misconduct pending amongst the ranks. Once the dust had settled and CID had completed its investigations, a significant number of UCMJs[12] needed to be processed, nine of which were court-martials. As the new incoming first sergeant, I had my hands full and had heard enough.

I did not want to know anyone's names except the one NCO that

---

10   NCO and soldier that are in "charge of quarters" or the barracks and company area

11   Army's Criminal Investigation Department

12   Uniform Code of Military Justice, thus "UCMJs" are cases needing to be processed

was the group leader of "The Incident" and the soldier that started the chain of events by skipping physical training that morning. I did not want to know any more of what had happened back at Fort Hood. As far as I was concerned, that was the past, and we needed to focus on the future. The company was arriving in a day, and I had to come up with a plan of how to deal with this information I had received from the XO and other sources. I went and found a place where I could sit and think about what I really needed to focus on, and prioritized my efforts accordingly. First, I needed to narrow things down and figure out exactly why things happened the way they did. Obviously, a discipline issue existed, but why?

I came to the conclusion that the lack of continuity of senior leadership—both of NCOs and officers—was one reason. It turned out the company had three first sergeants within a twelve-month period, and the platoon sergeants had come into the company within the last few months prior to deployment, plus the LTs[13] were being rotated to fill other critical positions within the brigade—so there was no consistent senior leadership amongst the platoons until the final months leading up to deployment.

The other main factor was fraternization. The NCOs were treating soldiers like they were their friends, hanging out and compromising their integrity and morals on the weekends and evenings, and expecting the soldiers to respect them during work. They found it hard to enforce discipline once the friendship had been established.

My focus was on the NCOs. Soldiers will do what the NCOs let them do and get away with. I didn't know exactly who to blame for this meltdown, and it really didn't matter, but I did know who was going to fix it. The responsibility to fix this rested squarely on the shoulders of the NCOs and myself.

Not all the NCOs were bad; as a matter of fact, the majority of the NCOs were awesome. It was just a fraction of them who were immature or just plain weak leaders. Most of them had a

---

13   Lieutenants

ton of combat experience and had been promoted quickly. What they lacked was the maturity of being a leader in the garrison environment, combined with the lack of continuity back in the garrison with the senior leadership: they had no steady leadership to show them what "right" looked like, so they did not know how to act or lead in a garrison environment. The Army had been at war for roughly five years at that point, and for a lot of guys, the field and war was all they knew. You tell an NCO to go and do a cordon and search of the entire city of Killeen, Texas, and they would do it and impress you when it was all over with. However, you tell the same NCO to come up and do some monthly performance counseling (effectively) and they wouldn't know what to do.

The other issue was that soldiers and leaders tended to use the excuse, "We're at war, going to war, or we are in a war zone," for not instilling discipline and letting little things slide. That type of thinking could have ended up being a cancer within the unit that slowly ate away at it until something catastrophic happened. It could have gotten to the point of an international incident, or worse, a war crimes committee.

Discipline is the foundation of our Army and is needed at all times. This unit needed someone to lay that foundation.

CHAPTER 2

BOOTS ON THE GROUND

MY QUIET TIME WAS over and I knew how I wanted to tailor my leadership style to fit what I thought would work for the current situation. I knew the company would arrive that evening; I was ready. HQ and Supply had the living arrangements squared away. We had a breakdown of the daily training for the next few days, and the XO had a list of maintenance priorities. The company came in around midnight. The buses had dropped them off a few hundred meters away from the barracks area, and we were standing there waiting as they came off the bus.

The first person off the bus was CPT Chapman, and I saluted him, shook his hand, and welcomed him to Kuwait. The platoon sergeants (PSGs) appeared shortly after and I gave them a quick rundown on the buildings and housing situation and told them to get accountability of all equipment and bags, break down into platoon formation, and give me an "up" when they were good to go. While I was waiting for the ups from the PSGs, I talked with CPT Chapman and within minutes had a good feeling about him and the situation we were about to embark on. The PSGs gave me an up on equipment, and I gave them instructions to link up with their platoon representatives that would guide them to their areas.

Once settled, I wanted the PSGs to link up with me in my area for a rundown on the timeline for the next day's activities.

The PSGs made it over to my living area pretty quick, and we did short introductions and started into the business at hand. We only had a few days to figure each other out, and I wanted to figure out who they were as leaders, what their experiences were, and what they were bringing to the fight, as I knew they wanted to know the same about me. The first thing I looked for in the meeting was their right shoulder: did they have a combat patch (not that a combat patch really meant anything, but it would be a conversation piece for later)? As I surveyed the four guys sitting in front of me, I started with the HQ PSG/Company Master Gunner SSG Lane. SSG Lane, from what I knew, had a mechanized background and had fought in Iraq as a squad leader on his last deployment. He was a master gunner and certified on the A3 versions, which reassured me that we would be able to utilize those Bradleys to their maximum potential. He was also wearing a 1st Cavalry patch on his right shoulder. First platoon, platoon sergeant was SFC Hamilton. He was a newly promoted sergeant first class, and was also a squad leader on his last deployment with the same unit, but did not finish his tour due to being wounded by an improvised explosive device and was evacuated back to the States four months into his tour. The second platoon, platoon sergeant was SFC Ciniceros, and he had only been in the unit for a few months before being deployed. He was a career light infantry soldier and had just finished up an assignment as a drill sergeant at Fort Benning, Georgia. He was wearing a 10th Mountain Combat patch on his right shoulder. Lastly, third platoon, platoon sergeant was SFC Reynolds. He was a career mechanized soldier, and he, too, recently came off of drill sergeant duty at Fort Benning. He was without a doubt the most experienced PSG and mechanized NCO that I had in the company.

The meeting was short but I accomplished my goals: I needed to do a face-to-face and try to get some sort of opinion on the NCOs that would help me make the necessary adjustments within the company. I also needed something to reference in the morning when I started talking to CPT Chapman and finding out his thoughts on the PSGs and platoon leaders.

After the PSGs cleared out and went back to their platoons, I was able to have a few moments with the commander and make some small talk. It was late, he was tired, and there was no need for a long drawn-out conversation. I had plenty to digest with the PSGs and figure out exactly how I was going to approach the company with my leadership style. Too hard could really breed resentment, and too light would make the guys think I was a pushover and that they could walk all over me. But if you go in too soft, it is hard to ramp things up. Decisions, decisions …The decision was made to go in hard—harder on the NCOs than the soldiers. If the soldiers were not performing to standards, it was the NCOs' fault, not the soldiers' fault.

I gathered the NCOs in a remote area away from all the soldiers and any distractions, and put them in a half-moon formation around me. I then went down the list of issues within the company, line by line, incident by incident. I didn't mention any names and told them I really didn't care (for the moment). As far as I was concerned, the incident did not happen and we had one thing and one thing only to focus on: THE SOLDIERS. We needed to get them straight, we needed to get our personal equipment straight, and we needed to get our vehicles straight. I told them the UCMJs were not going to go away and eventually they would have to pay the piper. However, I was going to put all the paperwork back into the tactical box, seal it, and forget about it until we were well settled into a routine within Iraq. Then and only then would I start sifting through the paperwork and start processing the UCMJs. My suggestion to the ones that were on the hit list was to be squared away and prove to me, their soldiers, and the rest of the chain of command that they were an asset and not a liability. Things could brighten up for them or get really bad: their choice.

Resentment from them was not a worry; these guys did not

need a nice guy, they needed leadership from the senior NCO in the company.

The rest of the day was spent unloading connexes and getting all the equipment unpacked and back to the platoons so they could start working the load plans within the vehicles and getting ready to start the mandatory training. I was finally able to sit down with CPT Chapman, and we had a good talk. I gave him a run down on my background and my family situation, and he did the same. By the end of our conversation, I felt that we were going to make a great team and do good things as a unit. I could sense that he really cared about the soldiers and knew what made them tick. Out of all the officers I have ever met throughout my career, he was the most impressive as far as getting to know and care for the soldiers. The soldiers could sense that he truly cared, and when a soldier knows you care, there isn't anything he won't do for you.

During our talk, I did not ask him about any of the UCMJs. I did, however, ask him to give me a rundown on the officers. He started off with first platoon, Second Lieutenant Boeka, West Pointer, Ranger, Airborne, Sapper, and a physical stud. LT Boeka had joined the company a few days prior to the unit departing Fort Hood for their JROTC rotation, so he was able to work a little with his platoon and get some advice from LT Moffitt. CPT Chapman then went onto second platoon and 2LT Kalar, who was young and eager and was also the newest addition to the LTs, having just arrived in the company prior to its deployment. Lastly, CPT Chapman described third platoon's PL, Second Lieutenant Dan Ebarb, and he, too, was a West Point graduate, Airborne and Ranger qualified, but like LT Kalar, he had just arrived prior to the unit's deployment and did not get to work with his men during the JROTC rotation. In the conversation, CPT Chapman also mentioned that LT Moffitt was a West Point graduate. That made four of the five company officers West Pointers. I was fired up knowing I had both officers and NCOs in the company that would not have been better if I had handpicked them.

As the day went on, I made my rounds. My first stop was to the barracks area where the dismount squads were doing classes with the medics on first aid and the platoon forward observers were giving classes on call for fire. I was able to sit in on a few classes, not to learn, but to see how the interaction was with the troops and the slice element (slice elements being the medics and FOs[14]). I then went to the connex area and checked the downloading of the connexes and the platoon boxes.

It was only 1000 hours and the temperatures were already into the low hundreds, and the temperatures within the connexes were at least 110 and getting higher. The wind was blowing and kicking up dust and sand, and making it just a little bit more miserable than it needed to be. The guys had to unload the boxes inside the connex because they were too heavy to pick up and move to the outside. They had a chain of soldiers formed so they could pass the items down the line and get it out of the connex with little to no effort. As the items made their way down the line, I figured that to be a good opportunity to look at our equipment and see what we had. As I was watching the equipment come out of the connex and get passed from soldier to soldier, I started noticing that there were no bumper numbers or platoon markings on any of the equipment.

I wondered how the Bradley crews were going to tell their equipment from the other crew's equipment. When you have fourteen Bradleys in your company, and you have fourteen sets of BII (basic issued items), and each set of BII consists of about 150 items—ranging from a small little grease fitting to a sledgehammer—and you pack it all into boxes that are not separated or organized, there are going to be issues. It wouldn't be that bad if everything was the same, everyone had their items, and everything was 100 percent operational, but that was not the case.

Naturally, when it came time to issue the equipment, a massive argument ensued about whose equipment was whose. Now that we were only a few short days away from being in Iraq, that 5/8-inch wrench that wasn't that important at Fort Hood seemed pretty

---

14 Platoon forward observers for artillery: privates through sergeants

darn important now. Of course, everyone wanted the good tools and swore they had 100 percent of their tools when they were packed. We ended up having to consolidate all the equipment and reissue it out to the platoons, ensuring that each section had at least one of each tool between two vehicles so they could share. This was yet another distraction we did not need.

By the end of the day, we had the vehicles as squared away as they were going to get, and I felt confident that the XO would get us on the right path with regard to the BII shortages.

Unfortunately, my time was short with the commander and he along with the supply NCO left later that evening to go to Iraq. The next time I would see the commander would be on Forward Operating Base (FOB) Warhorse. It was now up to the XO and me to get the company squared away for movement north in just a five-day period.

The XO and I got into a good working routine. The XO was focused on doing the coordination of the vehicle movement up north and the last minute weapons' upgrading and inspections. He also was trying to get our night-vision goggles, aiming lasers, and driver's night sights fixed. I was focused on the mandatory training and also some other opportunity training when time permitted.

Somewhere around the third day, we were able to load up the vehicles with all the crews and run them out to some forsaken part of Kuwait to test fire our 25mm cannons and coax machine guns. This was also another opportunity to see and gauge the proficiency of our crews and how well they were trained. The plan was to set all the BFVs[15] on line by platoon and have each vehicle load and fire all their weapon systems and do a few engagement drills. It should have been an easy day but it turned out to be a painstaking experience that really put me on edge.

When we showed up on the range, we pulled all the 25mm for a quick inspection, and they all looked pretty good. We lubed the weapons, and I did some spot checking inside the various turrets.

---

15 Bradley fighting vehicle (armored personnel carrier, NOT to be confused with a tank)

Once the PSGs[16] and I were comfortable with that, we installed the weapons and bore-sighted[17] them. This was where the day started to go south. Due to the lack of tools, we could not load the feeders on the 25mm independently and had to pass what 14mm socket and ratchets we did have from crew to crew. This led to a major delay in getting the weapons test-fired. Then there were crews that were not proficient in loading and unloading the weapon systems, so that also led to additional delays and some on-the-job training. So the only thing we could do was suck it up and start the teaching right then and there. By the end of the day, I knew all our gun systems were working and/or we had identified the issues and would be able to fix them that evening when we got back to our camp. All our crews had worked out some of the bugs with their internal systems and would be able to do what they needed to do with more confidence.

The infantry squads had a chance to go out with the PLs[18] and work on some of their SOPs.[19] I left the squads on their own and felt confident that they would be able to reach their training objectives.

At that point, I was more concerned about the combined arms fight and the basics of effectively operating as a cohesive platoon and not as two separate elements of mounted and dismounted squads. "We support each other" was the mind-set I needed these guys to get into.

As the day came to a close, I had told the PSGs to have their platoons go eat chow and be back in an hour for some additional training. As it started to cool off in the evening, I wanted the crews and infantry squads to go to the motor pool and start doing crew drills and vehicle recovery drills. We did not have any company standard operating procedures set in place. I had talked to the PSGs earlier that day and did a detailed review of what worked

---

16   Platoon sergeants
17   Aligned the weapon sights with the impact/strike of the round
18   Platoon leaders
19   Standing operating procedures

for me when I was a PSG, and that they could modify the SOP to work for their platoons. Crew drills are an important part of the fight; we needed to be able to do certain actions without thinking. The one basic drill we went over that evening was mounting and dismounting the vehicles. It sounds simple: get on and off the vehicle. But you have to take into consideration the firepower you have on the ground, security, the order you get on and off the vehicles, and where the squad leader is. It changes for different scenarios and missions so it benefits everyone to know the basics and that it is a science, not a thoughtless task. We also practiced hooking up a tow bar to the vehicles while under fire, how to best utilize the vehicles for cover, how to evacuate a downed crew member out of a vehicle, fire drills, and exiting the vehicle while it's on fire, and vehicle rollovers.

These were all good exercises to see the platoons and squads working together. I did not want to waste any opportunities. If we had time and the resources, I wanted to train. If something happened to these guys, and I knew I cut a corner and it was something that I could have prevented by taking a moment to train and teach them, I would not be able to live with myself. But I knew if I took the time and did everything I could do to get these guys ready for a fight with the time and resources available and something bad happened, I would be able to carry on with a clear conscience because I knew I did everything possible. That philosophy had gotten me through my last tour and it would get me through this tour.

Once the sun had set, the guys came back to the barracks to take showers and relax a bit before getting some sleep. I decided to do a walk around the area just to talk to some of the guys and see who they were and get to know them. With a company of over 110[20] guys, it was going to be hard to remember all of them in such a short period. I could identify them on a roster but to put a name with a face was hard to do in that kind of environment.

---

20   The company should have had 135 men but deployed short, as did the entire battalion.

24

The closeness I had with my guys as a platoon sergeant of only thirty-five was an awesome bond that I knew I would not be able to replicate as a first sergeant; nonetheless, I tried as hard as I could. As I did my rounds, I decided I would have a seat on a bench outside one of the barracks and relax for a moment. As I was sitting there taking in the evening, a soldier came and sat down next to me and asked how I was doing.

I thought to myself, *That takes a lot of guts. Who is this guy?*

"Fine," I said, and we started with the small talk.

He was a sharp-looking soldier, African-American, and had a certain leadership quality that was just natural to him. As we talked, I found out he was in Ramadi, Iraq, the same time I was, but he was with the Marines then. He had been wounded and evacuated to the States and ended up in California. While he was in California, he had finished his commitment with the Marine Corps and tried the civilian life for a while. Things did not work out as a civilian and he decided to join the Army and found himself at Fort Hood a short period later. I asked him what his rank was and if he was a team leader. He told me he was a private. I was puzzled, as surely a guy with his experience would have been a team leader and promoted.

"What happened. You get in some trouble?" I asked.

"Yes," he said, then went on to explain his situation and how he had been busted. Then he said casually, "It is what it is."

I was thinking to myself, *This guy could be a team leader in no time if he keeps himself squared away.* Before he left, I told him that if he worked hard and if he took care of his business and the soldiers around him, I'd take care of him; I don't hold grudges. His name was Private Clarence Spencer.

The rest of the night went on and slowly faded from business to relaxation. Around the backside of the barracks was another group of B Co soldiers, barely noticeable with the exception of the glowing cherry from the end of each cigarette and the slight sound of voices talking to one another. They were hanging out, sitting on the Jersey barriers[21] that separated the barracks from the road. No deep conversations—they were just talking to kill time until they were ready for some well-earned sleep. I stopped by the group for some small talk. I couldn't really see who they were in the darkness, but it really didn't matter; I just wanted to let them know that I was human and I was approachable. I wanted to make sure that all the guys, no matter what their rank, could come and see me if they had an issue and felt that they couldn't use their chain of command for whatever reason—they could talk to me directly.

Night is a time soldiers typically enjoy; it's a time when you can sit back and recap the day's events and plan for the next day's activities. For soldiers preparing for a deployment into Iraq, quiet time is not always a good thing. It allows your mind to stray off course and start to wonder about the "what ifs."

The very next day, I started the company physical training routine. Some people were less than enthusiastic at first but this was one of the only times I could really see the platoon sergeants, platoon leaders, and squad leaders interact as a whole with their subordinates. It was a good time for me to indentify the physically weak and the strong, the fast and the slow.

This particular morning, we were going to do a slow short-distance run down the main street of the camp. There are few experiences that can beat running alongside an infantry company full of guys that are all running in step, motivated, and singing as loud as they can. The energy that radiates from the formation is awesome. I sang a few of my favorite cadences and then let the younger guys take over. The run was not long or meant to kill anyone; it was a cohesion run.

When we got back to the company area, the platoon sergeants had the task of setting up some small platoon competitive events. The platoons competed against each other in various weapons assembly, disassembly, and function checks, and push-ups and sit-

---

21   Cement barriers seen in the States as road dividers

ups. We also had a competition to see which platoon could recite the Soldier's Creed and the NCO's Creed the best. There were no prizes, no days off, the only thing there was to gain was the bragging rights of who did what. Man! That was a great morning.

The rest of the day was more training. The company was again split up and the infantry squads went out and continued to train on MOUT,[22] and I again went out with the crews to do the mounted live-fire exercises. The platoon leaders had again gone out to continue to work with their squads and ensure they were getting their SOPs down with the squad leaders (SLs), while the platoon sergeants stayed with the mounted section.

Typically, when a mechanized platoon is operating and has troops on the ground, the platoon sergeant runs the mounted section, while the platoon leader runs the dismounted elements. The platoon sergeant is responsible for main support by fire and handles the reporting back to HQ since the Bradley has a great communications platform, and he is also in charge of the casualty evacuation. The platoon leader, on the other hand, is the leader on the ground and works with the SLs and takes on the responsibilities of maneuvering them in accordance with the commander's intent or how he, the platoon leader, needs them to maneuver.

Temperatures for that day's training were well above 110. We had conducted a fifteen-kilometer movement with the Bradleys to the range where we were going to conduct our offensive operations. The movement went well and was just another small piece of the training. During the movement, I ensured the drivers were buttoned up (hatch closed), and the gunners were down and scanning their sectors. We practiced different movement techniques on the way out, including action while stopped (herringbone formation is when the vehicles pull off the side of the road; they would provide local security by picking up sectors at the twelve, three, six, and nine o'clock positions with the TOW[23] missile launchers up).

We made it out to the range earlier than expected, and we still

22 Military operations in urban terrain
23 Tube-launched, optically tracked, wire-guided missile

had to go over the guns and do the last-minute coordination with the civilian MPRI[24] range folks. Since it was 110 degrees out, I told the mounted crews to go ahead and ground their individual body armor, helmets, and tactical vests while they conducted their final maintenance and filled out their pre-fire check sheets. No sooner did the guys ground their gear and start on the day's tasks, than the battalion command sergeants major pulled up in his vehicle. He pulled me aside and commenced to chewing me out for having my guys being out of uniform.

"Out of all the companies that need discipline instilled in them, yours is at the top!" he shouted. "But you have them out here like they are at a picnic! You get them back in uniform, and if I ever tell you this again, I will fire your ass!"

He then got into his vehicle and left. This was only the second time I talked to CSM Harris since I had been a 1SG and that was a one-way conversation.

In hindsight, when I told the guys to take off their gear, I remember getting quizzical looks from a few of the guys but then they just executed. I came to find out that the quizzical looks came because the 1-12 lived in their full battle rattle while in the field and they knew it. But me, being the new guy and not knowing the unit standard operating procedure, and oh by the way being the 1SG, no one said anything to me. That was one of many counseling sessions I was going to get over the next fifteen months.

The trip up north was now less than twenty-four hours away. I started giving the platoons a little more freedom to focus on the things they needed to without having me breathing down their necks. I began to work with the XO on getting maps and the transportation piece set. We had to finalize the flight manifest for the majority of the company, get the connexes repacked for shipment, and also get the Bradleys ready to be loaded up on trucks and sent north. The manifest turned out to be easier than we'd thought since we were loading the entire company on one aircraft

---

24 Military Professional Resourcing, Incorporated (former US military personnel that facilitate training for the units when they rotate in-country)

and flying north. I thought for sure we would break them down and piecemeal them over, just in case the plane got shot down or crashed on takeoff so that we would not lose an entire infantry company in one accident. Not the case. We were all set to depart at one time.

The vehicles were to get loaded "as is" on the trucks, and we just had to make sure that all the shackles were in position and all the sensitive items were secured. The guys started clearing out the rooms and packing up their rucksacks and duffels, sweeping the floors, and mopping, while others cleaned up the outside of the barracks. I decided it was time for me to pack all my equipment and get ready. I realized I still had a laptop computer that was the brigade's, so I decided to walk up to the brigade TOC and turn it in. As I walked into the TOC, a meeting was just finishing up, and all the commanders, S-3s, and other staff officers that I got to know while I worked there came over and congratulated me on my promotion and new position then wished me luck. I then found the supply NCO, turned in the laptop, and left the TOC area. On the way out, I came across the brigade commander Colonel Sutherland. He came over to me and shook my hand, then congratulated me and said, "You did not get the company by default." Then he jumped in a vehicle with a few other officers and left. I was thinking to myself, *What the hell did he mean by that?* Then I headed back to the company area to prepare for movement.

"Sound off when you hear your name called and grab your kit and move onto the buses," I shouted once everyone was in line. "Aparicio!"

"Here, First Sergeant!"

"Avila!"

"Here, First Sergeant!"

"Brooks, Charles!"

"Here, First Sergeant!"

"Brooks, Robert!"

"Here, First Sergeant!"

The roll call went on until everyone was loaded and the platoon sergeants gave me one last thumbs-up before the buses took off. Typically, I would just tell the PSGs to get their guys on the bus, but everything had to be in alphabetical order, making it slightly harder than it needed to be. As the buses pulled out, the hats got pulled over the heads, the iPod earbuds went in, and we settled into our seats for the ride to the next leg of our journey.

An hour later, the soldiers were bounced awake when the buses left the smooth surface of the highway and turned onto the rough rippled dirt road leading into Ali Al Saleen Air Base. As the buses moved down the dusty trail and began winding their way through all the jersey barriers, the soldiers started packing all their creature comfort items away into their patrol packs. The buses came to a halt. The guard from the checkpoint climbed aboard, gave the bus the once-over, and then waved us and the other four buses behind us through the gated compound.

The airbase was brightly lit like any other city or airport would have been. The buses pulled up outside the warehouse-turned-airport terminal, and the soldiers poured off the buses and went straight to the outhouses to relieve their bladders and get in that last cigarette. Others just milled about, then slowly started to line up in formation, get their follow-on instructions, and prepare for yet another head count. The temperatures outside were still in the hundreds and the night gave little relief from the heat.

We grabbed and organized the soldiers that were on the pallet-building detail, and sent them to start palletizing all our rucks and duffle bags with the load master from the Air Force, while the main body went into the building. Once inside the building, we were on lockdown until the plane came. Our stay at the airbase was relatively short and uneventful.

Next thing we knew, we were walking across the brightly lit tarmac onto the awaiting aircraft. This was something new I had not seen before. The seats were commercial airliner seats bolted to pallets, and the pallets locked into the floor of the plane. This idea was brilliant and functional, and sure beat sitting on a nylon cargo seat. We all loaded up, strapped in, put our earplugs in, and once again settled into our seats for an hour or so flight into Balad, Iraq. This time, I could feel the tension in the air, both with the flight crew and the guys. The rear of the cargo plane slowly raised and locked out all the heat and ambient light from the outside, and the A/C slowly started to cool the inside of the plane. It was a normal, noisy, and shaky takeoff. We climbed to altitude, leveled off, and set course into Iraq. We flew with our body armor and helmets strapped on until the plane leveled out and was at cruising altitude. Then we took the helmets off and tried to relax.

As the plane's engines steadied into an almost hypnotic rhythm, most of the soldiers drifted off into a light sleep. I sat quietly in my seat, observing the crew of the aircraft going about and doing their checks while illuminated only by the glow of various interior red, blue, and green lights. Then, without warning, the plane jerked to the left. We could see and hear explosions and flashes of light outside the fuselage. Then came another quick jerk back in the other direction. Then the plane went into a corkscrew descent— and then more explosions and lights.

Are we hit? I thought.

As I surveyed the flight crew for a look of panic on their faces, I came to the realization that this was just another day at the office for them while conducting their evasive maneuvers to avoid surface-to-air missiles or ground fire. Next thing I knew, we were on the ground. I never even felt the wheels touch down on the ground among all the evasive maneuvers. I also think it was a way for the Air Force guys and gals to have a laugh at the expense of a few unsuspecting Army grunts. Either way, they must be doing something right, as I haven't heard of one getting shot down yet.

As the plane taxied down the runway, the rear ramp slowly opened and let the hot evening air back into the plane. The only thing you could see out the back of the plane was the maze of blue lights that lined the runway. The plane pulled into position under blackout conditions (no lights) and parked. Then a forklift-type vehicle came over and pulled off our pallets of gear and carted it away. That process took about twenty minutes and allowed us time to get organized and stretch our legs. Once the exit was cleared, a soldier came on and instructed us to follow him to the small group of buses parked off in the distance. Once on the buses, we were shuttled to the terminal so we could be counted and linked up with our bags. Once in the terminal, we got our bags and broke down into smaller groups, also known as serials and chalks. We were going to fly into FOB[25] Warhorse on CH-47s, also known as Chinook helicopters.

Once we were situated on the ground, had our bags lined up in an orderly fashion, and had the schedule of flights and hard times we needed to be on station, I let the guys go find a twenty-four-hour chow hall and grab something to eat. The time was about midnight, and we had a long night ahead of us. We hung out in a gravel parking lot until it was time to move on to our next leg of our journey. Everyone was too anxious to sleep, so the typical bull sessions about everything under the sun started. I just sat there on my bag and quietly listened as I went over the flight manifests that were going to take us to our new home. We had to transport the company in two separate lifts, so I sent third platoon and half of second platoon ahead with myself and a few of the HQ guys. I left the rest of second with first platoon, which was coming on the last lift.

The buses came pulling in, and at the direction of a female specialist who had a voice like a mouse, we jammed ourselves into them with all our bags and rucksacks. We then proceeded to the tarmac and downloaded the buses. The helicopters were already spun up and there were "VIPs" already on the flight, which caused us to bump people and their bags. I had broken down each flight into a logical order to get onto the helicopters: I had two groups of soldiers and planned for one group up one side and the other group up the other side. We could all carry our bags on and be good to go. Not the case. The VIPs had too much baggage, so we had to bump[26] bags to another flight, then we had to bump

25   Forward operating base
26   Move to another flight

soldiers. It was a complete goat rope and turned my thought-out plan into a nightmare before the wheels of the helicopters ever left the ground.

We eventually got situated into the seats, the rear ramp rose slightly, and the helicopter started to move down the runway to a fueling point. Then we had to get off while the bird refueled, then load up once again for our final flight into FOB Warhorse. The bird sat there increasing the RPMs of its engines and suddenly jerked and shot up from the ground, pitched forward, and off we went, low and fast over the airbase and into the darkness. We flew only a few hundred feet off the ground as not to present much of a target. As I looked out the back ramp, I saw one of the other birds even lower than we were. The earth sped past at a hundred miles per hour. As I looked down upon the sporadically lit houses, I couldn't help but wonder what the next year had in store for me. Would it be worse than my last tour … easier … the same? God only knew.

CHAPTER 3

RIGHT-SEAT RIDE

EVEN THE MOST HARDENED of passengers got edgy at the sudden flashes of lights and instant explosion of flares shooting out from the side of the chopper, and the sudden jerks and rapid descent. The helicopter touched down, but the engines barely slowed and kept their high pitch just enough to keep the bird on the ground. We scurried off the back of the chopper into the darkness of night, dragging as many bags with us as we could. The crew chief tossed the rest out the back ramp. Moments later, the bird increased the engine speed and sprung up, off the ground, into the darkness to get the rest of the company. Silence fell over the landing zone (LZ) for a split second. It was then interrupted by trucks pulling into the LZ, and CPT Chapman and SSG Morales appearing from the darkness.

CPT Chapman was really excited about getting us on the ground and was starting to feel whole again. There is nothing worse than being separated from your men in a combat zone and surrounded by strangers you don't know and do not feel comfortable around. CPT Chapman came over, shook my hand, and told me to load up our bags on the truck, then we would walk the guys back to the barracks after a quick "Welcome to Iraq" brief. The briefing was in a large, beat-down pavilion area, and was uninteresting but thankfully short. After the brief, we lined up in single file and left the pavilion area and headed to our new home. CPT Chapman was pointing out certain landmarks and buildings as we walked, but I really couldn't see a thing and was disoriented. I tried to pay attention and get my bearings but knew it was going to look different in the morning. The walk to the new company area was around a half mile, but we made it there rather quickly. As we approached our new living area, I was glad to see it was surrounded by these massive cement walls that were twenty feet tall, and within the walls of this miniature fortress within a fortress, was our new company area. Our living area consisted of little eight-by-twelve trailers joined in groups of four. There must have been fifty or so groups. The area was not all B Company's, as we ended up sharing with HQ company. Each trailer housed two to three soldiers, and if you were a sergeant, you shared with another sergeant. The platoon sergeants, platoon leaders, XO, CO, and I all got our own rooms.

The supply NCO, SSG Morales, had my area squared away, and it was right next door to the commander's and XO's rooms. The rooms led out into a porch area that had a few lights slung over a two-by-four beam on a makeshift roof. We sat out in the light, and the commander started right into the business, which was fine by me. He had confirmed that we were relieving the engineer company as briefed earlier. The big problem was that an engineer company has fewer people. This meant fewer rooms for our soldiers to get into. The supply guys could not get the room allocations squared away prior to us showing up, so there was already one SNAFU.[27] Not a big deal, though, as the CO explained that the third platoon was leaving that night to go out to the Government Center to link up with the platoon they were relieving, so they could start to learn the ropes. I was thinking to myself, *Are you kidding me? We just got here, and we're expected to send a platoon outside the wire and they haven't even seen the battle space in the daylight?*

---

27 Situation normal all f---ed up

A lot of my thoughts went back to my last tour in Iraq. That was the only Iraq I knew, and it seemed as if every time we went out the wire, we were getting into it with the enemy, either by way of IEDs, small-arms fire, snipers, or a combination of all three. So I was a little anxious about having to go outside the wire, when we had not even received a basic load (210 rounds) of small-arms ammunition yet. But the decision had been made by the unit we were replacing. I knew CPT Chapman wasn't too happy about it, either, but it was the only option given to us.

From that point on, we were full throttle getting third platoon ready to roll. We had to issue ammo that the supply guy had managed to collect for the guys going out, plus grenades and batteries for the NVGs,[28] while soldiers topped off camel backs, canteens, and conducted last-minute PCCs[29] and PCIs.[30] Mo, the supply NCO, tried to scrounge up some maps for the guys too. This is a prime example of when it pays to be proactive and not put things off until the last minute (e.g., weapons maintenance, turning in a broken piece of equipment, tying off a piece of equipment, or ensuring your rucks are packed according to the packing list). The unit had been manning the Government Center (GC) the entire time they had been over here and didn't get into any major enemy contact. Having heard that report kind of put me at ease, but I still felt like we were going out the wire half-cocked.

Third platoon loaded up all their equipment on an LMTV[31] and mounted their personnel in a few gun trucks, then started shuttling the platoon out to the GC. The other platoons had arrived, and as soon as they hit the ground, our second platoon loaded up on trucks and were immediately attached to D Co 1-12, which was an M1 tank company in our battalion. I could not have ever imagined such a fast pace: the guys didn't even get a chance to get their equipment out of the company connexes and they were already

---

28 Night vision goggles
29 Pre-combat checks
30 Pre-combat instructions
31 Cargo truck (light multi-purpose tactical vehicle)

being task-organized to another company. The entire process was not helped due to the fact it was dark, we were all unfamiliar with the entire forward operating base (which is the size of a small city), and we had no forewarning.

As the night sky turned to day, we received the report that third platoon made it out to the GC with no issues and was getting settled in. Second platoon made it to D Co with no issues and their guys were starting to show up to our area to get their platoon equipment out of the connexes they shared with the other B company platoons. First platoon was able to get into their rooms, throw their bags into a corner, and make it to the chow hall. The XO, CO, and I started getting a plan together for unloading the Bradleys from the trucks, getting the essential platoon equipment out of the connexes, and making it down to the new company command post.

The M1 tank platoon we were supposed to get from D Co (Dealer) still did not show up, but I figured they would come find me eventually. I had other things to worry about at the moment, like finding the engineer company's first sergeant and figuring out the NCO piece of the pie. I made it to the company area after a few wrong turns and was picked up by a guy I flagged down for directions. It turned out he was actually from the company we were relieving in place (RIP). I jumped into the HMMWV, and we took off toward the company command post (CP). The condition of the HMMWV shocked me. As I looked at this disgusting HMMWV, I thought to myself, *I hope this isn't what they are using on patrols.* Belts of corroded ammo had been thrown on the floorboard, ammo cans both full and empty rattled around in the back, the blast door was opened with an ammo crate half in and out, smoke grenades were stuffed up on top of the radio, and a new combat life saver bag (CLS) bag was jammed in a corner of the vehicle. All this was alarming to say the least. Everything in that vehicle that was not strapped down would become a projectile if it took a hit. This situation was totally avoidable with the use of just a few straps.

It turned out the company command post was on the complete opposite side of the FOB as our barracks. I don't think you could have tried to get us farther from our barracks. This made absolutely no sense and was completely counterproductive to operating an efficient CP, and managing time and personnel. The only upside of our new CP was that it had been freshly built, and it had a nice, large conference table centered on a large five-by-eight-foot satellite image of the area we were to be working in for the next twelve to fifteen months. I was glad to see a nice map, the radio operators (RTO) station looked somewhat operational, and the general area was clean and orderly. I asked where their 1SG was, and they said he had already redeployed with the torch party back to the States.

You could have knocked me over with a feather! What? The 1SG left his company behind! I was left to RIP with an older sergeant that really wasn't tied into the mission. It was pretty obvious he didn't know what was going on when he gave me his version of what was happening in the company sector.

As I studied the huge map in front of me, I asked various questions: "Where are the US observation posts over-watching the main supply routes in and out of Warhorse?"

"There are none," he told me.

Then he pointed out the Iraqi army and Iraqi police checkpoints they "visited" on occasion. I found it odd that the MSRs[32] were not over-watched to prevent IEDs from being emplaced. In most sectors with predictable heavy US vehicle traffic, if you did not over-watch the MSRs, you would be taking IEDs all the time. That was like giving the insurgents a free pass to kill Americans. Even with the OPs manned 24/7, we still took IEDs in Ramadi during my last deployment. I thought it was foolish not to have US OPs out there at least working in conjunction with the IA and IP.

I asked what main routes and alternate routes they would take to the GC. He pointed at one route called "Route Gold" that went along the river, through numerous little villages, through a major built-up area, and then to the GC. Everything about the route felt wrong. It coursed through several low-traffic rural areas with plenty

---

32 Main supply routes

of places to be engaged by IEDs or even ambushed, then through a major congested and populated area with many choke points and minimal area for maneuvering, and finally running back onto the MSR where it then turned into yet another choke point. There they had to dismount the vehicles in a highly populated area and make coordination with the IP to open the gates and let them into the compound. I saw the potential for IEDs, ambush, and sniper attacks, but the NCO showing me the route did not see any issues with it. He went on to tell me, "We went that way to avoid all the other IP checkpoints on the main route."

I rephrased what he had just told me and said it back to him, trying to spark an acknowledgement that it was not tactically sound: "You mean to tell me that you guys intentionally go into an area that is not over-watched by ANYONE and has great potential for IEDs and ambushes to avoid the hassles of the IA and IP checkpoints that you are supposed to be watching anyway? And they do it ALL the time?"

At that point, I was finished talking to this individual.

We did get our tank platoon, and I was not disappointed. The platoon sergeant, SFC Malo, was a well-rounded E-7 who had been with his platoon for most of the pre-deployment training back at Fort Hood and prior to that was a drill sergeant. He had no recent combat experience, but his two wingmen were veterans from the CAV's last deployment. The M1 tank platoon leader, 2LT Joe Sparks, was a young Ranger-qualified, infantry lieutenant from Alabama State University and a product of its ROTC program. Having an infantry branch LT in charge of a tank platoon this early in the deployment was odd, but I took it as a good thing because the tankers were not going to do their typical M1 tank job. The majority of their job, so we thought, was going to be grunt work. The unit prior to us seldom rolled their M1 Abrams or Bradleys but instead choose to roll around in gun trucks. I was not a big fan of gun trucks. My philosophy was, "Why bring a knife to a gunfight, when you can bring a Bradley or a tank?" But I also understood the political aspect of the BFVs and M1s ripping up the roads, and intimidating the population. Then there was the financial and maintenance aspect of operating them all the time. M1s and Bradleys are maintenance intensive and were not built for the day-to-day abuse of a 365-day rotation. These vehicles were made to go in one direction and destroy everything in their path, and once they got to the limit of advance, they were to hold the ground. In this current fight, these vehicles were getting thousands of kilometers put on them, and they just wore down over the deployments. It was expensive to keep them on the road, and it took intense time and manpower.

I could see the point of gun trucks, but I also saw the need to keep the heavy armor out and about, and maybe mix it up a bit out on patrols. Maybe run all gun trucks one patrol, then run a mix of gun trucks and armor, and then maybe run all heavy one time. It would have been a good way to keep the enemy guessing: they wouldn't know exactly what was going to come out, and it would be hard for them to get a picture of our capabilities.

CPT Chapman agreed with me on the heavy armor/gun truck mix, but for the time being, we would roll in gun trucks until we were able to plan our missions accordingly. CPT Chapman also decided that the tank platoon needed more personnel in order to be effective on the ground. It's never a good deal for the infantry company when we give up a platoon of thirty-five guys and in return get twelve. Not a good return on our manpower investment. A fully manned tank platoon has sixteen soldiers, four per tank, but we got only twelve.

With twelve guys, we could only man four gun trucks at any given time, but there would be no one extra to go on leave, fill in for someone who was injured, sick, or placed on detail. Manning the gun trucks was one thing, but the platoon also had to conduct dismounted operations and needed the personnel to be able to do both, because you just couldn't park the trucks and leave them unattended. The commander cross-leveled SSG Hass's infantry squad from third platoon, as this would address our manpower concerns and allow them to maneuver on the ground when necessary. It also gave them some infantry expertise. SSG Hass was in 3/101st Airborne with then LT Chapman on a previous deployment. I felt better knowing we had a few experienced infantry NCOs in the tank platoon to help them with what needed to be done on the ground.

As evening fell on the third day, we were busy trying to finish up all the hand receipts on the theater-provided equipment. Theater-provided equipment is the special equipment not needed in the States or too expensive to issue, so they leave it in country and as the units rotated into Iraq, they would sign for the equipment and use it for that year and sign it over to the unit that relieved them.

In true Army fashion, instead of doing property transfer in the least amount of steps, we introduced layers and complexity by taking engineering equipment ourselves and then transferring it to our engineers (or just letting set in place, unused). As we were finishing up the last of the hand receipts and getting ready to call it a day, someone walked over and told us that the brigade had taken its first KIA. That kind of news, no one wants to hear. Without having to ask, he anticipated the next question and said, "6/9, it was 1SG McGinnis." Then he went on to say, "From the initial reports, 1SG was out conducting a night-time mission when his gun truck was hit with an IED. It evidently ripped him up pretty bad. They could not get the bleeding under control, and he died shortly after the blast."

Silence fell over our group as we let it sink in.

No matter how much you try to prepare yourself for casualties, you are never prepared mentally for the first one in the brigade, battalion, or company. Bad news like that is a slap in the face for a lot of people: "Wake up, damn it! They are playing for keeps."

Over the next few days, third platoon remained out at the GC. First platoon and our new second platoon were doing the right-seat/left-seat rides[33] in sector, and the commander was out rotating from platoon to platoon trying to get a feel for the area of operation (AO) and also meeting with the local leadership.

I, on the other hand, stayed back and was trying to get the company CP set up and our own operating systems in place. I did find a good NCO from the engineer unit to talk to, and he gave me a decent perspective on what was happening in sector. He did not like that they were in "over-watch" mode.

It wasn't the company's fault they had to do the over-watch; they were just following orders from higher up, which were to let the Iraqis handle their own business and for US forces to stay in over-watch.

He also took me out to his special connex and showed me some of the equipment we would be getting. That's when I found out that taking over from an engineer company did have certain perks. Engineers have some cool toys that grunts would like to have. For instance, we signed for a cargo truck that had a crane on it, a bridge layer on a M60 tank chassis, a CEE (combat earth excavator) also know as a bucket loader/back hoe, and a connex full of various engineer equipment (e.g., C-4, detonation cord, blasting caps, TNT, time fuse, robots, blowers, metal detectors, etc.), along with a few other items that I thought would come in handy if things heated up. What soldier wouldn't want to have all of that?

As the time clicked by, our guys started taking over more of the roles in the platoons and going out on patrol. The engineers' soldiers slowly faded out of the picture until it was all B Co guys out on patrols, all third platoon at the GC, and the engineer company removed from the operational picture.

We were a few days from being 100 percent on our own, but we had one final joint operation to conduct with the Iraqi army and

---

33   A process in which small groups of the inbound unit's leadership would go out on patrol with the current unit's leadership to learn the routines within sector and meet key leadership within the community to slowly be immersed into the region and to transition their soldiers into the mission while the current unit slowly phased out their guys.

a few of the key leaders from the engineer company. I was not at all excited about this operation, which was to be a battalion-level cordon and search of the city of Tahrir. The US was supposed to be the outer cordon of the area while the IA pushed through the city and searched the houses for weapons and other items that could pose a potential threat to the US and coalition forces.

All the key leaders—squad leader and above—gathered in the company command post for the operations order given by the engineer company commander. As we sat there waiting for the OPORD[34] to begin, I looked at the map and realized there were no route names on the map, no graphics, no control measures, and we had no hard copy of the OPORD.

The operations order lasted about ten minutes. The commander did a generic OPORD that did not include any detail of how we were to execute. It was just a, "We're going to get in our trucks, leave at 0630 hours, set up here while the IA do what they do, and when they're done, we will come back. Any questions?"

I am thinking to myself: *Yeah! What about PCCs/PCIs,[35] rehearsals, CASEVAC,[36] recovery procedures for downed vehicles, order of movement on and off the objective area, the enemy situation, communications plan, air support, and pretty much the entire five paragraphs of the five-paragraph operations order?*

I was totally disgusted with the engineer commander. How could a leader of men conduct himself in such a manner in front of outsiders? I thought to myself, *If we don't get anyone killed on this mission, it will be a surprise.*

As assumed, the mission was a complete goat rodeo, and the IA didn't do anything productive. We took a few incoming mortar rounds, but when the shooting started, the IA quickly declared the mission a success and pulled off the objective, which effectively finished the goat rodeo.

---

34 Operations order to coordinate actions before, during, and after the mission
35 Pre-combat check / pre-combat inspection
36 Casualty evacuation

Amazingly enough, we did not get anyone killed, and I breathed a bit easier knowing we did not have to do anything with this company again. But the good times kept coming with the engineer commander. The hand receipts were a complete train wreck, and the XO was at his wits' end. I asked the supply NCO, SSG Morales, what was going on and if I needed to talk to their supply NCO and get things straight. He told me the company supply guy was not there and there was a PFC in charge.

"When will the supply NCO be back?" I asked.

Mo said, "He went back to the States already."

Apparently, he had left with the 1SG and left the entire property book update in the hands of a private first class. None of this madness surprised me, and I just shrugged my shoulders and figured the engineer company commander wasn't going to leave the country until my commander was 100 percent satisfied with the property books and not a second sooner.

I assume the engineer commander thought CPT Chapman was just going to do the wink-wink on the hand receipts and sign without inventorying. Wrong! Now it was time to settle up. It went down to the wire, but CPT Chapman was eventually satisfied and signed.

As the day was coming to a close, my handheld radio attached to my hip crackled with the excited voice of my RTO, CPL Lunt.

Quisssh!

"Black 9, this Bone Main. The GC took sniper fire, and they have one person wounded, over."

"Roger that," I said then ran to the closest radio, which was at the BN HQ's tactical operation center (TOC) to hear the radio traffic that was coming in.

As I busted through the doors of the TOC, I saw CPT Chapman there and thought, *Damn, how'd he beat me here?* CPT Chapman had an expressionless look on his face when he made eye contact with me. Without me asking, he said it was LT Ebarb. He had been shot in the neck, and they were trying to evacuate him off the roof but were having some difficulties getting him down. We sat there, helpless to do anything but listen to the radio traffic.

Third platoon was doing everything humanly possible to get LT Ebarb off the roof. It was one of those things that you don't think about until it happens: what if someone gets shot on the roof? What are we going to do? How are we going to get them down? It's easy to say we will carry him down, but until you actually do it with a 180-pound limp body, under enemy fire or the threat of, while trying to keep the casualty stabilized, it gets a bit complicated.

Once he was off the roof, they did a vehicle evacuation to a small outpost called FOB Gabe that housed the Iraqi army, MTT teams, and a Special Forces unit on the compound. The helicopter was already there when the vehicles showed up and got him evacuated to Balad only moments from arriving on the camp.

We were able to breathe easier hearing the radio transmission, "Wheels up." He was in the MEDEVAC crew's and God's hands now, and there wasn't anything we could do to influence the outcome.

Later that evening, CPT Chapman flew to Balad with COL Sutherland and CSM Felt to check on LT Ebarb's status. As they walked into the hospital ward, they were guided by the Army nurse to LT Ebarb's bedside. LT Ebarb was conscious, and before CPT Chapman could say anything, LT Ebarb started apologizing for getting hit. CPT Chapman was speechless: what do you say to someone that is apologizing for getting shot in the neck? LT Ebarb was more worried about his soldiers and the additional burden they would endure by not having a LT, than about his own wounds.

I went out to the GC the next morning to talk to the platoon and see what happened. I was mad and disappointed with myself for what I soon saw. When I climbed up on the rooftop with SGT Bowlby so he could talk me through the sequence of events, I looked around and was in disbelief at what I saw. The fighting positions were inadequate and provided next to no cover. The distance the soldiers had to walk in the open to get to any of the three positions was about fifty to seventy-five meters, and once they were in the positions, they were silhouetted against the

45

entire city. I was furious at myself for not getting there earlier and checking the force protection.

Once on the rooftop, we scurried along the roof's edge and got to a vantage point where he could walk me through the entire sequence of events. SGT Bowlby told me that they had gone onto the roof to meet LT Mohammad, the IP supervisor. They were to discuss the fortification improvements and come up with a plan on how the IP and US soldiers would accomplish the tasks together. As they were walking across the rooftop, LT Ebarb suddenly dropped to the ground, rolled over onto his back, and was looking up at him asking for help. At first, he thought LT Ebarb had been shocked or electrocuted by one of the hundreds of electrical wires that were strung all over the rooftop.

"I never heard the shot," SGT Bowlby told me. "Doc Nguyen was up on the roof in a flash, and moments later had the pressure dressing on and went looking for the exit wound, got the LT stabilized, and started the chaotic evacuation process."

We talked in detail about what went wrong with the evacuation and how to fix it so it did not happen again.

Within the next forty-eight hours, third platoon, under the supervision of SFC Reynolds, put first aid bags in all the positions and several litters and ropes were staged throughout the rooftop. They rehearsed getting the casualties down from the roof both during the day and at night, and most of all, implemented numerous counter-sniper measures. We had pushed out thousands of sandbags to fortify the positions on the rooftop along with some ballistic glass (bulletproof) from gun trucks. We also brought out camouflage nets to drape over the positions to prevent the guards from silhouetting themselves. Third platoon also lined the rooftop with plywood to mask the movement of the troops as they moved to their positions. All of this work was done at night to minimize the exposure, and the guys rested during the day between their rotations on guard. From that point on, third platoon had their position wired tighter than ever, and they built that place into a solid fortress that they continuously improved upon. There wasn't a time I went out there that I did not notice something new that enhanced their fighting capabilities or force protection. Defensive positions are never finished. You make continuous improvements until you leave them.

It's ironic that the LT was shot while in the process of trying to figure out how to fortify the rooftop to prevent just that.

On the ride back to the FOB, I started to flash back to my first deployment. This deployment was eerily like the beginning of my last deployment. In 2004, we had not even completed the transition of authority, and we had already lost a platoon leader. Third platoon, C Co 1/9 IN, 2nd ID was out doing a recon of a town where they were going to do a mission. They were on top of a bridge overpass, out in the open, looking into the city, when insurgents opened up with a machine gun and raked the platoon. A round had hit LT Brown in the femoral artery, and he had bled out while they were evacuating him. The only difference was that LT Ebarb would live—but be paralyzed from his chest down.

The commander and I were forced to make a tough decision on what to do with third platoon: whether to take them off the GC and let them run patrols without a PL, or keep them at the GC and let them finish with the fortification of the GC, rotate the NCOs out to right-seat ride with the other platoons and wait for a new PL to show up, and then and only then, bring third platoon off of the GC to start running patrols and send another platoon to the GC.

We both agreed to keep third platoon at the GC until the new PL got there and then give him a week or so to get to know the area and his men before they started running patrols. The GC would be a permissive environment and allow the soldiers to learn their new PL as well.

This decision was based on the information I had received from the rear-detachment commander telling me they had a LT on the ground, and he would be over within a few weeks.

Well, a few weeks went by and still no PL. I called and found out it would be a bit longer; the LT that was in the rear burned a urinalysis test and would not be deploying. Now we were really hurting, but there was nothing we could do except wait for a new PL.

CHAPTER 4

FIRST RAID

WE STARTED TO GET into a rhythm with patrols, debriefs, reports, maintenance, and the other day-to-day operations. Things were calm and there had been no enemy contact. I made it a point to take these opportunities on every patrol that went out the wire, to observe the squads doing their pre-combat checks and inspection. I'd also spot check load plans on gun trucks and check the cleanliness and lubrication on the crew-served weapons. It wasn't long before the guys had a good standard operating procedure of checks and briefs before they went out the wire. I only had to periodically chew out someone.

There was a lot of work that needed to be done in the CP. We went full tilt trying to get everything straight and get our internal intelligence cell functional.

We made our fire support officer (FSO), 2LT Duplechin, our company intelligence officer and our link to the BN S-2. The company's senior forward observer (FO) NCO, SGT Matthews, was the link to our platoons through his three platoon forward observers. The plan was to use the platoon's forward observers as the designated platoon intelligence specialist, and they would work with the same platoon day in and day out. As the platoons got specific intelligence during a patrol, it was the forward observer/ intelligence specialist's job to specifically annotate it, bring that information back, and link it with other information that was being gathered either through the company or battalion.

The company commander, LT Duplechin, or I would try to connect the dots and generate missions for the platoons. At the same time, LT Duplechin would package up all the information and send it to BN. It did not take long for the entire fire support team to take charge of this mission and make it their own. After a few weeks of us teaching the FSO—what to look for, and what questions to ask—he had his systems in place, knew the questions to ask, and most importantly, learned to anticipate CPT Chapman's and the platoons' questions.

Now that the intelligence cell was running smoothly and the platoons were out getting their feet wet and picking up the tempo and intensity of the missions, I made my next order of business getting us some maps.

Even though we had that massive map in our company command post, it had no roads, route graphics, or route names marked on it, except for the main roads. It did have a few checkpoints listed by numbers but no road names for the intercity. I assumed it was the company we relieved that had failed to annotate detailed graphics, so I went to the BN TOC to see what maps they were using, since I did not want to reinvent the wheel. When I went to the battalion S-2, he handed me a fist full of maps. I opened them up, one at a time, and none had any road names on them. After a quick stop by BDE HQ on the way back, I had come to the conclusion that with the exception of the major MSRs that went through our sector, there were no route names designated for any "in town" roadways.

Units had been operating in that sector for over five years, and no one had made standardized map graphics to detail the smaller road networks within the city. I found that simply amazing.

It is only common sense when doing missions to reference road names rather than a bunch of forgettable checkpoint numbers that aren't sequential. I did not want to wait on battalion or brigade to make graphics and push them down to us, because if I did, it would be too late. I decided that we would make our own graphics and send them to higher.

I went and grabbed one of the PLT FOs that went by the name of Specialist Nash. He was a solid soldier, pretty smart when it came to computers and, most importantly, the mapping program that we were going to need to make new maps. I told him we were going to make an entire new map with route names, landmarks, boundaries, IA and IP checkpoints, and a bunch of other information. I said it as enthusiastically as possible but failed to get the desired response. You can imagine his enthusiasm: not so much.

To give him a bit of motivation, I told him when he was finished, he could name one of the routes. He kind of smiled at me and gave me a look that said, "I'll never be finished with this job, so I really won't worry about what to name a route for my own personal reward."

Specialist Nash was on the night shift, and every morning from that point on, when I came in, he would give me a rundown on his progress and tell me about any issues he was running into.

He would then ask, grudgingly, "Is there anything else, Top?"

"Nope," I'd say.

Then he would quickly gather his stuff and head toward the chow hall before I changed my mind. This routine went on for about three weeks until he finally got to name his road: "Route Nash."

Once we got the maps completed, we sent them to battalion and brigade. Eventually, everyone in the Diyala Province had the set of maps that SPC Nash had done: Aviation, Special Forces, MTT units, EOD, and as the troop surge came in, they got them as well.

I found myself getting restless while working in the CP and had to get out and see what the platoons were up to and how they were working together. At first, I tried to give them some breathing room so they could get their SOPs down without me hovering over them.

The commander was rolling out every day, sometimes two or three times a day. I figured it was time to give him—and me—a break, so I started jumping in on various patrols. I still didn't go out nearly as much as I wanted to, due to the fact I had to handle a metric ton of administrative issues, learn the ropes as a new first sergeant, and keep the battalion out of our business so the commander could focus on his job.

One of the priority missions for our platoons was to do patrols around the GC to find out any information on the sniper that shot LT Ebarb. We were not just going to take this on the chin. It turned out that our BN S-2 intelligence section got some information on the "Jasim brothers" that lived close to the GC. They supposedly were the ones who shot LT Ebarb. Based on that information, we were going to do our first company mission: a raid on the suspected snipers.

We started sending out platoons a few days prior to do drive-bys on the house, take pictures of the area, and get the neighborhood used to seeing military traffic around so when it was time, they would not be alarmed.

Once the commander got the reconnaissance completed, he started to do his operations order (all five paragraphs). He took a few days to ensure we had everything we needed. There was no pressure to rush and get this mission accomplished, so he took his time to ensure everything was right.

The HQ soldiers built a massive sand table for the operations order. The sand table had houses made out of cardboard and grid lines out of yarn, streets were painted onto the dirt, routes were marked with different color yarn, and they used little wooden blocks with the bumper numbers written on them for vehicles.

CPL Lunt was the NCO in charge and was one of the key players in the HQ platoon—and my go-to guy. He kept me out of trouble with all the daily reports and tasks that I would tend to push aside while focusing on bigger issues; he was a detail-oriented individual, and it showed on the sand table.

It was around 1600 hours. HQ platoon was putting the finishing touches on the sand table, and the commander was going over his notes and familiarizing himself with the sand table. The platoon leadership was starting to gather around the sand table, with maps and notebooks in hand. Everyone was on time.

After a quick head count, CPT Chapman started to brief the platoons: "Enemy situation: intelligence reports ..."

The operation order lasted about forty-five minutes and was detailed and well thought out; it left everyone with a clear understanding of what they were doing, when they were doing it, and, for certain jobs, how they were going to do it.

Once we finished the OPORD, we executed some walk-through rehearsals with the key leaders to double check the flow and work out any concerns that were not previously identified during the written portion. We adjusted a few minor details, rehearsed the withdraw from the objective, and talked through the handling of detainees.

The platoon leaders and platoon sergeant split off to go brief their guys. The mission was going to start at 0230 hours with a time on target of 0300 hours. When doing a mission like this, it is best to do it early in the morning. The majority of the time, the target is at the house sleeping, plus there is less traffic on the roads and less distractions, as far as people out and about.

With a hit time so early in the morning, it was hard to get any sleep prior to the mission; at least for me it was. Some guys have a button on their backside, and the minute they sit down, they are asleep.

I went back to my room, cleaned and lubed my weapon for the second time, mounted my NVGs on my helmet, checked my laser and my NVGs, filled my camel back, double checked my magazines, put a fresh battery in my radio and got a radio check with the CP, stacked everything neatly next to the door, and lay down on my bunk—and stared at the ceiling. I checked my watch, took in a deep breath, exhaled, sat up in my bunk, and went outside to have a seat on the porch.

Restless and excited, I decided to relax outside and look for an opportunity to talk to some other restless soldier. The time dragged by for what seemed like hours, but it was finally go time.

The platoons were out doing last-minute checks on their soldiers and getting communication checks with each other and the CP. I was riding in the back of a Bradley that belonged to first platoon, so I went over and linked up with SGT Bolton, the team leader, and asked him where he wanted me to sit. He pointed at a spot next to the turret, out of the way, so I would be the last one out and wouldn't get mixed up with his guys as they dismounted the vehicle. That was fine by me; it gave me a chance to look at the squad leader's visual display that shows what the gunner sees through the gun's thermal sight. The M2A3s were still new technology to me, and I was fascinated at the thought and imagination that went into those vehicles.

I reached into my rear pocket and pulled out the one magazine I had specifically for locking and loading, then I checked the rounds, slid it into the magazine well, pulled the charging handle to the rear, and let it slam forward. I made sure I heard the round slide off the top of the magazine, then closed the ejection port cover with my right index figure and gave the forward assist a few taps with the heel of my gloved hand. Then I double checked the safety with my thumb and climbed inside the back of the vehicle.

I sat there and watched the soldiers climb in one by one as the team leader (TL) checked them over one last time. Once we were all crammed into the vehicle, I looked at the TL. He gave me the head nod and said, "CLEAR!"

I slammed the turret shield door with my fist a few times, and the driver hit the switch that kicked the electrical motor that pumped the hydraulic fluid through and raised the thousand-pound steel ramp. With a dull thud, and the metallic click of the ramp locks securing the door, we were set.

The back of a Bradley is a dark, dusty, and hot place. The only lights come from the SLD, the slight green glow coming from the NVGs reflecting off your eyeballs, and maybe a few turret lights. There isn't any outside light, and you can't really see anything.

The driver put the vehicle into reverse and gave it some gas. I could hear the engine whine and the tracks started to snap and pop, grinding the dirt and rocks into a fine powder between its road wheels. Then it jerked to a stop and I heard the metallic clicks as the driver put the shift lever into drive and started rolling forward. It was anything but a smooth ride in the back; you get slammed around left and right, bounced up and down, and vibrated to the point your teeth feel like they are going to lose their fillings.

Once we made it just outside the gates, the Bradleys stopped near the test fire pit, locked and loaded the 7.62mm machine guns, gave them a quick six- to ten-round test fire, and also loaded and fired a few rounds of the 25mm into the pit. With a *Buuuurrrrp ...* and a *BOOM-BOOM-BOOM!*

"This is Red 6, REDCON1."

Once all vehicles were test fired, we rolled out. In the back of the vehicle, I could feel it swerve its way through the serpentine barriers and then slow down until everyone made it out of the gate. We slowly picked up speed until we were barreling down the road at full speed. We could feel the engine whine and the tracks slapping the top of the vehicle's hull; it vibrated against the hardtop roads as the Bradley settled into an almost hypnotic rhythm.

Senses were on high, switched on and ready to go.

Unfortunately, we took a wrong turn or two and ended up approaching the objective area from the opposite side, which threw off the entire dismount plan. One of the bad things about being in the back of a Bradley is that you can quickly get disoriented. If you don't have good situational awareness, you can get out of that vehicle and have no clue which way to go, then end up in a very dangerous situation.

Fortunately, the squad leader display had a few different settings, and I was able to switch to the map that showed icons of the vehicle within the platoon and company. It had the maps transposed onto it, basically a high-speed GPS with Google Earth on steroids.

Since we'd already deviated from the original plan, I yelled to get SGT Bolton's attention so he knew how to dismount. He gave me the thumbs-up just in time to hear the clack of the ramp locks unlocking, then the electrical motor kicking in and the ramp coming down. Before the ramp slammed onto the cement, we were all off and in a loose 360 formation just off the side of the road.

All the other squads also made the appropriate adjustments to the dismount plan and moved to conduct linkup. As I sat there watching the green shadowy figures come into focus, I alerted the TL (team leader) that the squad was coming in. The SLs (squad leaders) and TLs did a quick map check; the SL pointed at the houses and off they went.

Everyone's adrenaline was pumping and their senses were on high: vision crisper, hearing sharper, minds focused on getting through that door.

I sat watching as the breach team moved into position, stacked on the wall, then took a millisecond to get set and *SLAM!* The door went flying open and the entire squad poured into the house. I secured the entrance and the squad went through the house gathering up the occupants and consolidating them into one room.

The same thing happened to four other houses simultaneously. Typically, if we had the manpower, we would do the surrounding houses around the target just in case the intelligence was off or the insurgents had different houses they slept in every night.

The squad had the house secure in a few seconds. We put the wife and the kids in one room and the men into another room to ensure they wouldn't talk to each other. Once everyone was separated, we searched the house, room by room, drawer by drawer, rooftop, outside, cars, sheds, outhouses, trash piles, and goat pens. EVERYTHING got searched.

The typical Iraqi house has the same stuff: a living room with a few low-riding chairs or mats to sit on, a kitchen with a propane burner and minimal pots and pans, big bags of rice, a freezer that usually stinks like rotting meat, a master bedroom with a big shrunk-type closet, some type of bed but more often than not a massive pile of foam sleeping mats, and a few other odds and ends.

We tore through all the stuff like a hurricane; everything went in the middle of the floor. Anything of interest got set aside and reported to the TLs or SLs. Once the house had been searched, SGT Bolton consolidated the items that he had questions about, then brought the head of the household over to start the questioning.

The interpreter was with the commander in the house next door, but fortunately, the head of the household spoke good English, so we started the questioning. We asked him about the nature of the relationship between him and the other two males in the house then followed up with where they worked and went to school. The questioning went on for about twenty minutes, and we brought the other individuals in one at a time to see if their stories matched. They were being deceitful so they were processed for a trip back to FOB Warhorse for further questioning.

As we went through the house, SGT Bolton called me over and showed me a piece of notebook paper that had an American soldier's name written on it with an address in Killeen, Texas. Why would this guy have a soldier's name written down on a piece of notebook paper? Of course, "Haji" (our nickname for the local males) had no idea what it was, or how it had gotten there. He didn't know anything about the Jasim brothers—even though we had them in the next building over. It was the usual: "Meester, meester, don't know."

Snake, our interpreter, came over from the other building, and we started to question the other two males we found in the house. These guys knew the game just as good as we did: they answered with minimal if any response at all and tried to give us enough so we'd leave.

Not a chance with Snake. This was Snake's sixth rotation with an Army unit, and it was hard to pull something over on him. Snake was only eighteen years old, but he had spent the better part of his life growing up with and working for the Americans as an interpreter, despite the risk it posed to him and his family. He shared all the same hardships as we did. He lived with us, ate with us, carried a weapon, and went on patrol with us.

As the questioning went on, we simultaneously searched the cars outside the house and the yard. We pulled anything that looked suspicious, labeled it, took pictures, and drew sketches. We blindfolded, tagged, and flex-cuffed the detainees, then brought them outside to be linked up with the others being detained. We then loaded up and began to pull out of the objective.

We had been there for about forty-five minutes and made it back to the FOB without any issues. Once back, we processed the detainees, compared notes, took more specific pictures, and asked more detailed and deliberate questions. We had our company-level intelligence personnel review the detainee packets and prepare them for transportation to the detention facility where they would be questioned and held for further processing or released.

We ended up with a few AK-47s, magazines with rounds, a few computer towers, cell phones, some unofficial passports, and propaganda. None of it was that incriminating, but we did not know what was on the computer hard drives. Unlike the States, few houses in Iraq had computers, so this was suspicious in itself.

Unfortunately, we did not find the smoking gun, and the rest of the items we pulled out were most likely not going to be enough to detain these guys for any significant amount of time. All houses in Iraq are allowed to have one AK-47 with one magazine per military-aged male (MAM). Propaganda is forced on the people, and some hang onto it just so they can show that they are loyal to the insurgency when needed. The passports all looked suspicious, even the legit ones issued from the States; there was no telling if they were counterfeit or real. Cell phones alone weren't enough to detain anyone and neither were the hard drives.

Completing raids and detaining people are frustrating tasks. The insurgents know how the system works and play it against us like a game. We, on the other hand, have to be like CSI in every house we enter in order to keep these guys detained and build a case. We call it "sensitive site exploitation" or SSE. If we didn't have an airtight case against the people we detained, they usually wouldn't even go to the bigger detention facilities and would get released a few days or hours later.

For the ones that did get sent to the bigger detention facilities for further processing, they still had a chance because they got to go to court in Baghdad and plead their case. We would have to send a soldier or NCO down to the Green Zone to testify against the defendant (aka, insurgent). If we did not have a rock-solid case on the insurgent, he or she would get released. In some cases, we detained people several times just to find them on the streets again, fighting us until death. Not only did this process frustrate us beyond comprehension, but it also became a major distraction in the weeks and months to come.

Later in the deployment, we acquired intelligence that the IP officer (LT Mohammad) whom LT Ebarb was to meet that afternoon may have actually been the one who coordinated the sniper shot that wounded him. It turned out that LT Ebarb himself said that LT Mohammad insisted on meeting him on the roof that evening to discuss fortification of the GC. Days earlier, LT Mohammad also gave LT Ebarb a bright green folder and Motorola radio with a larger-than-usual antenna so he could communicate with the IPs on the GC if he needed.

Seemingly innocent at the time, it most likely singled out LT Ebarb as the leader and identified him for the sniper. LT Mohammad never did show up that evening for the meeting.

It was likely that LT Mohammad had one of his associates call in the tip for the Jasim brothers in order to throw us off in another direction. The chances of the Jasim brothers being corrupt and also an enemy or competition to LT Mohammad was possible. LT Mohammad probably just used Bravo Company and our aggressiveness to eliminate or scare off his competitors.

Shortly after, LT Mohammad was shot dead by unknown personnel, and the legitimacy of all IA and IP leadership was highly scrutinized.

CHAPTER 5

KICKING OVER A HORNETS' NEST

THE PLATOONS CONDUCTED MISSIONS out to the numerous IP stations and compounds to do inventories with "civilian contracted US ex-police." They were supposed to be over-watching and mentoring the IP forces, but it was impossible for them to do their job due to the lack of security and corruption. The IPs lost all accountability of AK-47s, RPK machine guns, ammunition, police vehicles, fuel, rations, armor vests, radios, and all the equipment needed to man an army, police force, or insurgency. Most likely all these items slowly got pilfered and sold to the highest bidder as it trickled through the supply chain. By the time it made it to where it was supposed to go, there was only a fraction of what should have arrived. This not only happened with the Iraqi police, but it also happened with the Iraqi army. The corruption ran deep at every level and branch of the government. It was only a matter of time before this ticking time bomb would go off.

Kidnappings, beheadings, bombings, and sectarian violence rapidly increased. At one point, a patrol found thirty-two human heads lying on the side of a road that led into a village.

Baqubah's demographics were a mix of Shia and Sunni with a

small percentage of Kurds. The diversity of the city's population was the reason why they said at one time, "Baqubah is the model city for the rest of Iraq." On the outside, two religious factions were living in harmony and being productive citizens while participating in a democratic government that had been elected by the people. But, behind the scenes broiled a constant struggle for power among the two groups. It was slowly coming front and center, with both sides no longer feeling the need to conduct the struggle for power covertly.

The company area of operation (AO) had five major towns or cities: Zaganiya, Old Baqubah, Tahrir, Chibernat, and the static security position of the Government Center between Tahrir and Old Baqubah. The area stretched fifteen miles from north to south and five to eight miles east and west. The terrain ranged from densely populated urban areas to small farm villages with sporadic houses stretched throughout the countryside.

The Diyala River ran straight through the battalion sector and separated New Baqubah and Old Baqubah. B Company's area, Old Baqubah, was east of the river and A Company's area, New Baqubah, was on the west side. The land was either urban terrain built as any other city would be, or farm fields mixed with densely vegetated palm groves that ran from the river's edge. The entire area was spider-webbed with irrigation canals feeding the lush green palm groves, orchards, vineyards, and the many farm fields that had been used to grow food at one point in time. There was very little open desert within ten miles of the Diyala River. The cities were alive with activity: shops were open for business, the few open gas stations had lines that stretched a mile long, police were on checkpoints, and the IA were manning others. At initial glance, it appeared like it was a normal city trying to recover from years of war and oppression under the dictatorship of Saddam's regime.

The priority for the platoons was to find the town leaders and talk to them about town security, schools, water, electricity, medical needs, and any other concerns the locals had. Once we identified the needs, we constructed a plan to support their needs, then started to foster relationships with the people and build their trust in us. At the same time, we started collecting significant actions (SIGACTS) reports throughout the BN's AO, then we tied them with reports in the company AO and slowly built an operational picture. Our company sector was broken down into humanitarian projects: wells, schools, clinics, etc.; security: IA and IP chain of command, needs, training, missions, cars, police stations; political and enemy: suspected terrorist groups operating in the area, agenda and safe areas, opposition.

As the platoons started talking to the town leadership and security, things began to unravel, and we started getting tips on arms caches, smuggling, kidnapping cells, crooked cops, and other insurgent activities.

All the violence in our sector, with the exception of the sniper incident with LT Ebarb, was aimed at the different religious elements and tribes within the area. Nothing had been directed at us—yet.

As the platoons conducted more operations, the picture became clearer on what was really happening within Baqubah. The government-run IA and IP were fighting each other behind the scenes both politically and militarily. Plus, various insurgent groups fought for power among each other. Within those groups, some locals were supporting AIF[37] (Sunni), while other local insurgent groups were supporting Al Sadr Militia (Shia). Lastly, the hardcore foreign fighters were pulling the strings and fueling the fires on both sides. The foreign fighters came from all over: Syria, Egypt, Afghanistan, Morocco, Jordan, Iran, and pretty much everywhere in the Middle East.

Our next significant mission was based on information we had obtained through local government forces. This led us to believe that both the Al Sadr and Sunni political offices were a cover

---

37 Anti Iraq Forces, which includes members of al-Qaeda

utilized to launch attacks against rivals within the area. In and around both offices were weapons caches and storage areas.

This operation was called a "cordon and knock" due to the political sensitivity. We would come in soft, cordon off the immediate area, and go in and talk to the officials. We'd ask to be taken around the offices and the general area to confirm or deny for ourselves the report's validity.

CPT Chapman decided to use second platoon (color designator white) to do the initial mission on the political offices. LT Sparks was the PL, and SFC Malo was the PSG, while staff sergeants Wallat, Davis, and Hass would be manning their gun trucks with their crews. That would give second platoon five gun trucks and about twelve to fifteen personnel to put on the ground to facilitate the inspection and provide outer security with the gun trucks. In theory, we were supposed to bring some IA and IP with us, but being that this was a politically sensitive mission, they did not want to participate, which was fine by us.

LT Sparks wanted to commence the mission when all the key players were present at the political offices, so he planned for the mission to start around noon, at the Al Sadr political office. The platoon would show up unannounced, then do a cordon around the building with four of the gun trucks. The fifth gun truck, with LT Sparks and interpreter, would go in with a small element to establish contact with the head of the office. They would then be escorted by the officials through the building. Once LT Sparks was satisfied that there was nothing incriminating, he would pack up and go to the Sunni political office and complete the same mission. That way, both political parties would be treated equally—so we thought.

The first stop was the Al Sadr political office. The platoon pulled up as planned and attempted to make contact with the official. The official was not there. The only people that were in the office were security guards, and they were not being cooperative. LT Sparks asked the guards to show them around, and the guards refused, which obviously put LT Sparks on alert. Finally, they made a guard show them around the office through threat of bodily harm. As the guard reluctantly moved through the building, everyone was on high alert. LT Sparks called for more soldiers to enter the building. Once the other soldiers came in, they spread out and went through the offices and the surrounding buildings. They located several stockpiles of propaganda, first aid equipment, IED materials, torture tools, metal detectors, uniforms, black masks, RPG rounds, RPG sights, AK-47s, PKM machine guns, ammunition, radios, and various other items. Upon these discoveries, LT Sparks ordered the six guards detained and then policed all the contraband to bring it to the Government Center, where third platoon would watch over them until first platoon arrived to pick them up and take them back to FOB Warhorse.

First platoon was en route from FOB Warhorse to the GC to pick up the detainees, and second platoon was already on the move to go to the Sunni political office. LT Sparks was almost to the Sunni political office when he heard a monstrous explosion that rocked the entire area. The explosion had come from the direction of the Al Sadr office. Moments later, we got word from the IP that the Al Sadr political office had just been blown up. Second platoon was just about to pull up to the Sunni political office when the streets erupted. They started taking machine-gun fire from several different directions: rooftops, streets, and alleyways.

LT Sparks and SFC Malo broke their elements into two sections and started to maneuver against the insurgents. SFC Malo's section killed the insurgent that was firing on them from the rooftop. LT Sparks and SSG Davis's gun truck engaged the insurgents south of them down the street and in an alley. Upon the reports of second platoon being in contact, first platoon, armed with a section of Bradley fighting vehicles, left the GC to reinforce second platoon. As second platoon began maneuvering and advancing on the small insurgent elements, another group began to fire on them with an RPK. Now they had three different groups of insurgents firing on their platoon. Two groups were engaging from west to east onto the platoon, and the other group was firing from south to north.

With the BFVs coming from the GC, LT Sparks coordinated with them to move from the south and flush them out into the open so they could be engaged by either the Bradleys or LT Sparks' section of gun trucks. The insurgents were so focused on the HMMWVs up north that they never heard the Bradleys turn the corner. They had gotten caught out in the open and paid the price. The lead Bradley opened up on the group with its 7.62mm machine gun and cut two of them down instantly. The section of Bradleys drove up the alleyway and stopped to clear the dead bodies and grab up the weapons of the insurgents they'd just killed.

With the threat in the south eliminated, LT Sparks and SSG Davis joined the other gun trucks, fired, and maneuvered onto the AIF in the west. They paralleled one street south of the street SFC Malo and his section maneuvered on. As the sections bounded down the streets westward, an enemy fighter turned the corner and opened up on a gun truck with his AK-47. He was met instantly with a burst of .50-cal and almost cut in two by SGT Crowley, the gunner of SSG Hass' truck. The enemy suffered four dead and soon realized they'd just picked a fight that they were not going to win. They wisely decided to fade back into the population and lived to fight another day.

First and second platoon consolidated all the enemy's weapons and policed the dead and wounded bodies of their enemy so they could be processed for identification at the secure GC.

Follow-on reports indicated that when second platoon was at the Shia office, the Sunnis decided it would be a good time to launch an attack on the Shias, being that we (US Army) just disarmed their opposition and left them defenseless. It also made it appear that the US Army was working in conjunction with the Sunnis to defeat the Shia in that area. We had been set up again.

Apparently, members of B Co 1-12 CAV weren't the only ones who felt like we had been set up—and things were too corrupt to continue. Shortly after the political office explosion and subsequent shootout, our BDE had pushed down the order that all IP units were to be dissolved and shut down within the Old Baqubah city area. All political offices were deemed corrupt and dismantled as well. We'd had enough. What B Co was going through on the east side of the river, A Company—our brothers-in-arms—was going through on the west side as well.

The corruption was so deep that no one could trust anyone, and we could not do any missions without word being sent through enemy channels. We had reports of IPs setting in IEDs and setting them off on US patrols. We had radios that we confiscated and would listen in on with the interpreter as the US convoys and patrols would pass by the IP checkpoints. The IPs would call into their higher-ups, warning them that the Americans were coming. We had picked up weapons from dead enemy fighters that were clearly marked as IP weapons.

I can only speculate why all this was happening with us when it did. My theory is that the previous US Army unit had their hands tied and were forced to work with the IP and the IA. Yes, initially, the insurgency wasn't bad in Diyala on the surface, which made it the "model city." We (the US) were in a hurry to have a success story, so they/we rushed into Baqubah and stood up a government in time for the 2004-2005 elections without fully having the systems in place and the personnel vetted. In our haste, we inadvertently put corrupt people into power, and they decided to take advantage of this, lie low, not draw attention to themselves, and play the peaceful game while they quietly and slowly milked the system for money, weapons, supplies, and whatever else was getting thrown at them from the US. All the while, they were simultaneously building their own alliances and developing their strategies on how each group would gain power in the Diyala Province. The US focus prior to this had been Baghdad, Sadr City, Najf, Al Fallujah, Ramadi, and a lot of cities and towns in the south and out west.

The insurgents were like electricity: they would go with the path of least resistance and build their power where the US soldiers were not. The theory "more with less" or "economy of forces" was the reason for the mess we were in. We did not have enough soldiers to cover an area, and the insurgents took full advantage of this. I knew this during my first tour and again felt the aggravation of just not having enough. The analogy "wack a mole" is fitting to describe what we had been facing since the initial invasion.

How did anyone expect to keep the peace and instill confidence in the people of four cities and numerous farm villages with only two maneuver elements of fifty soldiers combined while another thirty-five were tied up in a static position at the Government Center? The insurgents smelled weakness.

Within a few days of the political office raids, we got word that our new platoon leader for third platoon—LT Pijpaert—would be on the ground that evening. That was good news. Third platoon was getting a little restless being out at the GC the entire time, and they were ready to get out and start patrolling. The rear detachment commander had sent me the new LT's officer evaluation brief with the LT's general information on it. I gave it a quick scan and didn't see anything out of the ordinary, except that this guy had only been out of IOBC (Infantry Officer Basic Course) for just a few weeks. He'd had just enough time to move his wife to Fort Hood, in-process the post and BN, do the mandatory training at Hood, jump on a plane to Kuwait—where he did another round of mandatory training—and fly into Iraq.

The only thing I could think was, *Hope this guy paid attention in school.*

The commander and I decided we would have a little fun with the new PL and hopefully put him at ease, since he was coming into a tough situation. We decided that I would be the commander, the commander would be the company clerk, and the company clerk would be the 1SG. That evening, we switched all the ranks and got ready to go get our new PL. The commander and I jumped in separate Polaris Rangers and drove to the helipad to await our new PL's arrival.

It was dark and hard to see. There was zero illumination, so when the helicopter landed and spit out its human cargo and their bags, it was pure pandemonium at the LZ. There were civilian contractors that had no clue what they were doing, soldiers coming in that had no one there to link up with, and contractors and soldiers trying to get on the helicopter before it took off. I sat there, carefully scanning for the lost-looking figure in the darkness, and then spotted him fairly easy.

I walked over, shined my flashlight on his chest to confirm it was him, grabbed him up, pulled him to the side, and gave him a quick, "Welcome aboard." He saluted me, which caught me off guard. I forgot I was even wearing CPT's rank; I just looked at him like he was nuts.

The chopper had taken off and the LZ fell silent. I told the LT to grab his bags and follow me.

"Yes, sir," LT Pijpaert replied.

I was thinking to myself, *This saluting and sir stuff isn't going to last long.*

I walked him over to the ATVs and told "Corporal" Chapman to grab the LT's bags and bring him to the company command post (CP). I then jumped into my Ranger and tore out of the gravel parking lot, shooting gravel all over them. Once at the CP, I grabbed some coffee and patiently awaited the arrival of our new LT. I had to tell the radio guys not to blow my cover and to keep the laughing down, or I would have to crush their testicles.

The company clerk showed up with LT Pijpaert in tow. I sat there and eyed the young LT carefully. I noticed he'd purchased his own tactical vest. I paused and gave him a dramatic look attached to an extended period of silence.

"Why the f--k did you buy your own load-bearing vest?" I yelled. "Is the Army equipment not good enough for you? Are you too good for the Army's equipment? Take that crap off immediately!"

As he was taking off his tactical vest, I yelled, "BAM!"

I told LT Pijpaert that the company clerk had just been shot in the leg, and he was bleeding out and needed a tourniquet.

"NOW DO IT!" I yelled.

LT Pijpaert nervously started to go through his kit to get the tourniquet and place it on his patient. As he snapped open his first aid kit, I noticed he still had the tourniquet in the plastic wrapper so I told him to stop. I asked him why it was still in the wrapper and told him that he needed to be ready 100 percent of the time and never wait to do something. I told him to grab his notebook and then took him over to the map board to brief him. I also yelled at the company clerk to get his goat-smelling ass over to the map board and take notes. I gave the new LT a rundown on our area of operation and told him about second and first platoons' firefight. With the exception of me pointing north when I was talking south and vice versa, the brief was pretty legitimate.

"Get the LT a weapon, ammo, room key, all his sensitive items, and have him meet me at my room in a few minutes!" I shouted at the company clerk. "And you better not be speeding on that cart!"

The clerk turned and motioned for the LT to follow him, and they left the CP. I heard him fire up the Ranger and take off for the barracks area. I gave them a few moments, jumped into the other Ranger, and quickly caught up to them. They were only doing five miles per hour.

As I passed them doing about thirty-five, I yelled, "Slow down!" and then blasted by them.

On their two-mile-per-hour drive back to the barracks, the clerk asked LT Pijpaert, "What do you think of the old man?"

"He's a pretty intense guy, isn't he?"

"Yeep."

Once they made it up to the barracks area, we told LT Pijpaert to stay outside, and we all went into my hooch, switched back to our normal ranks, and called the LT in. He entered, looked at us, blinked, and smiled. We all had a good laugh at the LT's expense and we welcomed him to the company. I could see a slight sigh of relief come over his face, knowing he did not have to work for a lunatic over the next year or so.

We kept LT Pijpaert around the company area for the next day or two and let him in-process the company and battalion. We made sure all his paperwork was good. His life insurance was squared away and updated, and the emergency contact information was good. We took him out to the range so he could zero his weapon, and we also made sure he knew the rules of engagement and got a good solid brief from LT Duplechin. He needed to know the enemy situation. Over the next few days, the LT went out on a few patrols with the commander and other platoon leaders. Once the commander was satisfied that the LT had somewhat of a clue, we took him out and dropped him off with his platoon. We told him he had roughly a week to get to know his guys, and then we were going to pull his platoon out of the GC and have them start running patrols.

Within a few weeks of the political office missions, the police stations in the towns of Zaganiya—B Company's northernmost town—and in Buhritz—E Company's southernmost town—were both blown up, overrun, looted, and burned—and any IP that didn't swear allegiance to the AIF was killed.

The hornets' nest had been kicked over.

Before I start into the next chapter, I feel the need to explain and describe to the best of my writing abilities what an improvised explosive device (IED) is and what it is like to be in an IED explosion. The media write and talk about the infamous "roadside bomb," but never really break it down in detail of its destructive powers. To the person that really doesn't know, it just sounds like a bomb is sitting on the side of the road and some poor GI that wasn't paying attention drove by and the bomb went off and killed him.

IEDs are typically quite the opposite of simple. The insurgents have to go to incredible lengths to acquire the materials, build the bomb, store it, transport it, emplace it, and then detonate it.

Where do the IEDs come from? Initially the artillery shells and various munitions used for IEDs were plentiful throughout the country, because hundreds of ammunition supply areas had been looted and left unsecure when the US invaded Iraq. As the years ticked by, the Iraqi military supply dwindled down, and the supply routes and smuggling increased from other bordering countries. In addition to border countries supplying IED materials, some also supplied their own version of the US Special Forces to come in and train locals and other fighters in the making of IEDs, new tactics, and technology—like the "explosive formed penetrators" (EFPs), and how to make homemade explosives (HME) that could easily be disguised and made to look like ordinary items.

Most IEDs must have the following attributes to be successful: explosive material (HME with shrapnel materials), initiation system (blasting cap), power source, safety switch/arming device/trigger, aiming point, camouflage, and emplacement technique.

A DBIED is a deep buried IED that is usually dug into the middle of the road and covered up with dirt, cement, or gravel that will blend the bomb site into near invisibility. The explosives range widely: 155mm rounds, triple stacked anti-tank mines, propane tanks filled with homemade explosives, oxygen tanks, or whatever is lying around. Sometimes, they will put their own form of shrapnel in it, like nuts, bolts, ball bearings, and nails. Another technique is to surround the IED with gallon-size soda bottles filled with an accelerant in an attempt to catch the vehicle on fire as the IED is ripping through the hull of the vehicle. Some DBIEDs have had as much as a thousand pounds of HME in it.

The insurgents emplace the IEDs by using jackhammers, catching tires on fire, and melting the black top. Then they scoop the melted materials away, emplace the IED, and cover it with the blacktop. The insurgents will also use backhoes, picks, shovels, explosives, and many other imaginative ways to create a hole to emplace explosives. They put them in drainage pipes, culverts, sewers, the side of the road, previous IED holes, bridges, overpasses, curbs, guard rails, hollowed-out trees, hollowed-out walls, and basically anywhere their enemy goes.

An SVBIED is a suicide vehicle-borne IED. This is usually some sort of transportation like a car, truck, dump truck, donkey cart, bicycle, motorcycle, moped, cop car, or ambulance. The vehicle is packed full of explosives and armed with multiple initiation devices. Sometimes, the vehicles are driven by jihad fanatics. More often than not, they are driven by someone who has had their entire family kidnapped and/or threatened, as in, if they didn't go blow up Americans, their entire family would die, most likely by getting their heads chopped off. Sometimes SVBIEDs are used back to back. The first one is to create a breach in a wall and/or casualties, and the second to hit the weakness created by the first one, or to target people coming to the aid of the dead and dying of the initial explosion.

VBIEDs have all of the same structural characteristics of an SVBIED, but the vehicle is parked randomly among other cars or somewhere where it can blend in on the side of the road. When a convoy or foot patrol walks by—*bang!*

Pop and drops are typically smaller IEDs (1-155mm) that are all rigged up and ready to go. The AIF can do a drive-by with a car or van that has its floorboards cut out, or a walk-by, and with little effort, emplace it in a pothole, guard rail, trash pile, culvert, mud puddle, or random piece of debris. It's usually detonated by remote control (cell phone or handheld radio). It was not uncommon for guys with children to go out and emplace these in broad daylight; on occasion, women have been reported with harnesses under their dresses that held a 1-155mm round.

IEDs can take on the appearance of many objects that can be any combination of explosives camouflaged in trash piles, cans, dead animals, light poles, cement blocks, trash bags, sandbags, MRE boxes, palm trees, palm tree branches, fake rocks, overpasses, guard rails, walls, tires, propane tanks, wheelbarrows, and anything else that could make it blend into the general area.

EFPs are explosive formed penetrator/projectiles. These are nasty and extremely deadly IEDs that shoot a super-heated molten ball of copper. Typically, when one of these goes off, someone's going to die. Reports and evidence indicate Iran has been supplying these to the insurgency.

An HBIED is a house-borne IED. This was the insurgents' answer to our raids on houses. The insurgents would get a house, pack it full of explosives, and bait the US into doing a raid on it. They would call in tips or have a few fighters in the house shoot at US troops and try to lure them into the front of the house as the insurgents ran out the back. They'd either wait until they saw a squad go into the house, or they would have it rigged with a victim-operated device in one of the back rooms to ensure they got maximum people into the house before it went off.

Daisy-chained IEDs or multiple IEDs are IEDs rigged to one area or one initiation device to cause a massive simultaneous explosion that covers a wide area (e.g., a landing zone for a helicopter). The insurgents study our tactics and use them against us. They anticipate our reaction to an IED, either exploded or spotted prior to detonation, and will use that information to lay a complex ambush or IED engagement. They will plant an obvious IED to be spotted by an unsuspecting patrol. Once the patrol is stopped, the insurgents have an easy target, especially if the soldiers leave the safety of their armor-protected vehicles. If they anticipated correctly, they are able to inflict mass casualties in one event and possibly hit the first responders when they come to the aid of the initial patrol.

Personnel Borne IEDs (PBIED) use materials that vary from military-style body-armor vests to homemade materials sewn together to make the initial vest. The vest is lined with PE4/C4 type explosives and embedded with hundreds of ball bearings or other shrapnel-producing materials, both in the front and back. It can sometimes have multiple detonation devices in case the suicide attacker has second thoughts or to ensure detonation. The individuals are recruited and/or have had families kidnapped and threatened with death if the individual does not carry out the PBIED attack. Attackers can be women or men. Women are less likely to be searched by fellow Muslims and stand a better chance infiltrating certain areas. The typical attacker will just blend in with a crowd, recruiting line, or political rally, or approach unsuspecting foot patrols, and blow themselves up.

IED detonation devices range from cell phones, base stations, or radios. They operate by remote control, pressure-switched (i.e., victim operated), infrared-style beams or heat sensors, or command detonation (i.e., hard wired to a power source with a switch that is initiated by an insurgent).

These are just a few ways the enemy has figured out how to effectively fight a war against the US.

The psychological effect on the American soldiers or Marines is a powerful weapon alone. After watching or experiencing multiple IED attacks, our minds train themselves to think everything will explode at any given time.

The insurgents have two valuable weapons on their side: time and the ability to blend in with the general population. The insurgents know our "Rules of Engagement"—what we can and can't do legally—and use that information against us. The insurgents can sit out in plain view, study the Americans day in and day out, look for weaknesses in our tactics, and wait or create an opportunity to exploit those weaknesses.

The ability to imagine an IED going off without actually having experienced such violence firsthand is limited. However, I will try to do my best to describe an IED attack. When an IED goes off, most of the time, it's unexpected. Some of the times, we are anticipating it but just don't know when or where. It's a tough feeling: we know there are IEDs out there, and we have to go down certain roads, trails, or bridges, and we can't stop and look at every single piece of trash, pothole, car, or person. Even if we could, the insurgents are highly skilled at blending the IEDs into their surroundings.

The following is one of my more vivid recollections of an IED blast. Approximately three 155mm artillery rounds buried in the road went off while I was conducting a combat patrol in a Bradley fighting vehicle. When the explosion went off, I felt the heat and saw the flash a millisecond prior to the actual force of the explosion. It happened so fast and so violently that my brain didn't have time to process what was happening until it was all over with.

The over-pressure of the explosion in such a confined space was like getting sideswiped by a car doing fifty-five while sitting still in a Mini Cooper. The heat from the blast flash burnt my face and lungs, and every little piece of dirt and debris became a micro projectile that peppered my exposed skin and my eyes. The thirty-two-ton vehicle got tossed like a toy and suspended in air for a split second, then it came crashing down. My lungs and mouth were full of dirt and dust; my uniform was covered in fuel and battery acid. My body's senses were completely out of whack: my equilibrium was off, I couldn't hear, and I was blinded by the dust and smoke looming in the air. My body's senses were dulled but the adrenaline was kicking in and the joy of knowing I was not dead was starting to register in my brain. I never lost consciousness and didn't have any broken bones, shrapnel, or missing limbs. Everyone around me was okay, considering the size of the explosion. I lived to fight another day. Unfortunately, many soldiers' stories ends with the flash of an IED.

IEDs come in all shapes and sizes and do not discriminate. They are set off on dismount patrols, HMMWVs, Bradleys, tanks, Strykers, and anything else the insurgents decide to target. The IEDs go off during the day, night, rain, cold, and heat. They can be planted and left in place for weeks, months, and years. They can take on the appearance of the normal environment around them and wreak havoc on not just military but an entire population.

CHAPTER 6

BUHRITZ: BONE'S NEW HOME

GETTING BACK TO THE story at hand, LT Pijpaert went out to the GC, met up with his platoon sergeant and platoon members, and for the next week, he started to learn who they were and how they worked together. Unfortunately, we did not have the luxury of time or a permissive environment. The PLs back at Fort Hood had met their platoons in a garrison environment, were able to build a bond with their men while conducting various levels of training, and could develop their working relationship and trust with the platoon members. LT Pijpaert would have to do it on the fly. No small task for any leader, especially for what was about to unfold.

It was December and the weather had already become cold and wet. The rain had managed to turn everything into a thick glob of muck that stuck to the soles of our boots like some space-aged adhesive and added an additional ten pounds per boot. The once powdery sand, now mixed with water and churned up by the wheels of the HMMWVs and tracks of the armored vehicles, was like cement that had not yet cured. The temperature during the day, mixed with the steel of an armored vehicle or the concrete of an unheated building, was enough to suck all the life out of us and make young men feel old.

The battalion commander, LTC Goins, had sent E Company (Wardog) into Buhritz based on the information that the Buhritz Iraqi Police Station (BIP) and the mayor's compound were overrun by insurgents, then looted, set ablaze, and destroyed with explosives. Wardog was told to go to Buhritz, regain control, occupy the IP station, and not to leave it unattended. Wardog was a combat engineer unit that was outfitted with Bradley fighting vehicles and HMMWVs. However, due to the obvious need for boots on the ground, they, too, were not doing the traditional engineer job they were trained to do and had to serve as grunts like the rest of the battalion. When Wardog rolled into Buhritz, the insurgents were waiting and detonated several IEDs on their convoy, then engaged their patrol with small-arms fire as they moved through the choke point. Undeterred, Wardog moved in quickly, cleared the still smoldering building of insurgents, and proceeded to set up their hasty defense. Not waiting for a counterattack, they began fortifying their position until the next part of the mission could be planned.

About a week into Wardog's stay at the BIP, Bone got the word to relieve Wardog and occupy the BIP for an indefinite period of time. Upon us relieving them, Wardog would take over the GC mission, which would free up our other platoon that would desperately be needed to do this mission effectively.

CPT Chapman and I got a platoon together and rolled out the next morning with a mixture of Bradleys and gun trucks from first platoon. The commander had his own gun truck, and I brought out my gun truck, which was a HMMWV with a remote-controlled .50-cal machine gun on top (called the CROW).

I had CPL Lunt as my driver and SPC Kennedy, the company arms room specialist, as the .50-cal gunner in the back. The patrol made it out to the BIP without incident but the once bustling urban area now looked like a ghost town. The entire route was eerily quiet; shops were closed with their steel doors pulled tight. With the exception of the occasional dog or stray donkey, no one was moving—but we could feel the eyes of the insurgents watching.

That only meant one thing: the AIF were in town and were planning attacks, and the civilians stayed in the house so they wouldn't get caught in the crossfire when things went south.

The long road out to the BIP ran north and south, paralleling a palm grove and canal on the west side of the road and the city of Tahrir on the east side. There was no way to prevent ourselves from telegraphing our movements; there were two deadly choke points (bridges) that the enemy knew we had to go over in order to get to the combat outpost (COP). The terrain favored the insurgents; it was easy for them to engage and fade away into the palm groves or the city. There was one way in and one way out. This was not a good situation to be in, and the AIF in the area knew it and wanted to lure us in.

Almost immediately upon Bone's arrival at the BIP, we were greeted with the *thump-thump* of mortars being fired off in the distance and then a slight crackle as the projectile cut through the air, over our heads, and *CRACK!* There was only one explosion outside the compound and then silence; the other must have been a dud. Immediately after the mortar rounds hit, the snapping of rounds over our heads and impacting on the cement walls of the police station made it very clear that the insurgents were not happy with us being there. The Wardog soldiers on the roof followed up with their own barrage as the entire rooftop exploded with return fire. After about thirty seconds of return fire, a cease fire was called, and we went about our task at hand of surveying the area and figuring out what we needed to be successful.

The entire city of Buhritz was a tactical nightmare. It only had three entrances into the city. One was from the north that paralleled the canal; one was from the east and entered the city in the southeastern part of town; the other was from the south, and it also paralleled the canal. In order to get to the southern entrance, we had to cross over the Diyala River fifteen miles out of our sector. The Diyala River flowed north and south and was the western boundary of Buhritz. So really there were only two ways in, and the eastern route had nothing but open farm fields, canals, and the road that was also forty-five minutes out of our way. There was no way to alternate the route, which created an opportunity for the AIF to engage us at their leisure.

The only way to combat this dilemma was to put observation posts (OPs) and checkpoints (CPs) on those routes 24/7. Without them, we would be an easy target.

The IP station was located in the upper northwest side of the city. It was built within the last year as a project to pump money into the economy by hiring local people to build the station and employ locals to man the police station. The police station's compound had a good 360-degree defensive perimeter around it. As far as barriers, it had HESCO baskets, which are big eight-by-six-by-six cubes of chain link reinforced with a strong cloth-like material to keep the dirt from coming out. They are enclosed on all sides except top and bottom. They fold out and act as a basket for bulldozers and backhoes to fill with dirt. They come in various sizes, and once filled, they make a solid six-foot wall of dirt. The outside of the compound was outlined with the HESCOs and then smaller four-foot ones placed on top to give it some height. On top of that sat steel pickets, concertina wire, and barbed wire. The entrance was made for trucks, not Bradleys and tanks, so that had to be adjusted. The west side of the compound ran up to the edge of the Diyala River and was separated with HESCOs as well. All four corners of the compound had bullet-riddled steel guard towers at them that stood fifteen to twenty feet tall; they were great targets for the local AIF.

Across the river stood a massive palm grove in A Company's sector, and it allowed the AIF easy access to our compound. They had the ability to hide in the vegetation out of observation from helicopters or unmanned aerial vehicle (UAVs).

Outside the HESCOs, the north, east, and southeast sides were city, and the south side was nothing but a few random houses and another massive palm grove that stretched all the way into the southern part of Buhritz. This palm grove was our most dangerous area. It was thick with vegetation and had many spider trails that weaved their way through the thick palm underbrush, along with sporadic farm fields that were most likely there for hundreds of years. The locals knew these trails like the back of their hands and used them with ease.

The IP building itself was 75 percent destroyed. When the insurgents overran the IP station, they burned all the vehicles, looted all the police equipment, set the building on fire, and then blew up most of it. The building had one wing that had seven smaller rooms and a two-story second wing, which was the largest and appeared to be the main area. The AIF had planted explosives throughout and collapsed the majority of the larger building. The mayor's two-story house, which was across the street and outside the compound, was also destroyed with explosives, and 80 percent of that building was collapsed.

We decided that we would set up the living quarters and our company TOC in the burned-out, rubble-filled portion of the BIP. We initially set up two OPs on the roof of the partially collapsed building of the IP station, one OP facing south and the other OP facing west across the river. An additional two OPs were set up in the mayor's house, one facing east and one facing north.

We also decided that we would have to cover our main supply route in and out of the area. It was imperative that we over-watch the two small bridges and the road. They were our ONLY way of crossing over the canal that separated us from the main road. If those bridges were damaged, we would be cut off and would not be able to be reinforced, conduct casualty evacuations, or engage in any regular resupply operations. To cover those two bridges, we would have to over-watch them with a section of either Bradleys or M1 Abrams tanks.

The BIP was not large enough to house the entire company. At best, we could get two platoons plus the HQ element in there, which worked out fine. We still had to conduct missions in Old Baqubah, Tahrir, and Zaganiya, and we still had to come up with a maintenance rotation plan to ensure we could sustain operations for an extended period of time.

The decision was made to keep one platoon back at FOB Warhorse to conduct operations in Old Baqubah, Tahrir, and Zaganiya, while the other two platoons would be in Buhritz: one on force protection and the other conducting offensive operations.

We divided our headquarters platoon into two sections so that we did not have to take from one of the maneuver platoons to escort us around on the battlefield or make logistical runs. Having the two Bradleys in HQ platoon (commander's and XO's), we also had the FSO's Bradley, and I had the gun truck with the remote .50-cal. One section would consist of the company XO, the commander, and myself, and the FSO made up another section. If needed, we could flex to support the mission and add firepower to the platoons.

LT Moffitt and I drew up a large supply list and started to scrounge. The battalion headquarters element was helpful and gave us what we needed, if they had it. We started piling and loading the generators, antennas, extra communication equipment, water buffalos, engineer equipment, fortification materials, light sets, and power transformers. The extra crew served weapons, ammo, camouflage nets, fuel cans, detailed maps, and more sandbags than we could imagine, hauling it all on anything that had wheels to get it from there to the COP.

The only thing we had was the shell of a burned-out and blown-up building. We wanted to maximize our time at the outpost and minimize our road time and trips that took us out of sector for supplies; we wanted to become self-sufficient as quickly as possible.

The commander and FSO started getting all the information we could gather on our new area of operation (AO) and find out exactly who we were up against. An AIF group called "The 1920s Revolution Brigade" turned out to be our main opponent. We did not have a lot of intelligence on them, but we did know that they were Sunnis, they had the power within Buhritz, and their hold stretched into parts of Tahrir and Old Baqubah. Among the AIF of the 1920s Brigade, they had many foreign fighters, al-Qaeda hardcore extremists, and the local male population. The strength of the 1920s Brigade at that time was estimated to be between one hundred to one thousand AIF fighters and support personnel within the area. The wide estimate of fighters indicated that we didn't completely know what was going on enemy-wise because it was constantly changing. Someone considered a fighter one day might not be tomorrow, and vice versa.

We decided to focus the majority of our energy on the defensive posture of the COP and the mayor's house. We wanted to get in our heavy weapon systems, do sector sketches, fortify the OPs, and get our TOC and communications working. While all the defensive operations were going on, we still had to conduct our patrols and offensive operations in Old Baqubah, Tahrir, and eventually Buhritz. B Co's combat power to conduct operations was as follows:

PPLT	Vehicles and Crew	HMM WVs	Squads (7-man)	FO	Medic	On Leave	Work Detail
1st	4 BFV	6	3	1	1	3-4	1
2nd	4 M-1	5	1	1	1	1-2	0
3rd	4 BFV	5	2	1	1	2-3	1
HQ	3 BFV	2	0	1	1	1-2	1

In the rear, and at times out at the COP, we would have our vehicle recovery section and our maintenance team. The numbers above were only accurate if we had 100 percent of our equipment operational and 100 percent of our soldiers on the ground. Thus, our mission was going to get complicated in the weeks and months to come.

In addition to our requirements on the ground out in sector, each platoon had a minimum of three to four soldiers either going on leave, on leave, or coming home from leave. It was mandatory to send the soldiers home regardless of what our situation was on the ground. We had to abide by that ratio if we were to get everyone home in a twelve-month period. In addition to the leave, we still had work details that had to be filled with soldiers back at FOB Warhorse that consisted of perimeter guard, gate guard, chow hall guard, and a few other random duties that everyone was tasked for.

As the company first sergeant, I tried to fight these work details tooth and nail but to no avail; we still had to send precious manpower on details for the FOB. I would be furious when I came back to the FOB. I would see soldiers that never left the wire (aka Fobbits),[38] worked nine-to-five jobs, and took off on Sundays. Their biggest dilemma was figuring out what to eat for dessert when the chow hall ran out of cherry pie. Why we couldn't take some of these guys and gals to pull gate guard and tower guard was beyond me. My fix for this issue was to task each platoon to give up one to two soldiers per platoon that were not performing well out on missions. We would make these guys our FOB Warhorse force-protection detachment. I figured they would be less of a liability on the FOB than they would be out running patrols.

The manpower management took an unimaginable amount of time over the next ten months to keep on track. I tried to plan the leave roster to accommodate the soldiers the best I could so they could make it home for the birth of a child, anniversaries, birthdays, weddings, etc., and still meet mission requirements. It was a delicate balance and only got harder as missions increased, emergencies on the home front occurred, and casualties started to

---

38   A slang term used to describe soldiers that work on an FOB and never deploy on missions

mount. It was difficult for me to tell someone, "No, you can't go home to a funeral … No, you can't be there for the birth of your child … No, you can't have an extension on your leave because your wife is leaving you … No, you can't …" The majority of the guys understood what needed to be done in order to accomplish our missions. They were the meaning of "selfless service, dedication, and loyalty." It was clear and went without saying that if a guy went AWOL, was late coming back from leave, or took his time leaving Kuwait, he would be hurting his buddies back in Iraq. With the exception of a few incidents, 95 percent of the guys made it back on time and did everything possible, once they were in Kuwait, to get on the first thing smoking back into the AO and rejoin their platoon.

The building of a combat outpost was uncharted territory for all of us in the company. It had the makings of an urban defensive position, but we had to plan for long-term operations that mainly consisted of offensive operations. At first, we had no support as far as the conventional assets. Since our engineers were doing an infantry job, we had no engineer support and ended up learning how to drive Bobcats, bulldozers, and bucket loaders, and to operate the crane on our cargo truck. We had our infantry squads have a few soldiers each get cross-trained on the cargo vehicle and its crane. That allowed us to shuttle out two blast walls at a time from the FOB. Then we would start fortifying the building to protect it from mortar and rocket fire. SSG Grant, our maintenance chief, had our M88 recovery vehicle crews out at the COP using the winch on their vehicle to raise and set in the large twenty-foot concrete blast walls around the COP. They also used their vehicle to crush all the burned-out police vehicles, and then used the spade and the winch to neatly stack all the cars in a corner of the compound, nice and neat like in a junkyard back in the States. Everyone was moving with a purpose and knew it was only a matter of time before the insurgents figured out that we weren't just going to hang out for a week or two and go back to the FOB.

As first and second platoon were working out at the COP, third platoon went back to FOB Warhorse to get their Bradleys and gun trucks loaded up and ready for patrols in the rest of Bone's sector.

Since this would be the first time third platoon would be out in sector, CPT Chapman wanted to go out on a few patrols with them and see how they operated with their new PL.

The commander's intent was to get himself out into the town, talk to some of the local leaders, and then go into the city and meet with one of the Iraqi army commanders working with the company. The patrol was planned to be "low budget" and "routine." Needless to say, LT Pijpaert's first trip outside the wire was quite the experience and anything but "low budget" and "routine."

Third platoon had huddled around the company's designated briefing area just outside the command post. It was a big four-by-eight plywood box up on stilts. It had swinging doors on it that, when not in use, we could lock up so no passers-by could see what was on the board. I would use it to post the recent activities in the area of operation, new enemy tactics, weather, and other general information that would help the PLs. The board was also equipped with a dry-erase board, satellite image of the cities, a regular map, intelligence updates, and other mission-essential data.

For the mission brief, LT Pijpaert briefed his guys on what they were going to do and how they were going to do it from beginning to end, and it took about twenty minutes. Then he went into his contingency planning.

CPT Chapman was carefully listening to everything the LT was saying until he was distracted when the radio operator came out and handed him a message from battalion TOC. It referenced a meeting that was going to take place later that day. Not wanting to deal with the distraction, CPT Chapman acknowledged the RTO and continued to listen in on the remainder of the briefing. Satisfied that the guys had enough information to be successful while out on the mission, LT Pijpaert told everyone to mount up, get final radio checks, and then get into the order of movement.

The excitement level was high, and I could feel a slight bit of tension in the air. Even though the mission seemed routine, it always had the potential to go south in a hurry. Vehicles were cranking up, and the smell of diesel exhaust fumes lingered in the air. I could hear the crackle of radios mixed with the sounds of the .50-cal machine guns' receiver-and-feed systems being worked back and forth, getting the lube into the nooks and crannies. Guys also did other last-minute, nervous, pre-combat checks on whatever was within eyesight. Then the drivers pulled out one by one and jockeyed the vehicles into the order of movement for the patrol. I gave CPT Chapman a wave and went back into the CP to track their movements.

The patrol left the wire, and was just getting settled into the patrol route and adjusting the vehicle interval, when all of a sudden, a massive explosion detonated center mass on the second vehicle.

BOOM!

The LT's vehicle had gotten hit with an IED. The IED detonated on the driver's side of the vehicle and blasted the ballistic glass with 155mm shrapnel and shattered the window, sending tiny splinters of glass throughout the cab of the HMMWV. The driver, SGT Baron, was wounded in the face and neck. The LT seemed to be okay. But the vehicle was instantly disabled and rolled to an awkward stop on the road. Moments later, the patrol was engaged with AK-47 fire. The turrets of all the HMMWVs erupted with the sound of heavy automatic machine gun fire. They were returning fire at an enemy position near a palm groove six hundred meters away.

CPT Chapman tried to get a situation report from LT Pijpaert on the company radio. But LT Pijpaert was already on the platoon radio telling his guys to abandon the vehicle and prepare to "blow it in place" so it would not land in the hands of the enemy. Upon hearing the radio transmission, CPT Chapman grabbed his weapon and scrambled for the door handle of his truck, then jumped out and ran to intercept the guys from tossing some Thermite grenades into the vehicle and burning it to the ground.

As the firing slowed down and the casualty was stabilized, it was decided that SGT Baron's wounds were not life threatening. Minus the engine in the gun truck being inoperative, the HMMWV could roll and be towed (self-recovered) back to the FOB. The soldiers of third platoon sprang into action. They hooked up the tow bar while the gunners pulled security on the rest of the area. Within minutes, they had the vehicle hooked up, personnel cross-loaded, and were heading back to the FOB.

Once back at the FOB, the vehicle was towed back to the motor-pool area and dropped off. CPT Chapman and LT Pijpaert linked up at the company command post to do an after-action review (AAR). The main topic of discussion was the blowing up of a HMMWV. CPT Chapman was pretty fired up and was wondering where in the heck that command came from. It turned out LT Pijpaert had briefed "blowing a vehicle in place" as a contingency in his patrol brief, but CPT Chapman had been distracted for that split second when the RTO had come out and handed him a message. He obviously never heard the "blow it in place" briefed as a course of action. One thing was for certain: CPT Chapman listened to every patrol brief without interruption from that point on.

It only took a few days for the insurgents to start shooting mortars and small-arms fire at the COP in Buhritz. Initially, it wasn't that accurate, but as the days went on, they got the ranges set on the mortars and their small-arms fire also grew more accurate. To prevent anyone from getting shot by sniper fire, we shifted the majority of our "out in the open" fortification process to the evening time, to use the cover of darkness to our advantage. We also set up several designated marksman positions throughout the buildings to kill anyone that was an imminent threat to us. Additionally, we had one section of Bradleys up north over-watching each other and our MSR,[39] and one single Bradley oriented down south just outside our COP. These were a show of force and acted as a blocking position that prevented any possible vehicle-borne IEDs from driving up

---

39   Main supply route

close to the COP and exploding. Our OPs over-watched the single Bradley so that no one could sneak up on it and throw a satchel charge or IED underneath it.

Within seventy-two hours of occupying the COP, SFC Hamilton and I were in the TOC when we heard a ten- to fifteen-round burst of machine-gun fire right outside the COP. Immediately after the burst of gunfire, the company radio crackled.

Quisssh ...

"Bone X-Ray, this is Red 2. We just engaged and killed one individual wearing a black ski mask, armed with an RPG, one hundred meters south of our location, over."

SGT Williams, SPC Osborne, and SPC Aparicio were manning the Bradley that was oriented down south, and they had made the first confirmed kill in Buhritz. They were scanning their sector when, no more than a hundred meters away, an insurgent wearing a black ski mask jumped out from the side of a building and knelt down to engage the Bradley with an RPG. The crew identified the AIF before he could get settled to aim and fire the RPG, and mowed him down with the coax machine gun of the Bradley. SGT Williams was LT Boeka's wingman, and was also part of the same crew that got the kill on the machine-gun team during the political party mission in Old Baqubah.

Enemy contact continued to increase as the days and nights clicked along. Within the first week, we had killed five to six guys between Buhritz and Tahrir. The Bradleys and tanks that were up on the north side over-watching the MSR had killed a few AIF at night, while the enemy tried to emplace a 155mm artillery round/ IED. The OPs located at the mayor's house engaged one AIF east of their position. The AIF were moving tactically from house to house with AK-47s and appeared to be setting up to take some shots at the OPs. The OP watched one guy go behind a house and then come out the other side wearing a black ski mask and shooting his AK-47 at the OP's position. The OP cut him down with a burst of M240B machine-gun fire.

We initially went out, grabbed the bodies, and searched

them, and got the weapon system or IED material right after an engagement. But we started taking more and more precision small-arms fire so we just left the bodies lie there in the street where they fell and watched them to make sure no one came by and grabbed the weapons. If they were foolish enough to do so, we would kill them, too.

If we killed a local fighter and the families knew, they would come out (usually a female, since they knew we were less likely to shoot them) and wave in our direction either by hand or sometimes a white flag. They would pause, pray, and inch their way toward the body, hoping not to get shot, but also willing to risk it in order to bury their family member according to the Islamic tradition of getting them in the ground before the sun goes down. It was crazy to think we were still trying to be culturally sensitive to someone we just smoked, but we were (sometimes).

Around the first week of December, LT Boeka was at the southern OP and pulled down the street about a hundred meters farther than normal to get a different angle on a road. He had no sooner gotten to his new vantage point and *BOOM!* Bright flash, loud crack, and an orange fireball billowed into the sky, mixed with concrete, dirt, flying trash, Bradley armored track skirts, and reactive armor tiles. The BFV was instantaneously immobilized. The IED blew the front end of the Bradley four feet into the air, slammed it to the ground, dislodged the 800-pound final drive, sheered all twenty or so ¾-inch bolts from the hull of the Bradley, and ripped it from the transmission. The heavy steel track coiled up on itself and jammed into the road wheels, locking the BFV from going forward or backward on its own power. Moments after the IED had detonated the vehicle had shut off, the explosion cracked the fuel tank, the vehicle leaked its fuel onto the ground, filled the hull of the BFV full of fuel, and poured out of every conceivable hole.

Quisssh ...

"Bone X-Ray, this is Red 6. We just got hit with an IED one hundred meters south of our OP's position. No casualties at this time, but we will need recovery assets. Exact BDA[40] on victor unknown, but the vehicle will not run or move on its own power, over."

"Red 6, this is Bone X-Ray. Roger. We will be sending out a Bradley and a dismounted element to link up and tow you back to the COP, over."

We had just lost our first Bradley. The blast was so concentrated that it buckled the hull of the Bradley, ripped the final drive area apart, and dislodged the turret from the ring mount. When the dismounts went out to secure the site, they searched the area for clues to give us an idea how the IED was activated, powered, concealed, and any other information that would assist us in stopping it from reoccurring. We also needed to gather the evidence to educate all the soldiers. IED-making material, when separated from all the components, can look like everyday household items: wire, a battery for a remote control car, a cordless telephone receiver, a garden hose, nine-volt batteries, light switches, tape, cell phones, etc. So it was important for us to know what we were looking for when we went into a house and searched for the IED-making factories.

The specific IED that blew up Red 6's vehicle was what we called a victim-operated IED. It was a string of wire that had surgical tubing with metal clips crimped onto the tubing with the wire soldered to it. The wire ran to a nine-volt battery, and from the battery, the wire ran to a blasting cap stuck inside a 155mm artillery round that was stacked next to two other rounds. So when the BFV ran over the surgical tubing, the metal clips touched each other, completed the circuit, sent a charge to the blasting caps, and set off the IED. If the BFV was a few feet off the road, the blast probably would not have been so bad, but when the IED went off, the Bradley's right side of the track was sitting right smack dab on top of the IED, so it absorbed the brunt of the blast. If this had

---

40   Battle damage assessment

been a gun truck, the front right passenger, LT Boeka, would have certainly been killed.

Victim-operated IEDs were a reliable, cheap way for the insurgents to beat our electrical IED counter devices, if concealed properly. It also limited the insurgents' risk of having a triggerman near the blast site. The largest risk for an insurgent on any IED was emplacing it. Once that was done with a victim-operated IED, they were free to do other activities and not have to over-watch the IED.

SFC Hamilton and a squad of infantry recovered the vehicle and dragged it back to the COP's compound where we waited for the recovery team to come out and drag it back to the FOB. Once back at the FOB, the vehicle was dropped off near our maintenance area where the mechanics verified whether it would be fixed or scrapped. This vehicle was too badly damaged and didn't return to the fight. Once the vehicle was rendered non mission capable, we stripped it of all its good parts, pulled the reactive armor, communication equipment, all the ammunition and TOW missiles, tools, and other random equipment that could be used later, then locked it inside the connex, and waited for a replacement vehicle.

The battalion did not have any extra Bradleys sitting around, so we ended up giving first platoon the XO's vehicle to maintain their combat power. The XO ended up using the FSO's Bradley that didn't have the bench seating in the back, but had an excellent communications platform and more storage space in case he had to do logistical operations.

To ensure we kept a presence in Tahrir and Old Baqubah, the commander planned missions for the platoons to conduct on their way into FOB Warhorse and on their way out to the BIP. We would also conduct random missions in between the rotations to try to keep the insurgents off balance the best we could.

Third platoon, along with Bone Recovery, rotated into the BIP to relieve first platoon so they could go back to FOB Warhorse and execute some personal and vehicle maintenance over a two-day period. The rotation plan was for the platoons to do four days out at the outpost and two days back on Warhorse. It really turned out to be a day, maybe day and a half, by the time they conducted their missions in and out of the COP. The platoon's days back on Warhorse were filled conducting vehicle and weapons maintenance, personal hygiene, dropping laundry off to supply, catching up on some sleep, and maybe making a phone call or sending an e-mail, then it was back out to Bone X-Ray.

The two platoons that were out at the COP would share the workload over a four-day period that consisted of manning the radios, the four OPs, and the QRF (quick reaction force) consisting of two Bradleys and one squad.

The MSR security was the most labor-intensive mission (two Bradleys, M1s, or sometimes even gun trucks), but was necessary to protect our routes in and out of the AO. We would also have to conduct combat patrols to include small kill teams (ambushes), surveillance, and counter-surveillance.

If that wasn't enough, the platoons still had to conduct the daily supply runs, generator maintenance, and burning trash and a platoon's worth of feces.

The commander, XO, and I would try to rotate out with the platoons the best we could so that we had two key leaders on the ground out at the COP and one key leader at Warhorse to handle anything that sprung up back there that needed our attention. This was a particularly difficult task to keep everything and everyone on track. The average soldier at best got about two to four hours of sleep per day and that might have not been straight sleep. The Bradley and tank crews had it the worst out of all the personnel. The crews were stuck inside their vehicles for four, eight, twelve, and sometimes twenty-four hours, depending on the mission, before they could rotate out and head back to the COP. This went on for months in varying intervals. The Bradley and M1 crews had become skilled at urinating into water bottles, defecating into garbage bags, and occupying their time. The static positions were the most dangerous of all missions, as the enemy knew where you were and when you would be there, and after a while it became too risky for the crews to go outside to urinate; we knew the insurgents were watching us, waiting for a crew member to be exposed so they could launch an attack with precision small-arms fire (via snipers), RPG, or just open up with a burst of machine-gun fire. It would only take one time to let our guard down.

We found an alarming number of AIF in that area and it made for a target-rich environment, but they were still determined to kill Americans. At one point in time, SGT Green from third platoon was sitting in his Bradley over-watching the MSR when he decided to smoke a cigarette. As he popped his hatch to let in some fresh air and release the cigarette smoke from the turret, he heard a metallic bang and realized an AIF soldier had been hiding near a wall a few feet behind the Bradley and was patiently waiting for someone to open the hatch so he could lob a grenade into one of the open hatches. Fortunately, SGT Green did not open the hatch all the way and the grenade landed and wedged itself between the gunner's hatch and the Bradley's optics box, which we call the "Dog House." When the grenade went off, it rocked the Bradley turret and shot shrapnel everywhere. The most damage occurred to the sighting system of the Bradley and rendered the vehicle inoperative for a few weeks while we waited on replacement parts.

As time unfolded, we unfortunately had less of a waiting period for replacement parts. Our "bone yard" started to fill with the burned, blasted, and twisted steel wreckage of Bradleys, M1 tanks, HMMWVs, and pretty much anything that was on the roads throughout the battalions and brigade's sector.

CHAPTER 7

TURNING UP THE HEAT

IT WAS NOW MID December and Bone's occupation of the Buhritz IP station was a major obstacle for the AIF, and they did everything in their power to persuade us to go elsewhere. Unknown to us at the time, the 1920s Revolution Brigade used Buhritz as a safe haven, logistical hub, training area, and staging area to launch attacks into Old BQ and Tahrir.

Third platoon was scheduled to relieve first platoon so they could go back and conduct maintenance, swap out vehicles, and replace the Bradley that had been blown up the night before. Third platoon had called the COP and told the RTO that they were departing FOB Warhorse, would be out shortly, and to let first platoon know they could start getting their guys ready to roll out and get the PLs track-ready to be towed back in by Bone Recovery. The COP compound was so small that we could not fit all the vehicles in it at once. A platoon had to stay out on the main road and wait for the other platoon to pull out. Then they could pull into the compound, unload the vehicles, and stage them for follow on missions.

The weather was starting to turn from unpleasant to dreadful. The temperatures were dropping into the forties during the day and hitting freezing at night. The rainy season in Iraq was upon us and had turned the once powder-fine dirt within the compound to a thick muck that had the consistency of manure.

Once first platoon had their disabled Bradley hooked up to the M88 recovery vehicle, they headed back to FOB Warhorse. As the Bradleys, gun trucks, and enormous M88 churned up the brown muck and weaved their way through the barriers outside the compound, third platoon waited patiently out on the main road, scanning their sectors, waiting to pull down into the compound and waddle their way through the mud into the cold, damp, burned-out shell of a building we called home.

We were trying to make it as comfortable as possible. We had brought out a few potbelly stoves that could run off of wood, diesel, or gas, and also some electrical heaters to try to warm up the sleeping areas and TOC so the guys had some type of relief from the dreary weather. The electrical heaters drew too much amperage and kept blowing the circuit breakers on the generator, and the potbelly stoves had not been completely assembled due to missing parts and first platoon having to go out on a recovery mission the evening prior.

One of the first orders of business for third platoon was to conduct a logistical run with LT Moffit to FOB Gabe. Since FOB Gabe was closer to the combat outpost (less than five miles) than FOB Warhorse, FOB Gabe would become our primary logistical support facility to include helipad, chow hall, and rifle ranges, and it also housed an IA army unit/military transition team and Special Forces unit that we would work with on multiple occasions in the future. They had the ability to provide us with all our logistical needs and were willing to help us out since the personnel that were operating FOB Gabe were also the officers and NCOs that had been pulled from our brigade to support the MTT teams, including CPT Austin, MAJ Karcher, and SGM DeValle.

Once third platoon had gotten settled in, LT Pijpaert organized a patrol to go to FOB Gabe. There were two Bradleys: the XO's crew with SGT Martinez as the gunner and PFC Romero as the driver, and SSG Embry's crew. SSG Fili and a driver would man the LMTV (cargo truck), and LT Pijpaert, SPC Simmons, and PFC Birdsall would be in the HMMWV.

The patrol personnel gathered into the small congested area of the company command post for a quick patrol brief and a rundown on what route they were going to take (not like there were many choices), order of movement for the vehicles within the convoy, radio frequencies they would operate on, and contingencies if they should be attacked. Once briefed by the XO, the crews went out and fired up their vehicles, programmed the radios to the appropriate frequencies, and got radio checks with one another and the command post (CP). Once radio checks were completed, they pulled outside the COP, got into the order of movement, and proceeded to FOB Gabe.

Quisssh ...

"Bone X-Ray, this is Black 5. I have four vehicles, eleven personnel, departing Bone X-Ray en route to FOB Gabe, over."

"Black 5, this is Bone X-Ray, roger, over."

"Black 5 out!"

As the vehicles pulled away from the COP, they paused until they were a good interval from each other and then headed north toward the section of M1 tanks from second platoon that were over-watching the bridges and the route into the city. As the patrol approached the bridge, they slowed down to make the sharp ninety-degree turn onto the narrow bridge. The vehicles had to stop and cross the bridge one at a time since the bridge's weight capacity was not known, and we did not want to risk collapsing the bridge or have two vehicles on one choke point at a time. The XO's lead vehicle crossed over the bridge, made the left turn onto Route Gold, started to creep north at a slow rate of speed, then waited while the rest of the vehicles crossed. The second vehicle was LT Pijpaert's. It made the left turn off of the bridge onto Route Gold, and started to head north with the XO's Bradley. The third vehicle was the LMTV with SSG Fili and the driver PFC Myers. The LMTV crossed, and then it was SSG Embry's Bradley with SPC Daughtry as the gunner and PFC Avila as the driver. The trailing Bradley just started to make the turn off of the bridge onto Route Gold with the rest of the vehicles when SSG Embry looked forward. He saw an eruption of blacktop road, flames, smoke, and dirt slam into the driver's side of the vehicle. It lifted the front left side of the vehicle up into the air and enveloped it into a cloud of dust and debris.

"IED! IED!"

LT Pijpaert's vehicle had just gotten hit with an IED. As SSG Embry scrambled for the hand mic to call and see if they were okay, a second larger explosion slammed into the front passenger's door of LT Pijpaert's vehicle.

The cab of the HMMWV instantly filled with dirt, smoke, and debris; the entire crew was disoriented and choking on the thick, cordite-laden air. LT Pijpaert was screaming for a SITREP from his crew members and simultaneously searched for the hand mic that was hidden in the dust.

At that point, everyone on the patrol waited breathlessly for the report from the crew. That temporary pause waiting for the radio to break squelch seemed like an eternity.

"Black 5, this is Blue 6. No casualties, and the vehicle is still mobile, over."

At that moment, everyone on the patrol let out a deep breath and relaxed slightly, knowing everyone was okay, with the exception of being knocked around a little.

"Blue 6, this is Black 5, roger. Glad you guys are okay. We'll continue mission to FOB Gabe, out."

The turret gunners were traversing back and forth, scanning their entire sector for a triggerman or RPG gunner, anything that looked suspicious (in those situations, everything looked suspicious). Nobody was out walking around, shopping, or driving. All the local shops had their heavy steel security doors pulled shut and locked; the city looked like a ghost town.

With their vehicles in line and their thoughts back amongst them, they reported REDCON1 (Ready Condition 1) and slowly started to head north again until everyone had their intervals set.

As the convoy turned east onto Route Vanessa, LT Moffitt noticed that the once-manned IP checkpoints were now vacant and that the busy marketplace was empty, with the exception of a few mangy stray dogs scrounging around for some scraps. Once the entire convoy pulled onto Route Vanessa, the four-vehicle convoy put the pedals to the metal and started toward FOB Gabe.

Quisssh ...

"Bone X-Ray, this is Black 5. We are heading east on Vanessa, time now, over."

"Black 5, this is Bone X-Ray, roger, out."

From Route Vanessa, it was a straight shot to FOB Gabe. The vehicles just started to pick up speed and *BOOOOM!*

"IED! IED!"

An IED exploded in between the LMTV and SSG Embry's Bradley. SSG Embry's vehicle headed into the smoky debris cloud like a NASCAR driver blindly maneuvers his car through a smoking wreck on nothing but hope. *BOOM!* Another IED detonated squarely center mass of SSG Embry's Bradley. The multiple 155mm artillery rounds slung hot shrapnel into the thick steel plates of the Bradley's side armor and jutted the thirty-two-ton vehicle like it had just been sideswiped by a train. The concussion rocked the entire crew. The Bradley stayed on course and continued rolling in the direction of FOB Gabe.

Quisssh ...

"Black 5, this is Blue 3. We were just engaged by multiple IEDs at the intersection of C Avenue and Route Vanessa. No casualties and vehicle is still mobile. We'll Charlie Mike, over."

"Blue 3, this is Black 5, roger. I'll call into higher, Black 5, out."

As the four-vehicle patrol approached the gates of FOB Gabe, the crews could breathe slightly easier, but not much, knowing they still had to go back the same exact way. As the Bradleys and trucks weaved their way through the gates of the FOB, the guards that were manning the gates looked on with astonishment at the damage to vehicles. They knew all the explosions they'd just heard had been aimed at destroying the vehicles that were now driving through the barriers. Although the vehicles looked awfully bad, every one of them was still mobile and could make it back to the COP.

The vehicles pulled up in the gravel parking lot outside the chow hall to load up some rations, and the crews got out and surveyed the damage. LT Pijpaert's HMMWV had the entire front passenger door pushed in three to four inches, which explained why his elbow was now throbbing in pain since the adrenaline was wearing off. The ballistic glass was smashed and spider-webbed, the front engine hood was shredded with particles of fiberglass sticking out of the jagged edges, and the portion of the rear deck (trunk) was penetrated in several areas where the thin steel was easily sliced opened by the hot jagged shrapnel. With the exception of the oil sight glasses and hubs on two of the road wheels being cracked, a shock absorber being cut in two, and the steel side skirts being gouged, the Bradley was in pretty good condition.

LT Moffitt, LT Pijpaert, and the crews looked at the damage inflicted by the AIF and all agreed that it had been skilled fighters trying to kill them, given the accuracy of the IED detonations and how the blasts had been directed for maximum effect on its target.

The questions we asked ourselves were how and when did they emplace these IEDs? With the exception of the two IEDs on Chuck Avenue and Vanessa, the other two IEDs that went off on Route Gold were directly in the area we were specifically over-watching with a section of Bradleys or M1s to counter IED emplacement. How did they get those IEDs in there? Did they emplace them previously? Did they somehow avoid our surveillance? Where were the trigger men? These were all questions we would be asking ourselves for quite some time.

The guys loaded the vehicles with cases of water, MREs, sodas, Gatorade, energy drinks called "Ripits," and various other food products. Once the vehicles had been loaded up, they moved over to the fueling point to fill up the twenty-five-gallon fuel cans that were needed to run the generators and stoves. This routine would be done about every three to four days. The fuel-guzzling M1s alone went almost daily for fuel. We wanted to bring in a fuel truck, but the compound was too small and the threat of indirect fire from mortars and rockets was high. If by chance a round did hit the fuel truck, it would have ignited the 5,000 gallons, causing us to evacuate the compound, and that was not an option. Once the fuel cans were full and secured in the back of the LMTV, the convoy lined up and called Bone X–Ray to let them know they were heading back.

Quiiisssh ...

"Bone X-Ray, this is Black 5. Mission is complete. We are leaving FOB Gabe and are en route back to Bone X-Ray, over."

The vehicles weaved their way through the barriers, headed out to the main road, and started to get their intervals before increasing to convoy speed of thirty-five to forty miles per hour. The crews were on edge as they passed by the IED blast sites that detonated on SSG Embry's vehicle. They strained to look for a spotter or triggerman through the maze of buildings and alleyways. The convoy moved down route Vanessa and turned onto Route Gold without incident. Knowing they had M1 tanks over-watching their movement down Route Gold, the convoy moved a bit quicker, feeling a little better and more secure. The convoy passed by the blast site that blew up on LT Pijpaert's HMMWV and again breathed easier once past the site.

Soon the vehicles slowed to a crawl and one by one made the turn onto the bridge. When LT Pijpaert's vehicle approached the bridge to cross, it was instantaneously swallowed in a dust cloud and rocked by an enormous explosion unlike the previous ones. This IED's force almost flipped the vehicle on its side as the explosion blossomed out of the ground like a miniature nuclear detonation. The HMMWV appeared to be suspended in midair for a moment, came crashing down violently, and then slowed to an out-of-control stop. SSG Embry thought to himself, *They're dead, all of them, dead. No way did anyone survive that explosion.*

LT Pijpaert and the crew were knocked around pretty bad and could not get the vehicle to start or steer. No sooner had they gathered their wits about them than the HMMWV door flew open, and SSG Fili emerged out of the dust and smoke cloud to assist in the medical evacuation of the wounded. To his surprise, everyone for the most part was unharmed, with the exception of SPC Simmons, the gunner; he experienced the majority of the explosion's concussion in the unprotected, open turret.

The guys were assisted out of the HMMWV by SSG Fili and SPC Myers, then positioned around the vehicle in a 360-degree hasty perimeter to pull local security just in case the AIF had a complex attack set up. The M1 tanks that were over-watching the area were also on high alert while LT Moffitt backed his Bradley up to the HMMWV to hook up a tow cable and drag the HMMWV back to the COP. With the steering out and the vehicle not running, it was a challenge to get the vehicle over the bridge and back through the serpentine barriers of the COP. Eventually, though, the vehicle was secured within the compound walls.

At that point, it was mid December and we had already lost two HMMWVs and two Bradleys—one Bradley permanently and one temporarily. The vehicle temporarily down was the one that'd had a hand grenade thrown on top of the turret and had the sighting system blown up. LT Boeka's Bradley had been lost due to the IED just outside the COP. We had three soldiers wounded in action, two of which would not come back: LT Ebarb and SGT Baron. SGT Baron went AWOL when he went home on leave shortly after being wounded and was never heard from again.

The IED attacks on our logistical patrol indicated that the enemy had prepared well in advance for us to come down into the Buhritz and Tahrir sector. We suspected that the entire IP station attack, and subsequently overrunning of the compound, was a tactic used to draw US forces into the Tahrir and Buhritz area for a close-in fight. It also told us that they were well trained, funded, supplied, and determined to stay.

After the five IED attacks, we were able to get engineer assets from outside the battalion and brigade to bulldoze the sides of the roads along Route Gold, clearing it of all trash and debris that could be a potential hiding place for an IED in the future. The insurgents were using the city of Tahrir as their main area of operations to base attacks on the convoys and patrols coming and going from Buhritz, and then slip back into the urban labyrinth to fight another day.

To try and counter the AIF activity within the town and on the outskirts, we started to conduct unsystematic nighttime operations where we would take our Bradleys and tanks (under blackout conditions) and set them on both Route Vanessa and Route Gold to patrol up and down, observing all the alleyways and streets. The optics on the Bradleys and tanks were, to say the least, awesome, and we had the capability to see across the city at night. Even more importantly, we could engage whatever we saw with either 25mm, .50-cal, 7.62mm, or the M1's 120mm with high-explosive rounds, or a round we called a "can round." This was short for a canister round that had a thousand ball-bearing-type projectiles on the inside. When fired, it was like a massive shotgun that killed everything in its path. The can round was a great weapon for clearing alleyways and areas within a palm groove … as we would find out later.

At first, we had a superior advantage while doing these operations. The insurgents were not used to having company downtown at night. They did not know what our capabilities were with the Bradleys and M1s, and did not realize how far or effectively we could see at night. When we first started doing these operations, we would see squads of AIF walking randomly through the city streets carrying AK-47s, RPKs, and various other weaponry without regard to the US forces in the area. This only lasted a week or so until they realized that we could see down every single alleyway, rooftop, and across the city from one end to the other. We killed multiple insurgents every time we went out doing these types of missions until they started understanding our nighttime capabilities and were a little more vigilant.

Between the increased presence of B Co 1-12 hunter-killer teams, the Apache helicopters (known as air weapons teams or AWTs), and the assortment of other enablers our units were given, we were putting the hurt on the insurgents and disrupting the way they were conducting business. We forced them to reevaluate. They could not move like they once did, and every time they did move, it was really hazardous to their health. They did not know when or where we were. It was a deadly game of cat and mouse. The insurgents still had the advantage of time, and because we were not able to sustain any high level of pressure on them (massive area and limited personnel), they could just wait us out.

The insurgents were a versatile foe, could adapt rather quickly, and countered our maneuvers and tactics just as well as we could adapt and adjust to their tactics. The fighters we were up against were well trained and dedicated to the jihad. They were not going to be underestimated, and we had to stay on our best possible game to keep them guessing. Our biggest problem was the geographical location of the combat outpost. As mentioned earlier, it could not have been in a worse place.

Shortly after the IED attacks and all the night missions, I had one of my first experiences in Buhritz on how adaptive and cunning the enemy was. I went out on MSR security and over-watch with CPL Lunt and SPC Kennedy inside our armored HMMWV. We positioned ourselves directly in front of the bridge on the west side of the canal so we could over-watch the bridge known as CP 414, along with Route Gold. Shortly after getting into position, we took a few rounds of small-arms fire from the south that impacted on my door. My best guess was they were trying to shoot the optics out on the remote .50-cal. As we were searching for the shooter to our south, an AIF with an AK-47 ran from a building directly to our twelve o'clock about 150 to 200 meters away, then sprinted down an alleyway. Our initial instincts were to pull forward and try to position ourselves to get the "squirter" as he ran down the alley. But I paused for a split second and thought, *Why did he just run out in front of us? He could have stayed in that building all day.*

Something wasn't right. Instead of crossing over the bridge, we stayed on the west side of the canal and headed north to try to get eyes on so we could kill him. Naturally, he was gone.

A few hours later, the mayor's compound was engaged with heavy machine-gun fire, and I received a report that we had one wounded soldier from second platoon. I was told he was shot in the head and still on the roof. So I called for a tank to pull down and relieve us so we could go to the mayor's house, then treat and evacuate the soldier. Once we got there, CPL Lunt, SPC Kennedy, and I worked our way to the rooftop. Once we got to the location of where the casualty was, I expected to see a mess, but instead there was a delirious trooper lying on the ground with head trauma but no bullet wound. It kind of puzzled me, but I wasn't going to play CSI on the rooftop. I figured he had gotten hit in the head with a flying piece of cement or something along those lines. We got him off the roof and back to the COP.

Shortly after, LT Sparks and SFC Malo brought their tanks down on the east side of the canal and unleashed a few 120mm main gun rounds into the buildings that housed the insurgents. First platoon showed up and immediately cleared the wood line and a row of buildings to the east of the mayor's house, then they started to work on another set of buildings. As they were pushing down one of the streets, they saw a van speed away. They had just missed closing in on the group of AIF fighters.

Reports from some of the citizens indicated that the vehicle was used to evacuate the wounded. We found blood, bandages, and other items, indicating we had wounded or killed some guys, but we couldn't get to them before they evacuated.

Later that evening, the tanks were coming back from FOB Gabe after refueling, and as they turned the corner on the bridge at CP 414, the second tank in the convoy was hit with an IED. This was the same bridge we were over-watching. *How did they get an IED into that location?* We had cleared that area with bulldozers and route clearance and had over-watched since then. The one thing I did know for sure was that the random AIF who ran down the alleyway was NOT random—he was bait. They were trying to bait us across the bridge so they could blow the IED on an HMMWV instead of a Bradley or a tank. If we would have pulled across the bridge another fifteen feet, they would have killed at least one of us, most likely CPL Lunt. As for SGT Rodriquez, his skull had been fractured. He was eventually evacuated back to the rear, and later sent to Germany, then back to the States. We never did confirm what had hit him in the head.

It was 22 December, and we were moving into our third week in our new home. The insurgent activity had slowed down to harassing fires either by small arms or the occasional mortar round that would be lobbed toward the compound. The platoons were getting into a rhythm and were steadily building up our defenses at the outpost, so I figured it would be a good time to go back and start wading through the UCMJ paperwork. We were also starting to send soldiers home on R&R leave, so I also wanted to make sure the leave process was going smoothly. Plus, I wanted to conduct one-on-one counseling with the guys before they left for home to stress the importance of coming back on time—and not getting into trouble when they were home.

I had hitched a ride back with first platoon in the early morning hoping to get a hot meal before the chow hall closed. After being out at the COP for so long, I'd gotten used to the black-sooted walls, the dilapidated buildings that were half blown up and crumbling around me, and the constant cold that chilled my bones. So when I got back to the FOB, everything looked extra clean and orderly, including the prestigious Fobbits with their wrinkle-free uniforms, squeaky clean skin, and weapons slightly coated with dust and never oiled. As we made our way to the chow hall, we had to stop off at the clearing barrels, and there were a few Fobbits in front of us that smelled like perfume and soap. They kind of looked crossways at the group of us for being dirty with an expression like, *How dare you come to the chow hall soiled.*

One of the trademarks of being out at the COP during the winter was a sooty face and uniform blended with matted hair from wearing the fleece watch cap twenty-four hours a day. Between living in a burned-out building, using half-working potbelly stoves, and burning charcoal at night in the guard positions to try and get some warmth, we were always going to be black and coated with soot. It was a trade-off that all of us were willing to make. We sparingly burned every bag of charcoal that we could get our hands on. My supply NCO, SSG Morales, was a charcoal-scrounging genius (I think the chow hall people thought we were having big barbecues). The charcoal was a great source of heat for the guards. At nighttime, they could dump the charcoal into ammo cans that had holes punched into the sides and tops, and it would burn for a long time but did not throw off any light that would give our position away or interfere with our night-vision goggles.

After some good chow, a few cups of coffee, and a little conversation with some of the guys, I worked my way back to the room to take a shower and change into some clean clothes. Then it was off to the company CP for some paperwork and other administrative issues. I started to sort through the UCMJ and decided to deal with the company grade issues and work my way to the bigger stuff. There were a few guys that had some issues with drinking and other smaller infractions that I could test the legal system on and get a rather quick turnaround and thus start chipping away at the discipline issues.

I sorted through an immense amount of paperwork over the next day and a half, and wrote up some standing orders for personnel when they were on leave and listed a variety of emergency numbers and e-mails in case there was some kind of delay or emergency. They had no excuse not to call or e-mail and give us a heads-up so we could plan for their absence. I also worked on promotions for the lower enlisted and the specialists that were recommended for the NCO promotion boards. It was hard not knowing the guys like I should, but I did see a set of promotion orders that I had no problem recommending the month prior: Clarence Spencer. He had done nothing but impress me since I initially met him in Kuwait sitting on that bench when he told me he'd been a Marine then enlisted in the Army. He always looked like a soldier, had a great attitude, clean weapons, and I especially noticed his willingness to help out his fellow soldiers. That was an easy one to promote, and I was glad to see his orders sitting there. I set them aside because I wanted to make an example out of him—how a soldier could overcome adversity if they kept a good attitude and proved to be an asset. I also wanted CPT Chapman to be there; he, too, thought much of "Spence" and wanted to share in the occasion.

As the day slowly turned to evening, I passed the reins off to SSG Lane, CPL Lunt, and SPC Kennedy. These NCOs, along with the other guys back on the FOB, were doing awesome work with keeping the paperwork and distractions to a minimum so we could focus on the bigger picture downtown. Starting the next day, they would make it out to the COP more often than being back on FOB Warhorse.

Before I left the company CP, I told them they were going out with me in the morning and to get the gun truck ready; we were going to start working and augmenting the tank platoon so they had a little bit of extra manpower. They were getting worn down, being the smallest element out at the COP. Upon hearing that, CPL Lunt and CPL Kennedy were fired up and ready to get away from the FOB and the shenanigans that surrounded it.

There is nothing worse than staying back on the FOB, listening to the radios, hearing all the action going down, and listening to the stories when the guys rotate back for showers and a hot meal. As "TOC Rats," they tried to convince themselves that it was a necessary evil that the administrative tasks needed to be accomplished; however, they just didn't totally feel like part of the team. They kind of got the feeling of being the supporting cast not the leading role (which they were, but the production would never happen if it wasn't for them). I knew that I needed the best of the best in the TOC: I needed people that could operate independently, take the initiative, and handle tasks with minimal guidance; that's why they were there. Unfortunately, there were a few guys that had to be placed in HQ so they were not a danger to the guys out on patrol. They needed "extra" attention that distracted the A-team players within HQ platoon.

The following morning came quickly, and the weather had taken a turn for the worse. The temperatures were in the thirties to forties with a misty haze hugging the ground. The cloud cover was real low, less than a hundred feet, locking in an extra layer of dampness that cut through our clothing and went straight to the bone. We were not scheduled to leave for a few hours, so I headed to the company CP to wrap up a few things before I went out to the combat outpost. Upon arrival at the CP, I heard the radios crackle with the report that the COP had just taken two mortars rounds: one landed outside the wall and the other landed inside the compound; no casualties were reported. I didn't really give it much thought since they randomly launched a few mortar rounds to harass us in hopes of getting lucky. Then they'd run and hide before our helicopters or counter-battery would find and kill them. We called it "shoot and scoot."

As I walked through the CP, another report came in about two more mortar rounds landing in the compound, one on the roof and the other in the tiny compound. That got my attention. The rounds were landing in the compound, two for two; that was unusual. Then another call came in, two more rounds had landed. The rounds were now landing in the compound and slamming into the building. Concrete mixed with shrapnel cut through the air as the OPs continued to call in the reports. I told the RTO to call the air weapons teams and see if we could get some air support into the area and try to locate the mortars, or at least send them packing with the sounds of the rotors as they came on station. The RTO called, but the AWTs had all been grounded due to no visibility with no estimated time on station. Upon hearing that, it immediately registered that the insurgent mortar teams knew that the aircrafts were not flying. They didn't have to break their mortar tubes down, leaving time to adjust and bracket their rounds into the compound.

For the guys on the compound, they could tell that different-sized rounds were falling. The 60mm mortar rounds were deadly but really didn't pack much of a punch unless it was a direct hit or landed pretty close to its intended target. They were favored by the AIF since they were relatively small, concealable, and easy to transport and set up. The AIF initially started with the 60mm rounds, but then the 81mm rounds started falling. Those really got their attention, as they were a much larger explosion than the 60mm mortars. The AIF had followed up the 81mm barrage with automatic machine-gun fire, raking the observation posts and the buildings that housed all of B Co.

Quisssh ...

"Bone Main, this is Bone X-Ray. We are taking continuous mortar and small-arms fire. OPs are reporting the sounds of the mortars being fired from the north, west, and south, and the small-arms fire is coming from the south and east of our position. OVER!"

As the RTO gave the report, I heard the explosions and machine-gun fire in the background.

Once the AIF got their range with both the 60mm and 81mm mortars, they started dropping rounds onto the compound. Round after round exploded on top of an already structurally unstable rooftop, rattled the observations post fortifications, and slammed hot shrapnel into the sandbagged walls. The initial barrage fired ten to twelve mortar rounds. Then it tapered off to a sustainable rate of fire. They dropped rounds at random intervals with no less than two rounds shot every time they fired to catch us out in the open. The intensity of the small-arms fire was increasing. They were trying to get the OPs to either put their heads down or abandon their positions, so that they could maneuver on the COP.

We had two squad leaders in the COP, and all the Bradley sections had already been out in sector. SSG Fili and SGT McGrath, both from third platoon, met on the rooftop, and from there, they witnessed multiple gunmen running around about 300 meters from the COP's location. Muzzle flashes from AK-47s were everywhere. They immediately returned fire and tried to eliminate every target in sight. The enemy fire, both small arms and mortars, was starting to get more accurate and consistent than we had usually experienced; some of the rounds impacted near the guys on the rooftop. Upon hearing the reports, I, along with everyone, expected the fighters to do a show of force and slip back into the city. We were all wrong: they stayed to fight.

While all the reports of the fighting were getting pushed up through the battalion radio network, the battalion sergeant major, CSM Harris, was out with his maneuver element[41] doing battlefield circulation. He heard the traffic come over the NET and decided that he would go to the COP and help reinforce the outpost with his guys. As his patrol changed course and headed to B Co's outpost, they got hit with an IED as they turned onto Route Gold. The IED shot shrapnel into the sides of the doors and punctured two of the HMMWV's tires. As they continued down Route Gold, they were hit with small-arms fire before turning onto the bridge and that flattened yet another tire; they continued mission and limped the vehicle into the COP compound.

While the squads were on the rooftop slugging it out with the AIF, CSM Harris and his element pulled into the compound. No sooner had they gotten out of the HMMWVs than they heard *WISSSSH-BOOM!* A mortar round landed and blew up right in front of the driver as he was getting out of the driver's compartment. SPC Gardner got hit in several places with shrapnel and fell to the ground in pain. SSG Fili, witnessing the impact, rushed to help drag SPC Gardner to cover so the medic could get to work on him. As the medic (Doc Nguyen) started to cut Gardner's clothing away to expose the wounds, he could see where shrapnel had cut through his right leg and also his right side below his armpit. SFC Reynolds had heard the report of the casualty and pulled his

---

41   A maneuver element usually consists of four to five HMMWVs on patrol as a unit.

section of Bradleys into the compound to help with the evacuation of the wounded soldier to FOB Gabe.

Since the Bradleys had pulled off of their positions to conduct the MEDEVAC, there was a gap in our sector's coverage until the other section of Bradleys would be able to flex down to the south and take up SFC Reynolds' positions. The enemy took advantage of this and increased their fire from the south and north.

As the MEDEVAC was going on, the squads continued the fight on the rooftops and from every opening of both the IP station and the mayor's compound. They were engaging with their M4s, M249 (squad automatic weapon), and M240B (7.62mm machine gun). Our MK19 grenade launcher got jammed. SGT McGrath and a few guys worked on it while also covering the sector with their M4s and M203 grenade launchers. As they were scanning their sector, they spotted a group of AIF and attempted to kill them by firing an AT4. One of the guys took steady aim, put them dead in his sights, folded over the secondary safety, and started to gently squeeze the trigger with his thumb. While trying to control his breathing, rounds were impacting all around him. *POP! Click!* Nothing! MISFIRE! He re-cocked and tried to fire again. *POP! Click!* Misfire again! All attempts to fire the rocket failed.

The outpost continued to call for AWTs back to the company TOC. We had to tell them they were not available, but we were trying to get fast-movers on station. F/A-18s were out in sector, but we had to go through the approval process through the brigade HQ to get planes diverted from their initial flight plan and rerouted into our sector. Within minutes of the request, the fast-movers dropped in on our radio frequency. Shortly thereafter, it was determined that the enemy was too close for the fast-mover support. With the weather being as bad as it was and the large ordnance, it was too risky to drop so dangerously close. We then decided to have the pilots conduct low-level passes and hit the afterburners in an attempt to try and unnerve the insurgent fighters and take cover. The planes did it, and it worked for a moment.

As the F/A-18s were doing their low-level passes, SGT McGrath was trying to work up a call for fire mission to drop some of our own mortars and artillery on the AIF. SFC Reynolds and his Bradley section returned from the MEDEVAC mission and were back on the frontlines. SGT Fili quickly got them on the radio and guided them into a position to take out the house they were trying to previously fire on with the misfired AT4 rocket launcher. As the Bradleys pulled down to take out the house that had an AIF machine-gun position in it, a 155mm artillery round impacted dangerously close. That had been a round fired from the call for fire mission SGT McGrath was calling up. The round had impacted 200 meters away from the Bradley. Noting the impact of the round, SGT McGrath made the adjustment and called in another round. That one landed even closer to SFC Reynolds' Bradley. The decision was made to check fire on the indirect and use the TOW missiles of the Bradley to engage the entrenched AIF within the buildings and tree lines.

We had zero confidence in getting rounds on target that close and not blowing up our own guys. The TOW missiles were more accurate and caused less collateral damage, which at that point in time we were still worried about. The confidence of our mortars and 155mm artillery would later be regained, and the AIF would pay hell, but for now, the lack of artillery and mortars were to their favor.

The Bradley's TOW launcher rose slowly with the whine of an electrical motor and locked into position. SGT Wall indentified the building they were receiving fire from and gently squeezed the triggers on the gunner's hand station. As he said, "On the way," with a pop of the launch motor igniting and a woosh of the flight motor, the missile left the launcher and flew directly into the building. It blew a fireball, bricks, and debris thirty feet into the air. The missile had done its job: creating a massive hole in the side of the building and forcing the AIF firing to cease.

The AIF, though, were getting more audacious and moving about with no regard to the fire that was raining down on them from the buildings and Bradleys. SSG Fili had control of a 180-degree perimeter from south to north by way of the west, and SGT McGrath had the north to south covered by way of the east. CSM Harris' soldiers filled in where needed, and CSM Harris helped organize the ammo redistribution and continuously went from position to position to ensure everything was in order, and he helped out where needed. One section of tanks was in the north covering the route in, and the Bradleys were in a staggered dogleg formation covering east to south and reinforcing the mayor's compound that housed SGT Fuller and his fire team.

Knowing if the tempo of the firefight continued, the combat outpost would be out of ammunition by noon, so I started working on getting more ammunition from the ammunition supply point (ASP), I was getting everything I could get my hands on—once I convinced the disgruntled ASP warrant officer that there was really a war going on and that we needed ammo NOW! He actually asked me, "Why didn't you submit a request forty-eight hours out?" It almost got to the point where I was going to pistol whip him and take the ammo without his help.

CPT Chapman was briefing LT Boeka on the situation, and SFC Hamilton was trying to get his guys recalled and ready to roll out. It was going to take some time. First platoon's Bradleys were in the middle of maintenance. The vehicles' tracks were disassembled in order to replace worn track shoes and the infantry squads were scattered about the FOB doing various other jobs. At best we could leave in forty-five minutes to an hour. To make matters worse, MAJ Karcher was in heavy enemy contact in Tahrir. He was conducting an operation with his MTT units and IA, and had our tank platoon supporting his operation.

After the TOW engagement from SFC Reynolds' section of Bradleys, they tried to push farther south and get a better angle on some of the side streets, but there was concertina wire blocking their advance. SSG Fili saw that the Bradleys were held up by the wire and organized a fire team to maneuver down to the Bradleys' position and move it. SSG Fili grabbed PVT Myers and PVT Snead, who were over-watching the front entrance to the BIP. They huddled up on the side of the Bradley, came up with a quick plan, took in a few deep breaths, and darted out into the open to the concertina-wire roadblock. As soon as they exposed themselves in the open, the enemy started to walk their machine-gun fire onto their position. SSG Fili laid down some suppressive fire with his M4 while PVTs Sneed and Meyers wrestled with the razor wire, but the enemy fire was too intense. SSG Fili ordered the PVTs back to the side of the Bradley. Once back, they started to suppress the enemy one more time. PVT Meyers launched two M203 grenades into the enemy's position, and SSG Fili and PVT Sneed followed with rounds from their M4s. Meyers got a couple of good hits on the AIF position, and they retreated. A second attempt was made, and they were able to pull the wire from the road and open the path for the BFVs to maneuver farther down the road and wreak havoc on the AIF.

The AIF continued to fire RPG rockets, machine guns, AK-47s, and mortars onto the positions from the east and south east; there was no doubt the AIF was going to take full advantage of the weather and had every intension of overrunning the compound. The fight had now been going on for over three hours, and it was 1200 hours. The rain had not let up and made everything miserable. The soldiers were covered in mud, the weapons were covered in mud from being bounced from position to position, the ammo belts were contaminated, and despite the gunners' best efforts to keep things clean, sand particles were getting into the feed trays and causing weapons to jam. The small walkie-talkies (ICOM radios) we had to communicate from OP to OP had gotten wet, were intermittent at best, and made the coordination between OPs difficult.

The machine guns were starting to get sluggish from firing so many rounds, and the carbon was building up on them. The decision was made to go to the gun trucks, pull the guns that were mounted on the turrets, and swap them out with some fresh, clean guns. SGT McGrath reported that all the ammunition and AT4 rockets that were stockpiled in the company area were already used, and the gun positions were going "black"[42] on ammunition. Hearing that report, SSG Fili and CSM Harris, along with a few guys, started going into all the gun trucks looking for any ammunition that was missed. LT Pijpaert called and asked MAJ Karcher to push the tanks down one at a time to drop their spare 7.62mm ammunition off at the outpost.

SSG Davis' tank was the first to pull down into the compound and drop ammo. The compound was really tight and maneuver for a M1 tank was restricted so SSG Davis got out of his tank to guide the M1 backward and butt the tank right up to the entrance of the building so the infantry guys did not have to expose themselves for an extended period of time, and so the gunner, CPL Barta, could easily pass the ammunition from the tank to the dismounts. As the tank was being backed up, CPL Barta was in the turret hatch guiding the tank backward as a second set of eyes for SSG Davis. Once the tank was set in position, SSG Davis started to climb up on the tank to help pass ammunition down when he was slammed viciously to the ground by an explosion. A mortar round had landed directly on top of the tank. Shaking off the explosion, SSG Davis climbed back on top of the tank to look for his gunner and noticed the damage to the hatch area. The round had landed right next to the hatch and killed CPL Barta instantly. The lifeless body fell back down inside the turret to the horror of the loader, SPC Davis (aka Li'l D), and the driver, PFC Patrick. SSG Davis looked into the tank and reflexively yelled for a medic.

SPC Nguyen, ran out to the vehicle but first glance told him no amount of medical aid would do any good. CSM Harris and SSG Davis, along with the medic and SPC Davis, helped remove CPL Barta's body from the turret, then placed him in a body bag and prepared him for evacuation out of the COP and back to the FOB. The one thing you didn't want to do was leave a fallen brother

---

42   Out of ammo, less than 25 percent of basic load

out for others to see. If at all possible, we wanted to get him out ASAP.

The tank turret was covered in blood and could not be occupied; so the tank was parked off to the side and left to be dealt with later. But we'd lost a good man ...

CPL Jonathan Barta, Killed in Action, 23 December 2006, Buhritz, Iraq

CPT Chapman and I were still on the FOB with first platoon. I was in my HMMWV listening to the radios while CPT Chapman was giving the patrol brief and getting ready to roll out. I was initially relieved that the tanks were being pulled down to offload ammo, and then I heard the traffic that no one ever wants to hear: Bone X-Ray had called Bone Main and reported they had one KIA[43] and gave the report with the battle roster number of the soldier that was KIA. Knowing the order of battle roster numbers, I automatically knew it was not a B Co soldier but rather a soldier from D Co with the name starting with a "B." After a quick confirmation on my roster, I went and grabbed CPT Chapman and pulled him aside.

"Sir, we just had our first KIA. CPL Barta was hit with a mortar round and killed. Third platoon is bringing him back now."

CPT Chapman took it with little emotion and just sat there and absorbed it for a minute. Then he calmly said, "Hang tight, do what's needed to be done back here with mortuary affairs, and hitch a ride back out to the COP with the third platoon's Bradley section."

While I did that, he said that he would get the ammo resupply and first platoon re-enforcements out to the COP. We split ways and CPT Chapman went over to first platoon to brief them on CPL Barta and the change in the situation. At the conclusion of the brief, they mounted up and rolled out.

As the commander took off with first platoon, I walked over to

---

43   Killed in action

BN HQ to brief them on the CPL Barta and give them an update on the current situation, then I walked over to the mortuary affairs area and awaited the arrival of the Bradley section. The mortuary affairs' guys were there, and I told them they had a soldier coming in and to get ready. I went over to a pile of sandbags and just sat there waiting for the Bradleys. Once the Bradleys pulled up, I walked over to the vehicle and helped them carry the body off of the vehicle and into the tented examination area/processing table to confirm the identity of the body since there were no ID tags. What was racing through my mind was not good. How was I supposed to confirm the identity of a body of a soldier that had no distinguishable features, a soldier that his mother would not even recognize? But, after the business was finished at mortuary affairs, I told the Bradley crew to go over to the wash rack, hose out the back, and meet me over at the staging area, and we would leave from there. The weather had not improved, and there was no hope for any air support.

It was now about 1600 hours; the firefight had been going on for seven hours. Losing daylight, the insurgents increased fire with RPGs and heavy machine guns. They made one last large assault against the compound and got within hand-grenade range near the mayor's compound.

SGT Fuller was still manning the mayor's house with his fire team and had reported to SSG Fili that there was a group of insurgents in a vegetated area east of the COP and about a hundred meters from the flank of a Bradley. The Bradley could not depress the gun barrel enough to identify the enemy position. Hearing that report, LT Pijpaert, SSG Fili, SGT McGrath, SGT Croley, and PFC Sieger started to maneuver to reinforce the area. SGT Fuller was observing and provided a support-by-fire position. They had an M240 machine gun, their personal weapons, and a few hand grenades. SGT McGrath and SGT Croley bounded forward to set up a local support-by-fire position on a burned-out car while SSG Fili and his guys moved forward to set up the machine gun.

As SSG Fili advanced, he was slammed to the ground. SGT

McGrath yelled back to LT Pijpaert, "SSG Fili's hit, and we need a medic." But then he saw SSG Fili get back up, covered in mud and looking for something that had fallen into the muck. It turned out that SSG Fili had tripped on a small piece of concertina wire and it slammed him to the ground, jarring his NVGs loose and knocking them into the mud. He found them and continued to set up the machine gun.

PVT Sieger then came up with the ammo belt, but while doing his individual movements trying not to get shot, he had dragged the rounds through the mud, which would have jammed the gun if not cleaned. While SSG Fili attempted to clean the rounds, the rest of his guys started suppressing the area and allowed SGT McGrath to bound his fire team forward. The enemy had relocated and SGT McGrath lost track of where they had maneuvered to. SGT Fuller saw the AIF reposition and attempted to mark the enemy position with his M203 grenade launcher, but the rounds were not exploding because the close proximity would not let the rounds arm. The enemy started to fire again, and rounds began impacting around the group of soldiers. The squad was able to identify the muzzle flashes and started lobbing hand grenades, and SGT McGrath got the machine gun up and started spraying the area with 7.62mm rounds.

It was now almost dark as the commander and first-platoon Bradleys came lumbering down the road and reinforced the elements of third platoon. The insurgents quickly started to pull back into the city. Once at the COP, CPT Chapman weighed the decision to conduct a counterattack that evening or in the morning. The decision was made to wait it out. If we had any more wounded, we would not be able to fly them out due to the weather, and we knew the insurgents had laid scores of IEDs in hopes of luring us into their kill zone.

CPT Chapman had gathered the platoon leaders together to go over the plan for a counterattack in the morning. While the commander went over the plan, I started to coordinate the relief. I had first platoon start relieving third platoon from their positions so they could get some rest, take a break, clean weapons, redistribute their basic loads of ammunition, and do a quick recap on the day's events. Third platoon had endured eight straight hours of incoming mortar rounds, machine-gun fire, and RPGs. They fought for eight straight hours against a force that was numerically superior, well trained, disciplined, and able to maintain command and control on a higher level than previously thought. The intense combat had taken its toll on the guys. As their adrenaline started to wear off, they faded off into an exhausted sleep.

As the night slowly transitioned to an overcast but much-improved day, we could see the glow of the sun shining over the horizon. It was a good morning for a counterattack. Throughout the evening, CPT Chapman and LT Pijpaert worked on a plan to push out from the perimeter of the COP, clear the city from north to south, then swing back through and clear the palm grove from the east to west, and then push back north to the COP.

It was a good call to wait until morning; the conditions had been set. We had everything we needed: we had AWTs (two Apache helicopters), air MEDEVAC if needed, enough troops to hold the compounds while third platoon pushed out and provided a QRF and medical ground EVAC, artillery support, UAV on station, and most of all, time to plan. In the planning process, we identified three areas of interest that we plotted on the map. These would be third platoon's objectives. The first area lay directly east from the COP, where the AIF had infiltrated and came within hand-grenade range of the mayor's compound. The second area was a place we had called the "White Castle." It was a massive three-story building that was five hundred meters south of the COP and was a prominent building positioned on the corner of the main road leading into town. It was used as a rallying point for the AIF in sector and was also a jumping-off point for them to conduct attacks. This was also the building we had fired multiple TOW missiles into and AT4 rockets the day prior. The third objective was the palm groves. Thick and virtually impenetrable, these groves featured small spider trails that had been cut through the palm centuries earlier. Thus, this was a main infiltration route that the AIF used to get in close to attack the southern flanks of the COP and then retreat under the cover of thick foliage.

As third platoon was doing its last-minute checks and ensuring everyone had the plan, a few mortar rounds landed in the compound, followed by small-arms fire impacting the walls of the COP. I went to the rooftop to see what was going on, and by the time I made it up the ladder, it was an all-out firefight again. First platoon had been in position all night, waiting for their opportunity to put a little smackdown on the AIF. If the enemy was willing to come out, we were willing to kill them. I went to the west position overlooking the river and the palm grooves. I made it into the half blown-up room that housed one of the M240B machine guns as rounds starting impacting on the southern portion.

The one gunner that was on the M240B was attempting to clear a malfunction but really had no idea what he was doing. Rounds continued impacting all around the building. I was lying on the ground yelling at him to take the weapon off the tripod and get behind some cover as he tried to clear the malfunction. I was waiting for a bullet to smack him square in the melon. I low-crawled over, jumped up, helped him unlock the weapon from the sandbagged tripod, and we hit the ground. I cleared the malfunction, repositioned the weapon to the south, and started laying down a wall of steel into the palm grove. I fired at least 150 rounds into the palm grove. When I stopped, the AIF unleashed their own hailstorm of bullets. This went on for about 600 rounds, or a few back-and-forth volleys. I'd either killed them or they'd run out of bullets. Air weapons team came on station shortly after and things calmed down quite a bit. As I started to reposition the weapon back into the tripod, I looked at my assistant gunner and it was the company NBC[44] guy. I thought to myself, *What the*

---

44   Nuclear, biological, chemical specialist

hell is he doing here? Turns out he was up there just trying to be helpful because the primary M240 gunner went to help out his team leader rebuild an OP position that had been damaged in the mortar barrage the day earlier.

Third platoon cleared the area east of the COP and found no dead AIF and no blood trails, just a few pieces of equipment. As they were working their way back to the COP, more small-arms fire erupted from the White Castle, the second objective of third platoon that morning. It was just what we had been waiting for. We had the Apaches on station, and within a minute, CPT Chapman confirmed the grid and target description, and authorized the Apaches to launch their Hellfire missiles at the house. Moments later, the sound of thunder erupted overhead as the missile ripped through the air and slammed into the building. It was immediately followed by another missile. As the smoked and dust settled, we could see the building's top two floors had partially collapsed onto each other, but the building was still standing. Third platoon pushed south—over-watched by the careful eyes of the Bradleys—to clear the building and conduct the search for intelligence that may have been left behind by the AIF.

The gates into the compound were locked, so they called the Bradley vehicles down to ram the walls and create a breech so they could funnel into the buildings and fight it out with any remaining insurgents. SSG Fili , SGT McGrath, and SGT Bowlby stacked on the walls and waited nervously as SFC Reynolds had his driver ram the walls and knock them down. Once the walls fell, the squads rushed through the open compound and prepared to assault into the building. Within moments, they were inside the building and clearing each floor and room systematically. Occasionally, SGT McGrath's pistol-grip Mossberg shotgun could be heard blasting through locked doors.

"CLEAR!" someone shouted.

Nothing was in the building, with the exception of a copy of the Koran lying in the middle of the main room's floor.

The frustration mounted, knowing we had killed or at least

wounded some AIF in that building, but they could not find any evidence except shell casings and some random equipment. Again, no bodies, no blood trails, nothing. The Army has consistently pitched that, "We don't use body counts to measure success." We would say the same thing; however, seeing the AIF die for their cause made us feel better.

After clearing the building, third platoon maneuvered across the canal and entered the palm grove to start clearing from south to north back up to the COP. As the squad entered the palm grove, it was bogged down by the thick, heavily vegetated underbrush. Wanting to avoid the main trails, the men found it excruciatingly painful trying to cut through the underbrush. To make matters worse, they found various barbed-wire fence strands interwoven into the trees and underbrush, making it impossible to see. Each soldier shouldered a pack and gear that averaged about a hundred pounds. They were tired, wet, muddy, and trying to sneak up on an enemy that had more than likely played in the same palm grove as kids. The situation felt almost impossible.

It had taken half the day, but the squads had finally broken through to a huge rock wall. After some effort, they managed to get up the wall and identify a few AIF scouts. The Apaches were called in to engage the enemy scouts, but the squads were dangerously close. The scouts heard the Apaches and wisely decided to break contact and fade back into the boundaries of the city. With the sun quickly fading, the patrol made its way back to the COP without incident and was able to locate a few campsites that the AIF used for observation and staging areas. Their operations and tactics were similar: just as we had our OPs, they had theirs. They made sure we did not slip into the palm groves and send patrols out to attack them, which we would do on many occasions in the future.

Once third platoon was back inside the COP, we decided that we would keep first platoon out and the majority of HQ platoon, and rotate second and third platoons back to FOB Warhorse along with CSM Harris and his element. They would leave first thing in the morning.

The next morning, second platoon, third platoon, and CSM Harris' element were awake and ready to roll well before the sun was even up. They were ready for some hot chow, hot showers, and a little warmth in general. They had been running hard for three solid days and were ready for a break. The patrol made it back to FOB Warhorse just as the sun was coming up. The guys dropped their equipment in their rooms and headed straight to the chow hall. As the platoon approached the clearing barrels, most of the Fobbits didn't even want to make eye contact with the guys. Unfortunately, one not-so-wise female made a comment to SGT McGrath about the men's appearance. SGT McGrath quickly, decisively, and verbally squashed her attitude as the rest of the platoon carried on with their business of clearing weapons and moving into the chow line. It was Christmas morning 2006.

It was later determined that the attack on Bone X-Ray had been a coordinated attack between the AIF in Tahrir and the AIF in Buhritz. The insurgents planned the attack hoping that it would draw some, if not all, the coalition forces from the Tahrir offensive operations into Buhritz and relieve some of the pressure off of the AIF elements that were being attacked by MAJ Karcher's MTT and IA forces in Tahrir. Their plan failed.

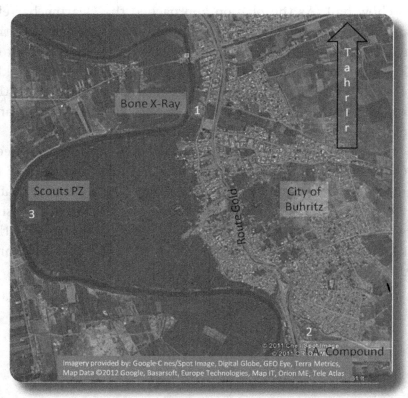

Buhritz

Old Baqubah (OB)

Tahrir

CPT Chapman at the Buhritz IP station with one of many photographers throughout the tour. (US Air Force photo by SSG Stacy L. Pearsall)

SPC Steven M. Devries—a medic with 1st Platoon, Company B, 1-12 Cavalry Regiment, 3rd Brigade Combat Team, 1st Cavalry Division—points toward the origin of small-arms fire to a fellow Soldier, March 28, 2007, in the Tahrir neighborhood of Baqubah, Iraq. Soldiers of 1st Platoon, Co B, and Iraqi soldiers encountered sporadic fire for about two hours during a house-clearing mission in Tahrir. (US Army photo by SSG Antonieta Rico, 5th Mobile Public Affairs Detachment)

SFC Michael Davenport and SPC Miguel Luzunaris, both of 1-12 Cavalry Regiment, 3rd Brigade Combat Team, 1st Cavalry Division, exit an Iraqi army compound in the village of Bob al-Durib after meeting with the IA and concerned local citizens on the security status of the village in the Diyala Province, Iraq, Oct. 24, 2006. (Photo by CPT Richard Ybarra, 115th Mobile Public Affairs Detachment)

US Army SGT James Bowlby reports the current situation as PFC Benjamin Cunningham scans his sector on a rooftop located in Baqubah, Iraq, June 19, 2007. Both soldiers served in B Company, 1st Battalion, 12th Cavalry Regiment, 3rd Brigade Combat Team, 1st Cavalry Division. (Photo by Senior Airman Chris Hubenthal)

From front to back: 1SG Colella, CPL Pester, SPC Ralstone, people of interest 1,2,3, and CPL Sieng. (Photo by PFC Hendricks)

GEN Raymond Odierno at COP Adam during an awards ceremony for the Chargers 1-12 CAV, 1 CD. (Photo by SPC Ryan Stroud, 3-1 PAO US Army)

Outside the Forward Operating Base Gabe aid station, SPC Orlando Garcia, 1st Platoon, Company B, 1-12 Cavalry Regiment, 3rd Brigade Combat Team, 1st Cavalry Division, and an Iraqi soldier, with the 5th Iraqi Army Division, await news on the condition of two soldiers wounded during a firefight in the neighborhood of Tahrir, March 28, 2007. One American soldier and one Iraqi soldier were wounded when their unit came under attack with small-arms fire while conducting clearing operations. The firefight lasted about 2 hours. (US Army photo by SSG Antonieta Rico, 5th Mobile Public Affairs Detachment)

SSG Eric Ross, SSG Alan Shaw, and SPC Leeroy Camacho—all assigned Company B, 1-12 Cavalry, but cross-attached to Company D, 1-12 Cavalry, 3rd Brigade Combat Team, 1st Cavalry Division. The memorial is covered by medals, patches and coins as a way of soldiers showing their respect for the fallen warriors. (Photo by SPC Ryan Stroud)

CPT Austin taking a break during one of the last missions of our tour. (Photograph by CPL Cabreja)

Fire team clearing a vegetable cart of its contents in order to evacuate SGT Graham after he was shot in the stomach during a firefight in Old Baqubah. (Photo by Senior Airman Chris Hubenthal)

PVT Eric Rundquist (left) and PVT Jason Taylor (right), both with 1st Platoon, Company B, 1-12 Calvary Regiment, 3rd Brigade Combat Team, 1st Cavalry Division, hold on to a strap inside a Bradley fighting vehicle after the Bradley hit a roadside bomb. The soldiers were en route to the Forward Operating Base Gabe medical station after one of their fellow soldiers was wounded when they encountered sporadic sniper fire for about two hours during a house-clearing mission in the Tahrir neighborhood of Baqubah. (Photo by SSG Antonieta Rico, 5th Mobile Public Affairs Detachment)

SPC Cabreja (left) and Doc Devries (right) during a seventy-two-hour operation in south Buhritz. (Photo by Bob Gee)

US Army SGT William McGrath and PVT Daniel Brothers, Bravo Company, 1-12 Cavalry Regiment, 1st Cavalry Division, launch a grenade toward a house after coming under fire in Buhritz, Iraq, on Feb. 15, 2007. (US Air Force photo by SSG Stacy L. Pearsall)

Left to right: SGT McGrath, SSG Fili, and PVT Brothers from Bravo Company, 1-12 Cavalry Regiment, 1st Cavalry Division, watch the Iraqi army raid a house after a firefight in Buhritz, Iraq, on Feb. 15, 2007. (US Air Force photo by SSG Stacy L. Pearsall)

1SG Colella back on FOB Warhorse after a rotation out at COP Adam toward the later part of the tour. (Photograph from personal collection)

Soldier with 1st Platoon, Company B, 1-12 Cavalry Regiment, 3rd Brigade Combat Team, 1st Cavalry Division, as he guards a street in the neighborhood of Tahrir in Baqubah, Iraq, March 28, 2007. (US Army photo by SSG Antonieta Rico, 5th Mobile Public Affairs Detachment)

CHAPTER 8

TOUGH TIMES

CHRISTMAS HAD COME AND gone with little or no attention at all; it may as well have just been another day. Since the assault, we were busy taking notes, comparing what went right and wrong, and making major improvements on the combat outposts and fighting positions. We figured the COP building and compound had been hit with a conservative estimate of seventy-five mortar rounds. The AIF had three separate mortar-firing positions configured in a triangle within a 500- to1,000-meter ring around the COP, which was attacked by no fewer than a hundred AIF who were supported by an additional seventy-five to a hundred AIF.

The week after the assault, we brought in some new support and new equipment. First, we had a new piece of equipment called the LCMR (lightweight counter mortar radar). The LCMR triangulates the rounds as they are fired and then in flight toward its intended target, and within a short period of time can give us a pretty good idea where the round was fired from. With the information the LCMR gave us, we could then conduct counterfire on the enemy's position, which in turn put pressure on them to relocate after they conducted a volley of fire. Then they would have to resort back to the "shoot and scoot" techniques. Our BN fire support officer, LT Jacobs, along with LT Duplechin, had gone up to the rooftop, installed the radar, and instructed the platoon FOs and RTOs on how to use it. It was a good piece of equipment and had little impact on the other operating systems or the way we were conducting business. I just wish we'd had it prior to the assault.

The ultimate piece of support came in the form of a 120mm mortar track with a section of mortars from our BN mortar platoon. The "Maniac" mortar platoon would take turns rotating out to the COP in groups of three soldiers every three to four days, and over time, these guys would end up earning the respect of all Bonecrushers. These guys were awesome; not only did they have the ability to fire 120mm's of death at our enemy, but they also were additional bodies to help man the company TOC and assist in the daily operations. They had to be ready at a moment's notice to conduct counterfire, so why not use them as RTOs, too? They were a welcome addition to the team and really loved being able to get out there in the fight doing what they were trained to do. Not one of the guys was over the rank of sergeant, but I had the utmost confidence in them.

When I found out the mortars were being attached to us, I asked the Maniac element to take the base plate off the side of their track and any other distinguishable mortar equipment and hide it so the AIF scouts would just see a M113 come into the compound and not a mortar track. I did not want to advertise the fact that we had our own internal indirect fire assets; the enemy would find out soon enough.

Along with the mortar track and LCMR, we had thousands more sandbags come in, as well as ballistic glass, an extra generator, fuel, ammo, claymore mines, lumber, power tools, various size blast barriers, and other medical supplies to set up a full-blown company aid station and medical evacuation vehicle so we did not have to use a Bradley. The aid station was not just for the wounded but also for day-to-day illnesses. Docs Devries, Nyugen, McCullough and Pecko—our company medics—were the best out there and knew they had to do everything possible to handle a mass-casualty scenario, so they made it one of the best field aid stations I had ever seen.

We at times looked like a construction company (minus doing everything with "full battle-rattle" on and weapons slung over our backs): we had circular saws going, cranes hoisting blast walls, the sounds of hammers pounding nails into two-by-fours. Hell, the XO even scrounged up a Bobcat mini-bulldozer (minus an operator). Bone had transitioned from fulltime infantry company to grunts moonlighting as construction engineers. It was amazing, to say the least.

We had guys that would pull four hours of guard duty, do a six-hour patrol, and then come back, eat, and go out and do whatever needed to be done: building frames to hold the ballistic glass or overhead cover, shuttling sandbags to the rooftops, burning human waste, servicing generators, doing vehicle and weapons maintenance, and everything in between.

Some guys like SGT Bolton took on the additional task as Bobcat operator or cargo truck operator. Other guys had been cross trained on how to drive and gun on the Bradleys and tanks to help cover down for wounded personnel, or when someone went home on leave. The official Army licensing and training went out the window. While guys were out on observation posts and MSR security, they would bring out inexperienced gunners and would use that time to go over all the equipment with the vehicles. If we had an inexperienced Bradley or tank commander, we would set him up with a squared-away gunner and have them together go over various things within the M1s and Bradleys. It was a slow but deliberate process that would really make B Co a well-rounded "do all" company over the next twelve months.

In addition to the cross training, we would also take the mounted crews and have them join in on dismounted operations so they were still in touch with what the guys were doing on the ground. It really helped when you knew exactly how the other guy operated, and it afforded everyone a great perspective on how to best support the man on the ground, or the guys in the Bradley or tank. Among all the cross training and different jobs, I think the best benefit was changing things up and preventing guys from getting complacent, as we consistently challenged the status quo.

The one thing that was starting to trouble the commander and me was the lack of external support. It was obvious the battalion was strung out way too much and had been assigned a sector that in reality needed a brigade to cover down on, and the brigade was in the same predicament with the additional task of rebuilding the Iraqi army and government.

It was hard to be a leader and have soldiers come up and ask questions like: "Why are we operating bulldozers and cranes? Where are our engineers? Why can't we go on the offensive and destroy the enemy? Why can't we get more units in sector? Why do we have to go back and pull perimeter guard when we need everyone we can get out here at the COP?" All these questions were valid and were the same questions that the executive officer, commander, and/or I had asked to varying degrees to various people throughout the chain of command. It was obvious we needed more units in sector, and we knew the chain of command understood our struggles. It was apparent they also knew we needed more assets on the ground but we had to ask the question: "When are we getting more support?" We would always be given the expected answers of "Everyone is short on personnel" or "We are working on getting help." I knew they were, but it just didn't make it any easier. We needed support then and there, not three months later.

The Army breeds an environment that makes it hard to admit you can't handle something. No one wanted to be the "weak link" or the company, battalion, or brigade that had to have outside assistance to accomplish its mission.

Based on the situation we fell into, things were fine on the surface, but once you started kicking over rocks, it became very apparent that we did not have appropriate resources to handle what was about to unfold. I remember someone in the Pentagon saying, "Do more with less." That philosophy works well when you're the CEO of say Walmart, but really does not work well when you are fighting an insurgency. The guy that said that was eventually replaced with a set of "fresh eyes." It did not take a General Patton to figure out that we needed more people on the ground; I had been saying that since 2004.

Every time we did anything on the offensive, we would receive direct fire or indirect fire, and we knew the roads were littered with hundreds of IEDs. We wrestled with the knowledge that we could push our way down into the heart of the insurgent stronghold of Buhritz, but in doing so, we would surely lose a few Bradleys, tanks, and soldiers in the operation—and also then not have the manpower or resources to hold our ground once we were on our objective. So we would have to leave and have everything we just fought for fall right back into the insurgents' control. The commander and I both did not like the idea of fighting for ground more than once at the expense of soldiers' lives and resources. This was a marathon race, not a sprint, and we had to be in it for the long haul. We would go down there but it would be after we had set the conditions and planned a deliberate operation. The current location of the COP was like being up against your own end zone every single play and still trying to score a touchdown.

Our battalion commander, LTC Goins, was a good man, and he had a great group of supporting officers. The BN XO, MAJ Segriest, and BN S-3, MAJ Poznick, were doing their best to get us what we needed. We did not go without material resources if they had it or could get it; it was ours. The precious resource we really needed, as always, was troops on the ground. So they gave us the BN sniper team, which was an awesome addition to our abilities to put the hurt on the insurgents in sector.

After the Christmas jihad, we ended up with some pretty good assets to put the screws to the AIF in our sector and give us a little breathing room. The sniper team was led by a young staff sergeant named Pina, and he had about six other shooters. They were all young and eager to prove their worth in a fight. These guys had stayed out at the COP on a continuous rotation and racked up kills both day and night. They would do deep infiltrations into enemy safe areas, set up their hide positions, get a kill or two, and either exfil[45] at night on their own or wait until a squad or Bradley section could come and assist with their exfil back to the COP. This technique was something I learned from my last tour. In Ramadi, one of our platoons had unknowingly been compromised going into an ambush site and had given the AIF a chance to set up their own ambush and ambush our guys when they exfiltrated from their objective.

Sometimes, just making it public that we had sniper teams and small kill teams in the area was effective. We were doing everything we could to get into the AIF's heads and make them think twice before they did something. Given our lack of boots on the ground, we supplemented our fighting abilities with tools such as UAVs used in conjunction with our internal 120mm mortars or our 155mm Howitzers back on the FOB. UAVs would spot the targets and we would drop mortars on the AIF. Plus, we had Apache gunships pretty much around the clock if needed, BN snipers, BN mortars, and our Bradleys, tanks, and infantry guys. We had gathered a wide array of enablers to assist B Co in its mission and were doing everything we could to keep inflicting as much damage on the enemy as possible. The one thing that made it somewhat acceptable not to launch a massive offensive was that we were killing several insurgents daily—but they just kept coming.

Apparently people outside the chain of command were taking notice of all the enemy kills we inflicted, along with the IEDs found every day, whether detonated or found, as well as the mortar attacks that Bravo Company was experiencing. We got notified we were going to have some reporters come into the COP and do an article on our company and its current situation. From my personal experience, I found reporters to be disruptive to the way we do our daily business and typically they never brought anything good. The words being taken out of context, the misquotes, and the hidden agendas were things I really did not welcome. I knew

---

45   Exfilitration (extraction)

there were good reporters out there. Unfortunately I had seen more bad than good. I always approached them with skepticism and tried to vet them the best I could by finding out what newspaper or magazine they were with, Googling their names, and reading previous articles to figure out what kind of slant they were putting on their stories. Then I would try to match them up with a platoon that would give them what they wanted with little or no issues. What I did not want to do was give them free rein of the company without some sort of oversight. Reporters have a way of finding that one dude that has absolutely no idea of what is going on or is the one disgruntled employee, and then latching on to every word he says and making him the company representative—that was something I would try to avoid.

New Year's Day had come and gone with little to no fanfare. I think a few of the guys shot a star cluster or two from their OPs at midnight and broke squelch with a subdued, "Happy New Year, yeah." With the arrival of the new year and reporters, we followed up with what we had hoped to be a good news story on how we were trying to win the hearts and minds of the people by treating them with "dignity and respect" by passing out Beanie Babies to some of the kids around the houses near the COP and within our so-called safe areas. LT Duplechin was not only our company intelligence guru, but he was also tasked to work with the civil affairs people and get some goodies to pass out around the town. The only thing that had been passed out to any local since our arrival was hot lead. So we needed to try and let them know we were more than just fighters.

Third platoon got tapped to do the "humanitarian mission." They would pass out book bags, coloring books, soccer balls, stuffed animals, and various other kid-oriented items, and we would also try to talk to the parents and find out what was going on through their perspective. We had a platoon of IA soldiers come from FOB Gabe with the "Gorilla" MTT team to help hand out toys and show the people that Iraqi forces were out, operational, and working jointly with US forces.

We had quite the production going on. We had an Iraqi army platoon, reporters from both the Army and the civilian newspapers, civil affairs people, and naturally four Bradley fighting vehicles and two squads of infantry.

As the band of do-gooders left the walls of the COP, it took less than twenty minutes and one Beanie Baby before gunfire erupted and they were in an all-out firefight. Incoming machine-gun fire impacted all around and was followed up with the woosh and thunderous explosion of an RPG in a nearby building. The infantry squads took cover around buildings and walls, the civilians disappeared, and the Bradleys jockeyed for position on the enemy. The third platoon squads were trying to identify the enemy while the IA soldiers fired wildly into the air and into the alleyways, making an already bad situation worse. SGT Bowlby and LT Pijpaert were able to ID where some of the enemy fire was coming from and marked the position with fire from a M203 grenade launcher from SGT McGrath and SPC Barton. They then called SFC Reynolds' Bradley over and talked him onto the target. With the target identified and positive ID established, the Bradley let loose with a five- to ten-round burst of 25mm high explosives, and the enemy fire stopped. Because the enemy was well outside our (and I use this term loosely) "safe zone," and with all the other personnel we had in tow, we did not bother going down to conduct BDA. Instead we chose to continue passing out the toys and other children's items. We did not want the AIF to have a victory by stopping us from our mission.

The reporters had gotten more than what they had bargained for and found themselves asking to leave a little earlier than expected. I had to inform them there were not any scheduled movements to go back to the FOB, and I was not about to pull someone off of their recovery process to come and get the reporters early. They would just have to stay as planned and ride back with a platoon as they rotated out. As it turned out, the extra day or so out at the COP was a good thing for the reporters. They got to take some great pictures and actually talk to the soldiers, building somewhat of an understanding of what the guys went through. The following days went by with little action and the reporters were sent back with third platoon as they rotated in.

Usually it only takes a few days to find out what kind of story the reporters wrote. If there were questions on what had been published, you could expect a message telling you to report to a higher-up for a debrief and a full explanation on how the words were misconstrued or misquoted. The butt-chewing was the best you could hope for, or a mixture of a butt-chewing and a letter of reprimand—and, in an extreme case, packing your bags and getting reassigned. Fortunately for us, the article showed the unit in a positive light. The reporters wrote about a tough job getting accomplished by some tough guys that had the odds stacked against them. It was a great article and it eventually brought more attention to the deteriorating situation in Diyala Province, and more specifically, Buhritz.

About the same time the first reporters came to Buhritz, I found myself getting more and more frustrated with the lack of support. I remember thinking to myself, *How could this be happening? We are the United States of America. We have the best army in the world with the best and brightest leaders, so why are we outgunned and outnumbered in this pitiful example of a town no one has ever heard of.* I would not dare say those thoughts out loud but I had to ask them to myself and try to find answers, then relay the answers to my soldiers and try to preempt their own questioning, because I knew that if I was thinking it, they were thinking it.

CPT Chapman and I had some serious discussions about manpower and how we were going to sustain the current operational tempo. It was an almost impossible task to keep doing what we were doing for the unforeseeable future. We just did not have the manpower, and our soldiers and equipment were both getting run into the ground. We had discussed getting the IA unit from the south and co-locating them with us. The IA compound was on the complete opposite end of Buhritz, and housed an Iraqi army company. We had only been down there a few times and didn't interact with them much due to their location and current mission. They did not come through our sector, either, and ran their logistical operations from the west, so we rarely saw them. The IA compound, like the COP, was in a disadvantaged position and allowed the enemy to exploit their weaknesses. I could see the reasoning behind the location if it was "peace time operation," but for the hostile environment that was presently upon us, the location was a disaster. We thought that if we could sell the idea to higher headquarters and have them authorize the co-location of the IA and US forces, we could act as an MTT unit on steroids and eventually go on the offensive. We both agreed and ran the plan up both the IA and US flagpoles—without so much as a nibble. No one wanted to give up ground nor reduce the footprint of US Army units in Buhritz, so it was back to hold until further notice.

CPT Chapman and I had decided to expand our perimeter of the COP and take over a house that was diagonal from the mayor's blown-up shell of a house. The house wasn't perfect but it was large, built well, three stories high, and with sufficient standoff from the road. It was also separated from the city by a large canal that would give us good protection from a suicide car ramming our compound walls. The main purpose of the house was to give us better fields of fire, more protection, and most of all, a larger perimeter and more space to fit our soldiers, vehicles, and other support assets. The secondary purpose was that if we did eventually end up getting an Iraqi army or Iraqi police unit, we could put them in that house and consolidate our US soldiers in the old IP station.

The plan was to take over the mayor's decimated house and finish blowing it up, then bulldoze it flat and use that area as a parking lot in between the two buildings. We went over and conducted a recon to confirm the house would suit our needs, but we ran into one small issue: the family was still living there. We had never seen the family come or go, and we had cleared that building several times, but never did we see a family there. No worries, though, as we told them they had until noon the following day to get all their household stuff together and get out.

CPT Chapman went back to the FOB and let me handle the delicate eviction process. The following day came, and I gathered a few soldiers and an interpreter and we went over to the house to see if they had left. I knocked on the side door. No answer—and it was locked. I went to the front door and it was locked. I knocked. No answer. Starting to get annoyed, I went back to the side door and told the guys to stand back and I fired three to four rounds into the steel door and lock assembly, and then kicked the door in. The family was huddled on the stairs and shocked to see we were back and we really meant what we said and were ready to move in.

As you could imagine, they were not too happy about being kicked out of their home in the middle of winter, and I was not really happy about doing it, but it was for the greater good: keeping my guys safer and making us more effective. The lady of the house was screaming, crying, and slapping herself. The man of the house was ready to break down too, and their girls were also in shock. After about an hour of yelling, screaming, and trying to convince them to leave, I called more soldiers over to start fortifying the positions. They first consolidated all the family's belongings and put them into a room, so eventually when they were able to get their household items, they could. I tried to handle the situation as diplomatically as possible (minus shooting their locks out), given the circumstances. I even wrote them a note to use in the future to reclaim their house.

But it just wasn't clicking with the family. I finally got frustrated and told the guys to start bringing in the construction materials and to start building. As the soldiers began fortifying, they started breaking the window and door glass out, so that just in case a rocket or mortar exploded, it would be less shrapnel flying around, plus it also allowed the sandbags to rest in the window sills. We did not steal anything (however, we did borrow their heaters for an extended period) and as sandbags came in with tripods for machine guns and grenade launchers, the family got the hint that they were not going to talk us out of evicting them, and eventually they left their house. The house was made into a fortress overnight.

We did most of the work in the evening when it was dark so we did not have to worry about the snipers and random pop shots. The next day, we had a new place to call home.

/////

A few days had passed from the "Toys 'R' Us" mission and the eviction ordeal. I had rotated back to the FOB. We were getting our first group of soldiers back from R&R leave, and I wanted to see how the process went and see if anything needed adjustments that we could make at our level.

Among those supposed to be back was SGT Baron, LT Pijpaert's driver who had been wounded. I asked PFC Berg if he had seen him since they were both on leave together and he told me he had not. (On a side note, PFC Ryan Berg was a solid kid. I recalled hearing a story about how the company was doing combatives for physical training [UFC style] and he had broken SGT Wall's arm by accident. I remember thinking, *Damn, if he did that by accident, what could he do on purpose?*) So, I started making calls back to the rear-detachment commander and asking if anyone had heard from SGT Baron. We really needed him back—we needed everyone back. One person missing from the platoon was one too many. I called the platoons and had them make arrangements to get their soldiers picked up and told SFC Reynolds that SGT Baron had not made it back. He informed me that he probably wouldn't be back and most likely went AWOL based on some of the information coming from guys in the platoon. Sure enough, we never heard from him again. SGT Baron will have to live with those demons for the rest of his life.

While back on FOB Warhorse, CSM Harris informed me that CPT Chapman would be doing a change of command sometime in March or April, so I wanted to get all the UCMJ paperwork finished before the new commander came onboard. I had decided to stay back on the FOB for an extended period to plow through all the UCMJ issues and numerous other administrative tasks. It was day two of me being back on FOB Warhorse and we were working down in the company CP when a massive explosion, only a few hundred meters away, rocked the CP and knocked various items off the walls and shelves. It came in the direction of the track gate, so I grabbed one of the RTOs and we jumped on the Gator to drive out and see if we could help. As we were heading in the direction of the gate, we smelled chlorine, but by the time it registered in our brain that it had been a chlorine bomb that exploded, we were hit with a concentrated invisible cloud. It instantly burned our lungs and irritated our eyes so we turned and headed back to the CP to call it up on the radio over the battalion net.

By the time we made it back, someone had already called it up. Luckily we'd had no casualties at the front gate. I sat in the CP for a minute and tried to figure out what to do next. It wasn't every day you got hit with a chlorine bomb, so you didn't know what would happen to your body. I knew I got a lung full of it, so I decided that the RTO and I would go to the battalion aid station to get checked out.

When I walked into the aid station, it was like a mass casualty scene from a movie. There were fifty or so people, mainly support personnel, getting breathing treatments. Their living areas were right in line with the direction of wind and all of them had been hit with the chlorine vapor. We checked in, got a breathing treatment to clear our lungs, and off we went. I could not get out of there quick enough. I had accomplished my task: get us checked out and get it annotated in my medical records, just in case my lungs blistered up and I died. However, I think some Fobbits thought of it as a way to get a Purple Heart or a trip out of FOB Warhorse.

Third platoon rotated out to the COP the following day and it was business as usual. This was my last day back before I headed back out to the COP. I was gaining on the UCMJ legal paperwork and getting other administrative issues squared away, including the added task of submitting the paperwork to stop SGT Baron's pay. I took a break and rode up to the maintenance area to check on the repairs of the Bradley that had gotten the hand grenade tossed on top. Our company mechanics were really good at what they did.

They had the call signs as "Bone Wrench" and "Bone Recovery," and did everything they could to keep our vehicles running and up to standard.

I took a special interest in the Bradley maintenance piece, which I think the majority of the mechanics enjoyed—with the exception of the team chief. I think he resented the fact that I knew my Bradleys and would not let him baffle the XO or myself with technical jargon. But he did like the fact that if my crews were not pulling their fare share of their duties or not doing what his team wanted them to do, I would jump on them too. So it was a good tradeoff for the most part. Any way you slice it, I was making sure the Bradleys were getting taken care of. I would also make my way over to the M1 maintenance area on occasion just to let them know I was interested in their maintenance too. I would sometimes ask crews from other companies questions, and once I got answers, I would go over and ask the questions to our tankers just so they thought I knew some stuff about the tank. I liked asking them if they bore-sighted. If they replied yes, I would ask them what the barometric pressure was to see if they were trying to pull one over on 1SG. When I ripped off a question like that, seeing their surprised expressions was priceless.

It was now Jan. 9, 2007, and the weather had taken a turn for the worse since our arrival in Buhritz in early December. The days back on the FOB all tended to start out pretty much the same way every morning. I for one don't know how the Fobbits could do it. I had left my containerized housing unit (CHU) to head down to the company command post. The TOC crew was building shelves and still organizing the CP to fit their needs. SSG Lane was doing various tasks around the CP; he generally ran things back on the FOB and I stayed out of his business. I was spending more time out at the COP, and I didn't want to come back for a day or two and stir up his flow and then leave, so I just let him go about his business.

With the UCMJ monkey slightly off my back, and, slowly but surely putting the troubled past in the rearview mirror, I started a new task: awards. After the Christmas siege, I felt inclined to write up some awards. I could not let the heroics of that day get lost and go unrecognized. I started working on several Bronze Stars and Army Commendations with Valor awards, for SSG Fili, SGT McGrath, CSM Harris, and several others who had risen above and beyond the call of duty. With all the negative UCMJ that was on the horizon, it would be good to have some positive events to help counterbalance things. Over my years in the Army, I had witnessed too many heroic actions go without recognition because it got put off. So, if I did not commit to writing up those awards, I would have put it off and regretted it later.

I left the company TOC on the Ranger ATV. I needed to get some information from BN legal about one of the UCMJ packets I was working on. I was about halfway there when my handheld radio broke squelch.

Quiiisssh ...

"Bone 9, this is Bone Main, over."

"Bone Main, this is Bone 9. Send your traffic, over."

"Roger. Bone X-Ray reports they have taken small-arms fire from the east of OP1 (our new building) and they have one WIA, over."

"Bone Main, this is Bone 9, roger. En route to your location."

I did not want to get details over the radio, since the handhelds we had were not secure. I gassed the ATV, flipped a U-turn, and raced back to the company CP. As I walked through the door and into the CP, the group of six or so soldiers who were huddled around the radio speaker parted ways. CPL Lunt gave me the update:

"First Sergeant," Lunt said, "third platoon, BBB #### (the battle roster number for the individual soldier), wounded in the shoulder. Doc Nguyen has bleeding controlled but patient is fading in and out of consciousness. Blue 9 is pulling over to OP1 time now to evacuate casualty back to FOB Warhorse."

"Have we confirmed whose battle roster number it is?"

"Yes, it's PFC Berg."

"How'd it happen?"

"SSG Sonkowsky's squad was heading out to do a patrol in the

151

local area, and they were also going to conduct a crater analysis where an incoming round had impacted earlier that day. When the patrol left the gated compound, they were immediately hit with a burst of machine-gun fire. Everyone made it back inside the compound, but when Berg went to shut the steel door, he was hit with another burst of machine-gun fire. The rounds went through the steel gate and hit him in the shoulder."

"Did they kill the shooter?" I asked.

"No reports on further contact with the shooter."

I told CPL Lunt to call it up to battalion and ensure that they told the aid station to get ready for a litter urgent casualty coming in.

"I'm heading to the front gate to tell the guards not to hassle the Bradleys as they come in the gate," I said. "You give me a call when they are at the traffic circle."

"Roger, First Sergeant," CPL Lunt said.

I took off for the front gate and briefed the guards to let the Bradleys through and then positioned the ATV so once the section of Bradleys came through the gate, I could take off ahead and block the traffic at the intersections so as not to slow down the Bradleys or cause an accident.

It seemed like an eternity waiting for the section of Bradleys to get there. Once CPL Lunt had called me, I looked at my watch: it had taken fifteen minutes to make it to the front gate from the time they left OP1 in Buhritz. *Not bad time,* I thought, then I started analyzing things in my head as I was waiting to see the Bradleys snake their way through the barriers.

Okay, it's a shoulder wound. May not be that bad, but bullets do weird things once they hit the body. A shoulder wound ... and the bleeding has been controlled, but Berg was losing consciousness, which is never good. And they never said they found an exit wound.

I felt so helpless, waiting and waiting. Finally I heard the whine of the engines and saw the exhaust plumes. Then I saw the first Bradley. They were coming into the gated area fast! The distance from the gate to the aid station was about a half mile, but through a few congested areas, including the PX parking lot. As I was flying through, someone yelled at me to slow down, but I didn't pay them any attention and continued on with the mission to block the four-way intersection. I did a power slide into position and let the Bradleys go screaming by me, then fell in behind them.

As the Bradleys pulled into the aid station parking lot, the lead Bradley did a power slide right in front of the doors and was met by a team of medics with a stretcher. No sooner did the Bradley come to a stop than the ramp was on its way down. I just stayed out of the way. There were plenty of medics to handle the business. As they pulled SPC Berg out of the back troop compartment, I saw that he was unconscious, with his T-shirt ripped and dangling from his body. His eyes were open but not responsive as they put him on the stretcher. All the color had left his skin, and I knew it wasn't looking good. Doc Nguyen followed the team of doctors, nurses, and medics into the aid station and told them everything that he had done—including CPR—while in the back of the Bradley en route to the aid station. SFC Reynolds came walking from around the front of the vehicle with a look only a father could have for one of his sons that had just been wounded. I left him alone to walk it out.

As I went into the aid station to see what was going on, I was met by a crowd of people. Some were from our chain of command and were trying to get an update, some were just being nosey, and others were trying to do their job. I linked up with Doc and he told me Ryan had stopped breathing en route. Also, he did not have a pulse, or, when he did, it was really weak. I thanked him and we walked out to talk to SFC Reynolds. Doc had told him the same thing he had told me and we just waited outside silently for any follow on information.

I told SFC Reynolds to go wash out his Bradley, and I let Doc go and change his clothes and take a breather before they headed back out to the COP to await word. I think we already knew what the outcome was but you never give up hope ...

PFC Ryan Russell Berg, Killed in Action, 9 January 2007, Buhritz, Iraq

Later reports said that the bullet had entered his upper shoulder, hit his collarbone, and ricocheted down then pierced an artery that led to his heart. Nothing could have been done to prevent his death. Gone but not forgotten; rest in peace.

Third platoon rotated in that evening. LT Duplechin and SSG Morales, our supply NCO, had the unfortunate task of clearing out PFC Berg's room and all his personal items. We wanted to get everything out before his roommates came back in.

The entire room-clearance procedure was starting to put an additional stress on the small detachment we had back on the FOB. Every single piece of property the soldier had needed to be inventoried on several forms (all handwritten) then packed, sealed, and shipped—and it had to be completed by an officer and witnessed by an additional person. We already had to process personal items from LT Ebarb, SGT Baron, CPL Barta, and now PFC Berg. The full complexity of this task was just starting to rise to the surface. This was something that you couldn't train for while you were back in the States. Sometimes it was even hard to tell whose property was whose. We made it mandatory for all soldiers to inventory their own equipment and post the inventory in their living area "just in case." It may have sounded a bit morbid at the time, but later on in the deployment, those inventories would help us out in ways I could not have imagined.

My focus shifted from awards and UCMJ to a memorial service and trying to figure out how we would rotate third platoon out from the COP again. The rotation and maintenance schedule was really starting to get off balance. First platoon was skipping its maintenance days and spending more and more time out at the COP. The soldiers and vehicles were getting worn down. Third platoon was spending more time back on the FOB, but no one wanted to be back there, and I am certain they would have much rather been out at the COP, as I would have been. Second platoon, the most under-strength platoon we had, was spending an enormous amount of time out at the COP and in their tanks on constant MSR security.

Memorial services and the "hero flights" were the most somber and least looked-forward-to event, but necessary. The hero flights were typically conducted in the evenings at the helipad that everyone used to fly into and out of camp. The battalion that had lost a soldier would have every soldier that was not performing a critical job report for the hero flight and gather at the graveled area leading up to the cement helipad. The companies would have their guidons out front and both the commanders and 1SG would be out in front together, which seldom occurs in any other formation. A HMMWV designed to be a field ambulance would pull up and back into a parking area, where it would be greeted by the chaplain and the pall bearers from the individual's company and platoon. There would be no flag-draped coffin or any fancy ceremony; just the soldiers who truly cared and loved their comrade-in-arms—and more than likely were with him in his final hour. These men would lift and pull the black body bag out of the ambulance and carry their fallen brother to the awaiting helicopter. As the soldiers slowly passed by the formation, we would snap to attention and render a salute. Sometimes, with those in front of the advancing formation, you could see the tears in their eyes and the pain on their faces as they tried to stay strong and fight back the emotions that were screaming to come out. Then the six men would place their brother into the chopper, say a few words, render a salute, and rejoin their company.

The helicopter crew would then strap the bag down as gently as possible, do their crew checks, and crank the engines on the birds. The slow whine of the turbine engines and the turning of the rotor blades seemed hypnotizing. As the blades spun faster, the whopping noise would drown out the sound of the engines. The Blackhawk or Chinook would spring up from the ground, do a hard bank, and head out into the darkness. We would salute one final time until the helicopter could not be seen or heard.

After our brother had left, the battalion commander would gather the battalion formation together and offer words of praise and wisdom and a Bible verse or two. It was hard on everyone. I know LTC Goins took each and every loss personally. As for me, the spinning of rotor blades and the gravel crunching under the boots of the pall bearers as they walked past are things that will be burned into my brain for the rest of my life.

The memorial services were even harder. They were forty-five minutes to an hour long, and we had to conduct full rehearsals several times prior to the actual event. The stiff new desert combat boots, weapon, and combat helmet, with the dog tags dangling, were a tough sight to see. We would try to get the best picture we could and then put it in a frame under the display. We would also enlarge one and put it on an easel at the front door so people could see who they were memorializing. The final roll call, "Taps," the twenty-one-gun salute, the playing of the soldier's favorite song, a video montage, and finally the eulogy given from his closest friend ... it was sometimes too much to bear. Once the memorial service was over, we would all line up, take turns rendering our final salute, and then the immediate chain of command and friends would line up on the path out of the gymnasium to thank people as they left the service. From the 25th Infantry's Division—General Mixon and CSM Taylor on down—they would file by and offer their condolences.

The services for CPL Barta and SPC Berg (both posthumously promoted) were the first of many memorials to come. If given the chance, I will never listen to "Amazing Grace" ever again.

The following days were marked by various small skirmishes and hit-and-run gun battles in both Buhritz and Tahrir. The air weapons teams became a permanent fixture in our area of operation and were basically our eyes in the skies 24/7, and if they were pulled out of sector, we would get a UAV. The attack helicopter squadron went by the moniker of "Wolfpack" and the various Apache attack helicopters teams went by color codes: white, red, blue, and black, as did our platoons. The AWTs were our eyes deep south and west, and they became proficient in getting the "keyhole" shots down alleyways, and most importantly, preventing collateral damage. The Wolfpack would also land and come into our TOC on FOB Warhorse and show us various gun-camera footage. We would share feedback on our interpretation of the fight and get updated graphics so we were all on the same sheet of music. The air and ground integration could not have been better. The working relationship over the months to come would be strong and influence the fight in many aspects. They would learn the initials RSC[46] and PC[47] well.

We also had a small victory in the external support realm. Battalion was able to get us some external engineer support. The engineer unit's call sign was "Blade." They had several bulldozers, bucket loaders, and cranes, as well as manpower. They were a sight for sore eyes, and we were happy to have them come into sector. I couldn't say they felt the same way, though. They did not even make it into Buhritz before being hit with an IED on Route Gold, and their lowboy trailer caught on fire. To their credit, the Blade element quickly disconnected it from the truck and heroically saved the dozer from going up in flames as they drove it off right before the trailer was engulfed in fire. Their actions and how they handled the situation told me immediately that we were dealing with some squared-away troops. The IED also helped put the situation in Buhritz into perspective for the engineer unit.

We had a laundry list of work priorities for the engineers. We wanted them to push our perimeter out a few hundred yards by bulldozing back the palm grove to our south a few hundred meters and bulldoze a few buildings and bricks walls to clear our fields of fire. In previous attacks, they were used as cover by the insurgents and severely restricted our fields of fire. We also wanted to beef up our HESCO basket perimeter and also bulldoze the field off to the east of our compound. The engineers had their work cut out for them. Luckily their equipment was "up-armored" and provided

---

46   Robert S. Colella
47   Pete Chapman

them some protection from small-arms fire. The insurgents made it a sport to shoot at the engineers on a daily basis. We initially did the heavy exposed work at night to lessen the exposure to the enemy. But with the amount of work that needed to be done in the short time periods we had the engineer assets, we made the decision to run the engineer operations as hard and long as we could. The construction of the defenses went surprisingly well with the exception of the occasional harassing fires. The engineers knocked down the building and walls, fortified the HESCO baskets, reduced the mayor's complex to a flat parking lot, and then moved to the palm grove—and that's when things started going bad.

With the constant rain and the palm grove's location next to the river, the water table was pretty high. As soon as the two bulldozers broke through the top layer of soil, they were swallowed up and stuck to the point they could not be recovered by the assets we had on the ground. To make matters worse, the one bulldozer was disabled after it got stuck by enemy small-arms fire. It was a massive chunk of buried dead weight. We brought out our M88 recovery vehicle to attempt to pull them out of the muck but could not break either vehicle free from the earth's clutches. The one was stuck directly behind the other and limited the angles we could get with the M88. We would have had to pull our perimeter wall down on the south side of the COP to get the proper angles, and given the current enemy situation, that was not an option. It was decided that we would leave them stuck in place until the enemy situation improved and we could get other assets in to recover the vehicles.

With the current fight and amount of losses we were taking, I started making a few personnel changes. I had scored a deal with HHC's 1SG Franklin to take on an E6 named SSG Nicholson. He had been wounded on his previous tour in Iraq and had a profile that limited his duties, but he had armorer experience and wanted to come to the company. I thought that was a great way to free up SPC Kennedy and send him to third platoon. With that deal worked out, I was able to cross-level a few guys from the HQ platoon to help with the shortage of manpower that third platoon was experiencing with the loss of Berg and Baron. I gave up SPC Kennedy, the company armorer, and a kid named PFC David Lopez. He was a guy that was rather large in body mass, and his physical abilities were limited. However, he was an intelligent and motivated trooper and was licensed and experienced on the Bradley, so it was decided to send him to third to be a driver.

Third platoon had just rotated out with first platoon and was once again manning the COP and getting ready to do another logistical run to FOB Gabe to pick up supplies. I was working with the engineers and supervising the perimeter fortification as the section of Bradleys had left for FOB Gabe. About two minutes after they left, I heard and felt an explosion that I just knew was meant for one of those Bradleys that had just left. I rushed into the command post to get a situation report.

Quiiisssh ...

"Bone X-Ray, this is Blue 2. Blue 6 just got hit with a massive deep buried IED as we were crossing over the culvert near the bridge at CP 414. I have no communication with Blue 6 track at this time. We need QRF at this location time now!"

SFC Reynolds was already getting his section fired up and rolling before I could tell him. They made it to the IED site in minutes and started the reports back. They had one serious casualty: the driver, PFC Lopez. The gunner and LT Pijpaert were knocked around pretty good but still functional. They were trying to get the casualty out of the hatch but were having difficulties because of leg wounds sustained during the IED blast. They could not get him out of the "hell hole" (the tiny passageway leading to the driver's compartment) for two reasons: one, was he was too big to fit; two, the IED blast was so powerful that it buckled the hull and pushed the battery box out and obstructed the path out the back. Regardless of the driver's weight, he would have to be removed from topside by way of the driver's hatch.

We had an additional issue: the evacuation route was now blocked by the immobilized Bradley resting inside a massive IED hole. I told SFC Reynolds to bring the casualty back to the COP and we could stabilize him there while they worked to tow the destroyed Bradley out of the path and free up the evacuation route. They had the driver back to the COP within minutes, dropped him at the front door, and went back to the blast site. We put Lopez on a litter and carried him over to a set of sawhorse-style stilts, which elevated him up to about four feet. Doc cut away his pants and stripped him down to his underwear, then gave him a shot of morphine to help take the edge off of just having his leg bone snapped in two. The morphine kicked in instantly and he was high as a kite. As we were working on his leg and open wounds, PFC Lopez started talking about his underwear and how sexy they were. I figured he was going to be just fine.

Meanwhile, SFC Reynolds had the road cleared and returned back to the COP. We had Lopez loaded and on his way back to FOB Warhorse in no time, followed by a helicopter flight to Balad Airbase then to Germany, and then Texas. He had been in third platoon for about three days.

The IED that had destroyed Blue 6's Bradley was a perfect example of how fanatically determined the AIF in Buhritz was in killing US soldiers. The IED was emplaced within 300 meters of the COP and less than 200 meters from an observation point that was manned 24/7. They had found a weakness in our security and exploited it. The insurgents could only have accessed this location undetected by crawling into position. The IED crater was later determined to have had at least three to five 155mm artillery rounds in it. Not only did the AIF have to drag the 155mm artillery rounds into position, but they had to run a detonation device and dig the side of the road out to complete the task. I was just thankful they detonated the IED on a Bradley and not an HMMWV. If they had, that entire truckload of personnel would have been killed.

SFC Reynolds and his section returned to the COP in less than an hour. We were focused on getting the destroyed vehicle back to the COP so it could later be dragged back to FOB Warhorse. Night had finally fallen on a very long day. We had just gotten the Bradley back into the secure perimeter of the compound. We had one last task to do, and I decided to call Blue 9G to have them drag the roll of track that had been blown off of LT Pijpaert's vehicle back to the open field near OP1 before they went into position for their turn on security with their Bradley. Blue 9G was SFC Reynolds' gunner who was training to be a Bradley commander and was taking SPC Barton out that evening to conduct cross-training, and had SPC Sieger as a driver.

Quiiisssh ...

"Rollover! Rollover! Bone X-Ray, this is OP1, we just observed a Bradley roll over into the canal south of our location."

Upon hearing this, I ran out of the command post—no gear, just a handheld radio and my 9mm—and jumped into one of the gun trucks that were parked outside. I cranked it up and slammed it into gear and started to pull away but was stopped by SSG Embry beating on the window for me to unlock the door. I stopped, he jumped in, and I floored it in the direction of OP1 and road up onto the road that paralleled the canal so I would not miss the vehicle as I headed south. The cement canal was very deep and had sporadic vegetation along its bank. I wanted to go quickly but forced myself to go slow so I did not miss them. As I drove down the canal straining my eyes in the darkness, the headlights caught SGT Green as he was crawling out of the canal to get help. He was soaked, his eyes big as baseballs. I asked where everyone was and he said in the vehicle. I told him to stand by and ordered SSG Embry to get on the radio and give the CP a report.

I turned and looked into the canal and saw the vehicle's underbelly peering up at me. The rear troop door was open, and the taillights were submerged under the dark rushing water but still illuminating. I looked at the edge of the canal, moved upstream a few meters, judged my distance, and jumped into the black abyss. The water was like ice and threw my body into shock as it took my breath away. I worked my way into the darkness of rear crew compartment to find SPC Barton trying to get to the driver's compartment to free SPC Sieger. The canal water was filling up the back of the Bradley and flowing through. We only had a few feet of room to keep our heads above water. Everything that floated in the back of the vehicle was pushed by the canal's current into the driver's hole. We would try to move it but it would just flow back into the driver's compartment.

At some point, SSG Embry joined me, and we started a chain to toss the equipment outside of the vehicle and clear the way. Once it was clear, I dove under the water and tried to swim my way into the driver's compartment but it was blocked. I tried it again but still couldn't get to Sieger. I couldn't even feel him. My mind raced to figure out what was blocking the path—whatever it was, it was solid. SSG Embry and SPC Barton stayed in the crew compartment to keep trying to get to Sieger, and I maneuvered my way outside the Bradley and worked my way around the front of the vehicle to see if by chance we could get to the driver's hatch. The current was strong and moving fast due to all the rain, and I was worried about getting washed downstream and ending up either drowned or deep in enemy territory, so I grabbed hold of the side skirts that had cable footholds and maneuvered my way toward the front of the vehicle. But the Bradley had rested on top of the hatch, so the only way we were going to be able to get to Sieger was by getting the vehicle back on its side or upright.

I made my way back to the troop compartment to see how SSG Embry and SPC Barton were making out, but no luck. I crawled up out of the canal and made it to my HMMWV to call the tanks that were out on MSR security to come down one at a time and drop off their tow cables. I had also called X-Ray and told them to get an M88 recovery vehicle down there and to also send QRF. I was concerned that the AIF would take this opportunity to launch an attack on us while we were in the middle of a rescue operation.

I assumed risk on the MSR security and had a section of tanks pull down on the east side of the canal and told the other section of tanks to stay on the friendly side (west side). We also had a squad of infantry on the ground. Once we had gathered all four tow cables from the tanks, SSG Wallat and a few of the dismounts, along with SSG Embry, worked on linking the tow cables together. I jumped back into the canal to get the tow cable and shackles of the Bradley and then worked my way back up the canal walls to hand the newly acquired items off before sliding back into the water to go to the front of the vehicle to hook the cables up to a lift shackle near the driver's hatch. I was joined by SGT McGrath and SPC Meyer, and they helped guide the now hundreds of pounds' worth of cable into position. We then crawled out of the canal and hooked the cables up to SSG Wallet's tank and he attempted to pull the Bradley onto its side. The tank started to pull the Bradley as hoped, but just as the driver's hatch was ready to break the water line, one of the shackles broke and the Bradley rolled back into the water. I yelled for another shackle, and it seemed as if it appeared instantly and out of nowhere. We rejoined the cables and tried it again.

The tank was able to pull the Bradley onto its side and then some, past the point where the driver's hatch was just outside the water. The tank then locked its brakes, leaving the entire weight of the Bradley suspended by just the haphazardly put-together cables. I was really nervous about the cables breaking or the shackles busting and rolling back into the water trapping one of the rescuers inside the driver's compartment or crushing him under the water, so I minimized the people in the water to SGT McGrath and SPC Meyers and myself. By this time, the adrenaline was wearing off and hypothermia was setting in. My limbs were numb and I was shivering out of control, but I was not going to stop moments from getting our guy out.

The driver's hatch was jammed shut and could not be opened by the latch. We yelled for a tanker's bar (pry bar) and, just like the shackle, the bar appeared instantly and out of nowhere. SPC Meyers and SGT McGrath worked on prying the hatch open, and just as it seemed like it was not going to work, it popped open and water rushed out. I slipped back into the water from the muddy canal edge and worked my way to the driver's compartment, where I was met by SGT McGrath. We could get to Sieger but we could not pull him out, as his foot was stuck under the instrument panel. SGT McGrath went into the driver compartment and was able to free Sieger's foot as I steadied him, thinking to myself, *If that cable breaks we will all be dead.* God, though, was looking over us and kept the cable strong.

Out of nowhere, one of the mortar guys jumped into the canal, started screaming "Sieger! Sieger!" and slapped the water. I grabbed this young soldier and told him, "Shut up and quit freaking out!" He was just making an already bad situation even worse. We needed a rope, and as with the other items, it appeared out of nowhere and we were able to pull Sieger up the side of the canal and into a waiting Medic Track where once again Doc Nguyen was waiting.

As we were working our way out of the canal, SGT McGrath lost his grip and got caught in the current and began getting washed downstream. Luckily I had seen him and was able to reach out and grab hold of his hand a second before he would have been out of reach. The right place at the right time; just a few inches prevented another tragedy.

CPT Conely from A Co arrived with the QRF and the M88 recovery vehicle and helped LT Pijpaert with the recovery of the vehicle and the additional security until we could reorganize ourselves.

The entire rescue effort took about thirty to forty minutes from the time the vehicle had rolled into the canal until we had Eric out of the hatch. I had heard of stories of miracles of people being brought back to life after drowning, especially in frigid waters, so I had a small glimmer of hope. But no miracles were to be seen that evening. Specialist Eric Sieger was pronounced dead at FOB Warhorse aid station shortly after his arrival.

SPC Eric Sieger, Killed in Action, 1 February 2007, Buhritz, Iraq

That evening, LT Duplechin came out to the COP to relieve me so I could go back and get warmed up and change out my equipment. The entire time, I had my 9mm pistol with me and it never came loose.

The Fort Ruckers safety team came out and did an investigation, taking statements from the crew and myself to try, to figure out what had happen. The investigation was not to cast blame on anyone; it was to figure out why it occurred and how we could prevent it from happening again. Vehicle crew members drowning was unfortunately a common occurrence in Iraq. There are so many canals with weak or no shoulders at all on the roads that parallel them; they often give way and the vehicles slide off into the canal.

The Army did buy small tanks called Aqua Lungs that were filled with air and strapped inside the crew compartments of all vehicles after that incident, but they provided little comfort. As many items were purchased and rushed to the frontlines, unless trained on and practiced with, the soldiers would not be able to use them when it mattered or would be reluctant to use them. So they just ended up being ornaments, or stuffed in a connex somewhere on a FOB.

Once the Bradley made it back to FOB Warhorse, I went down to the motor pool to try and figure out what was blocking the path and preventing us from going into the driver's compartment. I examined everything on the vehicle. Unfortunately the vehicle being upright made the examination hard to figure anything out, especially after the platoon had already been down there to get the sensitive items out of it and moved things around. However, I did notice that the battery box that sits behind the driver's hatch was broken. I saw the broken latches that normally held the four massive batteries directly behind the driver's position. I knew that was what was blocking us from getting to Eric. I figured that when the vehicle had rolled over, the latches broke—or they were already broken—allowing the battery tray to slide out, jam, and block our path. When the vehicle was eventually uprighted, the battery tray unjammed itself and slid back into position.

CHAPTER 9

CITY OF DEATH

FEBRUARY 2007: IT DIDN'T take long for the AIF in sector to plan another high-profile attack. We had received reports indirectly from the MTT unit on FOB Gabe that the Iraqi army unit in the southern sector of Buhritz was under attack and needed help. The MTT unit themselves did not have enough forces to push down into Buhritz so it was decided by BN HQ that the scout platoon manning the Diyala Media Center in the east would come in and assist the IA in repelling the attack.

We were hoping that the scouts would be able to push in and reinforce the IA with little to no issues, but we also knew that the route to the compound from the east was not over-watched by the IA, so the insurgents had free rein on the road to do what they wanted. If B Company had to push in from the north, it would be a tough fight, as the route down to the IA compound was littered with IEDs on both sides of the canal, and it would be a shooting gallery as the company tried running the gauntlet from the north. I kept my ears glued to the radio to follow what was going on.

If the assault on the IA compound was anything like the assault on our compound, the IA soldiers were in for a serious fight. The scouts were sent in from the east and only made it within a few kilometers of the IA compound before being hit by a deep-buried IED, destroying the Bradley and setting it on fire. The insurgents had also dug in a blocking obstacle with heavy machinery and tied that into a canal, which basically made the route to the IA compound impassable without major engineer assets.

Upon hearing that the reinforcement effort from the east failed, we figured we were next. We mounted up a patrol and went to FOB Gabe to talk to the MTT unit commander, MAJ Perkins, as well as CPT Austin. The MTT unit had a platoon of IA with seven to eight HMMWVs, and we had one platoon that could go down and reinforce the IA compound. My concern, along with CPT Chapman's, was that at least twenty-five to fifty IEDs lay along the narrow route south. I told the major that if we went down there without setting the conditions first, we were undoubtedly going to lose soldiers and several Bradleys and gun trucks, without question.

Our other concern was manpower: What would we do once we got down there? What was the plan? No one really seemed to think that issue through. Bravo Company didn't have enough manpower or logistics to stay down there once we did make it. I was worried about fighting our way down there, paying a heavy toll in men and equipment—both of which we were already short on—then be stuck with another tactical blunder of an isolated outpost. We had addressed our concerns about the placement and support requirements for the IA compound in the past and requested they move up with us in the north so we could mutually support each other, but that request had fallen on deaf ears. Now we were faced with the worst-case scenario.

MAJ Perkins was getting sporadic reports from the IA compound via cell phone, saying that the majority of the IA had already abandoned their post by dropping their weapons, taking their uniforms off, and leaving. The ones staying were the officers and they had no option to leave; if they abandoned their post, they would be tracked down and killed by the AIF, so they had to stay and fight. They also reported that they had several wounded personnel. We had attack helicopters and UAVs on station but no one to coordinate fires, so the air assets were basically useless, unless the insurgents came out in the open and could be identified, and they knew better than that.

MAJ Perkins called the BDE HQ and asked the hard questions. "What do we do when we get down there? How long should we plan to occupy? Will more IA come in? What is the plan to fix this so it doesn't happen again?" This still did not address the physical location of the IA compound, and it seemed like no one but the commander and me understood the poor location choice. Nonetheless, we were told to go down and reinforce the compound.

I was furious! If we lost any more guys and any more Bradleys— which we were certain to do—and gained more land mass responsibility, we would be spread too thin, and would be combat ineffective. "What are they thinking?" (Not sure if I asked that out loud or to myself!) I knew CPT Chapman was concerned, but at the same time if we didn't go down there, we just signed the IA officers' death warrant.

Once we got back to Bone X-Ray, we started getting our plan and resources together. We called BN and requested as many EOD teams as we could get. This would be a deliberate route-clearance mission and would take time; we could not afford to go down there haphazardly.

Luckily we had already been war-gaming the attack into the south and were planning an operation around 10 February with the Alamo and Ghost elements out of FOB Gabe, just a few long days away. So all we had to do was modify it to fit what resources we had available. As we were making final adjustments to our plan, the MTT unit lost communications with the IA soldiers in the compound, which was not a good sign. With the plan completed, CPT Chapman briefed the plan to LT Boeka, the squad leaders, and the section leaders of first platoon. What we planned to do was divide the force in two sections: one on the east side of the canal and one on the west side of the canal. This would allow us to mutually support each other with fires from either side. The Bradleys would lead, with the infantry squads providing flank security on the east and west to flush out any would-be trigger men or ambushes. The movement would be slow and deliberate—we were in no hurry to get someone killed. The only missing piece of the plan was explosive ordnance disposal teams—EOD. They were inbound but we only had one team coming, as that's all there was in sector.

The vehicles all lined up on their respective sides of the canals. I was manning the COP with a small contingent of HQ personnel and a handful of soldiers from second platoon just in case the enemy tried to attack once the main body pushed south. The insurgents were waiting for the push from the north. No sooner had the vehicles line up on the roads than machine-gun fire erupted from the south and southeast, followed by an RPG zipping past the COP and exploding into the palm grove. The Bradley crews started to push south a few hundred meters and set up an over-watch. As they scanned their sectors and the road for any possible indications of IEDs, SGT Williams and his gunner, SPC Osbourne, identified one IED after another. SGT McKinney and SPC Sieng reported the same in their sector. The AIF had obviously been planning and preparing for this operation for some time. They wanted us to come south and pick us apart as we did. We called the report up to higher and waited for EOD to conduct linkup. The problem was that we only had one EOD team but needed two—one for each side of the canal.

We were then told to hold in place and wait for further instructions. At that point, I was having a mental struggle: if they stopped us, I would be relieved that we were not going to lose any vehicles, soldiers, or both. However, that would come at the expense of losing an IA compound and what little trust they had in us. Then I started to struggle with the thought of turning back. We had committed to a fight, and there was no turning back. If we were to stop our advance, we would be sending a message of weakness. We would surely embolden them with two victories: one with the overrunning of the IA compound, and the other of driving us back into our own compound. But why lose soldiers and equipment for a lost cause and an IA compound that was a strategic nightmare? Live to fight another day? Surely these were the questions being asked many levels above me—or at least I hoped so.

Moments later, we got a change of mission and were told to cancel the operation and move back to the Bone X-Ray. The Apache helicopter pilots sent a report that the compound was being overrun. The pilots reported seeing civilians and kids going into the compound first and then the AIF had mixed in with them. The choppers could not engage without killing women and children so the only thing they could do is watch from a distance. AIF knew if the Apaches did engage and kill women and children, that would have given them a third victory that day: bad press and a political tool to use against America on Al Jazeera News. The UAV was on station and videotaped the entire tragedy as it unfolded.

I later watched the video and felt my heart sink, knowing that anyone in the compound associated with the IA had surely been killed—and all the IA equipment there was now in enemy hands, including a DShK (Dushka) .50-cal machine gun that we would end up dealing with later. The entire compound was looted at a leisurely pace. Several IA vehicles, including an M113 armored personnel carrier, were burned in place, and the Iraqi flag was hoisted down by a band of thugs.

That day was a lose-lose situation. The decisions that had to be made were not in any playbook, training scenario, field manual, or troubleshooting matrix. When I look back on that day, I can't help but think, *What would have happened if we had gone down there?*

From that day on, I could feel the tension with some of the soldiers. Some would ask me flat out: "First Sergeant, when are we going to be able to go on the offensive and take the fight to the enemy? It feels like we are getting nickeled and dimed to death, literally." Others understood and helped others to understand. Everyone was getting a bit stressed: the constant firefights and the long hours out on OPs either in vehicles or in gun emplacements were taking a toll. The rotations back to the rear were spent doing everything we could do to keep the vehicles in working condition, and maybe getting one or two e-mails off to the home front to keep that part of life going too. All the family members were stressed out as well. They were getting the reports back at home either through the rumor mill or the TV and newspaper. Baqubah and Buhritz were plastered all over the headlines.

The home front started to be my next focus of the battle. I was trying to keep the Family Readiness Group (FRG) in the information loop and had established contact with a few of the soldiers' wives participating in it. The one thing that I really regretted was that I'd never met these women and my wife had not had a chance to meet them, either. Nevertheless, I made contact and started sending newsletters, trying to give updates and squash the rumors. I was very careful in finding a balance between the doom and gloom versus the bright and cheery. The number one question from the wives was about the three-month extension. I could not confirm or deny it, but I told them to prepare for the worst-case scenario. With the troop surge being announced, it was pretty much a for-sure deal, but we had not been officially notified. The threat of the fifteen-month tour had been circulating since we'd left the States. I basically told my wife to just plan on me being gone for fifteen months, and if I was home sooner, it would be a blessing.

At that point, we were in Iraq for roughly four months. I could not see how we were going to be successful if things did not change. It was going to be hard to accomplish minimum small objectives for the short term, let alone the long-term large objectives. The only available resource that the commander and I saw was the Iraqi army. I talked this idea over with CSM Harris and the commander talked to the S-3 and XO and eventually LTC Goins. Then we both talked it over with MAJ Karcher, CPT Austin, and MAJ Perkins, specifically about getting more IA troops. The biggest selling point was the "Joint Compound" being constructed as we spoke: it would be ready for move-in within about a week. The annihilation of the IA in the south was also a pretty good selling point.

We received some good feedback and felt confident that

we would be able to get a company of IA to come down to the compound. Now all we had to do was play the waiting game and see what unit they could get. Within a few days, we got word that they were going to commit a company of IA soldiers once they finished their training exercises, and we could expect them by the second or third week of February. That was indeed good news. Good news traveled fast, and I could almost instantly feel the motivation lift a few notches within the company.

The idea was to pair the platoons up with the IA platoons and augment our guys with the IA guys. We would take turns rotating them back to FOB Gabe and do some basic tactics training with them so that we fostered some sort of cohesion before we went out on a mission. Our team leaders would essentially become squad leaders and our squad leaders would in theory maneuver two squads with the help of the IA squad leaders. And if all else failed, we could at least use them to reinforce the force protection on the OPs. Anything was better than what we had, but only time would tell.

On 4 February 2007, I was on FOB Warhorse and as usual was sifting through my morning dose of paperwork. I came across PVT Spencer's promotion orders that I had set aside for a time when the commander and I could promote him together. We both thought a lot of him and considered it a good news story within the company. I yelled over to the RTO to see what time first platoon was heading out to Bone X-Ray, and they replied they were getting ready for the mission brief, just waiting on the BN sniper team to show up. *Damn good timing.* I yelled to the commander, "Let's go promote Spence."

I jumped up from my chair, went over to the one and only PV2 we had on RTO, and pulled his Velcro rank off his chest so the commander had something to pin on Spencer. We loaded up in the Ranger and drove up to the track line. Naturally it was muddy, overcast, and cold. The platoon was already gathered around for the mission brief, so once LT Boeka was finished with his back briefs, I called them to attention.

"Attention to orders!" I said. "The Secretary of the Army has reposed special trust and confidence in Clarence Spencer, hereby promoting him to the rank of Private E-2 on this fourth day of February 2007, effective date 1 January 2007."

Everyone hooted, hollered, and clapped. Everyone in the platoon knew and respected Spencer, and they were glad to see he was on the upswing of things. The commander said a few words of praise and turned it over to me. I congratulated Spencer, shook his hand, and then I yelled at everyone, half jokingly, to stay squared away and not get complacent. Soon, off they went, out to the COP for another rotation.

CPT Chapman and I went back down to the CP to start working on the offensive operation planned for the tenth of February. This was a rare moment that both of us were back on FOB Warhorse at the same time, so we made the best of it. Our sister company—"Apache" A Co—had its company commander and first sergeant back from their outpost.

These guys were a good pair: 1SG JD Daniels and CPT Chris Conely. They had a hard fight in sector and were throwing the smackdown on the Haj in "New Baqubah" on the west side of the river. With the rare opportunity of having all four of us together, we went to eat lunch and compare notes on what was going on and the different trends we were experiencing in sector. Though we had seen each other throughout the months at meetings, promotion boards, and various other briefings, this was an odd encounter, and we really did not have anything pressing. So we could actually just sit and talk. Next thing you know, here came the "Crazy" C Co commander and 1SG: CPT Clay Combs and 1SG Ramsdale, both awesome Americans. It was like a big party in the chow hall. It was good to see our comrades all at the same time. For a moment, I paused and thought, *Who is running things out in sector?* As the talk slowed down, the commanders went back up to the BN TOC and the 1SGs sat around and talked for a bit longer about manning rosters and personnel issues. We all knew that sometimes more could get done in an unofficial casual meeting than spending hours in an official structured meeting. Eventually we outstayed our welcome, and were basically kicked out by the chow hall personnel that catered and cleaned the facility. It was a good day.

I went back up to our company living area to survey the housing situation and try to reshuffle a few things. We had interpreters living in our area, and I figured if I could kick them out and send them down to where the other interpreters lived, I could make their room into a command post and consolidate all our operations near the BN HQ and our living area. Our company command post was on the other side of the FOB from our BN HQ and company housing area. I had wanted to fix the distance issue since I'd arrived there, but kept getting sidetracked. This move would make us much more efficient. I went down, checked out the interpreters' living area, and confirmed they had extra space. So I went up and talked to SPC Pester, our company communication stud, about extra antennas, and he assured me we would not be off the air for an extended period and that he could have all the other electronic gizmos like SIPRNET (secure Internet) and the BLUFOR Tracker. Once I lined up all the resources, I briefed the guys, evicted the terps[48] and put the plan into motion. The move was going to take about a week and would be slightly painful, but in the long run, it would make our lives much easier.

Out at the COP, first platoon had switched out with third platoon and started to get settled in. LT Boeka and SFC Hamilton started getting things organized. The COP was a flurry of activity. We had the engineer company—call sign "Blade 6"—out there, and they were working there nonstop. SSG Fisher and his squad headed over to OP1 along with the sniper team to occupy that portion of the sector. At the same time, the Bradleys unloaded and split up, with one on MSR security while the other manned the TOC and pulled quick reaction force (QRF) along with SSG Rojas and SGT Bolton's squads. The area had been taking random fire all day and

---

48 Interpreters

Blue 6 and 9 G's had a few kills earlier in the day. The Blade element even got a few shots off on some bad guys.

Shortly after getting settled in, OP1 called up some suspicious activity east of their sector. They were watching kids the age of seven or younger moving around from house to house with AK-47s, then they reported an AIF running east with an AK-47. The BN sniper, NCO SGT Black, asked for a volunteer to go up to the rooftop with him to see if they could get eyes on. Naturally newly promoted PVT Spencer volunteered. They grabbed their gear, saddled up, and headed toward the rooftop. The sniper led the way up the stairs, and Spencer followed. They remained crouched down behind a four-foot brick wall that went around the entire rooftop. As they peeked up over the ledge to see what was going on, a shot cracked by SGT Black's head. He turned to look and see if Spencer was okay but immediately realized that Spencer had been shot in the head. Black radioed for a medic, and within a millisecond, Doc Devries was up there.

Quiiisssh ...

"Bone 9, this is Bone Main, over."

"Bone Main, this is Bone 9, send your traffic over."

"Roger, OP1 reported taking sniper fire from the east and has one wounded, over."

I headed straight to BN since I was closer to the radios. As I walked in, I was met by CPT Chapman, and he said it was Spencer. He'd been hit in the head, and they were evacuating him now. I was in shock. The only thing I could think was, *Damn, we just promoted him.* CPT Chapman and I jumped into the Ranger and drove down to the gate to warn the guards that we had a casualty coming in and not to impede their movement. This was becoming all too much of a routine. I heard the whine of the engines, saw the exhaust smoke plumes, and then the vehicles barreled through the barriers. The driver had his hatch in the popped position because it was drizzling and his periscopes were all clouded up. We spun out and blocked the four-way intersection as the Bradleys went flying through; they weren't stopping for anything. If a vehicle had been hit in the intersection, I don't think the Bradley would have even felt it.

The gravel parking lot of the aid station was flooded from the previous rains and made it confusing for the driver since the markings were underwater. After a slight pause, the driver keyed on the medics standing by with the stretcher and pulled in. As the ramp went down, we observed Doc Devries giving Spencer mouth-to-mouth. Spencer's head was already bandaged and all we could do was help get him on a stretcher and into the emergency room. Once in the ER, Doc gave the on-site doctor a rundown of what had happened and also informed him that Spencer had a mouth full of sunflower seeds when he was shot. Doc turned and told me he tried to get them out the best he could but it was still causing difficulty. He then looked at me and the commander and said he didn't think Spencer was going to make it. He said his body stopped working but his brain did not know it yet. We went into the ER to see him. They had hoses up his nose and down his throat, and they put a fresh wrap on his head. I thought to myself about what Doc said: his brain was still working but his body wasn't. I blurted out, "Come on, Spence!" The nurse looked at me like I was a freak, talking to a dead man. They flew him out shortly after to Balad Airbase to try and work on him some more, but he was pronounced dead on arrival.

PV2 Clarence Spencer, Killed in Action, 4 February 2007, Buhritz, Iraq

Over the next three days, the commander was putting the finishing touches on our offensive operation, and I started to plan and prepare for Spencer's memorial; we set the date for 9 February. First platoon would stay out at the COP until the evening prior to the memorial ceremony. There was no need for rotating them out, as there wasn't going to be any hero flight. Third platoon needed the maintenance and downtime. They understood and knew they would be coming in for the memorial service in a few days.

LT Duplechin had the task of conducting the inventories, assisted by SSG Morales and SPC Larsen. Unfortunately we had gotten too proficient at inventories and memorials by that point. SSG Morales had the picture frames, display boots, new Kevlar with cover, blank dog tags and chains, and new M4 rifle with all the accessories in a case with a new bayonet. The only thing that had to be done was to stamp out dog tags and have the Kevlar band sewed. It turned into a battle drill: after you do it so many times, it just becomes muscle memory and you don't think about it; you just execute. My emotions were getting dulled; I thought that was both a good and bad thing: good because I didn't hurt as much; but bad because I was losing my compassion.

Right around this time is when I had it out with the battalion chaplain. He kept hitting me up for the names of the people that were going to be in the memorial so he could get the programs printed, and he also wanted to sit down with someone so he could find out information on who Spencer was so he could talk about it during the ceremony. I kept telling him I would get the information, that the guys were out at the COP, but he insisted and kept pushing like it was some report about logistics, not like it was about an individual, a comrade with friends that were at an outpost trying to do a dangerous job and hurting on the inside. The battalion chaplain was so detached from what our reality was that he didn't have a clue about what we were feeling. Not once did he ever come out to the COP: not for Christmas, New Year's, or any other significant emotional event—never! I actually requested another chaplain from another BN. I'd had enough of that specific individual.

I scored a really awesome picture of Spencer from SSG Rojas. So I had SGT Zufall—our unofficial company Photoshop expert and memorial slideshow tribute maker—spruce up the picture a bit. It was a picture of Spencer standing with all his gear on, with a M4/M203 launcher, just looking like a soldier. SGT Zufall faded the edges and we had the color of the font in red and yellow. It kind of looked out of place on the backdrop of an infantry blue background. I think only a few people understood why I chose those colors, but it seemed appropriate at the time, since Spence had been a Marine, too.

I had a few friends that worked in the brigade S-2 shop and they had a big old printer that they used to make maps and graphics and cold print color. A female NCO hooked me up and printed a large picture of Spencer then gave me some plastic board to tape the print to. It was a great picture of him and would really look awesome on the easel. Every memorial we did, we upped the standards. It wasn't a competition; I just felt the need to honor our guys the best we could, and like any mission you take on, the more you do it, the better you get at it.

It was now the evening prior to the memorial ceremony. Everything was in order and we were ready to execute the ceremony in the morning. The scouts and mortars manned the COP so we could have everyone else back. I briefed the rifle team that was going to conduct the twenty-one-gun salute. Then I briefed the ushers and did a final review with SSG Morales, and as usual, he had everything squared away.

LT Duplechin came up and asked if he could sing "Amazing Grace" at the ceremony, and of course the first question I asked was, "Can you sing?" He started to tell me about the band he was in back home and how he played the tuba in marching band in college. He then proceeded to flex his LSU tattoo and later showed me a calendar that had a picture of him at a football game playing in the band. He was so proud, he said, "Hey, Top, come check out the calendar I am in." I was curious so I went over to his CHU and he showed me a picture of the LSU marching band in the stands at a football game. I tried to find him and couldn't spot his picture. He then pointed to a body that has the face covered up by a tuba. "There that's me!" he said. I then pointed to another person playing the clarinet, someone who also had his head covered up. I said, "Look, LT, that's me! We were at the same game and didn't even know it." Then I walked out.

Anyway, back to the prep for the memorial service. Later that evening, I had some quiet time and decided to take a hot shower and try to get some rest. As I lay down and shut my eyes, my mind started to drift into the questioning of what the hell was going on and reflecting on the past four months and trying to visualize what our future was to look like. Then I started thinking about all the guys that we had lost, not only in the company but soldiers in the battalion. We lost our battalion scout, PSG SFC Haines, and his driver, SPC Mutz, in a fiery IED explosion that annihilated their HMMWV. Alpha company had lost a fine NCO by the name of SSG Morris, killed when an explosive formed penetrator (EFP) hit his gun truck while on patrol. E Co 215th, our support company, lost two guys, CPL Jonathan Schiller and SPC Richard Smith, in a massive IED explosion, and the MTT unit lost a few guys, plus the brigade had lost a few soldiers in various attacks throughout the area of responsibility. That was just the US side. When you added in all the Iraqi army, Iraqi police, and the religious, tribal, and insurgent casualties, it truly was a city of death. We were fighting every day and we were killing bad guys. We were disrupting their safe havens and safe houses, raiding their supply networks, killing IED emplacement teams. We had informants working for us, UAV drone strikes, Apache helicopters (AWTs) constantly in the air. We were putting the hurt on the AIF and they were still coming.

I fell asleep and woke up with the same question on my mind. *Why are we, the United States Army, not being reinforced? Aren't people reading the daily reports? Don't they see how many bad guys we are killing, and how many of our guys are getting busted up in the process?*

The president had announced in early January that there would be a troop surge, but the talk was Baghdad and out west in Al Anbar. No one mentioned Diyala Province.

On 9 February 2007, at 0700 hours, the sun was out and the sky was clear, I was up early and worked my way to the chow hall for some grub and a cup of coffee before I went to the gymnasium to see if they'd blocked it off and if the tarp had been laid down on the floor. Upon my arrival, everything seemed in order, so I found a spot on the steel bleachers that were pushed over in a corner and went over my notes as I waited for the detail to show up for the setup and rehearsals.

As in the past, the first few rehearsals were pretty rough at first, but started to smooth out as we went along. Slowly we made progress and added different parts and fine-tuned others. We eventually worked our way up to rehearsals with the chaplain, speakers, and color guard. A few hours later, the commander and I were ready to do our final rehearsals. Once the final rehearsals were completed, we were all ready for a break, so the commander and I stepped outside of the gymnasium to get a breath of fresh air before the start of the ceremony. As we stood there talking, I noticed a young soldier dart across the open field and stop and ask another soldier a question. The soldier being questioned turned and pointed over in the direction of the battalion commander, who was off in the distance near his vehicle. Identifying his intended objective, the soldier again took off running. Out of breath and trying to maintain his composure, the young soldier handed the battalion commander a note and then stood silently as the battalion commander read it.

As I was taking in what was going on around me, I turned and looked at CPT Chapman. Before I could say anything, he said, "Whatever it is, it's not good." He had taken the words right out of my mouth. My mind started racing. *What is it this time? Did someone just get killed? If so, who? What unit?*

As the thoughts sped through my head, CPT Chapman went over to see what was going on. As he approached, LTC Goins put his right hand on my CO's left shoulder and handed him the note. CPT Chapman opened the folded paper and read it. As he read, his head went from upright to a downward position, then he turned and walked toward me. As he handed the note to me, he asked, "When is it going to stop?"

Dreading the worst, I open the note and started to read the smeared ink. Not wanting to believe what I was reading, I read it again. An entire squad from B Company that was attached to

"Dealer" D company had just been wiped out in a massive house explosion. Three soldiers were missing in action, most likely killed in action and buried in the rubble. Three others were critically wounded, and two others wounded but stable.

There we were, minutes away from paying our respects for one of our soldiers, and we got the word that an entire squad from our company had just been wiped out, with at least three of the eight men killed in action and the remainder wounded. There was nothing we could do. SFC Cenicerous and LT Siggins were both squared away and could handle what needed to be done on the ground. Dealer Company and the battalion commander pushed all available assets to the location of the house explosion to help recover the bodies and secure the area. We had to stay and conduct the memorial ceremony. The ceremony lasted about forty-five minutes, and all I could do was think about what was going on with the recovery operations. That was the longest forty-five minutes of my life.

Once the ceremony ended, we did not line up for the usual condolences and handshaking. After CPT Chapman and I rendered our final salute to PFC Clarence Spencer, we headed straight toward the side exit door and busted into a dead sprint to the aid station. We made it there in record time. As we rounded the corner, we saw the majority of the platoon gathered around the side and rear of a Bradley. Some soldiers were completely covered in chalky dust, except where sweat ran down their faces (could have been tears). Some guys were bleeding from their hands from trying to claw through the rubble to get to their fallen brothers. There were two Bradleys sitting there all covered in masonry dust with big and small blocks of concrete scattered about on the engine decks and reactive armor. Some soldiers were trying to get accountability of equipment, others were staring off into oblivion, while still others sat quietly and smoked cigarettes and looked at what was going on around them.

What could you say to a platoon that just watched an entire squad get annihilated? Nothing—there was nothing at all you could say that would make any difference or comfort anyone. You just had to go and do what you were trained to do. We needed accountability of all the equipment: we needed to figure out what was there, what was missing, and then call it out to the soldiers working on recovering the rest of the equipment and personnel. As we started to organize the weapons and other equipment, one of the guys handed me an M4 rifle that was literally cut in half from the explosion. The recovered items were a pile of mangled equipment. Just looking at it underscored how massive the explosion had been. It was a miracle the entire squad had not been killed. The guys did a great job of consolidating the equipment and recovering the other casualties. They did not leave any immediate equipment behind for the insurgents to use as propaganda material. The accountability piece was good. It got the soldiers up and moving and thinking about something other than the house explosion.

While they were busy getting things back in order, I slipped over to the emergency room to get a situation report. Doc Wright was all blasted up with shrapnel to his face but he was going to be good. SSG Johnson had already been flown out to Balad Airbase; he was pretty bad but stable. SPC Larry was also wounded pretty bad and flown out.

The second platoon guys wanted to go back out and help with the recovery of their brother, but I told them no. There was an entire company, plus engineers, out there and they had things under control. I asked the guys what happened and they told me immediately: "It was a setup." They had gotten a tip from the IA on two houses that were suspected to be IED-making factories. CPT Carlock planned a company cordon-and-search mission for the next day. The tanks would provide the outer cordon, and the Bradleys were to roll up, drop the infantry squads, and move to a position where they could over-watch the squads. The first squad, led by SSG Heinz, would go in and secure the first house, then set up an over-watch and cover SSG Ross's squad as they maneuvered into the second objective.

The operation kicked off around 0700 hours, and everything

went according to plan. SSG Heinz's squad made it into their building with no issues and quickly cleared it. The building was abandoned and not habitable due to the fact it had been gutted from a previous JDAM guided missile strike. The walls were crumbling in some areas and non-existent in others. SSG Heinz had his teams set up in a 360-degree perimeter and called up to LT Siggins to report they were set, so SSG Ross and his squad could move into the second objective.

A few seconds later, SSG Heinz could see the squad move from the vehicles and disappear one by one into the fenced courtyard of the target house. Moments later, SSG Ross came on the radio and reported they had gained a foothold in the house and were moving to clear the rest of the building. Everyone waited in silence for the call, "Building secure," when an enormous explosion knocked SSG Heinz down to the ground and showered massive chunks of concrete down on top of everyone within a hundred-meter radius. As SSG Heinz stumbled to get back to his feet, he looked around for SPC Miller and PVT Hyde, who had been next to him prior to the explosion, but he could not find either one of them amid the dust and debris. As his senses started to come back, and the air started to clear, Heinz spotted part of a Kevlar helmet and a muzzle sticking out of a pile of cinder blocks. He started to dig and throw the cinder blocks aside to free the trapped soldier. Then SPC Miller appeared out of the dust and started helping uncover PVT Hyde, who was buried by what used to be a wall.

Once they freed PVT Hyde, SSG Heinz had SGT Castillo and his team move over to the demolished building, with SPC Miller's team following. Still dazed from the explosion, the teams stumbled in a foggy haze across the hundred-meter open area and entered into the partially collapsed courtyard that was littered with bodies and debris.

In the courtyard, they saw three bodies lying just outside the building. SGT Johnson looked to be busted up really bad and couldn't move, so they dragged him over to a corner and set up a casualty collection point. Then they grabbed SPC Larry, and he, too, was in really bad shape. The explosion had blown one eye completely out of the socket and he was going into shock. The third fallen man, Doc Wright, was not coherent after being peppered pretty bad with multiple shrapnel wounds to his face.

By that point, the Bradleys had pivoted and backed into the courtyard, and SFC Ciniceros and LT Siggins dismounted and started helping with the casualty triage and evacuation. SGT Shaw was lying in the hallway just as SSG Heinz and SPC Pachotta entered what was left of the house. Shaw's eyes were blinking and he appeared to still be alive, so they carried him outside and set him down with the other casualties. Then they went back into the house to find SSG Ross and SPC Camacho. First, they came across SSG Ross. It was obvious that he was dead so they carried him out, then set him on the other side of the courtyard and covered him up. Entering the building for a third time, they spotted numerous unexploded anti-tank mines scattered throughout the debris. Worried that one of the AT mines was going to go off, SSG Heinz told SPC Pachotta to go outside the building and help the others. After a thorough search, SPC Camacho was identified, buried under massive amounts of debris. It was apparent that he had been at the heart of the explosion's force. They would not be able to recover his body without heavy engineering equipment and EOD assets to deal with the unstable unexploded ordinance.

By then, SGT Shaw had died of his wounds in the courtyard, so he and SSG Ross were loaded into one Bradley, while the casualties and remainder of the squads were loaded up in the other. Then they all headed back to FOB Warhorse. SSG Heinz stayed behind to assist with the recovery of SPC Camacho, which they would end up doing after a few hours of work with engineer assets and EOD.

The hero flight that evening was well after midnight. I wasn't expecting many soldiers, and the only soldiers from our company that could be there were from HQ platoon and the actual Bonecrusher second platoon. The rest of our guys were all out at Bone X-Ray getting ready to conduct the assault down south in Buhritz. As I pulled into the parking lot, I saw more soldiers at this hero flight than any other I had witnessed. I was surprised—and relieved.

This hero flight ceremony was going to be especially hard, standing there and trying to watch and pay respects to your fallen comrades, while thinking about the families they were leaving behind. As I watched, the pallbearers filed by, one group after the next, carrying body bags that had fathers, sons, and husbands in them. Images appeared in my mind of the pain the families would soon feel when the casualty notification officer and an NCO came knocking on their door to tell them about the tragic fate of their loved ones. SSG Ross's wife was six months pregnant and had a few kids she was trying to raise already. SPC Camacho's wife was from out of the country and had a language barrier to overcome and had several children to take care of. SGT Shaw's family would not fare any better. All of them would be robbed of that one last glimpse of their loved one before he was laid to rest, and the kids would grow up not knowing their fathers or understanding how brave and admired they were from the guys they served with.

SSG Eric Ross, Killed in Action, 9 February 2007,
Baqubah, Iraq
SSG Alan Shaw, Killed in Action, 9 February 2007,
Baqubah, Iraq
SPC LeeRoy Camacho, Killed in Action, 9 February 2007,
Baqubah, Iraq

After the hero flight, I gathered the guys up in a horseshoe formation and said a few words of encouragement, but really, what could I say? After the formation, I slipped onto the ATV and slowly rode back to my room. Up to the point of closing my door behind me, I had been strong and shrugged off a lot of the madness, but when that door closed behind me and I was alone, I broke down. Watching my soldiers get blown up on an almost daily basis—and killed, wounded, or shot at—had taken its toll on me. Things felt out of control. I was losing hope. I was mad at God and I was mad at everyone around me, including myself. I wanted answers!

Why are we being subjected to this punishment! How can we keep going on if things don't change? Where is God in all this death and destruction?

I was having a breakdown and felt helpless. I wasn't worried about myself being killed. I just felt responsible for the deaths of my soldiers, but I did not know what more I could do to prevent them from dying. I tried to reason with myself that no one could prevent it—that it was war. But that wasn't good enough. (I am certain that every soldier who was part of this fight had broken down at some point, and this was my moment.) As I sat there alone, mad at the world, trying to make sense out of the craziness of war, I had a saying come into my thoughts: "God will only give you what you can handle." I remembered thinking to myself, *God must think I have a pretty big rucksack; he is dumping a lot of stuff in it.* Then my thoughts got really clear and I thought to myself: *God put me in this position; he wanted me to do this job for a reason.* After that simple one-sentence phrase, I suddenly felt like I was doing God's work and what I was doing was bigger than all of us. So I was not going to let him down, and I certainly did not want to let my soldiers down.

Up to that point in my life, I had not been a big Bible banger and really didn't know any Bible verses, so for that one sentence to come into my thoughts, it had to be purely God's way of giving me a little encouragement in my darkest hour.

Luckily my moment and realization came and went rather quickly, because the company was getting ready to kick off the major offensive into the south in a few hours and I needed to focus. This was the moment we had been waiting for. The battalion and brigade had given us what we needed in personnel, and we were ready to do some damage. We had an additional US Army platoon from our HHC scouts. We had the Alamo and Ghost elements from our IA MTT unit. We had all three of our platoons on the ground, plus air support—both rotary wing and fixed wing, including

A-10s and UAV—and even EOD teams, a BN sniper element, and reporters.

We were going to try something new in that I would be positioned for the operation. I would be located in the BN TOC and be co-located with the artillery officer, LT Jacobs, whom I called Big Jake (tall, ugly guy). Big Jake had control of the big guns, A-10s and the UAVs. The plan was for me to be able to help CPT Chapman by anticipating the needs of the company as I watched them maneuver via the UAV and then request support assets as needed. I also could watch the enemy and help interpret their actions to the UAV pilots, and also relay the information to the commander and if possible anticipate where they would need support and work with LT Jacobs as the commander worked the ground forces. What we learned in the past was that we could give all the graphics in the world to the UAV pilots, but unless you stayed working with them minute by minute, you would not be able to use them to their maximum capabilities. With my detailed knowledge of the terrain, AIF tactics and maneuver capabilities, and close knowledge of our own plan, it seemed like it would be an effective option.

The scout platoon, Bone's third platoon, and the EOD teams infiltrated under cover of darkness. The plan was to slowly build combat power throughout the night. Then, once we were set and started to push south, the Alamo element (IA Special Forces with US Special Forces) would air-assault in and seal off the east side of town and hit a few high-value targets. At the same time, the Gorilla element would leave FOB Gabe via their HMMWV gun trucks and fall into our rear formations and slowly integrate into the fight with our guys.

Everything was going according to plan until first light. The insurgents must have been anticipating our attack (anytime you mix IA in with a US mission, there is always a good chance your plan has been compromised). The instant the vehicles started to position themselves on their respective sides of the canals, the entire city erupted. Red 6 gunned down two AIF east of their position while the enemy was trying to fire an RPG at OP1. Other

AIF RPG teams fired RPGs at Bone X-Ray, with mortar rounds landing, IEDs going off, and the ever-present machine-gun fire sounding throughout.

I had the UAV loitering around a known major intersection and watched guys dragging tires out into the street and start burning them. I watched other guys running and directing what little civilian population was out there to disperse. I also observed one guy running toward our troops, before he stopped and picked up a bag on the side of the road that was prepositioned in a stack of tires—and then he pulled out a burka and changed into a woman's complete wardrobe with an AK-47 underneath. It was going to be a long day.

The Alamo elements air-assaulted in and occupied their objectives with little resistance. They killed a few AIF while they assaulted the buildings they were to strong-point in and blocked the enemy's withdrawal routes out of Buhritz from the eastern and southern portions of the sector. We started pushing south slowly, a hundred meters at a time. We anticipated this mission was going to take two to three days to move less than three miles.

It was now around 1025 hours and we had pushed a few hundred meters south and were in a good position to call in the Gorilla forces. They had been held up on Route Gold awaiting the word to launch. Just as they were getting the word to head south, they took precision small-arms fire from Tahrir in the east. They reported one person shot in the head. I immediately told the UAV pilot to move over and cover down in Tahrir and start looking for any AIF. We initially thought it was an IA soldier, but moments later the call came over saying it was a US soldier with the Gorilla MTT. Gorilla 3 had pulled out of their holding pattern and rushed the wounded soldier back to FOB Gabe where he could be airlifted out. They returned about thirty minutes later, linked up with the remainder of their unit, and pushed straight into Buhritz, where they immediately joined the fight.

About this time, the AIF shifted their mortar tubes onto the Alamo element in the east and tried to push them out of their stronghold so they could withdraw or reinforce. They dropped three rounds and managed to wound one of the IA Special Forces. I was searching high and low for the mortar tube that was launching these rounds but the AIF had gotten skilled over the past few months in eluding our air surveillance. I noticed a large crowd of thirty to fifty military-aged males (MAM) at a building southwest of the sector, but only saw a few weapons. There was a building shaped like a triangle and it seemed to be the focal point for the personnel in that portion of the city. All the individuals were going in and out of the structure, and cars were pulling in and out. We were straining to try to identify weapons or other indicators that would justify us killing them in accordance with the ROE. The UAV pilot spotted some weapons getting put in the trunk of the car. We called in a description to AWTs and Wolfpack patiently waited for the vehicle to move away from the crowded gathering area and fired a few bursts of 30mm cannon onto them and scored a few more kills for Team Bone.

Now FOB Warhorse was under a mortar attack. The AIF, for whatever reason, had managed to call for fires on FOB Warhorse and dropped eight mortar rounds. I think they were trying to distract us. It was barely a blip on the radar.

At 1237 hours, the UAV was picking up plenty of bad guys. I could see four AIF laying an IED along Route Yankees, and about 400 meters to the west, I could see another four guys with weapons slung on their backs in a courtyard of a house. AWTs were conducting refueling operations so I tried to get clearance to fire some mortars, but was denied due to collateral damage and because our guys were not directly threatened. I was starting to get frustrated; I felt like the ROE for this area was a little inadequate.

It was now 1400 hours, and LT Moffitt had been assigned the most important task of the entire mission: route clearance. If we had gotten bogged down with this, the entire operation would have come to a grinding halt. LT Moffitt was placed in charge of getting the EOD team to the specific locations in an expedient manor. The engineer/EOD assets, call sign "Havoc" element, did not expect to be this busy. The engineers had already blown six IEDs and were working on their seventh when their robot[49] got blown to pieces. Luckily the Havoc element had a few more robots, and it did not slow them down too much. Over the next hour, both Predator and Stalker had each killed several AIF emplacing booby traps and IEDs along our axis of advance. The AWTs came back on station and within minutes killed one individual that was still in the courtyard down south.

Then, at 1530 hours, White 9 and White 3 engaged and destroyed one white sedan on the northern portion of Route Gold. It had driven by and emplaced an IED in a previous IED blast hole.

Later, at 1606 hours, IA on the west side of the canal south of Bone X-Ray were hit with an RPG while clearing a building, reporting one KIA and two WIA. Alpha section Bradleys from first platoon evacuated the WIA and KIA back to FOB Warhorse. Shortly after, at 1630 hours, EOD lost a second robot while reducing their fifteenth IED.

As the casualties from the IA were being transported back to FOB Warhorse, we started making calls and gathering additional demolition equipment and batteries for the robots so that we could pass it off to the EOD teams once the Bradleys returned back to sector.

From 1630 hours until daybreak of day two—11 February 2007—the platoons strong-pointed in houses and over-watched the EOD teams as they worked throughout the evening, reducing IED after IED. Just that evening they completed over seven controlled detonations, reducing at least that many IEDs and creating a path for us to push farther into the AIF stronghold. The company task force pushed about one mile into sector on day one.

---

49   An EOD robot is a battery-operated, remote-controlled, and tracked device that had multiple cameras, a gripping claw, a light, and several other mechanisms that are designed to investigate an IED or a suspected IED, and also to place explosive charges to eliminate the IED—all without putting the EOD technician in harm's way.

Our first contact of day two came in the form of small-arms fire from the southwest, followed by an explosion next to Bone X-Ray. As the day ground on, the dismounts were making good progress. With EOD getting overwhelmed with IEDs, the infantry squads and Bradleys started reducing the IEDs on their own. They were finding the wires that powered the IEDs and would trace them back to the firing position or cut the wires or detonate the IEDs by hooking up a radio battery to the wires. Or, if they could talk a Bradley onto the IED itself, they would just let the Bradley shoot it with the 25mm. This technique was not preferred, but sitting in one position for hours waiting for EOD to make it over was more dangerous than taking the IED out themselves.

By 1200 hours on day two, the company task force had killed roughly twenty to twenty-five AIF and reduced another twenty-five IEDs (both conservative estimates; both the logbook and the radio transmitter operator were getting overwhelmed).

At 1310 hours on day two, the UAV spotted a house where ten to twelve AIF were gathering for what appeared to be a launching site for a counterattack, which put our soldiers in imminent danger, we had PID (positive identification of enemy and hostile act or intent). I called it into Maniac and they dropped four rounds of high explosives onto the house. Their accuracy was awesome, killing everyone inside! About an hour later at 1417 hours, AWTs engaged a two-man sniper team with a Draganov sniper rifle and scope. I thought to myself, *Hope that was the jihadist that killed Spencer.*

As the day continued and the company task force continued to push south, the direct engagements started to taper off slightly. Radio and cell phone intercepts reported the AIF had left a substantial force to fight it out with us, but the majority of the AIF had fled either west into the palm groves or south along the Diyala River. Our logistical lines were stretched dangerously thin, and we requested the QRF to come out to reinforce White platoon on MSR security so they could push into the south and help secure our supply routes.

At 1530 hours, the IA unit engaged and destroyed a VBIED that was set up on the side of the road and positioned in such a way that whatever vehicle it hit would be blown into the canal. AWTs fired one more Hellfire into a house, killing two AIF armed with a heavy machine gun before the sun started to set on day two. At that point, the company task force had made it two of the three miles south into the objective area. The rest of the evening was spent rotating vehicles out to pick up supplies and fuel, and doing the final preparations for the assault into the last mile of the city.

Even though the intelligence reports and cell phone intercepts said the majority of the AIF forces had left, we expected some of the heaviest fighting to occur on day three as we cornered the remaining forces and closed in on them.

Day three started out slow and deliberate; the tension in the air could be felt just as it could be read on the tired and expressionless faces of the soldiers of Team Bone. Everyone was glad to have made it this far into the town, but also knew that disaster was just an IED or machine-gun burst away. The farther we pushed, the harder the fighters that were remaining in town would fight.

As the sun started to crest over the palm groves and cut through the hazy smoke-filled air, the radios crackled with reports of squads and teams getting REDCON-1 and doing final coordination with the Bradley sections that would be over-watching their movements.

Slow and steady was the mind-set. The Iraqi army soldiers were a little jumpy as the day started, but the cool and deliberate demeanor of the US soldiers helped calm their nerves and eventually got them into the groove again.

Just a few hundred meters into the movement, the routes south started getting more restrictive due to low-hanging electrical wires and the narrowing roads that parallel the canal, causing the Bradley fighting vehicles to halt their push south.

With the Bradleys halted, the Iraqi army pushed their up-armored HMMWVs past the Bradleys to help support, with their heavy Dushka .50-cal. machine guns or their mounted RPK 7.62mm machine guns.

As the lead IA HMMWV slipped past the Bradley fighting vehicle, the partially exposed IA gunner waved and gave the thumbs-up to the dismounts that were tucked into the small alleyway protecting the flank of the Bradley. With the IA HMMWV in the lead and moving cautiously down the restricted paths, and the infantry squads to their flanks and slightly forward, the formations were now set and the coordinated movement could be executed.

Just as CPT Chapman was doing the final map checks and sending the front line trace of the friendly units up to BN HQ, a machine gun opened up from the east side of the town in the direction of the cemetery.

As the sound of bullets snapped overhead, the infantry squads moved into the courtyards and other available cover, maneuvering to positions that would allow them to indentify where the shooting was coming from. With the Bradleys unable to push into better positions for observation and positive identification, it was up to the dismounts to get "eyes on."

Within a few moments, first platoon was calling in a grid coordinate to the enemy machine-gun team in the cemetery and requesting a fire mission. Upon getting the PID and the eight-digit grid coordinate, CPT Chapman relayed the information to Charger 14, LT Jacobs. Just as luck would have it, we had an A-10 check in on station, and we had all the right conditions for an A-10 strafing run. Why not?

With the infantry squads in hard-standing buildings and accounted for, the Bradleys and HMMWVs a safe distance away, and the positive identification of the enemy in the cemetery, the conditions had been set and the final coordination between Charger 14, Bone 6, and the A-10 pilot had been made.

With the calm, cool voice of the pilot coming over the radio and the words "guns inbound," there was a momentary pause, then silence, silence, silence. Everyone strained to hear the engines or the guns of the A-10...

Nothing. Then ...

Buuuuuuuuuuuuuuuuuuuuurrrrrrrrrrrrrrrrrrrrrrrrppppp!

Five seconds and 350 rounds of 30mm later, it was all over.

By the time the first platoon infantry squads saw the rounds impacting the target area and could key the hand mic to give a report, it was all over. They could then finally hear the sounds of the Gatling gun and the roar of the Warthog's dual engines. The amount of death and destruction that could be delivered by the A-10 in such a short period of time and with such precision is indescribable. Needless to say, there was no more AIF machine-gun team in the cemetery.

There's nothing like starting your day off with a gun run from an A-10 and sending a message to the enemy that says, "If you come out in the open, we will kill you from 4,000 feet away, and you will never hear it or see it coming—just instant terror and death."

The rest of the day went pretty smooth, and the platoons had closed within a few houses of reaching their objectives. With the over-watch and coverage of the exfiltration route off the objective getting dangerously thin, the IA HMMWVs were being repositioned to cover down for the withdrawal of the infantry squads off of their objectives.

Just as the squads bounded into their final positions and maneuvered to cover each other's withdrawal, a thunderous explosion erupted from the canal area. Without a second guess, everyone knew one of the IA gun trucks had been hit with an IED. LT Boeka worked his way over to the IED site with a squad of infantry, but there was little that could be done. The main body of the HMMWV wreckage was flipped over onto its roof and came to rest halfway in the canal—engulfed in flames. Without a doubt, everyone inside the truck was dead.

Lacking the ability to extinguish the flames, the only thing the squads could do was wait until the HMMWV burned itself out. In the meantime, the IA were trying to figure out exactly who they'd lost. It turned out that not only was the gun truck crew killed, but several IA soldiers were near the vehicle when the IED was detonated and were missing in action—and later reported killed in action.

Day three was slowly coming to an end, but our worst fears had become a reality with the detonation of an IED and the loss of five IA soldiers. Task Force Bone had accomplished its mission and reached all template objectives; cleared thirty-plus IEDs; killed multiple insurgents, including a machine-gun team and sniper team; found multiple caches, including a mortar system and rounds; cleared and indentified safe houses, medical supplies, and facilities; and disrupted their day-to-day operations.

Frustratingly enough, we did not have the ability to stay and hold the ground we'd just fought three days for and TF Bone had to move back to its main area of operation. Within a few days, the insurgents were able to move back into their areas and reestablish their systems and defenses for yet another fight they anticipated in the future.

CHAPTER 10

STEEL RAIN

I'D HAD ENOUGH OF the FOB and was ready to get back out with the men. I knew the UAV was effective, and having a liaison from the company in BN HQ during the mission was a great technique, but for future operations, it would not be me. I could not help but feel guilty as I watched from "above" instead of being on the ground with my company.

I had one mission to do before I left, so I went down to the aid station to check out the "Combat Stress Team" (CST). I figured if I was going through all those emotions, my soldiers were too—and some didn't have Bible phrases and one-on-ones with God—so I wanted to at least get information on where they were and talk to the team and let them know who I was and give them a rundown on the company's history, just in case they did not know and some of my soldiers had come in.

I talked to the counselor and asked various questions, but the two big ones were, "What are your capabilities?" and "What can you do for my soldiers?" The answers were positive and reassuring—and then he asked me, "And how are you doing?" I was taken aback by the question, but told him that I was stressed but had things under control. He didn't leave things at that and asked me questions.

He was genuine in his concern, so I let my guard down a little and we talked for a while. I expressed my concerns and told him a little about the breakdown the evening prior. We talked about some coping techniques, and I felt pretty good about what he was telling me, to the point that I would go back and brief the platoon sergeants about the experience and have them start encouraging guys to either go and see the CST or recognize the indicators and know some of the coping skills and techniques so they could make suggestions to their soldiers.

After my meeting with the CST leader, I felt even better than before. I was on a new mission, and I wanted to do away with the stigma that someone was weak if he went to see the CST or chaplain and talked about what was bothering them or to just vent a little. I thought I had pretty good credibility in the company, and if I promoted it openly with specific soldiers, I thought they would benefit from it. And if I told them I went personally to see the CST, then it would make it easier for them to go in and talk to the CST as well.

On my way back up to the company area, I ran into one of the soldiers from Apache and he looked pretty distraught, then he told me that Apache Company had just lost a guy from SFC Davenport's platoon that was attached to Crazy Company and that Apache had lost a few guys from their recovery team.

Crazy Company had one of the farthest sectors in our BN's area of responsibility (AOR); their area was about thirty kilometers south of FOB Warhorse, and like the rest of the BN companies, they had nowhere near enough people to maintain such a massive area.

The night prior, SFC Davenport's platoon had been conducting SKTs along Route West Vanessa where the anti-tank mine/IED activity had picked up considerably. During that mission, they'd managed to kill two AIF while attempting to set in a double-stacked AT/IED. With their position compromised with the engagement of the two AIF, they returned to their COP around 0400 hours, but were sent back out to over-watch another IED emplacement site.

Just prior to daybreak, SFC Davenport's section rolled out of the KBS outpost heading north along Route Vanessa. The weather was bad and turning to downright miserable, which had an effect on the visibility. It was a light rain mixed with an early morning fog that hugged the roadways and canals that were running parallel to the main highway. The mounted patrol rumbled past CP 168 with the A33 vehicle in the lead and the A34 running trail and rear security. As they approached their assigned area, code-named "Cleveland," SSG Regis pulled off the road to bypass the specific portion of the road they were to over-watch. They parked about 500 meters north.

Humans are creatures of habit and the AIF were not immune to this fact. Once they found something that worked, they would stick with to varying degrees until it proved unsuccessful. The AIF liked to use previous blast holes within the road networks, as they could simply put their explosives in the hole and fill it with dirt and gravel to blend it in with its surroundings, leaving it there for weeks or months until someone unknowingly made the mistake of driving over it. The US response to the IED blast holes was to go and fill them with cement. As the cement cured, they would "brand" it with their engineer insignia so we knew it was our handiwork and not the AIF's. We called this "crater repair." The area they were to over-watch was a previous IED blast site that been repaired by our engineers and been branded with their branch insignia.

The weather progressively got worse and the optics on the Bradleys were starting to have difficulty cutting through the early morning haze. Not much longer after their initial setup, they received the call to return to base at KBS. Happy to oblige, they reversed the order of movement and headed back to the COP to hopefully get a little rest, as they been at it for over twenty-four hours straight. As they were rolling south, SFC Davenport had his driver swing wide to miss the crater repair site in the road and instinctively turned back to make sure his wingman cleared it too. As SSG Regis's Bradley approached the patchwork in the road, a fireball erupted underneath the Bradley, sending pieces of the vehicle flying through the air in a slow-motion volcanic eruption.

Seeing the explosion, SFC Davenport had his driver turn hard left into the field adjacent to the IED site and the downed Bradley. The A34 gunner scanned the entire area for a triggerman as SFC Davenport called the COP and informed them of the IED strike on the A33 vehicle, requesting additional personnel to reinforce him on the ground and to facilitate with the recovery of the vehicle. As he was talking on the radio, he saw SSG Regis and SPC McClellan both moving in the turret hatches, which was a good sign. SFC Davenport and the medic dismounted the vehicle and worked their way over to the A33 vehicle as the A34 gunner laid down some suppressive fire on the east and west side of the road in order to scare off any would-be ambushers or additional triggerman. SSG Regis was shaken up really bad; SPC McClellan sustained a head injury and was bleeding from his forehead. SSG Regis and PFC Taylor rendered first aid to SPC McClellan while SFC Davenport moved to the driver's hatch to check the status of PFC Cummings. Once atop the Bradley's driver compartment, he kicked the locking mechanism then popped the hatch free and swung it upward so it would lock in place. Anxious to get a status of the driver, he quickly looked down inside the driver's compartment but it was obvious that PFC Cummings was KIA.

The massive IED had detonated directly underneath the driver's compartment of the Bradley, ripping through the thick steel flooring of the hull and pushing the brunt of the explosion into the confined quarters of the driver's compartment, killing Cummings instantly. With the limited resources on hand and reinforcements still over twenty minutes away, SFC Davenport decided to get everyone out of sight, and put SSG Regis and SPC McClellan in the back of his vehicle until the area could be properly secured.

After what seemed an eternity but in reality was thirty minutes, the MTT unit from KBS COP and one M1 tank showed up on the scene to reinforce the IED blast site. Having them on the ground was good, but there was no way they were going to be able to recover the Bradley with what they had, so the decision was made to call for a QRF from FOB Warhorse with the M88. Moments later, they got the call that QRF was en route. The QRF that was coming to their aid wasn't the typical QRF; it was Apache's entire HQ element, plus A Co's commander—CPT Conely—1SG Daniels, and 1LT Gilory, each rolling their own Bradley with an M88 crew. They had just come back onto the FOB from a mission in New Baqubah when they heard the radio traffic about their A33 vehicle taking a hit. Once on the FOB, they grabbed the M88 recovery vehicle and one EOD truck and became the QRF.

As the makeshift QRF worked its way south, they dodged a few other IED hot spots and previous "crater repair" sites. SFC Davenport established communications with them and gave them an update on what to expect on the ground as they pulled in. The Bradley was catastrophically destroyed; the IED blast had torn off all the reactive armor tiles and scattered them in a forty-foot radius around the vehicle. The first layer of actual armor on the Bradley's hull had been ripped off, and the entire left side of the suspension was missing. The vehicle was either going to have to be put on a lowboy trailer or basically dragged back to the FOB.

As the QRF pulled in, CPT Conely quickly started assessing the situation. With the QRF and the MTT unit both now on site, they were able to secure the area properly and start the recovery of both the vehicle and the driver. CPT Conely and LT Gilory worked the security and vehicle recovery piece, and SFC Davenport, 1SG Daniels, and SGT Corona worked the recovery of the driver from his hatch, as they had to pry pieces of the twisted steel wreckage away in order to free PFC Cummings from its grip.

Within twenty minutes of the QRF's arrival, they were able to recover PFC Cummings from his driver's hatch and carry him over to 1SG Daniels' vehicle, where they placed him gently into a body bag, zipped him up, and secured him in the troop compartment in the back of the Bradley. CPT Conley said a quick prayer and then they shifted focus back onto the recovery of the vehicle, and assisted the M88 crew with getting the Bradley hooked up and ready for movement back to FOB Warhorse.

The M88 senior recovery NCO, SGT Siegert, took charge of the actual rigging and had the M88 positioned and ready to hook up to the tow bar. He, CPT Conely, and two other soldiers lifted the tow bar and ground-guided the M88 back until they were able to drop the heavy tow bar onto the tow hitch of the M88. Next, SGT Siegert got a chain off of the M88 and hooked it up to a protruding hunk of steel that was originally part of the suspension system but was now dug into the ground and needed to be removed prior to dragging the disabled Bradley back to the FOB. SGT Siegert secured the other end to SFC Davenport's Bradley and gave him the cue to pull his Bradley forward, ripping the hunk of steel from its mount. With the obstruction eliminated, they quickly packed up the chains then loaded everyone up into the Bradleys and got ready to roll. SFC Davenport would head south back to his COP with the MTT unit, and the M1 tank, CPT Conely, and his element would head back north to FOB Warhorse.

The order of movement north had CPT Conely in the lead, followed by the M88 towing the A33 vehicle, then 1SG Daniels' vehicle, EOD, and finally the A50 with LT Gilory and his crew.

The QRF element traveled about two kilometers when CPT Conely's driver spotted a patch in the road and veered around it. As they passed without incident, CPT Conely traversed the commander's independent sight to look at the M88 to see if it also veered and immediately saw the IED detonate on the M88. Seeing the explosion and the M88 turning into an instant fireball, CPT Conely yelled for his driver to stop the Bradley. He immediately jumped out of the turret and ran back toward the glowing fireball that was now kicking up twenty-foot flames. As CPT Conely ran back toward the fireball, he heard his interpreter yelling for water. He turned and looked, seeing SGT Siegert lying on the ground, completely engulfed in flames. CPT Conely ran to the A90 track and yelled for some water. Then 1SG Daniels handed him a fire extinguisher, and CPT Conely ran back and put the flames out that had completely burnt 100 percent of SGT Siegert's body. Just as the flames were extinguished, the A60 gunner opened up with the 25mm to the east and then almost simultaneously heard small-arms fire, so CPT Conely worked his way back to the XO's vehicle, which had a better communications platform to have the XO call in an air MEDEVAC. Once back to the vehicle, CPT Conely realized that they were not in an ambush, but rather, the rounds on the M88 were exploding from the fire.

As the XO called the MEDEVAC, 1SG Daniels and the RTO came and got the fire blanket out of the A60 vehicle then wrapped up SGT Siegert and carried him over to the low ground on the side of the road until the helicopter could pick him up. With the M88 settled awkwardly in a massive crater—and the front portion of the vehicle still completely enveloped in flames—there was no way anyone else inside the vehicle had survived. CPT Conely requested additional forces from the emergency reaction platoon, and also requested the BN QRF with three M88s to conduct recovery operations.

There wasn't anything anyone could do for the moment but secure the LZ for the MEDEVAC helicopter and wait for the arrival of the QRF with the additional M88 recovery vehicles. The MEDEVAC came in and picked up SGT Siegert then took off without incident while the recovery assets were still twenty minutes out. The M88 recovery vehicle was still ablaze so the only thing they could do was sit and wait for the flames on the M88 to die down and the QRF to show up.

Once the additional QRF assets arrived, they had a quick huddle and came up with a plan on how to recover the vehicle. The first order of business was to disconnect the Bradley from the M88 and drag it away from the fire. As they worked on disconnecting the Bradley, a platoon of engineers showed up with a bucket loader and started scraping dirt up from the side of the road and dumping it onto the burning vehicle. With only a few bucket loads, it got the fire down to a manageable level.

Once the fire was extinguished, the recovery teams hooked up an M88 recovery vehicle and attempted to pull the damaged M88 out of the IED blast crater. But the recovery vehicle could not get it to budge, so they had to hook up an additional M88 and pull simultaneously to get the destroyed M88 out of the massive crater. After further inspection, it was determined that they would not be able to drag the burned-up hulk back to FOB Warhorse, so they requested a heavy equipment transporter (HET) to come and carry the M88 back to the FOB.

When the HET and third M88 arrived, escorted by Wardog White 4, CPT Conely directed them to get the HET into position so that they could lift the disabled M88 up off the ground with the M88s then drive the lowboy trailer underneath it and lower the disabled M88 into position. It took some rigging and out-of-the-box thinking, but it was finally loaded and strapped down and ready for its final trip back to the FOB.

Once the entire recovery element had made it back to FOB Warhorse, 1SG Daniels and CPT Conley pulled over to mortuary affairs and dropped off PFC Cummings. The damaged M88 went to the sterile yard and was downloaded. The medics were then able to extract the remaining two KIA out of the troop compartment of the M88 then took them to mortuary affairs.

A Co / E 215th
PFC Branden Cummings, SGT John Rode,
SGT Carl Siegert, SPC Ronnie Madore,
Killed in Action, 14 February 2007

Out at the COP, it didn't take long for the bad news to hit on that front. CPT Chapman informed me that the Iraqi army unit that was coming to reinforce us had a "small issue."

"Oh yeah," I said, "what was that?"

"They had a mutiny!" he said.

Wow, that was not what I was expecting to hear.

He went on to say, "The IA said it was too dangerous in Buhritz and they told the commanders they refused to come into the sector."

CPT Chapman then explained that we were still getting a company of IA soldiers but it would take a little bit longer.

Surprisingly enough, later happened sooner than expected. We had a company of Kurds show up a few days after the mutiny. These Kurds had an excellent reputation as good solid fighters who were loyal to the cause. I went over and met with my counterpart and realized instantly these guys had pride and they were disciplined. They were all in uniform, they had their weapons and equipment squared away, they were clean looking and well kept (for the most part) and had what I considered the most important attribute of them all: CONFIDENCE. They did not care that they were in Buhritz, at least not for the moment. I think they also knew they were part of something special. They were joining an actual US Army infantry unit. They knew we would take care of business— and business was what we had planned.

The good news just kept coming: we received word that some VIPs were coming out to get a firsthand look on our situation. At first a lieutenant colonel from outside the brigade came out to Bone X-Ray and evaluated the situation and mission. He had a few pointed questions to ask CPT Chapman and then off he went. Next came a colonel, and after that, we got word that some retired four-star general was coming out to the COP. CPT Chapman and I were pretty fired up, as it meant people were paying attention after all. Well, the general turned out to be General (ret.) Jack Keane. He came out to the COP and did his "fact finding" with CPT Chapman. I kept my distance and worried about the insurgents getting uppity, seeing activity outside the ordinary happenings around the COP. I figured we would catch some small-arms fire or a few mortar rounds, but it never came. GEN Keane came and went, and CPT Chapman told me one thing that really stuck out in his mind. He said the general asked what made him come up with the idea of living with the Iraqi army? CPT Chapman had replied, "We had no choice." Before the general left, he said one last inspirational thing: "The entire country needs to be doing what you guys are doing."

After the VIP visits, we started conducting small offensive missions with the IA Kurdish element. They looked good and had confidence, but the true test would come once they got shot at and were put under pressure. Would they turn and run or would they stay and fight? The IA units were like any other army in the world: it really depended on who their leaders were. As expected, within their first few patrols, we got into it with the 1920s Rev BDE. The insurgents were anxious to show us that the large-scale operation we'd just completed would not slow them down and that they were back. They also wanted to demonstrate to the IA that they were not welcome and thus displayed a show of force to try and scare them away. The IA at first were a bit disorganized and fired wildly in all directions, but as the fighting settled in and our guys on the ground organized the fire of the combined US and IA squads—and the firepower of the Bradleys for support—the IA took note and emulated our guys. The Bradley also helped to instill confidence in the IA. They really liked the 25mm cannon—then again who wouldn't, as long as it's on your side. These joint offensive missions were geared toward one major goal: keep the pressure on the AIF and not give up what we just fought for. We knew we would not be able to keep eyes on the entire city and many of the IEDs would be emplaced again, but what we did not want to give up was our freedom to maneuver in and around the COP, OP1, and a comfortable distance east and south.

With the most recent offensive operation over and the addition of our new Iraqi friends out at Bone X-Ray, business was running a bit smoother at the COP, and our platoons were getting a little more quality time back on FOB Warhorse. I shifted focus over to the maintenance effort. The executive officer, LT Moffitt, had been doing an awesome job. He pretty much became a one-man wrecking machine. He'd been on a solo mission trying to get three replacement Bradleys in addition to coordinating the day-to-day maintenance on all our vehicles and weapon systems. Additionally he had taken on the daunting task of trying to get additional mission-essential equipment like additional night vision, extra radios and mounts for the LMTV and other cargo vehicles, additional uniforms, and whatever else we needed. One of the bigger, more imminent fights he had taken on was trying to get enough reactive armor for all the Bradleys, and he also tried to get more crew-served weapons for out at Bone X-Ray. We needed more machine guns since we would be conducting more offensive operations. We could not afford to leave our M240B 7.62mm machine guns in position back at the COP but we also didn't want to strip the firepower from the force protection there.

Our company was not designed to operate the way it was, and we were finding ourselves short on equipment or finding requirements for new equipment never used in an infantry company, like generators, carpentry tools, and cargo trucks (PLS). We were even trying to get the bridge layer working, not to mention the massive amounts of various communications equipment that were needed to be effective. We needed mainly vehicle radios and dismounted (IMBTR) military radios; we needed real Army radios for the observation posts. The batteries and dependability of the regular Army radios were far superior compared to the small handheld radios we were initially using. The regular-issue Army radios would allow us to talk to the Bradleys, aircraft, and anyone else, unlike the Motorolas we first used.

In addition to the observation posts, we had several different cargo vehicles for which we were not allotted communications, so we found ourselves pulling radios from various vehicles and switching as each mission dictated, instead of having designated radios for all the vehicles. Doing the radio switch was an XO's nightmare, trying to keep accountability of what radios were where, especially when it came time to do our monthly 10 percent and 100 percent sensitive-items inventories. Most importantly, we needed radios for our infantry squads and team leaders that would give everyone the ability to talk to Bradleys, EOD, M1s, and aircraft. The handheld Motorola or ICOM radios were not cutting it, and we found ourselves on numerous occasions in which the team leaders needed to coordinate with an element outside of his squad. We needed the good, long-range radios that were light in weight, durable, and used the same batteries as everything else.

During the first few months of the deployment, LT Moffitt would just jump on random convoy and head to Balad Airbase to turn in equipment or try to draw additional equipment. Later he and the other company XOs in the battalion banded together along with the BN S-4 (supply section) and started doing their own coordinated convoys to and from Balad. Our supply NCO, SSG Morales, and his assistant, SPC Larsen, who was an 11B infantry guy, would gun and SSG Morales would drive the HMMWV with the XO as the truck commander, and off they would go. The supply guys made our life as good as they could, as SSG Morales and SPC Larsen would pick up, drop off, and inventory an entire company's worth of laundry. Seldom did they ever miss a day. The guys would come in from the COP, and they'd drop off one dirty bag and pick up one clean bag. That was one less thing the guys had to worry about. They did many other things, but the laundry, as simple as it sounds, made life for that soldier just that much nicer.

We were lucky to have LT Moffitt on our team, but our luck was about to run out. Alpha company's XO had been reassigned for various reasons and A Co needed an XO, so who better to take an XO from than B Co? When I first found out, I thought someone was kidding me—not so much. It's not as if battalion would do it if they had other options, so I just rolled with the punches. That unexpected shift in personnel left us with the mighty LSU graduate and hard-charging field artillery officer, 2LT Jeremy Duplechin, as our company XO. This shift made perfect sense. We had an infantry officer, 2LT Sparks, as the platoon leader for our tank platoon. We had an artillery officer, 2LT Siggins, as our second-platoon PL that was attached to Dealer Company, so why shouldn't we have a 2LT field artillery officer in a seasoned infantry lieutenant's position? CPT Chapman and I talked it over and decided that we had faith in LT Duplechin and SSG Morales to take care of the equipment issues. I could pick up the slack on the maintenance issues and guide LT Duplechin through some of the maintenance pitfalls, and we were assured it was only temporary and we would get another LT in, so then we could bring up 1LT Boeka as company XO. But for right now, all the platoons needed every person they could get, so shaking up the leadership in this situation would be insane.

At that point in the deployment, Bravo Company was down four Bradleys, one M1A2SEP (tank), and several HMMWVs and Cargo trucks. We had lost around fourteen soldiers—seven KIA and seven WIA—with one AWOL. And we had given up our company XO for the greater good. However, we were gaining an IA unit out at Bone X-Ray, and we made it into a fortress comparable to nothing in modern history. Plus we were conducting offensive operations again. Things were looking better.

It was now the middle of February, and early one evening, CPT Chapman was over at OP1 with a few guys from the sniper section over-watching LT Boeka , SSG Fisher, and SSG Rojas while they were conducting a dismounted clearing operation south of Bone X-Ray. We had taken fire from a few buildings earlier in the day, and we suspected the AIF was stashing their weapons, ammo, and other equipment around that area to avoid detection by our AWTs or UAVs. It was almost dark so we decided to do a US-only mission, supported with a section of Bradleys. I was back in Bone X-Ray tracking the movements of the troops on the ground and conducting any coordination that needed to be done with higher HQ.

The patrol made it down to the buildings and cleared it without any issue. As they left the building en route to the second building, they were engaged by a high volume of machine-gun fire. Rounds started impacting all around the soldiers as they slammed their bodies to the ground for cover. They found themselves in a low-lying area between the two houses in a field. The patrol was separated, half in the low ground and the other half stuck in and around the first building. They could see red tracers as the rounds snapped past their heads. LT Boeka immediately got on the radio and called the Bradleys forward to suppress the machine-gun fire. As the Bradley's pulled forward to get an angle on the insurgents, they realized they were right on top of an IED and could not go down the streets any farther. Based on the observations from OP1, the Bradley section, and LT Boeka's firsthand observations, it was quickly determined they were caught in a crossfire with some of the enemy elements firing from a higher elevation down onto the dismounts. With the patrol effectively pinned down by machine-gun fire, and our Bradleys' advance halted due to an IED in the road, that gave the signal for the insurgents to open up on OP1's position with machine-gun fire.

At that point, I called for AWTs to come on station, but they were on another mission supporting some A Co soldiers in the west. I then requested the UAV to come on station and gave them the grid coordinates of our friendly forces and a few grid coordinates for the suspected AIF firing positions. The UAV was on station within a few minutes, though this specific UAV had no offensive capabilities. But sometimes just the sound of its propellers churning up the air and the buzzing of the engines overhead would be enough to deter the AIF from conducting operations. Not this time, though, as the enemy gunfire increased.

By this time, the sun had fallen and the day turned into darkness, with the exception of the red tracers cutting through the night. The fire was coming and going from both OP1 and the guys on the ground, with the occasional thumps of the 25mm cannon. The fire was still intense and the AIF gave no signs of falling back. They knew we could not move south or east without losing vehicles. The AIF knew they had a temporary advantage and planned on massing their combat power to exploit our guys in the open. They were basically daring us to come east and assault them, hoping we would fall into their ambushes of IEDs and keyhole shots with the RPGs.

Within a few moments of the UAV coming on station, they reported identifying multiple AIF firing weapons and emplacing even more IEDs to cover their withdrawal, in case we gave pursuit.

The UAV had given us a pretty accurate description of what we were up against, with the main firing coming from an intersection and at least two other independent firing positions from rooftops. I set my focus on the RPK machine gun with five individuals: one gunner, one spotter, one lookout, and two guys stringing in an IED. I asked the UAV pilot for a grid coordinate, and they gave me a ten-digit coordinate to their location, which in theory would put me within one meter of their location on a map. I double checked the grid and plotted the distance from our friendly forces and told our mortar team to go ahead and lay the mortar tube on that grid.

The mortar crew had not been out during the February offensive and had been eager to drop some rounds—and this was their chance. I told them to let me know when they were on target and to stand by. I called the commander and briefed him on the situation: I had a solid ten-digit grid on a group of AIF with safe distance from friendly forces, and I felt pretty confident we could drop mortars on these guys with minimal collateral damage. The rounds were dangerously close to our guys but some were holed up in a building and the others were farther away in low ground, so I felt we were pretty safe. The commander voiced his concern about accuracy and wanted to make sure the guns were laid in correctly. He told me to fire an illumination round first to verify they were somewhere in the ballpark. With a "Roger that," I told SPC Harris and the guys to go ahead and ready one illumination round on my command.

They reworked some of the gun data then hung the illumination round and fired it.

Boomp—Pop!

The AIF gunfire stopped when they heard the round, but once they realized it was an illumination round, they just started firing again. Satisfied with the accuracy of the mortar tubes, I told SPC Harris to load one high-explosive round and make it air burst. I gave the UAV pilots a heads-up to do some spotting on the rounds and gave the command to fire.

Boomp—Craaack!

Thinking it was another illumination round, the insurgents got a surprise.

The BN TOC called back excitedly, "Target. Target!"

I told Harris to go ahead and give me two more rounds but make them ground burst and then fire at will. Moments later ...

Boomp. CRACK! Boomp. CRACK!

The battalion TOC called: "Target, you got three of them. The others are wounded and moving east." The UAV followed the two wounded AIF back to a safe house; the other wounded man had dropped dead in the streets. The UAV loitered above, watching the AIF fighters run in and out frantically, trying to figure out what to do. The battalion TOC was giving us a play-by-play on the events. They watched about fifteen AIF come into the building, including the two wounded, and then moments later, a car pulled up and a few guys carried one wounded AIF out to the car and drove him off.

Upon hearing about all the fighters that were in the house, I asked for a ten-digit grid. There was a delay, so I asked again. I was ready to yell into the hand mic: "GIVE ME THE M-F'ING GRID!" when they came over the net and gave it to me. I was happy, and relayed the grid to the mortars and told them to lay it on. I double-checked the map, and SPC Nash checked the digital satellite imagery for anything out of the ordinary. The grid had plotted exactly where we had templated an enemy strong point. It was also across the street from an abandoned school that was known as a "point of origin" or POO site for insurgent mortar fire, so I had no worries about collateral damage. There were no civilians in this area, as they had moved out a long time ago when the AIF took it over as one of their frontline fighting areas.

Convinced we had no issues, I told the mortars to go ahead and fire one round and wait. I told the UAV pilot to observe, and once he gave me the "eyes on," I told the mortars to fire.

Boomp. CRACK!

"TARGET! TARGET!"

I told the mortars to go air burst on the next two. I figured the

211

first one was enough to get them out of the house but they would be scattering like rats, so I figured the airburst would give us the desired effect, like a big shotgun raining hot lead down onto our foe. The mortars fired two more rounds and they all landed right on target. We didn't get any immediate feedback from the safe-house rounds, but we knew at least twelve individuals were in the house, and only a few emerged and ran in various directions.

We were all fired up in Bone X-Ray. We just killed at least three AIF, with another twelve to fifteen AIF believed to be dead, wounded, or seriously considering another occupation. But getting to the destroyed safe house to assess the battle damage would have to wait. We did not want to get too strung out and then not be able to support ourselves in another sustained firefight. Battalion did not want to wait, though, so they ordered us to go down that evening to conduct BDA.

When we got the order, the TOC went silent. CPT Chapman thought for a minute and then told BN HQ to "send an EOD team because we have multiple IEDs to clear in order to get to the house, so it's going to be an all-nighter." Upon hearing that, we started gearing up to head down to the safe house. I grabbed my kit, although I was not thrilled about going deep into AIF territory after we just bombed them, just so we could count dead bodies and look for intelligence. I understood the need, but I figured by the time we got down there, the bodies would be gone and any information that had been there would be gone too. We knew of at least three IEDs and possibly more.

The EOD team showed up, and we found out they were a new team. We were expecting the Havoc crew from our three-day offensive, and we knew those guys were good. But we had not seen these new EOD soldiers in sector before. In fact, they looked brand new: they had shiny new equipment and the "What the hell did I get into?" look on their faces. The EOD team leader was a female, which kind of threw me off guard, but, hey, if she wanted to play with bombs, more power to her. SGT Watts, LT Boeka's gunner, told them exactly where one of the IEDs was on the map, so it was decided that the Bradleys would cover the EOD team as they cleared the IEDs. Then we would go down dismounted after they were cleared. What we didn't want to do was send our ground troops deep into the AIF area and have no way to conduct casualty evacuation or to reinforce them. Getting the road cleared was the number one priority.

The EOD team bumped down to our company radio freq (push) and SGT Watts guided them into the area where the IED was. We were all huddled around the radio speaker and heard SGT Watts tell the EOD, "Stop, the IED is right in front of you. Don't go any farther."

BOOOOOM!

Quiiisssh ...

"Bone X-Ray, this is EOD. We will have to come back tomorrow. Our vehicle was just hit with an IED, and we have two flat tires and the radiator is leaking, over."

Upon hearing that, we knew it was a wrap for the evening. We called the section of Bradleys back in and put ourselves in a holding pattern for in the morning. Once the Bradley section was back in the compound, SGT Watts came into the company command post area and said, "Check this out." He had been videotaping the EOD team in action and caught the IED explosion on video. We had no idea why they pulled down as far as they did, but we hoped they learned something, because they wouldn't last long around there doing things like that.

Upon reporting the IED detonation on the EOD vehicle, Charger 6, the battalion commander, LTC Goins, got on the radio and told us he was coming out in the morning with Charger 9. We all started to get worried. We started thinking about collateral damage since they were pushing us so hard to go down and do BDA. I started going over the "rules of engagement" in my head, making sure I didn't miss anything before we dropped those rounds. SPC Harris was worried, but I told him, "Don't sweat it. I told you to fire, so you were just following instructions." Silently I was worried for about a minute. *Screw it,* I thought, as I laid my head down on a stack of body armor and equipment on my cot. I did what I thought was right and it killed the AIF who were trying to kill our soldiers. If someone had an issue with that, I knew we would never win this fight.

The next morning came quickly, and as promised, Charger 6 and Charger 9 were pulling in the compound. I got up, put a fresh dip of Copenhagen in, and went to the coffeepot. I figured if I was going to get put in jail, I ought to be awake for it. When they came into the TOC, I could tell immediately that the situation was not bad. They were both grinning from ear to ear.

"Who was on the mortar last night?" LTC Goins asked.

"Specialist Harris and his boys," I said.

"Get them in here." LTC Goins said. "I got some coins I want to hand out. They did some fine shooting last night. We watched the entire engagement from the brigade TOC. They dropped every single round right on top of the insurgents. We saw EVERYTHING, and it was AWESOME!"

Man, it was great to see Charger 6 and Charger 9 all fired up and to see them out there giving the boys a pat on the back. They'd been just as stressed as everyone else, if not more. I had a company to worry about; they had a battalion to take care of. That was a great morale booster for everyone. Not a bad way to start the day.

On 21 February, as part of the early stages of the troop surge, the Army was kicking off an operation called "Fardh al-Qanoon" or "Operation Imposing Law" in Baghdad. The gains of those early operations were moderate at best as far as we could tell. However, what we did know was the more they started to push in Baghdad and Al Anbar, the more fighters we saw come into our sector. It became very apparent that the rally point for jihadists getting pushed out of their areas by surge troops would be the Diyala Province—more specifically, Baqubah and Buhritz.

Recognizing the insurgency's own troop surge into Buhritz and Baqubah, the battalion commander shifted forces around and assigned the Stalker element—our BN scouts—to our company. The BN scouts worked with us during the 10 January offensive and did an outstanding job, so we were excited to have them on board.

As February wound down, we were given several major tasks that were going to need our attention. The first task was to start conducting reconnaissance for other areas within Old Baqubah and Tahrir that would be good combat outpost locations. Once the troop surge had accomplished their missions in Baghdad, an element from 3rd Brigade—2nd ID Strykers and several other battalions size elements from the 82nd Airborne and the 25th Infantry—would start working their way into Diyala Province and would reinforce 1-12 Cav.

Before we could do any major movements or reconnaissance in Tahrir, we had to plan and conduct a route-clearance mission for C Avenue (aka, Chuck Ave). Every time we had gone into Tahrir, we'd been hit with IEDs. Since we had been mainly focused on Buhritz the past few weeks, we knew that the IED situation had gotten even worse in Tahrir.

The second mission was to start inventories and to prepare for a company change of command with CPT Marc Austin. The change of command really did not come as a surprise. CPT Chapman would have been in command for eighteen months by the time his change of command rolled around. What surprised me was that the entire time, I thought when B Co got a new commander, it would be a young captain named Sheldon Morris, but it turned out he would be taking over Apache Company a few weeks prior to B Co's change of command. I hadn't even considered CPT Austin, since he was on the MTT on FOB Gabe. I had taken that as good news, since I'd worked with CPT Austin back in the States. We had flown over together, and most of all, he was on the Gorilla MTT and knew the area and its current situation. I was still a little nervous, as CPT Chapman and I had managed to build a cohesive team in a pretty uncertain environment. We complemented each other's strengths and weaknesses, and communicated well with each other.

Then I had my personal mission: I was going home on leave.

Just like the change of command, there is never a good time to do it, just the best of the worst times. I had planned my leave when we first arrived in-country and obviously did not know about the troop surge coming. Even if I had, the timing would not have changed, because we had no definite time for the troops to arrive in our sector. So I just stayed the course and hoped for the best. The good news, I found out later, was that CPT Austin had already taken his leave and that CPT Chapman was going to take his leave after the change of command, so the company and I would not go without a commander on the ground the entire deployment.

With the troop surge happening down south in Baghdad, we were experiencing a major influx of insurgent fighters and supplies being pushed into our area. The insurgents were becoming even more aggressive with direct fire attacks with RPGs and small-arms fire on our OPs manning MSR security: OP1 and Bone X-Ray. SSG Embry's Bradley had been hit with an RPG while out on MSR security and the IA had taken a few casualties when an RPG slammed into OP1. The static positions took it on the chin pretty hard, with OP1 under constant small-arms fire. Both Bone X-Ray and OP1 took several mortar rounds a day, to the point that no one went outside during the day unless they absolutely had to. The direct-fire engagements on our patrols increased as well. We were consistently conducting offensive operations south and east of Bone X-Ray just to keep a good buffer around our perimeter.

All the platoons, including the Stalker platoon and Predator element, had conducted several reconnaissance and surveillance patrols east and south of Bone X-Ray to locate the insurgents' main infiltration routes into our sector. The platoons pinpointed several locations and planned multiple small kill-team missions to disrupt the AIF as they tried to infiltrate our sector. We did our pattern analysis and determined the best times and locations to send out our teams. We were having great success, but the number of engagements and the sheer numbers of AIF we were killing soon became alarming.

During the past four months in Buhritz—based on the company

having a total of 125 soldiers, including US attachments—we figured we were outnumbered two or three to one, but recent reports from the brigade and battalion intelligence cells had the numbers at five to one or higher in Buhritz alone, and we would soon find out that those numbers were conservative at best.

In anticipation of the troop surge pushing into the Diyala Province, we were given the mission to start looking for possible future locations in Tahrir and Old Baqubah. CPT Chapman and I started out with a map reconnaissance and the identification of several buildings that we thought we could use as combat outposts, but the pickings were slim. They had to be tactically sound locations that provided us easy access into all avenues of the city: be big enough to house a company-size element plus attachments; have good routes in and out that we could over-watch; and most of all, be defendable. The other major piece of this operation was that we did not want the AIF to know we were conducting recons of the buildings. If we made it obvious, they would know we were going to move in and then booby trap the building or just blow it up. So we decided to do the recons in conjunction with route-clearance missions and mixed it up with a few other random building searches that had nothing to do with our selection of a combat outpost.

The main building we thought would be the best was an L-shaped structure that had three stories on one side of the L and four stories on the other. It used to be a female college dormitory before the war. It had plenty of parking and stood in a good location, as it was mutually supported by the Government Center currently manned by the Wardog element. CPT Chapman had tasked the scouts to conduct surveillance on the building and see what kind of enemy activity was going on in there. In the past, we had taken fire from that building on several occasions and third platoon had launched two TOW missiles into it previously in the tour.

Route clearance started on C Avenue from Route Gold and moved north then east. The concept of the operation was to have two platoons of infantry move on each side of the main road network and to clear all the buildings and possible trigger sites, along with

217

providing over-watch on the route-clearance teams. We would also locate several positions that were optimum for the snipers to over-watch the dismounts' movement. The route-clearance teams would use all their specialized equipment to detect, mark, and reduce the IEDs, while the Bradleys cordoned off the roads and provided additional security and blocking positions. While all this was going on, we would have UAV and AWTs support throughout the operation.

The route-clearance mission started before daylight. The Bradleys pulled into their assigned positions, and the dismounts jumped out the back before the ramp made the *clunk* on the blacktop road. They moved like a well-oiled machine, with some soldiers pulling security, others stringing up concertina wire, and still others putting out traffic cones and signs. All of these were precautions to warn innocent civilians and provide the soldiers with a trigger line. Each layer was an increase in response: if a car passed the signs, they would get a warning shot; if they passed the cones, they would get a disabling shot; and if they crossed the wire—they would die.

With the blocking positions in and the security set, the dismounts started clearing buildings, rooftops, and alleyways. Once they made it to their first designated over-watch position, they called the route-clearance team to come in and start their tasks.

The route-clearance team (Havoc) came in and within the first twenty-five meters, they identified three IEDs: two surface-laid and one buried in the ground. It was going to be another long day. The first surface-laid was an ordinary-looking twenty-gallon propane tank with tiny copper wires running from it to a light pole, where the wires blended with other wires. The second was hidden in a previous blast hole with a small amount of trash thrown over it. Both surface-laid IEDs were reduced as planned. The deep-buried IED consisted of several Italian landmines, but they did not get a chance to confirm exactly what else was in the hole, because it blew up as they were investigating. Luckily they were using the hydraulic arm of the Buffalo[50] and the damage was minimal. However, it did blow the forks clean off the arm and severed the hydraulic lines, rendering the Buffalo combat ineffective. Havoc element did not let that slow them down; they still had some cool gadgetry to continue the mission.

A soldier's eyes are the number one defense against an IED—being able to decipher your environment and figure out what is there to kill you, what is normal, and to also take into consideration what is not there too. I think everyone has a "sixth sense" or "gut feeling." I just think they have to know when to listen to it and not be overly paranoid.

At that stage in the game, everything looked suspicious and with only little debate got a block of C4 placed on it by "Johnny 5," the EOD robot. More often than not, the explosions had secondary blasts, confirming it was an IED. The route-clearance mission lasted well into the early evening. Havoc element was "in the zone" and didn't let up. We had to call and have the QRF from battalion bring out more C-4 and batteries for the robot. Some of the IEDs were buried so deep and were so big that they destroyed the underground water lines and caused areas of the streets to start flooding. Other explosions rocked the front of buildings, knocking down walls and blowing out all the windows. By the time we finished clearing C Avenue and peered down the street, it looked like the surface of the moon, with craters everywhere, sidewalks uprooted, massive holes in the street that a car would get lost in, the median divider curbs blown apart with dirt and masonry scattered throughout, and light poles and power lines lying in the street, crumpled by the weight of the Bradleys running them over. It looked like hell. Any remaining civilians gathered their belongings and left in short order. They were listening to their senses: war was coming in a big way, real soon.

The route-clearance mission was the last mission the company did before I went home on leave. I had gone back to FOB Warhorse

---

50 Specialized route-clearing vehicle

to turn in my weapons and draw the stripped-down rifle with no bling-bling on it. I double-checked the manifest with SFC Riddick and put myself in a holding pattern to wait on helicopters to fly out to Balad. I was pretty excited but knew I would worry the entire time I was gone about what was happening "in country." My worst nightmare was that a soldier would be killed while I was gone. I did not assign an acting 1SG, as the PSGs were more than capable of doing what needed to get done, and SFC Reynolds had the final say in things out in sector if there was a debate amongst the NCOs. SSG Lane handled the business back in the rear with BN HQ, and CPL Lunt could handle the day-to-day business. I did plan a "Family Readiness Group" meeting while I was home, as I did not want to pass up an opportunity to meet the soldiers' families and take the time to explain to them in person, face-to-face, what was going on in sector. I also wanted them to be able to ask questions, no holds barred. I wanted them to know I was there for them as a resource and they could communicate to me if they had an issue. If the family was taken care of, that would be one less distraction for the men on the ground.

The choppers had been cancelled so I did not make it out the first night. With a full day off on the FOB, I naturally went down to our CP to work on the UCMJ and awards. Just as I was getting started, I heard the word "TIC"—and that word got my attention real quick, since it meant "troops in contact." I ran over to the RTO station and turned up the speaker. It was our scout element. They had just come under heavy fire while conducting a small kill-team operation south of Bone X-Ray in the palm groves. The five-man Stalker element led by LT Miller had been tasked to disrupt the infiltration routes leading up to Bone X-Ray from the south through the palm groves.

What I heard next sent images of the entire small kill team (SKT) getting their heads chopped off on Al Jazeera News: "We are cut off and have to push south."

I learned that when the Stalker element relocated from their initial position, they had been compromised by an old lady, and she tipped off the AIF about their presence. Unbeknownst to the Stalker element, the AIF massed forces and cut them off from their exfiltration route back to Bone X-Ray, positioning their forces to push the SKT even farther away from friendly lines and deeper into enemy-controlled territory. When the insurgents opened up on the SKT, they did so with such ferocity that LT Miller and the rest of the soldiers knew they were outnumbered and outgunned and could not fight their way through it.

The enemy knew that if they could push the Stalker element deep into the palm groves, they would eventually trap them against the Diyala River. The men on the SKT had one radio with a long whip antenna, two M203 grenade launchers, and their M4 carbines. After the initial firing had slowed, the insurgents attempted to maneuver on the Stalker element, which allowed the two M203 grenade launchers an opportunity to unleash some HE (high-explosive) rounds onto the enemy PKC machine-gun position. SGT Zimmerman and SGT Demuth killed two guys with their M203s and that allowed the SKT time to pack up and relocate to a better position. The Stalker element had just made the transition from combat mission to escape and evasion.

The farther the Stalker element was pushed south, the worse the communications got. For a period of about fifteen minutes, we lost total radio contact. I had called AWTs and got them on station. The canopy of the palm grove was too dense, and the pilots could not identify enemy or friendly but were at least able to bump down to the Stalker frequency and relay information.

As the Stalker element was pushing south, they captured two guys on a motorcycle they figured were enemy scouts, as any non-combatants would have left the area when all the firing started. They assumed the scouts were trying to locate their position so they could mass their combat fire and kill or capture the Stalker element. Not wanting to let these guys get away and not being able to kill them (unarmed), they had to detain them. They dragged these guys along for the next two kilometers to the river, where they were able to set up a hasty defense, establish radio communications, and call up a good grid to their current location.

Once I got the grid to their location, I was able to have the mortars out at Bone X-Ray drop a few 120mm mortar rounds on the path the scouts had taken to deter any enemy from pursuing them. I was also able to find a good clearing on the map that was within 500 meters of the Stalker position, so I told them to move toward the tentative landing zone. I also asked the AWTs to identify the LZ and tell me if it would work. In the meantime, as a contingency, CPT Chapman was coordinating with the Special Forces unit to do a river crossing with rubber boats or to conduct a ground assault into the palm groves (which would be the least preferred). If helicopters could not make it in, or if they got shot down while attempting to extract the Stalker element, we would have to go in on foot.

I had requested Blackhawks for the extraction, but the closest Blackhawks in the air had to come up from Baghdad. I didn't care if they were coming from Mars, as long as they were coming. I was told twenty minutes. Shortly after, I had an element that went by the call sign "Sidewinder" on the net. I relayed the grid to the LZ and also passed them off to Wolfpack Apache pilots and the Stalker element directly for coordination.

Everyone held their breaths. CPT Chapman had an assault force ready out at Bone X-Ray. CPT Conely had his guys ready on the west side of the river in case the Stalker element had to swim for it. And the helicopters were swarming overhead, waiting for the Stalker element to make it to the LZ.

While we were waiting to hear from the Stalker element, I was plotting on the map, retracing what had just occurred. The Stalker element had just moved four kilometers under fire, killed at least two guys, and dragged along two detainees for the better part of two of those four kilometers. Wisely, they left the detained men flex-cuffed near the river's edge before they made their mad dash to the rendezvous point.

As the Stalker element approached the clearing, each soldier was nearing exhaustion. Their muscles screamed under their heavy combat loads as they tactically maneuvered through thick palm brush and nearly impenetrable underbrush to make it to the clearing. Once at the edge, they established communications once again with the Sidewinder element and tossed a purple smoke out into the open field. Sidewinder identified it and swooped down into the tiny clearing, and no sooner did the wheels touch down than the five-man payload was on board and heading back to FOB Warhorse.

With the Blackhawks inbound, I grabbed a driver and a truck. We drove to the LZ on FOB Warhorse and waited for the Sidewinder element to land so I could thank them in person. But I never got the chance. No sooner did they drop our guys than they were up and in the air again. At least I had the chance to talk to the Stalker guys. I hadn't hugged too many soldiers, but when I saw those guys getting off that chopper safe and sound, I hugged every one of them.

Once back at the company command post, I got a complete debrief from LT Miller, SGT Zimmerman, SGT Demuth, SPC Gronberg, and SPC Rogers. All of these guys had fought ferociously for each other against numerically superior forces. With their training, mental coolness, physical agility, and tenacity, they outwitted a very smart and bold enemy that had the upper hand on them.

CHAPTER 11

THE SURGE

THE AIRPLANE TOUCHED DOWN in Dallas, Texas, around 1300 hours with a slight cheer from the soldiers on board. I was sitting next to a young soldier that was grinning ear to ear and telling me about all the beer he was going to drink and all the girls he was going to chase. I thought to myself, *How nice it is to be young.*

As the plane taxied down the runway to the terminal, the airport fire trucks were out on the runway, shooting a crisscross stream of water from their water cannons over and onto the plane as it taxied by. From my understanding, they only do that for the Dallas Cowboys after returning from a big game, the president, and returning soldiers. I had experienced it one other time when I had flown home from my first tour but thought it was an isolated event, but apparently they do it for every single "Freedom Flight." The warm welcome from the patrons and staff of the Dallas/Fort Worth airport was amazing. The majority of US airport personnel usually stop what they are doing, and people stand up, wave, cheer, clap, and go out of their way to shake your hands or give you a hug. It is a great feeling and makes you really feel appreciated to the point of almost being embarrassed because people are making such a fuss.

Nonetheless, it is 100 percent better than the way our returning veterans from Vietnam were treated. So thank you, America.

Once I deplaned, I ran into a sergeant from the Wardog element and he told me it was a two-hour wait to fly into Killeen, but his wife was there at the airport and said I could hop a ride with them. I jumped at the offer, especially when he told me they had an ice chest full of cold beer. The sun was shining, the temperature was beautiful, and it was nice to finally flip the switch back to family guy. The ride home was filled with beer drinking, cigarette smoking, and talks of motorcycles and parties. He, like me, was a big American motorcycle enthusiast and we chatted about the riding we were going to do once we got settled into the leave routine. I was almost home.

Once home, it was surreal. In less than a seventy-two-hour period, I transitioned from being in the most hostile area in Iraq—worried about getting five soldiers out of a palm grove so they didn't end up on the Al Jazeera evening news getting their heads chopped off—to a calm, organized house that was filled with the love and innocence of my beautiful wife and three-year-old daughter.

I did not have any major plans and just took the leave as it came. I only had a few "must do" tasks. Number one on the list was to meet the wives of the soldiers that stayed in the Fort Hood area during the deployment. I had been in contact with several of the women, including the wives of SGT Flores from second platoon, SSG Johnson from second, and SGT Sonkowsky from third. They set the FRG meeting to take place at SSG Johnson's house. There, I met several other wives, including SGT McGrath's wife, SPC Brook's wife, Lelo, and PFC Spencer's wife, Charlotte. To meet Spencer's wife was a great honor and it reassured me of the Army's commitment to take care of the families that had made the ultimate sacrifice. Though not a perfect system, it was and is still a system designed with the family's best interest in mind.

The FRG meeting went well and the main topics of discussion were the number of casualties the unit was taking, the troop surge, and the fifteen-month extension. Thank God all the topics already had an answer. I explained to them the casualties were a result of having a very determined enemy that had massed a large group of dispersed fighters into our sector, as well as the fact that we did not have enough soldiers on the ground to cover the sectors like they needed to be covered. However, with the troop surge, we would be able to have more boots on the ground—and more boots on the ground meant better security, and better security would help reduce the amount of casualties. Unfortunately the additional troops came at the cost of their husbands doing an extra couple months over there. I did not sugarcoat anything. I wanted to maintain my credibility with these ladies that cared enough to come to the meeting. I also knew they would talk to the other wives who hadn't come. I told them that we would engage in more fighting to take back the cities, and that it would obviously involve their husbands. But with them staying an extra three months, it would help us achieve our objectives and provide more security, not only for B Company 1-12 but for all the US forces in Iraq and the Iraqi people. We were really close to achieving our objective and it would take some sacrifice from everyone to attain it.

After the formal part of the meeting, we mingled for a little bit and I was able to talk to Charlotte Spencer. I found out she was a soldier in another unit back at Fort Hood and that her chain of command was doing everything they could to take care of her. She told me that the entire Casualty Assistance Program was, for the most part, an excellent experience, considering the circumstances. She went on to tell me that she knew something bad had happened to Clarence before she was ever notified of his death. She told me she was at a Super Bowl party with some of her friends from the unit, and something just told her subconscious that something awful had happened—and she knew it had to do with Spencer. She was a very brave and strong woman, and she was a great example for other wives and gave everyone around her strength, including me.

My other obligation was to mail some of LT Ebarb's equipment back to him. He had purchased his own optical sight for his M4 and had some special M4 ammunition magazines. Since the equipment was similar to military equipment, we could not mail it from Iraq, so I had to hand carry it and mail it once I got back in the States. I was also able to talk to him on the phone and get updates on his progress. He was at Walter Reed Medical and had nothing but high praise for his treatment. His spirits sounded reassuring and motivated, so he, too, was a great example for others.

The last military thing I had to do was order a bunch of "going away" plaques. No way was I going to let the XO, LT Moffitt, and CPT Chapman leave without the appropriate departing plaques from the company. I also ordered one for 1SG Daniels for CPT Conely. I had carried both A and B company's guidons home in my carryon luggage to get framed and matted. Along the way, I was worried something would happen to them, so I kept an extra careful grip on my bags the entire trip. A commander's guidon is presented to him at his assumption of command ceremony and goes with him wherever he goes throughout his tenure, and as tradition is replaced when a new commander comes on board. A faded and torn guidon is a badge of honor, especially one that has been in combat, and it should be displayed proudly for many years to come by the commander.

The rest of leave was spent doing menial chores around the house, relaxing, and spending quality time with the family the best I could. When home on leave, you can never fully relax, because when your mind is not preoccupied with something, it tends to drift back to the thoughts of what is going on back with the guys on the COP—and secretly wishing you were back. You can't relax fully because you know you are going back in a few days.

The two weeks went by quickly, and next thing I knew, Jennifer was scolding me about how I was not just going to slip out of the house and leave in the middle of the night without a proper good-bye. They were going to drop me off at the airport and that was that! We drove up to Dallas/Fort Worth, and the airport was kind enough to allow the dependents of deploying loved ones to go through security and wait with them in the terminal. I love

Texas! We sat in the terminal and made small talk as Abby watched the big planes coming and going. The time went quickly, and I was anxious to get back. Jen could tell I was getting jumpy, so we decided it was time. We walked to the final security checkpoint, said our good-byes, hugged, kissed, and cried, then departed ways. I fought back tears as I watched them walk out of sight, and then I went to a secluded corner of the airport, sat down, and wept.

With my soldier switch turned back on, the flight back over was filled with anticipation. I had not heard any news about the unit and was hoping the "no news is good news" rule was in effect. We touched down in Kuwait, shuffled over to the warehouse, and picked up our stripped-down body armor then went into the manifest for the flight back into Iraq. I was fortunate, as I was slotted on one of the first flights out that evening, so I found myself back in Iraq before the sun came up. Iraq, though, was where my luck ran out as far as the flights and getting back to FOB Warhorse.

I ended up staying on Balad Airbase for a day and a half before I was able to link up with a platoon from FOB Warhorse picking up some vehicles that had just had extra armor added. When I started talking with the soldiers on Balad, I found out that within a few days of me leaving on 5 March, HHC Company 1-12 Cav had lost three soldiers in a IED explosion on their HMMWV along Route Tora Tora near a place called Five Points. It was SPC Blake Harris, SPC Ryan Russell, and SPC Barry Mayo from the mortars—the same SPC Harris that had just a few weeks earlier been handed coins by the battalion commander for doing an outstanding job. Not that I needed a reminder of how bad things were in Baqubah, but that news wiped out any remaining "feel good" I had regained while on leave.

My stay on Balad wasn't too bad. My two best friends and riding partners back in Texas were stationed there with a COSCOM unit. MAJ Brett Swanke and SFC Bill Conwell were both in the same unit, and I was able to stop by and visit them while waiting to catch a flight. We were able to eat some chow and take the opportunity to talk over a few details on Bill's custom Panhead we were planning on building once we all got back to the States. It was time well spent.

While I was waiting in the terminal at Balad the first evening for my soon-to-be-cancelled Chinook ride to Warhorse, I was doing my normal people watching and took note of a *Soldier of Fortune* magazine cover a young trooper was reading. The guys on the cover had a 1st Cavalry patch on. As I looked closer, I realized it was my guys! *Damn, that is SGT McGrath and SPC Barton, while they were in a firefight in Buhritz!* I walked over to the soldier and asked him to see the magazine. He looked at me like I was crazy but then handed it over. I skimmed the article and was amazed. It's not every day you have guys from your company on the cover of *SOF*, so it was pretty cool.

After my flight got cancelled, I went to the PX in Fobbit Central to buy a copy of the *SOF* magazine but naturally they were sold out. I never did get a copy of that magazine. The time with Brett and Bill was good but the atmosphere on the FOB was painful. For example: when I went to the chow hall to eat with my buddies, I had to have a civilian contractor security geek from Uganda verify my weapon was cleared before I could enter the dining facility. Wow, I was a senior NCO in the United States Army and had to have some foreigner verify that my weapon was cleared! Are we that incompetent? That was wasted American taxpayer money and an insult to every leader wearing a uniform over there.

I eventually made it back to FOB Warhorse and it was like slipping on a pair of old tennis shoes—comfortable. Everyone understood and could relate to one another. Everyone (at least in the circles I traveled) talked the same language and knew about places like Buhritz, Tahrir, Old Baqubah, New Baqubah, Kahlas, Kon Bani Saud, and Zaganiya. I found out one of the reasons why I couldn't get a flight back was due to the fact that all the surge troops were coming in and the aircrafts' priorities were geared toward supporting them. That was fine by me. I was excited to see patches on the ground from 2nd Infantry Division and their Strykers rolling all over the place; guys from 82nd Airborne and the

25th Infantry out of Hawaii were also moving about. All the troops meant one thing: we were not in it alone anymore and we were going on the offense in a BIG way. I don't think they shared in my enthusiasm of them being in Diyala Province at first.

On 28 February 2007, I tracked down the commander and got an update on what had been going on in my absence. First, we did not have any KIAs while I was gone, but we had lost another Bradley and had one WIA. SFC Reynolds had a Bradley blown up on C Avenue and had his driver injured, but not serious enough to be evacuated out of country. After a brief rundown on my leave and the family, CPT Chapman dropped a few bombs on me.

The first was like a cluster bomb drop: we were now manning two combat outposts and 2nd ID had operational control over our company! CPT Chapman paused and let it sink in for a minute and then said, "We still had our COP in Buhritz and we had taken on an additional COP in Tahrir and had the warning order (WARNO) we would be manning a third on C Avenue." It turned out we had taken over the women's dormitory as planned—and we had also been given the follow-on mission to occupy a large house on C Avenue that was located south-central of Tahrir. That outpost would be manned by a platoon of US and IA soldiers and supported by the company.

The second bomb was that we were right-seat riding with Bronco Troop in Buhritz, and they were going to take over Bone X-Ray in a week. It turned out the Strykers with 1-12 Cav had come in swinging and launched a massive offensive as they rolled into the Diyala Province and Buhritz. A few of my guys told me they initially had taken some hard hits and had one KIA and twelve WIA. Additionally they sustained a significant amount of Stryker damage and at least one catastrophic loss. However, they did a quick azimuth check on the severity of the enemy situation: the numbers now were estimated to be 2,000 to 2,500 fighters within the Diyala Province and we knew how organized, fanatical, and hard core they were. The 5-20 IN Task Force regrouped and seized control of 95 percent of Buhritz over a one-week period, killing forty to sixty insurgents, capturing a suspected forty more, and clearing the palm groves over a three-day period while engaged in some of the fiercest close-up, in-your-face, jungle-style guerilla warfare reminiscent of Vietnam.

The insurgents were not on the run but they were executing a well-planned and rehearsed fight they had been anticipating for months. The AIF, all 2,000-2,500 of them, were going to have to deal with the entire 3rd Brigade, 2nd ID, plus elements of 1st Cav, 82nd Airborne, and 25th Infantry. It was only a matter of time before they felt the entire might of the task force squeezing them slowly and pushing them out into the open to be killed.

With elements of 5-20 IN battalion and Bronco Troop 1-14 Cav down in Buhritz, Bone Company as a complete unit with scouts from 1-12 had moved up to Tahrir and occupied the dormitory with the mission to hold and build. We were also told to prepare Tahrir for follow-on forces to conduct offensive operations. We initially thought we would go into Tahrir with 5-20 within a few days of occupying COP Adam, but the decision was made to wait. The conditions for success had not been set and the decision had been made to bring 1-23 IN SBCT and the rest of 3rd Brigade 2nd ID command element into the Diyala River Valley and Baqubah proper. Bringing in the additional forces would allow us to contain the AIF forces in both Apache's sector in New Baqubah and B Co's sector in Old Baqubah and Tahrir. With the incoming 1-23 IN SBCT, the entire Task Force structure got shifted around. Bone was tapped to give up an infantry platoon to the 5/73rd from the 82nd Airborne up in Zaganiya. Those guys were up there and really needed some heavy forces to help them out in anticipation of the insurgents moving into the northern sectors as we continued to push from the south inside the cities. So we reluctantly gave up our first platoon.

With only three platoons, two of which were out at COP Adam at any given point, we reverted back to conducting large-scale operations while platoons were coming and going back for refit operations and we had all the platoons on the ground at one time.

The rest of the time, we were over-watching and conducting a extensive amount of small kill teams and ambushes that gave us the highest payoff, troops to task.

I stayed in on FOB Warhorse for a few days after returning from leave to catch up on the three week's worth of not-so-missed administrative duties, and to go and meet my new bosses: LTC Antonia and CSM Huggins, along with their XO, and S-3. They were all professional and took us in as one of their own and treated us well. I could sense this was going to be a good relationship right from the beginning, and for that I was thankful. Sometimes when you get cross-attached to a unit, they take that as a green light to treat you like their "red-headed stepchildren" or they just don't fully understand how to implement you into the fight. Luckily LTC Antonia new exactly what he wanted us to do, and with both CPT Chapman and later CPT Austin being highly competent leaders, it made it that much easier to use us as part of the team, and in some cases, as the main players. I don't think the patch on our left sleeve was ever an issue or even thought about; it was all about what was in our hearts and the guys on your left, right, front, and rear: "One team one fight."

Once I finally made it out to the Tahrir outpost, known initially as "Bone Disney" but later named COP Adam, I was pleasantly surprised. This place was a four-star hotel compared to what we had just left. CPT Chapman had the engineers build us a massive perimeter out of HESCO baskets and Texas-sized blast walls. We had plenty of standoff from the general traffic areas, as well as parking for our Bradleys, tanks, Strykers, HMMWVs, and whatever else came into the compound. The engineers also brought in these massive cement towers that looked great, but you could not pay anyone to man them, due to the fact they were bullet and RPG magnets. We eventually fortified them with bulletproof glass and camouflage netting to conceal the guard's location and protect them from sniper fire. SFC Reynolds, SFC Malo, SSG Hamilton, and SSG Foster did a great job getting the initial layout of the building divvied up and the company command post squared away.

The physical layout was as good as we were going to get. Over the next few weeks, we continued to fortify the primary and alternate positions. We made sure that we had redundancy in our sectors, so if there was another assault on our COP like the one in Buhritz, it was going to be like unleashing a hornet's nest on the insurgents. We fortified, built, and improved every chance we got, in addition to conducting our patrolling and force protection schedule.

As we focused on the force-protection piece, we realized another aspect we had not been privy to in our earlier outpost: the battalion's S-5(the guys with the money). They were authorized to pump money into the local economy, so they worked a deal to buy us real mattresses and bunk-bed frames, coolers for our water and ice cream, and big generators (primary and alternate) so we could run all our electrical equipment that included a microwave and personal items. Finding electricians to wire the generator and run the electrical boxes was another challenge in itself. All the small comfort items made it like Christmas for the soldiers! We stayed busy making this place survivable and livable until the day we left.

As work continued on the new combat outpost, we also increased the pace of patrols, both mounted and dismounted. It was a target-rich environment and we wanted to take advantage of it and put our infantry squads and sniper teams to work. We used the 1-12 sniper teams, and SSG Foster and the 1-12 scouts also had designated shooters to over-watch our infantry squads as they patrolled within the city. The Bradleys and M1 Tanks patrolled the outskirts of the city, including up and down portions of C Avenue. The patrols were conducted simultaneously for mutual support around the clock. We were keeping continuous pressure on the insurgents within our sector until we were ready to put the full weight of 5-20 and B Co 1-12 on the AIF within the city.

*****

On March 7-8, 2007, Bravo 1-12 scout platoon was supporting an operation north of COP Adam in Old Baqubah (OB) in support of

5-20 IN conducting operations to secure several combat outpost locations in the OB sector. It was a screening mission along Route Tora Tora, and the scouts were tasked to prevent AIF forces from infiltrating and attacking the 5-20 IN forces in sector. However, the task also indicated that they were not to disrupt civilian traffic.

Quiiisssh ...

"COP Adam, this is Stalker 3. We need QRF out on Tora Tora NOW! We have a Bradley that has been hit by a suicide vehicle-borne IED and is engulfed in flames. Stand by for BDA."

The 1-12 scouts had gone minimum manning on the Bradley crews since it was a screening mission, so they had no one to immediately put on the ground to help with the crew evacuation. Luckily a Stryker platoon was operating nearby, and they saw the explosion and came to the aid of the crew. In a matter of seconds, the entire Bradley was on fire, rounds were exploding inside the vehicle, and the crew was disoriented from the explosion. A 5-20 soldier jumped on the burning Bradley and helped get the driver and gunner out of the vehicle. Then he went back with the help of a few others and tried to get the Bradley commander, CPL Schaffer, out of the crew compartment, but the fire was too intense.

With the two extracted crew members loaded in the 5-20 vehicles, the Strykers evacuated them to FOB Gabe. The Stalker element secured the area and awaited the QRF to come with recovery assets. We requested a fire truck to come from the Iraqi government but there was little that their inadequate firefighting equipment could do. The explosions were intense, the heat was intense, and all the scouts could do was sit there and watch as the Bradley burned to the ground with their brother-in-arms inside.

SGT Jason Shaffer, Killed in Action, 5 April 2007, Old Baqubah, Iraq

Once the vehicle burned itself out and was cool enough, the M88 recovery vehicle hooked up and dragged it back to FOB Warhorse, along with the SVBIED that had struck it, which would be examined. The vehicle was sent to the bone yard with the other blown-up hulks of steel. I and a civilian friend named Gary—who was with the Asymmetric Warfare Group doing some fact finding—jumped on the ATV and rode down to the bone yard to see what had happened. The report of a SVBIED slamming into the side of a Bradley but killing someone in the back seemed puzzling and did not make sense, so I went down to figure out what exactly happened so we could try to prevent it from happening again.

When I got to the wreckage, the first thing I did was find where the hull of the vehicle had been penetrated. Gary and I scoured the entire vehicle then looked underneath, and on the rear right undercarriage, we found a blast hole where the vehicle had been penetrated. That made no sense unless the SVBIED had some sort of extension rod with explosives attached to it. So we checked out the SVBIED, which was still in excellent condition, with the exception of it being on fire and the damage from the vehicle slamming into the side of the Bradley, but even that damage was not bad. We looked for an initiator and found none. The back was full of grain and the truck cab was full of everyday personal stuff. None of this was the usual indicators of a SVBIED attack. The most obvious of all indicators was not seeing a body in the vehicle. *So why did the reports say that? And how did this vehicle fit into the puzzle?*

After some discussion and the elimination of several theories, we had come to the conclusion that the vehicle was not hit with a SVBIED. It had been blown up by someone walking up behind the vehicle and placing an incendiary device—most likely a five-liter gasoline jug—underneath the vehicle. The incendiary was likely tied to a land mine or other explosive device and detonated by remote control or time fuse. The civilian vehicle that hit the Bradley was simply some innocent bystander that watched someone walk up and put the bomb under the vehicle and leave. The driver of the suspected SVBIED, in a panic to get out of the area, opened the door without shutting the vehicle off and ran from the scene, leaving the vehicle in drive—and it rolled into the Bradley as it exploded.

Static vehicle positions, and combat outposts, are the most dangerous. The insurgents have all day every day to watch you at their leisure and then wait for you to make a mistake and exploit it. That is exactly what happened. The scouts were over-watching each other but it only took a split second for the insurgents to slip that bomb underneath the vehicle and disappear into an alleyway.

From early to mid April, we continued to patrol as LTC Antonia and his staff coordinated with COL Townsend and the other units for the offensive into Tahrir. The plan was to launch two companies from 5-20 into Tahrir from the south and then have them push north to clear the city building by building. The scouts and mortars from 5-20 would seal off the eastern portion of the city, while two additional companies from 5-20 would push from the west portion of Tahrir and clear to the east. At the same time, B Co 1-12 infantry squads would clear from the northeastern portion of the city, including a massive university complex, while the mounted crews helped with the cordon and over-watch piece. We also planned to use the mounted sections to shuttle water and ice out, and bring wounded or detainees back.

Once Tahrir was cleared, the battalions would systematically clear each additional city (clear, hold, build) in basically the same fashion, leaving US elements behind in each area to work with the IA forces to maintain security and prevent the AIF from reentering the now-cleared city, as they had done in years past.

As we continued to build combat power to enter Tahrir and block off the western portion of Baqubah, the enemy attacks steadily increased. The insurgents had been waiting for this fight and now they had it. They were still inflicting a serious amount of damage by detonating hundreds of IEDs. And nothing was exempt from the IED blasts: it didn't matter if it was an M1 tank, Bradley fighting vehicle, or a Stryker—they were trying to blow them all up. The one question that kept us puzzled was how they kept getting the massive IEDs into position. We would clear streets one day, keep eyes on the area with small kill teams and patrols, and still have IEDs blowing up on them the next day.

With increased troops on the ground came an increase in intelligence. Some reports we were getting from the Special Forces units and our own intelligence said that the insurgents had been planning their defensive fight for months prior to 1-12 Cavalry and 2nd ID ever even coming into sector. Reports from various sources indicated the AIF had roadwork crews that would operate in broad daylight out in public: backhoes, jackhammers, and construction equipment you would see on any work crew on the roads—with the exception of the IEDs. They were even repaving the roads with new blacktop to hide the thousands of pounds of explosives underneath, running the wires under the cement and sidewalks and just leaving two little wires sticking out, or routing the wires into concealed firing positions with stereo jacks to expedite the plugging in of the initiator. The AIF's pre-surge preparation would haunt every soldier on the ground and in vehicles for the next several months.

Before any massive offensive could be completed in Tahrir, we needed to clear the routes into the city. The engineers from 5-20 IN were tasked with the route-clearance mission and we were tasked to provide local security for them. The Blade element came out to COP Adam as the sun was coming up, so we went over the plan with them and our White platoon. Between the section of tanks, infantry squads, and their own internal assets, they had plenty of firepower and protection on the ground to take care of business—or so we thought. Though nothing is routine, this clearance mission was nothing we hadn't done before, with the exception of the Strykers being included. The northern portion of C Avenue was cleared rather quickly, until they got to 41st Street. That intersection was scanned by a special vehicle that can locate the most difficult of IEDs to find. The Blade element was setting off charge after charge—one charge just to remove the blacktop and another charge to blow the IED ... and sometimes a third charge for any residual explosives, or just for good measure.

The explosions must have awoken the insurgents from a nap,

because after the round of explosions at 41ˢᵗ Street and Chuck Avenue, the insurgents came out in force.

Quiiisssh ...

"COP Adam, this is White 3. We just engaged and destroyed one RPG team, southeast of 41ˢᵗ and Chuck Avenue. It appears one of the Strykers was hit in the rear. Stand by for BDA."

Blade 26 came up on the radio and gave us a good situation report, saying they were going to continue the mission. As they continued to head west on 41ˢᵗ Street, they were engaged with small-arms fire while trying to deploy the Johnny 5 robot for yet another IED—but the robot was disabled by sniper fire. As usual, they deployed another robot to recover the first one—but it, too, was shot. At that point, the Stryker's brakes were not working due to the RPG that had hit them earlier. Since they were out of robots, they departed to get their vehicle fixed and load up with more robots before trying it again when it was dark. That left the White element out on 41ˢᵗ Street to over-watch the robots and make sure no one stole them while the dismounts headed back to COP Adam.

White 3's tank commander for that day was SSG Carl Haas. He was an 11B Infantry squad leader in third platoon but was cross-trained to be a tank commander so he could backfill the crews when SSG Wallat or SSG Davis went on leave. Not more than an hour after the Strykers left, White 3 called COP Adam:

Quiiisssh ...

"COP Adam this is White 3. I am observing individuals hiding behind a brick wall and attempting to lasso Johnny 5. I am going to fire a burst of .50-cal over in the direction to scare them off, over."

Buuuuuurp ...

"COP Adam, this is White 3. That should do it, over."

I called back out to the White 3 crew and gave them an "Atta boy!" We didn't need the insurgents running around town with one of our zillion-dollar robots. About thirty minutes later, White

238

3 called up and reported that the wannabe cowboys were trying to lasso the robot again.

Quiiisssh ...

"COP Adam, this is White 3. I am losing my patience with these ignorant SOBs, and they almost lassoed Johnny on their last attempt. Request permission to engage with main gun, over."

"Roger, you are cleared for main gun engagement. Just give us an 'on the way' before you let it rip, over."

Not more than a few seconds had passed and we heard "On the way!"

BOOM!

"That'll do it, over."

There is nothing like letting a 120mm smooth bore loose in the middle of the city. It really got people's attention!

The end of March and the first few weeks of April were as high tempo as things could get. We had a change of command for not only B Company, but also A Company. CPT Sheldon Morris was taking over A Co, and CPT Austin was coming to B Co. I was cleaning house in HQ platoon. At that point, we had mostly wounded soldiers in HQ, with the exception of the commander's personal maneuver element. One of the lone survivors was SGT Lunt. I tried keeping him as long as I could but he finally wore me down by continuously asking me when he could go down to a line platoon. I threatened him that if he asked me one more time to go to a line platoon, he would never leave and be in HQ for life. As much as I liked having a squared-away soldier like Lunt in HQ, it only made sense for him to get in his team-leader time while deployed, so I also rewarded him by sending him to a platoon of his choosing. Until SGT Lunt departed, he worked on training his replacement: Specialist Daniel Sieng. SPC Sieng had been wounded on his previous tour in Iraq and then had been blown up in his Bradley while out on patrol. He'd been shaken up pretty good and was ready for a change of pace, so he and SGT Lunt got to work on the training process before Lunt left.

It also worked out good for me, as we had just received three replacement Bradleys and I needed a gunner because we'd have an extra Bradley for a float vehicle—and I planned on using it until a platoon needed it. By then, we had about seven Bradleys blown up to the point that they were non-mission capable and were sent to the bone yard. We originally had Bradley A3 vehicles, and they were the best the Army could get, really state-of-the-art vehicles. Unfortunately, as the Bradley A3s steadily were destroyed we, started getting the Bradley ODS (Operation Desert Storm) vehicles that were older but still excellent vehicles. Eager to check out our new vehicles, I went over to the motor pool to check out the three new replacement Bradleys that had just arrived.

To my shock, they were Bradley M2A2s. The vehicles were old as dirt compared to what our guys had been using. It appeared these vehicles had been in country for years and abused regularly without any maintenance, ever. Most of the men had never even seen one like this, unless it was in a museum. The Bradley M2A2 had a manual range-indexing knob compared to the A3's laze-and-blaze. The thermal sights were red and very hazy compared to the crystal-clear optics of the A3—and the list went on and on. Basically it was like going from a Stealth fighter to a Cessna. I knew that we would have to set up a training program just to train the gunners on how to shoot it. Surprisingly enough, the vehicles ran well and the turrets—minus the communications—all came up to standard without any major issues. After a while, the guys actual enjoyed some of the simplicity of the vehicle, but there was no substitute for modern technology.

Personally I felt right at home with these vehicles, because I had "grown up" on them as a soldier over the years and had even deployed with the same style vehicles from Korea in 2004. We used them the entire time we'd deployed in Ramadi. The funny thing was, when we blew them up in Ramadi, we were getting the newer ODS versions and thought we were big-time then.

Now, though, the one thing no one had thought about was communication equipment and the differences between the new and old types of Bradley vehicles. The internal communications on the old Bradleys were set up as analog, but all the communication equipment—including the crew helmets—we had on hand was for digital communications. This was a major issue and basically rendered these old vehicles useless until we could rectify the problem.

Our company change of command would be coming soon, and we worked it so we would literally hold the fort down for A Co while they did their change of command, then in return, they would do the same for us. To my relief, CPT Chapman's framed and matted guidon had shown up in the mail just in time without a scratch on it. SSG Morales had the bakers at the chow hall bake a cake in the shape of a guidon then decorate it with red and white icing to "Cav it up." He also reserved a section of the chow hall for the reception, departure, and a recognition ceremony. This would be the first time we had the entire company together since we'd arrived in country six months earlier.

The change of command was a bittersweet moment in Bone's deployment. It was awesome to see CPT Chapman move on with his career, as well as see another young officer come in and take charge of a company and have his chance at the best job an officer could ever ask for. The guys really liked CPT Chapman and were proud to have him as a commander, and they were also nervously excited about the incoming commander. I assured them that he was a solid guy, but they would have to find out for themselves.

As the change of command drew nearer, we moved CPT Austin into the CHU area so he could start doing his inventories and get them straight before he signed the property books for the company. The property books were in much better condition than they had been six months earlier. We had to plan extra time for the platoons as they rotated back from the COP to lay out all their platoon equipment to be counted and serial numbers verified. All equipment had to be counted, from the tiny little grease fittings to the serial numbers on the Bradleys—what joy!

The inventories are a good time to really get an idea of who the commander is and how he will be. I have seen commanders come in and just sign the hand receipts, barely taking notice of the equipment and just going for the bare minimum, which made all the soldiers happy because they were home at a normal hour. But it made me nervous because this equipment was there to make his command successful, and one sure-fire way of having a bad command was to lose accountability of your equipment or to fail to maintain the equipment that the Army and taxpayers had entrusted you with.

I had also seen commanders come in and really dig into their equipment and take ownership of it right from the start, as it should be. Attention to detail went a long way, and everyone took notice. I had commanders count the points of each individual socket, or have a tape measure on hand to measure the length of a screwdriver. If the hand receipt said you had to have a twelve-point, half-inch socket and you brought over a six-point socket, you found yourself buying the right one! The good commanders not only looked for the accountability piece but they also asked "Does it work?" And if it didn't, then they wanted to know why it hadn't been turned in.

CPT Austin could have just signed off, taken everyone's word for it, and used the excuse, "It's combat and we don't have time for it." Then, later, he could have tried to write off the losses as "combat loss," but that technique would not have allowed him the time to see exactly what his company had to operate with. Thankfully CPT Austin did not take any shortcuts and took the "hard right over the easy wrong" from the beginning, and that put my mind at ease. As the company first sergeant, I would have failed him right from the beginning if I did not help him if he had veered off course. Inventories were not only about numbers, but it really told us what our capabilities were as a unit.

CPT Chapman set up CPT Austin for success with the company equipment and his personal crew and maneuver element. Bone 6 Delta (the driver) was SPC Cabreja, aka "Li'l C." He was an excellent driver and RTO on the ground, and he really took care of business. Bone 6 Golf (the gunner) was SGT Sisson. Then we had SGT Gary

Rojas, who was the designated dismounted security element for Bone 6. The commander had to be everywhere all the time, and we did not want to burden the line platoons with security so we made sure the commander had the best of the best on the ground with him at all times to keep him out of trouble.

It was now a few days prior to the change-of-command ceremony. Third platoon was out at COP Adam, and LT Pijpaert was doing a patrol with a squad and a section of Bradleys over-watching. The patrol was around the general perimeter of the compound, and they were trying to talk to any of the locals that had stayed in the area. It was mid afternoon when a long burst of machine-gun fire erupted from the south a few hundred meters from the patrol's position. The rounds skipped off the street and snapped by the exposed men as they searched for cover behind the Bradleys and in the small courtyards of the houses that lined the street. PFC Castelleon went down hard in the middle of the street with the initial burst of machine-gun fire. Doc Devries saw PFC Castelleon go down and ran out into the open to drag him to cover. As Doc Devries ran out into the open and did his combat slide next to the casualty, the Bradley pulled down to suppress and help evacuate the casualty. To Doc's surprise, Castelleon was conscious and talking, even though he had been shot in the head!

Quiiisssh ...

"Bone 9, this is Bone Main. COP Adam reports Blue 6 taking machine-gun fire in Sector W1 (Whiskey 1 = west) while conducting a patrol and has one WIA—BBC####. Casualty was shot in the head and is en route back to FOB Warhorse with a section of Bradleys from Blue platoon."

Upon hearing that, I pulled my battle roster out of my sleeve pocket and ran my finger down the list to confirm the ID of the casualty. Once I confirmed it, I rolled to the gate to escort the vehicle to the aid station as I had done in the past. The Bradley section made it to the gate in less than fifteen minutes from the time I got the call, and we were at the aid station minutes later. At the station, we saw this one female nurse; she seemed to always be on duty when we brought in casualties. I'll never forget the look she gave me as I stood in the waiting area that day. It was one of compassion and genuine concern for me and the entire company. The look she gave me offered me some confidence that our boys would be taken care of with people like her working in the aid station and looking after the troops as they came in all banged up.

A few minutes later, an ambulance pulled up to the back door and they shuttled Castelleon out to it for transport to the helicopter landing pad to fly him out to Balad. To my surprise, Castelleon was fully conscious and somewhat coherent. He talked to us as they loaded him onto the ambulance, and he even managed to yell out a "Bonecrushers forever!" then jibber-jabbered about some other stuff as they closed the doors. Morphine or not, he was still showing pride in his company and fellow soldiers.

It turns out he had been shot in the upper forehead and the bullet fractured his skull, then traveled to the right around the skull between his scalp and the skull bone, finally exiting out the backside of his head behind his ear. That was CPT Chapman's last full day of being Bonecrusher's company commander.

The following day, we had all the platoons back and started the company rehearsals pretty early. I didn't want to get too carried away but I wanted the ceremony to be fitting of a great departing commander and to show the incoming commander that we were squared-away professionals and proud to be in the cavalry. We had Bradleys lined up behind the formations and behind the podium. I had a big poster of the company mascot blown up and laminated on display in front of the Bone 6 Bradley. We had the battalion colors and a brand-new shiny red and white guidon to hand over to CPT Austin. The hardest part of that day was getting the platoons to sing "The US Army Song." It was like pulling teeth without any Novocain, but we eventually made our way through a few warm-ups to the point I thought they could sing it without butchering the song too badly. We were infantry, not singers, so it would have to do.

The ceremony went off without a hitch. The brigade commander, COL Sutherland, was there along with CSM Felt and a few other key personnel from brigade, with the exception of MAJ Karcher, as he had been seriously wounded in an ambush earlier that month while conducting tactical operations with one of the senior Iraqi army leaders in the area, and since then had been sent back to the States for recovery. Naturally all the commanders and staff officers from battalion attended. It was quick and painless. Even the singing didn't hurt too badly.

After the ceremony, we all headed down to the dining facility for cake and socializing. There we presented to CPT Chapman his going-away gift, but not before everyone in the company signed the backside of it with a silver Sharpie. Usually the outgoing commander disappears and the reception is for the incoming commander, but these weren't usual times. So it ended up being a combination outgoing-incoming lunch. It was just nice to see everyone together and nobody really cared about proper protocol. The lunch was short, as everyone had to get back to work. We were still setting the conditions to conduct the offensive into Tahrir and had some major route clearance to finish.

That evening, CPT Austin headed out to COP Adam, and I stayed back at FOB Warhorse. I got word that we were finally getting some fresh replacement soldiers from the United States. I was relieved to hear that news, as we were really hurting on personnel and no one had any soldiers to spare—to the point that I had quit asking. The company originally deployed with an average of only seven men in the nine-man squads to begin with. Between casualties, one AWOL, details, and various other distractions over the past six months, B Co was critically low on personnel. But now we would be getting six new soldiers, three NCOs, and three soldiers. With that many new soldiers coming in, it was a "must do" to come up with a thorough plan to integrate them. I did not want to assign them into a platoon and have them out on patrol the next day. It had to be a deliberate integration, starting with personal equipment inventories, and confirming all of their personal information, including the accuracy of life insurance and next of kin info. We learned quickly not to assume things were in order. I had to interview each one and figure out what their strengths were and how they could best be used in the company. Next was to issue them weapons and sensitive items based on where I decided they would be assigned within the company. Then we had to take them to the range both day and night and have them zero their weapons and do familiarization fire on ALL the weapon systems in the company. Then we had to give them "Rules of Engagement" classes and teach them the area of operation and what units were where and what AIF elements operated in that AO. We also had them man the TOC for a few days just to learn call signs and see how things operated to really get an understanding of what was happening downtown. Situational awareness down to the lowest private was essential.

The platoons were anxious to get the new guys and I was anxious to give them. However, I wanted to make sure they were squared away once they were in the platoons. It wasn't that I did not trust the platoons to do the right thing; it was that the operational tempo was so high, I was worried about them getting caught up in the "now" and some important information or process just getting pushed off until it was too late and the new guy either got killed, wounded, or hurt someone. That was not a risk I was willing to take.

Luckily, SSG (now promotable) Lane was back at FOB Warhorse with SSG Johnson to help get the replacements squared away and set up a solid reception and integration program. It seemed that once the initial replacements came in, it was a steady flow of replacements from that point on. We were not complaining—better late than never.

CPT Austin found himself conducting route-clearance operations in Tahrir his first day on the job. The task was to clear C Avenue, starting from Route Vanessa, and head south to Route Gold. The plan was for third platoon's infantry squads to go in first and clear the buildings that parallel C Avenue and then allow the

Bradleys to set up blocking positions. Once the blocking positions had been set, White platoon would seal off Route Gold and Route Vanessa with a section of M1s on each route. Then the Trail Blazer element would come in with their vehicle, called a "Husky," which looks similar to a road grader, but with a reinforced cab that is basically designed to absorb the blast of an IED while keeping the driver safe. The vehicle was essentially made to be blown up and to be easily rebuilt in sections. The Husky's job was to go in front of all the other vehicles and identify IEDs (something the Blade 26 element could not do on the earlier route-clearance mission).The Husky had a blower hooked up to the front of the vehicle so that it could blow all the trash and loose dirt away from a suspected IED to confirm or deny if it was indeed an IED or just a bag or box. The cab also had good fields of view and allowed the operator to have an unobstructed view almost all the way around the cab. Once the Husky did its job, the Buffalo vehicle could come in and interrogate the suspected IED site with the hydraulic arm, and if need be, deploy a robot to blow the IED.

At 0630 hours on 16 April 2007, third platoon's infantry squads pushed through the northern section of C Avenue. SGT Bowlby and his squad entered the fifth house and discovered a makeshift aid station for the AIF in the area. They found a significant amount of bloody bandages, clothes, and the signature al-Qaeda ski mask. Just a few houses away, SSG Fili found a hide position with cached sleeping bags, cold-weather gear, and water. These were all obvious signs that the AIF had moved back into that portion of town and that they had left just hours before third platoon entered the buildings. We suspected they were infiltrating in from the north, by way of Old Baqubah.

As both infantry squads maneuvered throughout their buildings to set up over-watch of the area, they could feel the ground shake from the vibration of the Bradley fighting vehicles pulling into position outside the buildings. SFC Reynolds was pulling outside of SGT Bowlby's building when, without warning, the earth erupted underneath the vehicle and swallowed it up in a cloud of dust and debris. The powerful IED stopped the Bradley instantly and blew off the front side of the building that SGT Bowlby's squad was in. Immediately after the IED detonation, the insurgents opened up with small-arms fire, sporadically hitting both buildings the dismounts occupied.

Upon the report of the IED and small-arms fire, B Company's internal QRF (A section, third platoon) rolled out from COP Adam to help secure the area. As the QRF rolled out to the north, CPT Austin (Black 6) and his crew left COP Adam and headed south to 41st Street so they had security on both sides of the downed vehicle. As Black 6 turned east onto 41st Street, they were engaged by a massive IED, elevating the Bradley into the air and then slamming it back down. It split the heavy steel track off its rollers and sprockets like a conveyor belt that had just snapped.

At 0830 hours, I called the battalion and requested battalion QRF to bring out two M88 recovery vehicles and also requested AWTs on station. We had a platoon of M1s, five Bradleys—two of which were destroyed—two infantry squads, and an EOD element. It was decided to have the Husky and the Buffalo pull down to clear the rest of the area before the M88 and the crews got out to hook up the tow bars. As the Husky pulled down to clear the path for the M88, it rolled directly over another monstrous IED, which blew the Husky into three pieces and tossed it through the air like a toy. You could see axles and tires mixed with blacktop, dirt, and smoke getting flung through the streets. The main cab of the Husky landed thirty feet away in a small dirt field from the IED blast crater and came to rest on its side. Everyone watched in horror; no one could have survived that—no one. The Trail Blazer soldiers in the Buffalo were already heading over to pick up the remains of the driver, but to their surprise, they saw the top of the crew capsule pop open, then the driver crawled out and staggered toward their Buffalo. It was a miracle—he was alive.

As the Husky driver was getting picked up, the White 3 tank was struck with an RPG. Though there was a thunderous explosion, it caused only minor damage. Taking note of the explosion, the

White 3 tank slowly traversed the turret in the direction of the RPG fire. The RPG gunner frantically raced to reload and fired wildly as the red tracers of the 7.62mm coax machine gun found their mark and cut the gunner down, leaving his body sprawled and frozen in an awkward posture, still gripping his grenade launcher as life slowly leaked from his wounds.

Then Redwolf 1 and Redwolf 9 from the air weapons team came onto station. They keyed in on the explosions and smoke, and immediately acquired four armed AIF moving into a house five streets southeast of 41st and C Avenue, so they requested clearance to fire. They confirmed with the HQ element out at COP Adam that we were clear of friendlies in that area and they launched two Hellfire missiles into the building. The scream of the missiles' flight motors zipped overhead, followed by an enormous explosion. It put a small piece of you at ease knowing that everyone that had been in that building had now fulfilled their destiny and given their life to the jihad. If the AIF in sector wanted to come out and fight, we were happy to oblige them. There was no way in hell they were going to come out and blow up three vehicles and not pay for it.

With the M1 tanks, infantry squads, and AWTs on station, the insurgents wisely slipped back into the shadows. LT Boeka escorted the recovery vehicles out to the site and CPT Austin rejoined the main element on the ground to take charge of the recovery process. Within thirty minutes, the company's mission went from route clearance, to offensive operations, to vehicle-recovery operations. The recovery of the vehicles was going to take the better part of the day. The Husky was in so many pieces that they needed to drag the parts out to Route Vanessa and load them on a lowboy trailer with the boom of the M88 recovery vehicle, just to get it all back to the FOB. Both Bradleys had been immobilized and thus had to be dragged back to FOB Warhorse, where they could be stripped of all useful parts and equipment and then sent to the bone yard.

The really frustrating part of the entire day was that we had just cleared that area with the Blade element a week and a half earlier and felt fairly confident that no IEDs were in that small section of street—and if there were, the infantry squads would have cleared the trigger men out. The IEDs were massive, and it would have taken an extensive amount of time, labor, and resources to emplace them. They had obviously been there the entire time; we just could not find them the easy way, and the insurgents had been taking notes on how we were conducting our route-clearance missions, then made their adjustments to their trigger-man positions and pushed them back much farther off the roads and dog-legged the wire a few times to throw off the direction of the wire. Later we actually traced detonation wires that crossed over the road twice to throw us off of which side of the road the IEDs were detonated from.

The other frustrating part was that we knew about the IED that CPT Austin hit; he just had not gotten the memo. The IED that took out his Bradley was the same suspected IED that the Blade 26 element had been working on when the robots got shot by the sniper before they could blow it. Luckily the Bradley absorbed the blast and no one was hurt seriously. I was disappointed in myself for allowing that to happen. Situational awareness is a must; I regret not sitting down with CPT Austin immediately and deliberately going over the situation downtown from my perspective. I assumed he knew about the IEDs on 41st. The company command post was highly accurate by that point on battle tracking and posting information in regard to suspected IED locations, known IED locations, and previous IED locations. We had a extra large laminated map board that had a big sheet of metal behind it, and we had magnets that represented all the platoons, vehicles, infantry squads, sniper teams, enemy units, and IEDs. Somehow the IEDs that blew up the Black 6 crew had gotten overlooked. One of my theories on how they'd been overlooked was that it had become so obvious to everyone that 41st Street was a NO-GO road, I/we assumed that everyone else knew. Obviously a new commander would not have known that, and when he tells his crew to go, they go—no questions asked. We made our adjustments and from that point on made extra sure that everyone leaving the wire was up to date on the latest and greatest information.

Part of the adjustment included taking a portion of the large command post and again setting up our own internal intelligence section. We made it into an isolated area for platoons to come in and plan, and also give their operations orders with no distractions, all with the latest information on enemy contacts, IEDs, high-value targets, new enemy tactics, and what had been happening in and around other sectors without having to ask for it. It was another system that we continuously improved. We initially built bench seating, had another large map printed, and then we displayed additional blow-ups of each sector in the city for detailed views and planning. We labeled and numbered every single building in the area and ensured that the AWTs got the same information we had on the ground. We had also put up a large dry-erase board with the five-paragraph operations format on it to help with the orders process. It was a great system and was also used for the debrief process and the after-action review following every patrol.

CPT Austin made it through his first full day in command and, through no fault of his own, managed to get himself blown up and have two Bradleys destroyed—each worth a few million dollars—a route-clearance vehicle annihilated, and two not so seriously wounded soldiers.

CHAPTER 12

TASK FORCE BONE

IN MID-LATE APRIL 2007, Bone received a new lieutenant in the company to backfill us since we had given up LT Moffitt, but at the same time we had to give up LT Duplechin to go to another company outside the battalion. So the decision was made to move LT Boeka from first and bring him to the XO's position. First platoon's new platoon leader was 1LT Karim Branford. LT Branford was a graduate from both Princeton University and Ranger School, which gave him a little credibility. The rest would have to be earned. With first platoon north in Zaganiya with the 5/73rd Scout Company, I was a little concerned about how they were going to use our guys. Based on my own previous experiences of getting attached to other light units, I was concerned they would not be used correctly. Within a week, I already started to hear rumblings and my concerns became reality.

First platoon had been out in Zaganiya for a week and rotated in for a maintenance day when SFC Hamilton raised the maintenance issue, saying that they were not getting enough time back on Warhorse to conduct quality maintenance and give the soldiers a little downtime. He also raised the force-protection issue at the COP and how things needed to be fortified; he had no building materials even though he had requested them several times. LT Branford also mentioned the only mission they had been performing was force protection and route security for days on end. I can understand why this happened, but it still should have been done in a manner that the crews conducting route security got some type of break so they did not get complacent.

Route security into Zaganiya was important, and I understood the concerns of the commander. We lost a Bradley out there earlier in our tour. The IED completely destroyed the undercarriage of the Bradley, and it wounded SPC Arenas[51] and shook up CPL Sieng pretty good. One long road ran about eight to ten kilometers of twists and turns, and it was impossible to observe the entire route into the little towns—and Zaganiya was all the way at the northern end. Again, it was a prime location for insurgents, as it only had one way in from the south, so the insurgents had the upper hand when it came to attacking US forces. They could attack at a time and place of their choosing. They proved this once again in early April when 5/73rd's S-4 was doing a logistical run into Zaganiya and his up-armored HMMWV was hit with a deep-buried IED that killed everyone inside.

Upon hearing LT Branford's and SFC Hamilton's concerns, I decided I would go out to the 82nd Airborne's COP and check things out firsthand. I figured we could help them out by loading up building and fortification materials we had been stockpiling, including some ballistic glass and hand tools to improve the OPs. We arrived around 2:00 a.m. and the main entrance was blocked off. No one had warned us of the change nor did anyone mark the route to the new entrance. The disgruntled RTO gave us directions to the alternate entrance but didn't bother telling us that it was flooded and impassable. So, naturally, we got the cargo truck stuck and it took us an hour to get all our vehicles through the entrance that was too small for Bradleys to begin with.

Now the vehicles were inside the compound, and a good

---

51 High-speed soldier who, after only two weeks working in HQ platoon, begged to go back to his platoon as a squad member and not a Bradley driver.

portion of first platoon's soldiers were covered in mud, including me. I was a bit disgusted and figured I would go and tell the RTO how bad the entrance was and to thank him for his unprofessional attitude on the radio. Shortly after my talk with the RTO, I met the company commander, CPT Kirk. Our initial meeting was less than productive.

Nonetheless, we unloaded our supplies and tools and went to work. SGT Graham, one of the new NCOs that had arrived with the replacements, had some great carpentry skills, along with SPC Garcia, and they made an awesome fortified OP position with ballistic glass and a machine-gun platform. Our guys filled sandbags and went to town as they had on two previous COPs. As the 82nd guys watched us banging out wood frames, sawing wood, slinging sandbags, and moving with a purpose, they slowly started to help until it was an all-out GI party getting the place fortified.

I had the utmost respect for the 5/73rd and their soldiers. The 5/73rd's commander, LTC Poppas, and his soldiers were some real ferocious fighters and had been putting the hurt on the AIF for months in the north with very little help from outside units. From that first trip up to Zaganiya, I made it a point to go there routinely to check on the guys and do some patrols with the squads. The 82nd Airborne liked to operate with minimum frills—but not the 1st Cav, unless it was absolutely necessary. The weather was getting hotter by the day and triple digits were already upon us. I scored a bunch of window-unit air conditioners and some generator light sets to power the AC units. The generators were on trailers but I had no way to get them out there. I explained my dilemma to CSM Harris, and next thing you know, we mounted up a patrol with his "maneuver element" and tossed a bunch of steaks in a cooler with a few charcoal grills and coals then headed out to Zaganiya to have a BBQ with the guys and drop off the ACs. We even made enough for the 82nd and showed them how to Cav it up a bit.

On 25 April 2007, a combat outpost manned by another company of the 5/73rd lost eight soldiers in a coordinated suicide vehicle-born IED attack on their outpost. Reports indicated that it was a well-planned and coordinated attack that targeted the outpost's perimeter. One vehicle packed full of explosives hit the outside walls of the COP and detonated, creating the initial casualties and confusion. Once the 5/73rd's first responders came to aid their injured and fallen comrades, a second larger vehicle rammed the same location and caused massive devastation on the now massed paratroopers. The insurgents were obviously taking notes on how we operated and started to adjust their techniques to how we responded to various AIF-induced actions. The targeting of reinforcements and first responders was becoming more frequent as the daily battles and attacks continued.

Meanwhile COP Adam was going through some changes with attachments and different task organization. We were giving up our 1-12 scouts effective immediately, and in exchange, we would be getting two platoons from 5-20 IN. Unfortunately we were not getting their scouts and mortars assigned to us for another week, so we just had to stick it out for a little bit with just third platoon and second platoon. To maximize our manpower on the ground in the infantry platoons, we returned the third squad that was on loan to the tankers to third platoon. We were getting replacements in, and White platoon had pretty much finished their R&R leave rotation. At that stage of the fight, we needed every guy we could get on the ground. The 120-degree weather was taking its toll on the multiple daily mounted and dismounted combat patrols, and with only one infantry platoon, we had to be smart.

We resorted back to the high-payoff tasks of inserting our small kill teams (SKT) throughout the city. We would infiltrate into specific locations and over-watch areas that we had templated on the map as enemy infiltration routes, supply routes, or hotspots for IED activity. We also conducted counter-reconnaissance missions. The AIF continuously watched everything we did, so we would have to be creative in our deception as we left stay-behind soldiers for the small kill teams or other various operations.

A typical SKT mission with Blue platoon would last anywhere from six hours to two days. Squads would leave some time in the late evening or early morning under the cover of darkness and work their way to their positions that they carefully selected based on recent enemy activity and intelligence. They would enter and clear the house. If there were occupants living there, they would gather them up and put them in a room and place a guard on them. They would then verify that they had good observation and also ensure they could defend the house if needed. Once it was confirmed that they could see the intended target area, everyone would get to work with their assigned tasks. Someone would have to mark the building on the roof for aircraft with strobes and orange panels (VS17), while others would barricade doors and set tripwires and flares. Others would have to establish communications and grid coordinates to call up to higher, and still others would be pulling security while some set up a rest area. Everything was planned before they ever left the COP, so there was little talking and minimum distractions. They tried to plan for as many different scenarios as possible, but some they just couldn't plan for.

One particular evening, call sign Trouble 2 called up that they had entered and cleared a house and were setting up. But they had to vacate the house shortly afterward because the stench of a rotting corpse overpowered them. They initially thought they could deal with it but wisely decided to go and set up elsewhere. You just never knew what you were going to find when you started going into houses and factories in Tahrir.

Once the SKTs were established, they sat and waited—and waited. Everyone would have their night-vision equipment out and ready to use at a moment's notice. Any equipment not being used was put away just in case they had to leave in a hurry. As the sun would start to rise, they would take turns putting their night-vision goggles away, turning their lasers off, and switching their clear lenses to their tinted lenses on their eye protection, all to prepare for a daytime fight. On an SKT, you had to be observant, as the AIF seldom came out and blatantly did something that could give you reason to shoot someone. You had to watch for the indicators. Usually, when emplacing an IED, the AIF would send out scouts first to survey the areas while trying to blend in with the general population. However, in Tahrir, the civilian population for the most part stayed in their houses or vacated town. Any male individual from the age of sixteen to sixty was considered suspicious, as well as any women dressed in the burka—just because we did not know if they were really women or not.

Once the AIF felt they were safe and could carry about their terroristic ways, they would prepare the IED site either by digging or using a previous blast hole. Unfortunately you couldn't shoot someone for just digging a hole and they knew this, so they would emplace the IEDs in stages. They would dig a hole and leave it there for a week or two, and then go back and drop the IED in it. The IED would already have the wire hooked up to it and be tied off to fishing line so they could run the detonation wire from a concealed position by pulling it with the invisible line without being observed—or it was looped and tied for later deployment. They would transport the IEDs to the hole by either hiding it in a box, bag, donkey cart, propane tank, vehicle with the floorboards cut out, underneath a burka, vegetable crate, car tire, or anything else they could carry and disguise from being recognized as an IED. Some AIF would surround themselves with kids or a group of people as they walked by and placed the IED into the hole. Homemade explosives (HME) made it hard to identify the IEDs because they could make the explosive and pack it into anything that would blend into the surroundings, just adding shrapnel. Knowing the indicators and being observant paid off. You usually had to look past the initial layer of what your eyes were showing you and your mind was telling you. Once you were able to look through the layers, you could really see the details of what was happening. Some guys could sit for days on end, studying their surroundings and memorizing what was out there and how people acted—and eventually they could key in on different body language and find that one indicator that gave them the right to shoot. Insurgents were not as willing to go hang out with those heavenly virgins as some would lead you to think, so being able to pop one took patience and good aim. That was when it paid off to have an M24 sniper rifle or an M14 carbine that was dialed in: you could split their wig in a crowd once you'd identified hostile intent. That would leave an impression on other AIF—and "good news" travels quickly.

Some guys had natural ability and could really put it on the Haj, while others never could pull the trigger in a situation like that. Most engagement opportunities in that type of situation were only a few seconds so you had to be on your "A" game at all times. It was also a technique to have alternate shooters and or a crew-served weapon as a backup if you had multiple targets (also known as "Tangos," if you want to be sexy). Once that round hit, the rest would run like jackrabbits to get out of the kill zone. War is an art; if you treat it as such, you can and will be successful. Al-Qaeda does.

SKTs would end their stay for several reasons. You may have shot and compromised your position. Your position could have been compromised because someone came looking for the people you had detained momentarily in their own house. Or you just ran out of time. The worse case was when your SKT was compromised going into position and didn't know it—and then the Haj turned the tables and attacked them or waited and set up his own SKT for when you left the position.

Midway through our tour, we received a report on an SKT from another unit that was actually being assaulted by the insurgents to the point that the AIF were in the same house slugging it out with the American forces in a close-quarters battle and hand-to-hand combat. While the US forces did end up repelling the attackers, it came at a high cost, as most every survivor had been wounded and several others had been killed. The number one rule is: DO NOT UNDERESTIMATE THE HAJ.

Between our platoons, and the scouts and snipers from 1-12, we were getting very proficient with the SKTs as we refined our techniques after every mission. The AIF, on the other hand, were getting cautious and good at concealing what they were doing and adjusting as well. With only having third platoon and SSG Pina's sniper sections on the ground until the 5-20 "Regular" soldiers showed up, we had to be smart about how we would operate.

The week went by with the usual daily firefights and harassing fires on the COP and patrols. Every time the patrols rolled out, we were getting into contact of some sort. But it was only a matter of time before the tables were turned and the AIF would be getting squeezed as the noose tightened.

The battalion-level offensive mission in Tahrir finally kicked off as planned. Two companies were used from 5-20 "Attack" company in the south and "Battle" from the west. Bone would push from the north while the 5-20 IN scouts ("Shadow") and the mortars ("Thunder") infiltrated in on foot from FOB Gabe and blocked from the east. It was a well-planned and coordinated attack on the city, and it left nowhere for the AIF to run. The companies were to enter and clear every single building block by block and street by street within Tahrir. There were several six- and eight-story apartment complexes, schools, college campuses, government buildings, and various other shaped and sized buildings. The key to the success of this operation would be to catch the AIF forces in the city before they had time to flee.

We'd received intelligence that they had booby-trapped houses and had various cars rigged with explosives along our routes— including the use of many of the techniques we'd seen in Buhritz, with tripwires and pressure-plate IEDs focused on killing the infantry squads, not the vehicles. The movement was going to be slow and deliberate. The mission was planned to last several days. At that point in an operation, you had the rest of your life to get it done.

From 25-27 April, the start of the operation was slow and methodical. Every few hundred meters on every street, an obstacle needed to be removed, either an IED, suspicious car, or suspicious wire running on a fence to a gate or a door. The insurgents made plenty of decoy IEDs along with the real ones to slow our advance. It was as if everything was going to explode around you, and to make matters worse, they left a significant amount of fighters in the city to slug it out with the attacking US forces as they dealt with each obstacle. By halfway through the first day, we were calling in artillery, Hellfire missile strikes from the helicopters, and JDAM guided missiles from the fast-movers, since there was no sense getting into a fistfight with the AIF. The 5-20 guys did a good job of finding the enemy and fixing them in position, then finishing them with the assorted smorgasbord of death and destruction they had in their arsenal. Once the munitions had taken care of the intended target, it was onto the next block where the fight was for the most part repeated in the same fashion.

At the end of the two-day operation, fifteen to twenty insurgents had been killed and an additional twenty to twenty-five captured. A disturbing amount of various types of IEDs had been found and destroyed. Several booby-trapped houses had been demolished. Also, several VBIEDs had been found and destroyed, including a fire truck that was rigged as a VBIED. An AIF HQ was also located, and valuable intelligence was gathered: we confiscated thousands of various anti-coalition propaganda pieces in the form of CDs and pamphlets. Multiple IED factories were located and destroyed, along with a significant amount of already-made HME (homemade explosives). Many other weapons caches were located, containing various weapons and munitions, including AK-47s, pistols, machine guns, RPGs, landmines, hand grenades, sniper rifles, scopes, radios, cell phones, IA uniforms, IP uniforms, body armor, suicide vests, medical supplies, maps, and blueprints of buildings and water treatment facilities—and much more. We dealt a devastating blow to the AIF in the Tahrir area, but the majority had fled prior to the US operation and lived to fight another day. They would return in the following weeks when the major forces moved on to other parts of Baqubah.

After the operation in Tahrir, the Shadow and Thunder elements were given a day to refit and then they were assigned to Bone. I was excited to get two more platoons in the company. More people on the ground meant more security. The Stryker platoons had roughly forty soldiers per platoon plus four Strykers in each platoon. It would give our guys a much-needed break. All the platoons had been running full throttle for seven months under daily combat conditions with no end in sight, and it was taking its toll, so the surge had come just in time.

I wanted the 5-20 soldiers to feel welcome and a part of the team so I made sure that the platoon sleeping areas were as squared away as possible and that we had adequate supplies on hand. An additional eighty soldiers out at the COP would be a logistical challenge. CSM Harris managed to get us a new Army mobile kitchen and assigned us a few cooks to rotate out to the COP. Even knowing 5-20 had operational control over Bone, 1-12 still took care of us with the administrative and logistical needs. The kitchen was impressive. It was totally self-contained and was all state-of-the-art cooking equipment. It was massive, but thanks to our large new compound, we could fit it in on the side of the building where it was not likely to draw fire, and we could feed our soldiers two hot meals a day. The mobile kitchen alleviated the worry of putting soldiers on the road to make a thunder run to FOB Gabe to get hot chow. It was an excellent addition to the outpost.

Another welcomed addition to the outpost was an Iraqi army company. Part of the clear-hold-build process was to insert IA units as quickly as possible into the newly liberated areas and show the Iraqi people it was going to be maintained jointly with IA forces—and then, as security improved, the IA would slowly take over. The only difference in this strategy from the past was we actually had enough soldiers on the ground to really provide security and eventually gain the confidence of the civilian populace by actually living deep inside the city 24/7. As expected, the confidence and trust of the civilian population would not come easily and would be something that would have to be fought for in the weeks and months to come. The al-Qaeda in that area had a stranglehold on the population and the citizens did not have confidence in the US forces to stay and provide security in a long-term capacity.

With the city of Tahrir cleared for the most part, it was then divided in half. The northern sector from 42nd Street north was Bone's, and from 42nd south was Battle's. While the companies continued to work Tahrir in their respective areas, Attack Company was working in Old Baqubah, trying to establish a foothold within. The Iraqi army unit that was living out at COP Adam with Bone was working with all three companies within sector on various operations, with a platoon rotating consistently with Battle Company in the southern sector of Tahrir.

On 29 April, the first Stryker platoon showed up in the early evening. I wanted to meet and greet each soldier as they came in, so I went to the front entrance of the COP and welcomed them one by one. I had their platoon area squared away and wanted to leave a good initial impression on them. One of the first soldiers to walk through the doors was a young guy named SGT Clark, a young NCO whom I had been stationed with in 1-9 IN C Company 2nd ID in Korea and subsequently deployed to Ramadi with. He was as shocked and relieved as I was, and we gave each other a bro hug as I welcomed him to the company. SGT Clark wasn't in my platoon, but he knew I took care of business the right way (most of the time), and I was certain he would tell the other Stryker guys that they were in good company.

CPT Austin also made it easy for the Stryker guys to feel welcomed, as he had a natural ability to project confidence as a company commander and put people at ease around him, which was a great quality as a leader. But the biggest and most impressive image that put the 5-20 soldiers at ease was the way our platoons and sniper sections operated. They were all business professionals and represented the true warrior image and spirit. There were no "We are better than you" egos, and our platoons were truly glad to have them on board and part of the team—and their attitude and actions reflected their feelings. Shortly after the Shadow element showed up, the Thunder element pulled in with their Strykers and I greeted them at the door and had a few of Bone's troopers guide them to their platoon areas.

SFC Hunsecker and CPT Lewis were the PSG and PL,

respectively, for the Shadow element, while SFC DelaCruz and CPT Jensen were the PSG and PL, respectively, for the Thunder element. All of these guys were professional and immediately put to rest any worries we had. CPT Austin huddled up the PLs to do a once-over of our world with them, and I grabbed up all the platoon sergeants and did the same with them. Then I gave them the tour and told them the do's and don'ts of the COP. If there was anything that would start everyone off on a bad note, it was doing something unintentionally to piss someone off. When you have 200-plus people living in a confined space and in a hazardous environment, you must have order, or things can go haywire quickly. That was a situation that no one wanted.

COP Adam was bursting at the seams with activity. With the addition of the IA unit of roughly 100 soldiers and the addition of the two Stryker platoons of eighty soldiers, plus our original soldiers, the snipers, cooks, communications and HQ elements, we had about 225 solid people out at the COP. CPT Austin made sure he went out on a few patrols with each platoon from 5-20 right from the start, as he wanted to be able to gauge their experience and how well they operated together. He was quickly impressed and reassured that they would be an asset not a liability. I made sure they knew everything they needed to know about how we operated with QRFs, Rules of Engagement, force protection, and just the day-to-day business of maintaining an outpost. Within a week, we were all operating as if we had been together for months—one team, one fight.

As the first few days went by, I was able to talk to most of the 5-20 soldiers. One young staff sergeant told me, "We had you guys pegged all wrong. We figured you guys were going to be like the other mechanized units we had worked with in the past and not get off your Bradleys or tanks. So we figured we were going to come up here and save the Cavalry." I found his honesty amusing. He went on to tell me how they had gotten used to rolling into an area and basically intimidating the insurgents to the point they would melt away with little to no fight, so they figured it would be the same in

Baqubah. However, within the first forty-eight hours, they realized it was a worst-case scenario.

Soldiers tend to always prepare themselves for the worst and hope for the best when getting ready for a big operation. As the missions progress, they start to realize that they had built it up and blown it way out of proportion and are typically relieved. Not the case with the operations in Baqubah. Unfortunately these guys' worst-case scenarios were now a reality.

After the young SSG finished telling me about their previous operations south of Diyala Province, he said, "You guys are all business. You have been fighting in this area since November with just a company; now there is a battalion-plus. Your company and its soldiers have all of our respect."

Up north in Zaganiya with the 5/73rd, first platoon was conducting platoon operations to clear an area of suspected AIF fighters, when a disagreement got out of hand between the platoon sergeant and the platoon leader. It led to the PSG leaving in the middle of the operation with his section of Bradleys and coming back to FOB Warhorse. Red 6 called Bone Main and requested that I come up on the radio. I could not believe what just happened. LT Branford told me that the PSG just left his platoon in the middle of an operation! There was no excuse and there was only one thing that could be done: relieve him of his position. I made my decision before SFC Hamilton was even back at the FOB. There was no way I could ever bend on leaving soldiers in the middle of an operation—NEVER.

In the environment we were dealing with over the past seven months, everyone had hit their breaking point at least once and lost their cool in some form or fashion. Typically they were better soldiers afterward. I found myself in many awkward positions as the main disciplinarian of the company, as I had to deal with certain situations differently than I would have in a more hospitable environment, for the simple fact we were so short on personnel and experienced leadership. The discipline within the company was at an all-time high and we distinguished ourselves repeatedly and were consistently commended for it by our higher HQ. Having said that, we still had some internal squabbles, and most could be and would be dealt with internally, but relieving the platoon sergeant was something that was going to have to be done. Upon receiving LT Branford's message, I went to CSM Harris and told him about the issue I was dealing with. He agreed and told me to go and find SFC Hamilton a job.

I went down to brigade and talked to a friend of mine, SGM Gill, who was the operations sergeant major of the brigade TOC. I explained to him the situation and assured him SFC Hamilton was squared away and just needed a break. SFC Hamilton had done a lot for his platoon and had been through a lot with the company, but it was time for him to take a knee. I worked out a deal to trade SFC Hamilton out with SSG Gallego, a squared-away NCO that I had worked with when I was the brigade master gunner. Gallego was a newly promoted SSG and needed to get his squad-leader time. I knew that second platoon over with Dealer company was still short several NCOs since the house explosion. So this move would work out pretty good. I could move SFC Lane, our company master gunner, to first platoon to take Hamilton's spot and get a new NCO for second platoon. It was as good a deal as I could get, given the circumstances.

I also shifted some HQ's personnel around when LT Boeka came to HQ platoon to be the XO, he'd brought his Bradley crew with him: SPC Diaz, his driver, and SGT Billy Watts, his gunner. That deal worked out well, since these guys had done their lion's share of the fighting and could do some good in HQ platoon. I had assigned SGT Martinez and PFC Romero to first platoon since they were the most experienced Bradley crew and LT Branford was the least experienced Bradley commander—thus they could balance each other out. Both SGT Martinez and PFC Romero were ready to get out of HQ platoon and back to the line platoons and the fight. There were constant personnel changes due to the wounded, KIA, non-battle injuries, unfortunate accidents, mental breakdowns, and quitters. The constant combat and stress was slowly taking its toll; we were nearing our eighth month in combat.

Just as all the personnel changes were going on, we got another NCO into the company fresh from the States: SGT Mulligan. I was going to send him to second platoon as well, but he needed to go through the in-processing within the company. SGT Mulligan struck me as a pretty sharp guy, and I asked him what rumors he had been hearing about the company while he was back at Fort Hood on rear detachment waiting to come over. He said he heard all the war stories from the guys that were over here and had been sent back for various reasons. Though some of the guys were legitimately wounded and recovering on rear-D, a bunch of guys milked some superficial wound or had some mysterious illness called THS (tiny heart syndrome). They could have deployed and/ or stayed over in Iraq and answered radios, pulled gate guard, or got chow for the warriors. They could have done some menial task that would not have interfered with their THS, but instead they went back to the States. They were the ones telling the biggest war stories, wearing the shiniest Combat Infantryman's Badge, and telling the greatest tales of how they broke the backbone of the insurgency before they were injured, but deep down when it was all quiet at night and they were all alone, they knew they were quitters and left their buddies hanging.

As SGT Mulligan got in-processed, I tried to reassure him that it was bad, but not as bad as people were making it out to be—and that things had gotten better since the troop surge. I told him he was going to make a logistical run out to COP Adam with me, as I needed a truck commander for the cargo truck and figured it would be a good time to take SGT Mulligan out and let him see the COP and meet some of the guys. I told him we would be leaving later that day and to get his equipment ready to roll and get a dismounted radio from the company CP for communication in the truck.

At this time, I had my own Bradley M2 basic version and crew, which really helped out with various logistical and tactical operations, including medical evacuations. CPL Sieng was my gunner/training NCO, and PFC Perry was my driver. Perry stepped on his crank earlier, and I had to move him into HQ platoon. I figured I could best keep an eye on him as my driver. He was thrilled to say the least. Being that I had my own Bradley, I could pair up with either the XO's or the commander's Bradley crew, or just borrow one Bradley and crew from the platoons and move independently as needed. I'd given up my gun truck to the Wardog engineers so they could use the remote .50-cal on their route-clearance Buffalo vehicle (and they got a kill with it the first day out, so I know it went to good use).

This particular movement was with the XO's crew, my crew, and the cargo truck. We left FOB Warhorse with me in the lead, then the cargo truck, and lastly the XO's vehicle. We were heading south on Route Vanessa and had just entered Apache's area, moving about twenty-five miles per hour and scanning the roads and center dividers for IEDs. I spotted some M1 tanks to our front, about 500 meters away, pulling route security. As we started to slow down, I heard a muffled explosion. I looked back through my rear periscope and saw a large dirt cloud in the air. The cargo truck was veering off the road and came to a halt. I radioed the cargo truck but got no answer. I tried one more time, but still no answer.

Great, I just got the new guy killed on his first trip outside the wire, I thought.

I told my driver to pivot 180 degrees and head over to the vehicle. As we pulled up, I crawled through the turret, grabbed my weapon, and dismounted out the back of the Bradley, then ran over to the cab of the truck. To my relief, they were both still alive—rattled, but alive. The explosion had knocked them around and they'd lost their hearing, so they could not hear me calling them. The vehicle was still running but had a flat tire and other minor damage, so I decided to keep going to the COP and deliver our supplies. By the time we made it to the COP, the tire was shredded and smoking as we limped into the compound. SGT Mulligan survived his first IED blast on his first trip outside the wire. He was still dazed as he walked into the COP so I had the docs check him out and see if he had a concussion. Once he got checked out, I walked over to him and told him, "See, it wasn't as bad as you thought it was going to be, now was it?"

It did not take long for the Shadow and Thunder elements to get their first kills under Bone's moniker, and they slipped right into the rhythm of patrols, SKTs, and targeted raids. They were out conducting their own personal wars on the AIF in sector. They found their share of IEDs, insurgent hide positions, firing positions, and caches within their first few patrols. The ability to have multiple platoons in sector every day several times a day was really putting the hurt on the insurgents. We established a pretty effective routine in that, whenever the dismounted patrols were out, they were always supported by the mounted elements. With the long-range optics and night capabilities of the M1s and Bradleys, in conjunction with AWTs, the patrols could maneuver and push the enemy from their positions. When they fled, the tanks, Bradleys, or AWTs could kill them when the AIF tried to reposition. Or if the AIF decided to stay and fight it out with the infantry squads on the ground, the dismounted squads could call big brother and we could kill the AIF with whatever we had on hand, either a 120 HEAT round from the tanks, a TOW missile from the Bradleys, or a Hellfire from the Wolfpack Apaches—or maybe even a JDAM from the Air Force. JDAMs were extra scary because the enemy never heard anything before the goodness fell upon them. Silence ... then a massive explosion as the earth erupted and swallowed the target in a cloud of fire and dust. The words "proportionate response" are left for interpretation. When the AIF is blowing up houses on you and sending suicide bombers to blow themselves up, or cars filled with explosives to ram the walls of your outpost, what is a proportionate response?

From 1-5 May 2007, with Battle Company in southern Tahrir, Bone in northern Tahrir, and Attack in Old Baqubah, the AIF had plenty of pressure on them. However, they still managed to mount an aggressive counterattack of sorts. The IEDs they had planted over the past year were now being initiated as part of their well-conceived plan to repel any US or coalition forces from entering the city. Attack Company had taken a few hard hits with some deep-buried IEDs on their Strykers in Old Baqubah, and we had taken a few additional hits on our vehicles. We had so many downed vehicles between the M1s, Strykers, assorted route-clearance vehicles, and Bradleys that we kept our Bone recovery team and the M88 out at the COP. When vehicles got blown up to the point they were not drivable, we would flex our Bone QRF, which was typically the M1 tanks or Bradleys with a squad of infantry, and send them to the downed vehicle for recovery. The Strykers did not have their own recovery vehicle, so the M88 came in handy.

Then, on 6 May 2007, at 1115 hours ...

Quiiisssh ...

"Regular X-Ray, this is Attack 6. We just had an IED detonation on Attack 37, vicinity Trash Alley and Market. The vehicle is on fire. We have seven US KIA, one reporter KIA, and one US WIA. We are taking heavy machine-gun fire from a mosque northeast of our position. Request support at our location, over."

Regular 6 called and requested additional support into Attack 6's area, but we were already scrambling our forces. CPT Austin was already getting his crew ramped up and getting another Bradley from Blue platoon, along with a squad of dismounts, a medic, and the M88 recovery vehicle. Black 6 rolled out of COP Adam seventeen minutes later.

We had the Shadow element come in from another combat patrol, and they had three detainees, but we would put them on ice and get ready to roll up into Attack's sector if needed. Just as Black 6 and his element rolled into Attack's area, Bluewolf AWTs came on station and launched a few Hellfire missiles into the mosque that was being used by the insurgents to shoot up the Attack Company soldiers as they tried to get to their buddies. The Hellfire missiles and Bradleys quieted things down but they could do nothing for the flaming Stryker. We had nothing to extinguish the raging fire, now fed by the Stryker's tires, fuel, and ammunition. The only thing we could do was to wait.

As Attack and Bone pulled security around the IED blast site, they spotted several other suspected IEDs. Then they had a report of another IED attack at Checkpoint 451 on Route Vanessa. The Trailblazer element had been dispatched to Black 6's location and conducted two controlled detonations on the IEDs, clearing the area for recovery assets to start doing their job once the fiery vehicle burned itself out.

As Trail Blazer finished their mission on Market and Trash Alley, I called them down into our sector to link up with the Trouble element that had just found several more IEDs in Bone's sector. It seemed as if IEDs were just showing up at will. The insurgents clearly were flowing back into Old Baqubah and Tahrir to conduct offensive operations. Various skirmishes throughout the battalion's sector went on throughout the evening. The AIF fired multiple RPGs onto an Iraqi police checkpoint around 0200 hours on 7 May 2007, killing three Iraqi police and wounding another four. We received multiple reports of both suicide vehicles and personnel-targeting patrols in sector, and a main route had been temporarily placed in a "Black" status, not allowing traffic on it until cleared.

On 7 May 2007, with the temperature at 110-plus degrees, Shadow rotated out of sector with Thunder around 0800 hours in the morning. CPT Jensen planned a joint patrol with seven of his guys, seven IA soldiers, and one interpreter for later that afternoon. At the same time, Bone's second platoon, with their M1 tanks, would be out conducting mounted patrols throughout the day and setting in blocking positions to assist Battle Company in the south while they conducted small platoon-level operations.

At 1400 hours, as Thunder 6 and Thunder 3 departed COP Adam for their mission, Battle Company's second platoon got into a short firefight with two AIF, killing one AIF with an RPG while the other got away. Battle seized a donkey cart that the AIF were using to smuggle weapons into sector. It had five pounds of HME, seven AK-47 magazines, three blasting caps, and an RPG launcher hidden in its contents.

Thunder completed their daytime patrol and headed back to COP Adam around 1630 hours, followed by White platoon's tanks. With the exception of Battle Company's mission, the patrols went on without incident. As the day started to come to a close, third platoon set out for mounted patrol with a section of Bradleys. They left COP Adam at 1705 hours.

Five minutes later, a thunderous explosion shook the COP. We all knew instantly it was an IED targeting third platoon's patrol, which had just left the COP.

Quiiisssh ...

"COP Adam, this is Blue 2 (SSG Schaffer). We were just hit with an IED between B Avenue and C Avenue. No casualties but the vehicle is disabled. We will need to be recovered, over."

Upon hearing the detonation, CPT Jensen rallied his platoon to go assist with the recovery of the downed Bradley that was only a few hundred meters away from the COP. The Thunder element, along with CPT Austin, made it to the downed Bradley within minutes. As the patrol approached the vehicle, sniper fire erupted and CPT Jensen went down. His guys immediately started to fire in the direction of where the shots had come from, suppressing the area while a few other guys dragged the captain to safety near a vehicle then administered first aid. CPT Jensen had been shot in the neck and had to be evacuated immediately. CPT Austin called for QRF (third platoon's other section of Bradleys at COP Adam) to bring the medic and more dismounts to the IED blast site. Shortly after, third platoon's infantry squad and Alpha section of Bradleys arrived on the scene to evacuate CPT Jensen and reinforce security in the area.

CPT Austin told LT Pijpaert that once he dropped CPT Jensen at FOB Gabe, he was to go back to COP Adam and get as many IA soldiers and vehicles as he could muster. Together they could start to clear the area and to look for the shooters and trigger men that might still have been in the area prior to the recovery assets showing up. While LT Pijpaert conducted the casualty evacuation, the rest of the Thunder element and third platoon's infantry squads started to clear the buildings in the immediate area.

Once the AIF smelled blood, they would do everything in their abilities to capitalize on it if we were not aggressive enough to push them out of their hiding places and keep them off balance.

Trouble 1 element retraced the IED detonation wires and found the trigger house, then conducted some intelligence gathering to try and figure out how they were getting the IEDs in on our guys. LT Pijpaert made it back from FOB Gabe and gathered about forty IA soldiers and three IA HMMWVs to augment third platoon in their clearing of the sector. The entire element started to clear east, building by building. They headed in the direction of the small-arms fire toward an area that was a notorious hotspot for insurgent activity, located southeast of C Avenue and 41st Street. This area made it difficult to gain the element of surprise, and to make matters worse, the insurgents had planned a defense in-depth with many IEDs aimed at destroying not only vehicles but dismounted personnel as well. Previously, during the battalion-level mission, Battle Company had taken a high volume of small-arms and machine-gun fire from that area, and Bone had as well over the past few weeks. The AIF managed to select the perfect location, set on the farthest boundary of two US infantry companies in sector, so the AIF were able to slip in and out during our lapses in patrols.

As the large impromptu clearing mission pushed through the vacant houses and abandoned retail stores, they found several more suspected IED firing locations. The soldiers had pushed through these same buildings on several other occasions in the recent weeks, but each and every time, it seemed as if they found more indicators of new insurgent activity. Finally the exhausted squads from third platoon and the IA squads made it to the intersection of 41st and C Avenue and set up in the buildings, "strong pointed" within all four corners of the intersection. Confident that the insurgents had been cleared, CPT Austin called the XO, LT Boeka, who was staged at COP Adam, and requested that he come in with the M88 and start to recover SSG Schaffer's Bradley.

With the buildings cleared, the intersection secured, and company XO on the ground, CPT Austin headed back to FOB Warhorse with the remainder of the Thunder element. The plan from Regular X-Ray was to bring Thunder back and cut the Shadow element's recovery short and send them back into sector.

Around 2200 hours, while the recovery efforts continued, the White 3 tank threw its track while out patrolling with its wingman. The track was thrown to the point that it could not be fixed and an additional M88 recovery vehicle had to be requested. Upon hearing this, I coordinated another recovery vehicle and crew from 215th Forward Support Battalion to link up with CPT Austin and his Bradley section to head back out to Tahrir to recovery the D-33 tank.

The recovery was an all-night effort, and by the time Black 6 and Black 5 had recovered the vehicles and headed back to the FOB, it was 0320 hours in the morning. Once back at FOB Warhorse, CPT Austin and his crew were finally able to get an hour or so of sleep before they had to go back out to COP Adam with Shadow element.

The next day, on 8 May 2007 at 0800 hours, the entire company had been strung out for well over twenty-four hours. So it was necessary to consolidate and reorganize how we were doing business. With the Thunder element getting pulled to go back to FOB Warhorse, the Shadow element's recovery was getting cut short. With third platoon now having yet another Bradley down, and second platoon also having another M1 down, we needed to pause and make adjustments. The pause had to be quick, as the AIF in sector could not be given any slack. It was obvious by now that our battalion-clearing mission had not been as successful as we had initially thought and that Tahrir had become the focal point of the AIF forces. LT Pijpaert was getting ready to do another patrol in sector that afternoon, as well as the Shadow element and second platoon with their remaining section of tanks.

SSG Fili took out SGT Croley and the soldiers that had been attached to the White platoon, since they were not as familiar with the terrain or as fluent on the ground as the other squads. Fili felt like he could assist them by showing them the lay of the land while they did a joint IA and US patrol.

After the patrol left the COP, they headed south and crossed over 41st Street, where they made contact with the section of M1s that were over-watching their movement. LT Pijpaert headed south a few more blocks and then turned east to head toward our southeastern boundary, where we continuously received fire. As the patrol crossed over 41st Street, they identified a building that had fresh anti-American graffiti on it, so they went into the compound to talk to the owner and check out the house. As the IA soldiers pulled security on the outside of the building, to the south they saw four AIF, with weapons, get into a white car and head east. They excitedly told LT Pijpaert's interpreter and he relayed the information. LT Pijpaert looked up over the small compound wall to see if he could spy anything. Not being able to indentify anything out of the ordinary, he turned to organize the squad for the next leg of their patrol.

Buuurp! Snap, snap, snap, snap!

A hail of accurate machine-gun fire erupted and impacted in the courtyard and against the walls of the compound. SSG Fili ID'd the three-story building that the fire was coming from and quickly had his squad return fire with the machine guns, an M203 grenade launcher, and their rifles. As SSG Fili's and SGT Croley's guys returned fire, LT Pijpaert called the White 6 tank (newly arrived 2LT Green) to move his tank section over to support and suppress the enemy building. Once the tank pulled into sight, the AIF machine-gun fire ceased.

LT Pijpaert and SSG Fili quickly came up with a plan to close in on the building. They did not want to attack directly from the direction they had just come, so the decision was made to do a bold flanking movement and loop around from the northeast down an alleyway until they could see the enemy building. So they briefed

Doc Nguyen and PFC Rivera, Davis, and Russell, and tried to tell the IA soldiers what was going on. Then they filed out from behind the compound walls and headed north. At the intersection, they took turns cutting the corner and heading east. The squad members remained staggered on each side of the road, and spread out, in case someone lobbed a grenade over a wall or an RPG was fired—then it would not take out more than one person. The plan was to use speed in the movement to flank the enemy before they had time to flee. The squad was to consciously move east in a traveling over-watch and then transition into a bounding over-watch as they headed south and made contact with the enemy. Just as the last IA soldier turned the corner to head east, all hell broke loose.

Burp! Burp!

Four insurgents came charging out from around a corner, firing their AK-47s at point-blank range straight down the alley full of US and IA soldiers. SGT Croley, Davis, and Rivera and an IA soldier went down immediately from the initial firestorm of bullets. Then an AIF heavy machine gun opened up from a rooftop down onto the alley as LT Pijpaert and Doc Nguyen attempted to run out into the open and drag Rivera and another wounded man back into one of the compounds that lined the street. But the fire was too accurate and intense, so Doc and LT Pijpaert turned and busted down a gate then fell into the compound. LT Pijpaert turned around—but Doc was not there. He looked out the gate down the alley, and only a few feet from the gate, Doc was hunched over, slumped against the wall, with a pool of blood next to him. LT Pijpaert yelled, but it was obvious that Doc was dead. SSG Fili yelled out that he and the wounded PFC Davis were in a walled compound diagonal from the LT's location across the alley. Lt Pijpaert gave him a situation report: Doc and Croley were dead, and PFC Rivera was still alive but out in the open. As LT Pijpaert was giving the SITREP, Rivera yelled "FRAGOUT!" and tossed a grenade over the cement compound wall—the wall being part of the house being used to support the AIF machine gun on the rooftop.

As LT Pijpaert assessed the situation, he felt a sharp pain in his chest. Realizing that he had been wounded, he slipped his hand inside his body armor to feel for a bullet hole and to look for blood, but he found neither. Not worrying about it, LT Pijpaert coordinated with SSG Fili to get a solid grid coordinate and a situation report so they could get help to their location. They knew White 6 and the Shadow element were nearby. They knew they had two US KIA, two IA KIA, and four US WIA, but they did not know where the other IA soldiers were, or the interpreter. LT Pijpaert called up the initial report to COP Adam, but the Shadow element was already marching to the sound of the guns and heading in their direction. The tank section was not sure of LT Pijpaert's location, so he had to talk them to it. The tanks made it there first and the Shadow element with Bone 6 showed up shortly after.

The Shadow element and CPT Austin, with his security element, had basically sprinted the eight city blocks from the COP to the location where LT Pijpaert and SSG Fili were. As SFC Hunsecker and his guys turned the corner into the narrow street, nothing could have prepared them for what they saw. Bodies lay everywhere, some motionless and others on their backs in awkward positions with their weapons at the ready, as blood flowed freely out of their bodies and into the streets.

SFC Hunsecker, along with CPT Austin's security element, set up security and called in a more accurate situation report, then called the Stryker vehicles onto their location to help evacuate the wounded. The Shadow medic and a few other guys started treating the wounded and stabilizing the casualties for transport. As they moved to check the soldiers, they were surprised to see that SGT Croley was not dead, but he certainly had been wounded the worst. Initial reports had him being shot six times. Then came LT Pijpaert, who was indeed injured. His upper chest wound was serious but it was hard to tell how serious while on the ground, so he was treated as critical and a litter-urgent along with SGT Croley, who we realized might not make it. Everyone else, with the exception of SSG Fili, had been shot at least once in various parts of their bodies, but none seriously life threatening. The entire triage process took about thirty minutes before they could get all the soldiers loaded and en route to the helipad on FOB Gabe.

Once the wounded were loaded and en route to FOB Gabe, the majority of Shadow element stayed on the ground to hunt down the ambushers. As they hunted for the AIF, they found no blood trails or other indications that any of the ambushers had been wounded or killed. As the Shadow element was assessing the situation, Battle Company was alerted to our south to assist Bone in tracking down the ones responsible. Bone already had every person they could spare on the ground, which wasn't that many because of the previous day's fighting. Regular 6 was on the radio, and he was massing every available soldier in the sector with the task of finding who was responsible and making them pay. They were not just going to ambush a squad and not have the entire might of the task force hunting them down. As the day slipped to night, the hopes of finding the ambushers were fading as fast as the sun was setting. Unfortunately we would not find the ones who were responsible for the ambush immediately but we would persevere in the months to come.

That evening, SSG Fili and I jumped on a Blackhawk with COL Sutherland and CSM Felt to fly to Balad Airbase and check on all the wounded. Everyone was still there when we arrived. SGT Croley was stable but sedated and unconscious, awaiting transport to Germany. LT Pijpaert was as high as a kite and barely conscious. PFCs Russell and Rivera were both awake and in good spirits, just happy to be alive. PFC Davis was back at FOB Warhorse, as he had been able to be treated locally. I walked through with SSG Fili and we talked to the guys. There was no need to tell them about SPC Nguyen. They had already known he'd died before they left the street that day. SGT Croley and PFC Rivera would end up getting sent to Germany and eventually back to Texas at Brook Army Medical Center. LT Pijpaert and PFC Russell would eventually make it back to FOB Warhorse.

The time up at Balad Airbase was short but reassuring. It helped SGT Fili and me to see that the guys were, for the most part, going to be okay, considering what they had just experienced. It was good to return back to FOB Warhorse with some good news. It was surely needed after the past two to three days. With the exception of SGT Croley, who was busted up pretty good, I was hopeful that they would all recover from their physical wounds rather quickly—maybe not 100 percent but to a point that was acceptable for them to lead productive lives again.

Doc had truly been loved by the entire third platoon. Just knowing he was out on a mission gave everyone a sense of confidence to go into harm's way, understanding that if they got wounded, they'd be taken care of by the best the Army had to offer. RIP Doc ...

CPL Dan H. Nguyen, Killed in Action, 8 May 2007, Tahrir, Iraq

CHAPTER 13

BATTLE DAMAGED

10 MAY 2007: THOUGH the Tahrir offensive was immediately deemed a success, with the past week's events, it was glaringly obvious we collectively failed in our mission to keep the city clear of insurgents. We anticipated that the AIF would infiltrate back into sector but grossly underestimated the extent to which they did. The main reason for the influx of AIF back into sector was that the city had not been sealed off nor was the flow of traffic in and out controlled. The reasoning behind leaving the city open and not sealing it off was to avoid stemming the flow of traffic. Plus we (not me or anyone in the ground fight in Diyala Province) wanted the general public to be able to resume their lives as quickly as possible without putting massive restrictions on vehicle traffic and foot traffic, which in theory would inflame the civilian population and breed resentment against the US presence within their city. However, the only ones who really took advantage of the open streets were the AIF.

After a short discussion with Regular 6 and 3, it was decided that we would seal off the entire city and make only one way in and one way out. We would block every single entrance into the city with cement barriers, mounds of dirt, and whatever else it took to seal it off. The checkpoints would be manned by IA and IP forces, and supported by Task Force Bone. The innocent population would just have to deal with the inconveniences and restrictions that were about to be placed on them, including a curfew that forbade anyone on the streets after nightfall.

With LT Pijpaert wounded and no estimated time of his return, it was decided that LT Boeka would go back down to the line and take over as the platoon leader for third platoon. We needed a PL more than we needed a company XO.

The entry and departure control points in Tahrir would be a primary target for suicide bombers, either on foot or in vehicles, so they had to be constructed smartly and manned even smarter. Third platoon was tasked with the job of implementing the barrier operations and sealing off the city, as well as the initial construction of the entrance control point (ECP) with the help of the IA/IP, while White was mainly pulling QRF and route security. The Shadow element and third platoon's squads ran the daily patrols within the city around the clock. The temperatures consistently reached into the triple digits, which in turn had a major effect on how we conducted our patrols. During the peak temperature times of 1100-1500 hours, the temperatures could reach as high as 120 degrees, and average civilians would stay inside their thick-walled cement houses and wait for it to cool off before conducting the rest of their daily business. However, if we did not send patrols out during the hottest times of the day, it would only be a matter of time before the insurgents keyed in on it, giving them the green light to conduct their missions. They had the luxury of wearing civilian clothing and blending into their surroundings, doing their surveillance from the confines of air-conditioned cars or buildings of their choosing.

The average US soldier carries a hundred pounds (conservative estimate) of mission-essential equipment on each patrol and is in constant threat of dehydration during triple-digit temperatures. One man can easily consume three quarts of water on a two-hour dismounted patrol. We also had the armored vehicles out 24/7, and those crewmen had to be careful of dehydration as well.

Being a crew member inside an armored vehicle, either a tank or Bradley, took a special kind of conditioning and mentality. The vehicle was considered your weapon and you could not leave it unless it was on fire. You basically lived in it at ALL times and considered it the crew's life-support system while out in sector. It was the firepower, resupply vehicle, casualty evacuation vehicle, and detainee transport, among hundreds of other things. The insurgents feared the Bradley more than the M1 Abrams. When they saw the Bradleys, the insurgents knew the infantry squads were around somewhere hunting them, while also protecting the Bradley. The Bradleys and M1s had their place on the battlefield and we would not leave them parked just because it was hot. For the armor crews, temperatures could easily reach 130 degrees inside, with no breeze and no escape from the additional heat generated from the diesel engine and electrical equipment. And they would be locked inside the vehicle for hours if not days on end. It took a special character and mind-set to be a crew member.

The Thunder element had not come back to B Company and they were going to stay under 5-20's control for future operations in New Baqubah, and the other smaller towns in A Co 1-12's side. At best, B Company had three squads to keep continuous pressure on the AIF in sector while the other two squads pulled force protection and rested. The average squad would pull a minimum of two patrols a day, lasting an average of three to four hours and a rotation on QRF. We would not maintain this schedule for long without driving our equipment and soldiers straight into the ground if things did not change. We were barely keeping our heads above water in reference to the Bradleys and M1s. We'd already begged and borrowed every extra Bradley and M1 tank that could be spared. To make our Bradley situation even worse, it was decided that we would have to take one to two Bradleys up to Balad Airbase over a five- to seven-day period and have underbelly armor installed. Evidently the deep-buried IEDs had gotten the attention of the Bradley folks and they came up with additional armor to protect against the DBIEDs. My Bradley didn't last long, and I gave it up to replace SSG Schaffer's Bradley, which was the most recent casualty.

LT Boeka and the rest of third platoon had the city sealed off within a couple of evenings. Now, with the city sealed off to random vehicle traffic entering and leaving at will, we were able to focus our energy on specifically targeted areas that we anticipated the AIF to infiltrate and exfiltrate on foot. Within twenty-four hours, we knew the barriers were working. There had been several attempts by the AIF to remove the heavy cement barriers in two locations. The AIF had managed to move several on the north side of C Avenue, but not to a point where they could get vehicles in and out. We figured we'd struck a nerve if they were going through that much effort to move the barriers. Within two days, we noticed a significant decrease in random enemy fire, as the insurgents had to be more selective with the way they planned their attacks and escape. It would not take long for them to adjust.

With the city effectively blocked off, CPT Austin started planning a mission to go back into the southeast boundary area and clear it out and deny the AIF that area as a safe zone. The mission was going to be a company-level mission and it was planned to last a solid twenty-four hours, as it would be a deliberate search-and-destroy mission/movement to contact. The good news was that we would get our first platoon back from Zaganiya in a seventy-two-hour period. First platoon would go to FOB Warhorse, conduct a forty-eight-hour refit, and head straight out to COP Adam to pick up where they had left off.

CPT Austin planned the mission for 18 May 2007. That would allow first platoon to get into sector, get familiar with the area again, and also get used to working with the Shadow element. Additionally it would desensitize the AIF in sector with the sudden increase of even more Bradleys.

It was nice to have first platoon under our control again, and they were glad to be back. The COP was starting to feel more like a home than FOB Warhorse. We had the TV room hooked up, with a sofa and some random mismatched chairs that looked like they came straight from the late '60s and early '70s. I was able to score some exercise equipment, as well, including a flat bench and an assortment of mismatched weights. CrossFit served as the main Bonecrusher physical training plan, so with a few weights and some imagination, we were able to get in a good workout. We had a homemade two-stall shower that the battalion welders rigged up for us, and I even got a barber shop going in the COP. With the increase of soldiers on FOB Warhorse, everything was crowded and I did not want our soldiers wasting two hours of their precious time back in the rear trying to get a haircut. So I went to SSG Morales and signed for a WWII barber's kit that we had been dragging around since Kuwait. It wasn't much, but it had clippers and scissors, and that was all we needed. My Iraqi first sergeant counterpart told me he had a guy that could cut hair and he introduced me to him. After we met, I had him do a sample cut on me and figured if he didn't slice my throat or scalp me, I would make him our company barber. It worked out pretty good. My soldiers got cheap, good haircuts, and saved some time getting it done out at the COP—and the Iraqi soldier made a few dollars, which I am sure his 1SG got a kick back on. Win-win for everyone.

Running the COP was like being the mayor of my own little city. I had to worry about security, sewage (burning the poop), water for hygiene, water to drink, entertainment, mail, laundry, safety (electrical nightmare as everything runs on 220 volts and nothing is even close to the standards of the US), and trash. Trash was the biggest issue when it came to my slum village with the Iraq soldiers and our guys. It was a never-ending struggle to keep the place from overflowing. We initially started to burn it, but I had health concerns about the fumes. Then we also started getting rats. Not all the trash would burn, so it began to pile up day after day, and eventually started to get out of control. The fix for the trash was to use a few of the hundreds of connexes we had on FOB

Warhorse to put the trash in. We would leave it on the PLS skid, and once it was full, we would get a soldier cross-trained on the PLS truck, and when they rotated out for refit, the platoon would tow it out to the dump on FOB Warhorse. Each platoon would bring in an empty one and haul out a full one. It was just another dirty job for the grunts.

With first platoon coming out, that meant we would send back the Shadow element for refit while we had all our original 1-12 platoons in one location since the change-of-command ceremony. Once first platoon went out in sector, it didn't take long for them to get a welcome call from the AIF.

Quiiisssh ...

"COP Adam, this is Red 1. We just got hit with an IED on 41st Avenue, approximately 100 meters west of B Avenue. The vehicle is on fire and we are evacuating, out."

Not waiting for a response, the crew abandoned the vehicle and ran to the safety of their wingman's track. With a first-platoon Bradley now destroyed and on fire, the other section of Bradleys departed COP Adam in record time to help secure the site. Once they arrived on the scene, the Bradley had fortunately burned itself out, but it was a total loss. The heavy-armored engine deck was thirty to forty feet away from the Bradley. The actual side armor of the Bradley had been blown off, with reactive tiles scattered all about. It was missing two sets of road wheels, and the engine and transmission had been blown from the mounts.

SFC Lane attempted to self-recover the vehicle and drag it back to COP Adam, but with the engine and transmission blown, it jammed the final drives to the point that it was like dragging thirty-plus tons of dead weight. SFC Hudgins, the new tank platoon sergeant, took a section out and successfully pulled it with the tank's turbine engines.

By that point, the number of vehicles we'd lost in sector had reached eleven or twelve Bradleys out of the eleven we had in the company (minus the four that were with D Co) plus replacements, and we had lost two of the four M1 Abrams. We lost a slew of wheeled vehicles that were not even going on mission anymore due to the fact that the IEDs that were going off would completely vaporize a HMMWV. The Strykers were a little better off, but we left them parked unless it was an absolute emergency. The risk of having the Bradleys out in sector was far outweighed by the benefit of the protection they provided the infantry squads when they needed them, which was significant. The amount of ground they could cover, either by physically patrolling or via their optics, was essential to keeping eyes on all the routes. It was a must to have them in sector patrolling 24/7; we had no other options.

The frustrating part was the amount and size of the IEDs, and the way they had been emplaced. These weren't little "pop and drops" that they could do a walk-by on and drop in a hole. These were hundreds of pounds' worth of homemade explosives buried under sidewalks, in sections of curbs, and under blacktop. The amount of preparation had to have been incredible and sophisticated, and the job must have been done over a series of months, if not years. The AIF were detonating massive DBIEDs on routes that vehicles had driven on for weeks and months without incident. But just when we thought the route had been cleared, another one would go off. C Avenue and 41st were by far our worst roads, and we had conducted several route-clearance missions on both routes, including dismounted patrols (not the preferred technique) scouting for IEDs and firing positions. Yet the AIF were still able to detonate them on our patrols on those roads.

CPT Austin received word that we would be taking over the entire city of Tahrir in a week in order to free Battle Company to go into New Baqubah and help with the clearance over in Apache's area of operation. To accomplish this, we would be getting another two platoons attached to our company. The platoons would be light infantry from the 25th Infantry Division. The intent was to augment them with the IA forces and have them responsible for the southern sector since it was not as hot as our sector in the north portion of Tahrir. Between two platoons of infantry and the IA, they had plenty of people to be effective in the southern sector.

Having control of the southern sector meant we could coordinate the daily patrols to mutually support each other more effectively. We were going to truly be a combined-arms fighting unit. We had M1 tanks, Bradleys, Strykers, light infantry, our Wolfpack attack helicopters, our own internal mortars and counter-radar, and finally an excellent relationship with the local ODA (Special Forces unit). What an exciting package of lethality we had under one company (I get excited just typing it)!

The brigade task force and all the surge troops were completely on the ground in the Diyala Province, and COL Townsend, the brigade commander for 3SBCT 2nd ID, and LTC Antonia set their sights on New Baqubah as their next target of the counter-insurgency fight. It was their plan to reinforce Task Force Bone with the additional two platoons and turn us loose on Tahrir. They also gave us the additional task of disrupting enemy activities in the Old Baqubah sector while Attack and Battle Companies flexed over to the western side of the Diyala River into Apache's area of operation and joined forces with 1-23 Infantry to clear not only New Baqubah, but also Majima, Katoon, and Mufrek. All four cities connected and were a significant piece of terrain in the counter-insurgency fight that would take weeks to clear from the grip of the AIF.

We set the date for 18 May 2007 for the search-and-destroy/movement-to-contact mission. We would have all platoons on hand and would be able to flood the area with every infantry soldier we could get on the ground. The Bradleys would advance into position to secure key intersections and terrain to support the infantry squads as they moved through the fortified areas and started to clear the area one building at a time. The fighting was going to be up close and personal, and with so many troops in such a confined area within the city, it would be absolutely essential that we conduct several different joint rehearsals and allow the platoons time to do their rehearsals at platoon and squad level. So long as everyone knew their jobs and who was on the left, right, front, and rear of them, they stood a good chance of being quick on the draw when needed and had a better chance of avoiding fratricide. Urban fighting and extensive planning to build situational awareness go hand in hand.

The concept of the operation was for our second platoon, with the M1s, and the third-platoon Bradleys to set an outer cordon on the western, northern, and eastern sides of the city to kill anyone trying to flee or coming in to reinforce the AIF within the city. Battle Company would do the same in the south, and we would have the AWTs on station providing us the aerial observation and fire support as needed. We would also insert our 1-12 sniper teams in various positions within the city to over-watch specific areas of interest and be our local eyes and ears. Once the outer cordon was set, we would conduct a bounding over-watch through the built-up areas as the platoons and squads alternated securing footholds in key buildings. Once the buildings were secure, we would bring the Bradleys in to secure that area and support the infantry on the ground as they moved to their next objective. All the infantry squads would be augmented with three to four IA soldiers. Back at COP Adam, we would also have a contingent/reserve force of third platoon's infantry squads to assist with QRF, casualty evacuation, and reinforcement of a platoon if need be. The mission would start in the early morning, and we would push south from COP Adam and then clear east on 41st Street until we crossed over C Avenue. Then we would start to push into the area where LT Pijpaert and SSG Fili had been ambushed, and then move into the heart of the AIF area near our most southeastern border.

On 18 May 2007 at 0240 hours, the Shadow element left first, with CPT Austin and his element moving with them to establish the initial foothold. First platoon left shortly after that, and they, too, were broken down into two separate maneuver elements, one led by LT Branford and the other by SFC Lane. We had roughly sixty to seventy soldiers on the ground maneuvering and ready to slug it out with the AIF.

Almost immediately, the infantry squads that had just left the COP Adam compound started calling in reports of gunshots and explosions from our OPs and Battle Company in the south. Regular X-Ray was sending intelligence reports picked up by the UAVs, stating that several individuals were running from rooftop to rooftop with weapons, around C Avenue and 41st. Our sniper sections reported several unarmed but suspicious personnel roaming around their areas while observing main roads. The AIF apparently had their scouts out and were ready for a fight.

At 0534 hours, Shadow element captured two AIF with several explosive boosters for RPGs and command wire that was ready to hook up to an IED. It was typical to catch AIF with bits and pieces of an item. It did not incriminate them as badly, and they could stash weapons all over the city so they could maneuver without making themselves a target. Shadow tagged these guys and sent a small team with the detainees back to COP Adam to be processed.

As the platoons moved through their respective areas, they would call up their checkpoints and phase lines to the RTO back at the COP and they would in turn write the situation updates into the logbooks.

0610 hours: Battle Company reported their third platoon was in contact.

0720 hours: Battle Company in contact.

0721 hours: First platoon took small-arms fire from a building southeast of the intersection of 41st and C Avenue.

Red 1 and Red 2 Bradleys were called forward to support the dismounts and engage the building that contained the AIF. The Bradleys pulled forward, their engines whining and their tracks popping as they positioned themselves for their engagement. A short pause ensued, then the 25mm cannon started spitting fire from the muzzles, punching holes in the building and spraying cement shrapnel throughout the confined rooms.

0749 hours: The Alpha section of first platoon's Bradleys made quick work out of the building, and the first platoon dismounts went in to clear it of any remaining AIF that foolishly decided to stay.

Shadow element crossed over 41st and C Avenue and was

going to strong-point their squads until first platoon cleared their buildings and bounded across C Avenue. Everything was going as planned, and the Bradleys were pulling into position to support the infantry squads for their next move.

At 0805 hours, a massive explosion rocked COP Adam. It came from the direction of the dismounts. Immediately every radio from every OP started calling in reports. Fearing another rigged house explosion, I called Bone 6 and asked for a SITREP, but got no answer. That immediately concerned me because SPC Cabreja was CPT Austin's RTO and never missed a radio call. Plus CPT Austin carried his own radio, and neither he nor Cabreja had answered. Then Red 9 (SFC Lane) called and told me they had one Bradley destroyed and three KIA. I paused for a few seconds, trying to absorb what I just heard.

Then I keyed the hand mic and said, "Are you sure there are three KIA. There is no chance they got blown out of the vehicle?"

"First Sergeant," SFC Lane said, "there is no way anyone survived that explosion. It engulfed the entire vehicle and vaporized it."

After hearing that report, I again paused and gathered my thoughts.

"What vehicle was it?" I asked.

"It was the Red 1 Victor, over."

Damn, I thought. That vehicle had carried SGT Martinez, SPC Nash, and SPC Romero. I remained composed and reminded myself how important it was to be the calm voice of reason on the radio. I was detached from the scene, and I was the person that could give the clear guidance to Red 9 until Black 6 made it to their location.

I told them to first secure the blast sight, and not to put anyone out in the open until we could adjust the plan. We didn't want to fall into a trap with additional IEDs going off or snipers picking off soldiers as they tried to recover the bodies of their fallen brothers. Shortly after giving the initial guidance, Bone 6 came back up on the net, out of breath but on the radio. He had run the entire way back to link up with Red 6 and 9. Once there, they organized and gave me an additional report on what we needed for recovery. I was told by Black 6 that we needed an M88 recovery vehicle, a lowboy trailer, and three cargo trucks with a crane to put all the vehicles parts in it. We were determined to pick up every single piece of that Bradley so that none of it would end up on CNN or Al Jazeera as propaganda.

I relayed the traffic to Bone main, and they started the process of gathering the resources to come out with QRF from battalion. Regular X-Ray and Attack Company both monitored the radio traffic when it was called up, and so did Grim Magic (a Special Forces unit). Attack Company came down form Old Baqubah to link up with CPT Austin and pick up the fight for first platoon so they could stay and secure the blast site and work the recovery mission, while CPT Austin continued the fight. The last thing we wanted to do was stop our momentum. We were going to clear that area, and nothing was going to stop us. The emotion of losing three of our soldiers would be tucked away and dealt with at a later time and date. Right then, we had a mission that needed to be accomplished.

As Attack Company linked up with Black 6, a ten-round burst of 25mm erupted. Red 2 engaged and killed two AIF with weapons inside a building. The AIF were trying to maneuver to attack our squads. That was Black 6 and Attack 36's cue to move out and continue mission. LT Branford and SFC Lane were more than capable of handling the recovery. SFC Lane called up and gave an update. They had recovered two of the soldiers that were still inside the turret, which was completely separated from the Bradley and blown forty feet away. The turret was on fire so they had to wait for the flames to burn themselves out. The Bradley was completely destroyed, with the engine blown out of it, the tracks and road wheels completely blown off and separated, the ramp gone, the thick steel floor peeled back like a tuna can, and the side armor and reactive armor tossed about the blast site like confetti. The blast crater was so large that a six-foot-tall man could stand in it and not be seen from ground level. The circumference of the blast hole was large enough to swallow a full-sized SUV. It was by far the worst IED I had ever seen or heard of. Destruction of that magnitude could not be described or comprehended without seeing it in person.

After about forty-five minutes of searching, they found the body of SPC Romero. It lay forty feet or so from the blast site. Now we had accountability of all the soldiers. Third platoon pulled down to assist with the evacuation of the soldiers back to the COP. SGT Wall pulled his Bradley down and placed them in the rear. Soon enough, I met him outside as his Bradley pulled in and we unloaded them into the parking area of the COP. SGT Wall and I made eye contact, and we didn't need to say a word to each other. We were both feeling the pain but we had a mission to do, so he loaded up, raised his ramp, and went back out. Again, what do you say to each other when you just had three soldiers killed?

SSG Anselmo Martinez III, Killed in Action, 18 May 2007,
Tahrir, Iraq
SGT Casey Nash, Killed in Action, 18 May 2007,
Tahrir, Iraq
CPL Joshua Romero, Killed in Action, 18 May 2007,
Tahrir, Iraq

CPT Austin with Attack 36 and Shadow element continued to clear the area. They found a car in which the backseat was covered in blood with an empty ammo can it. The car was parked outside a house that they thought was rigged with explosives, and shortly after that, they found a suspected IED: a command wire running into a pile of trash on the side of the road. With a suspected HBIED and surface-laid IED, they decided to have the Sapper 16 element come out from the 5-20 and blow at least the surface IED. Sapper 16 confirmed it was an IED and quickly conducted a controlled detonation. The house was noted and would be dealt with at a later time (JDAM through the roof).

1500 hours: By this time, Regular 6 and Regular 7 showed up

at the COP to see if there was anything they could do or help out with. We had everything under control, as we always did, and I think they knew it, but they wanted to be there in person to support us. The Special Forces team showed up at the COP too. They pushed into sector and helped gather some intelligence with their sources and scouts. The recovery of the Bradley was going to take hours. The Bradley parts were too heavy to load by hand, so the soldiers had to use the crane on the cargo trucks and the M88 recovery vehicle to pick up all the pieces and load them. By the time I was given the thumbs-up on the recovery mission and its completion, there was not so much as a water bottle lying on the ground at the site of the explosion. The only thing left was the empty crater. Soldiers are amazing!

The rest of the search-and-destroy mission went slowly and methodically, house by house, room by room, street by street. The platoons were at it for fifteen hours straight in 100-degree temperatures. They would move, strong-point, and rest. Then, if need be, we would push Bradleys to their location to drop off ice, water, and additional IVs and MREs (meals ready to eat). When conducting these types of missions in the extreme heat of the day, it was a challenge to balance out what you had to carry and what we could supply while midstride in the operation. We did not want to weigh the soldiers down with items we could easily bring to them when needed. We had become experts on indentifying the symptoms of being a heat casualty and also administering IVs.

Once we identified someone was going to be a heat casualty, we would find a suitable house, invite ourselves in, gather the family, if there was one, and explain to them our situation, then we would start administering buddy aid. We would strip the soldier down, give him some water, hook an IV up, and pump the fluids into his veins. Once the soldier felt good enough to continue mission (Charlie Mike), we would gather our medical waste, pay the family a few bucks for their inconvenience, and head out to finish the mission. When behind closed doors and hidden from the watchful eye of the insurgents, most local families would cater to us with

Chai tea, water, or bread and then grudgingly would take the money we offered. The money we had while out on patrols was a nice option to have. All the key leaders would carry $100 or so, for "incidentals" or "business expenses." It was a great way to pay people for things we might have torn up in the process of our job, and it streamlined the claims process and eliminated the "claims form" for small incidents.

As the sun slowly slipped behind the palm groves off to our west, the COP became a flurry of activity, with each squad trickling in from their mission on the verge of heat exhaustion. Once the infantry squads were in, we collapsed our outer cordon, and the vehicles came into the compound. I sought out SFC Lane, just to have a talk with him and find out his mental state. To my relief, he was okay, and being out there taking care of the business probably had helped him. He was fine, with the exception of a major gash on his face, caused when he had tripped and the butt of his weapon cut him clean open to the point he was going to need stitches, but it had all crusted over throughout the day, so they would have to reopen the wound to clean it and then hopefully sew it up. The bad thing about having a scar like that on his face is that every time he looks in the mirror and sees the scar, it would remind him of the tragic day he lost three of the finest soldiers the Army had to offer.

That evening was the hero flight. I rode back to FOB Warhorse with first platoon to help take care of business. I was totally numb to the hero flights by that point. I had no more feelings or emotions. It was part of the job God had selected me for. I still thought about the families and the hurt they were going to feel. SGT Ansalmo Martinez and SPC Joshua Romero were both husbands and dads that were leaving this world way too early and leaving plenty of things undone. SPC Casey Nash was a man's man. He was a field-artillery soldier who excelled at everything he did. He did not have to be in that Bradley that day, but he wanted to be. He wanted to be part of the team and contribute to the fight. Not that it made up for anything, but these guys went out with guns blazing. They had just gotten finished engaging two insurgents that were firing on the infantry squads just moments before their Bradley was destroyed.

With the help of third platoon Attack Company and Battle Company in the south, Task Force Bone accomplished their mission and finally entered and destroyed the AIF safe havens within sector. Three AIF were confirmed killed, two AIF were captured, and several small caches were found and destroyed. One surface-laid IED was found and destroyed, and one house-borne IED was found and marked for destruction at a later date. We also found the trigger house that was used to detonate the IED on the Red 1 crew. It gave us a better inside look into the way they were adjusting to our techniques. The AIF knocked several small peep holes in the apron around the roof to look through instead of peeking over the top. They built observation posts on roofs that had overhead cover, which could shield them from the eyes of our UAVs and the Wolfpack's thermal imagery. They had target reference points written on the walls to let other fighters know where the aiming device was for the IED. The AIF even had silhouettes of soldiers cut out of corrugated steel so that they had something for practicing their marksmanship skills. It was not surprising in the least. We knew we were fighting a smart foe that took their job seriously and treated it as we did: killing is both a science and an art. The insurgents had home-field advantage and continuity within sector that gave them an edge. We would change out every year, and all the knowledge and friendships that were generated over that year's period would be lost—and the next unit would start all over again. Though we did a changeover and tried our best to gain knowledge and maintain some sort of continuity, it was not as effective as we wanted.

With the troop surge and extensions on our tours, we were given the most valuable resources we needed: time and troops. We were going to finish the fight the right way. The AIF's days were numbered in our sector. The constant pressure we were able to put on them day after day was starting to take its toll. Nowhere in

Tahrir or Buhritz was safe for them, and they were slowly getting squeezed from every angle, which was causing them to fight even harder. The one thing they still had going for them was that they had the local population intimidated and unwilling to cooperate with US and IA forces. The only way we were going to get the support of the locals was to exterminate the hardcore al-Qaeda in sector. Then, once we gained the confidence and support of the local population, we could begin to turn the corner to achieving our objectives.

With the search-and-destroy mission complete, TF Bone assumed responsibility for the entire city of Tahrir with two COPs: COP Adam and Bone Zulu. The Old Baqubah COP had not been named yet. The Attack and Battle Companies of 5-20 IN were on their way to the west side to help 1-23 IN and CPT Morris with Apache Company. Attack Company had left a COP up in the north-central portion of Old Baqubah in the hands of Team Bone, and our initial plan was to hold it with a platoon and support it from COP Adam. The new COP was initially named Bone Zulu, but would eventually be called COP Romeo.

Within a week of being up there, we were running into many logistical issues that were not going to be fixed with brute force. Trying to support three COPs with enough equipment was starting to strain the system, and it was not going to get better. The biggest issue we ran into right from the beginning of maintaining all three COPs was the communications equipment. Running long-distant and effective communications from a fixed site was not as easy as parking a vehicle in a field and having someone monitor the radios. When you run an outpost, there needs to be a command post, and within the command post, you have to have at least two radios, preferably three: one on company net, one on battalion net, and another one so if you have to bump to an administrative or logistical NET, you can do so without losing communications with the main networks. In addition to just the radios to run a command post, you also needed generators, power converters, and a plethora of other odds and ends of communications equipment, including antennas.

The other companies took all their equipment with them so we were in a bit of a bind. Our company communications guru, CPL Pester, worked some miracles and was able to get communications but it was limited. The communications equipment was just the beginning of our struggle in maintaining three COPs spread throughout two cities with only six platoons. We did not let it slow us down too much. Hell, we were still better off than we had been a few months ago.

The COP down in the south was mainly manned by the two platoons from the 25th. One went by the call sign "Gun Dog" and the other by "Spartan." These elements were augmented with IA soldiers. Meanwhile our original two infantry platoons plus Shadow rotated between COP Adam and Bone Zulu.

It did not take long before we were fighting the AIF in Old Baqubah (OB). Attack Company was battling it out relentlessly with the AIF the entire time they were up in Old Baqubah. Just as they were making some good progress, they were pushed over to the west side of the river to assist with the major clearance operation of New Baqubah and the outlying towns. Intelligence reports indicated that AIF had some extensive logistical cells and training camps north of OB, and also indicated that there were several areas within OB that the AIF used consistently as staging areas to launch attacks on MSR Vanessa and into Tahrir. The fighters would then go back to their safe areas north of OB. However, the COP was standing in the middle of their exfil route.

The location of Bone Zulu was less than perfect, and both CPT Austin and I were concerned. It sat in a strategically valuable area, but it was right on top of everything within the city, thus lacking standoff from the surrounding buildings and alleyways. The location also didn't allow for us to deploy our forces effectively before they were in a high-threat area. OB's inner city was much more built up than Tahrir and had extensive alley and side-road networks that facilitated the AIF to using a maze to elude pursuing US forces. The AIF took full advantage of the absence of an entire Stryker company and commenced their attacks on B Co 1-12 before we could even get our first major platoon operation kicked off in OB. While first platoon's Alpha section was doing a mounted patrol in OB, the AIF managed to detonate a surface-laid IED on Red 2's Bradley, disabling it from moving. However, our guys could still shoot and communicate, and the wingman remained next to them for protection.

We got the call at COP Adam that Red 2 was disabled with no casualties, but in need of recovery. I just so happened to get another Bradley the day prior, and I had my crew out at COP Adam, so my crew and SFC Lane and his crew, with a handful of infantry guys and Doc Devries, mounted up to go recover Red 2's Bradley.

We left and headed up a main street on the west side of the city. The road ran all the way through to the Bone Zulu and Five Points intersection. As we headed north, we went nice and slow, as we figured the AIF knew we would be coming to recover our Bradley and would try to ambush us while we moved into sector. SFC Lane and his crew had the lead, and my crew came in behind his in our two-vehicle recovery team. CPL Sieng scanned over the rear deck at the six o'clock, and I watched through my periscope as we slowly crept north. An intersection lay ahead, one where multiple IEDs had detonated in the past. SFC Lane approached the intersection, and our nerves were tense. Everyone was on edge as the Bradleys slowly whined and clanked their way northbound. As the lead Bradley entered the intersection, I radioed SFC Lane and told him to just keep his eyes peeled. We were certainly in no hurry to get blown up. He made it through the intersection and just made it around a massive IED crater. I breathed a sigh of relief.

Then a vision of the earth erupting with flames filled my view. Chunks of blacktop flew through the air as it propelled the lead Bradley into the air, engulfing it in a cloud of smoke and debris mixed with armored tiles and other various parts of the Bradley. A thunderous explosion followed as the Bradley seemed to hang in air before finally crashing back down to earth with its antennas wobbling.

As the scene unfolded in front of me, the old familiar battle drill kicked in—one that I had executed time and again when I was a PSG myself: deep breath, scan, scan, scan, looking and straining to find a triggerman so I could release control of the gun and turret back to the gunner, and then key the hand mic and try to get a report from the crew inside the flaming Bradley.

Quiiisssh ...

"Red 9, this is Black 9, over," I said.

A long pause.

"Red 9, this is Black 9, over!" I repeated.

I waited.

Nothing.

With no response, I had the driver pivot-steer (turn on its axis) 180 degrees and back up to the ramp of the downed Bradley so I could jump out without exposing myself to the enemy. Just as we turned about, the radios lit up with SFC Lane's voice. He said the Bradley was dead and would not start. Just as he said that, we indentified some movement in a vacant three-story building that looked to be a perfect location for a triggerman. The gunner started lighting the building up with the coax machine gun as we deployed the smoke-grenade launcher on our Bradley to screen the dismounts and Doc Devries when they got out of the troop compartment and cross-loaded onto my vehicle. Just as CPL Sieng stopped firing and we loaded the soldiers up in the back of my Bradley, SFC Lane called and said he had gotten his vehicle running, with everything working fine. With another shorter sigh of relief, we pulled out and went to go recover Red 2.

At SGT McKinney's location, we pulled up, dropped the tow bar, popped the shackles off, and had the vehicle hooked up and ready to roll in a few minutes. We had all become too proficient at recovery operations in a hostile environment. It was an art, like everything else. With snipers and other hazards, it was always best to try to shield the exposed and vulnerable soldiers with the other Bradleys as they hooked up the tow bar, which weighed a few hundred pounds and took at least three people to get rigged properly. I liked to call it setting up a "cocoon" of steel.

Once the Bradley was back at COP Adam, we determined it would be heading to the scrap yard once stripped of its valuable parts. That left only one vehicle from first platoon that was an original vehicle we had come over with.

With the loss of another Bradley, and upon further evaluation of our situation—and our logistical and manpower constraints—Regular X-Ray decided that we would abandon the Bone Zulu COP. Then, once the city was cleared with the surge troops, another COP would be built in a factory that we'd indentified as being much more suitable for a joint COP/IA compound.

That was great news, and I was glad people were listening to us. We could still do patrols into that area either by foot, mounted, or both, and with the many alleyways and inner roads, we could use them to our benefit. We would not have to always have our Bradleys, especially if we had multiple areas to approach from. Plus we could use the Government Center to support and launch operations from. It was a good deal all the way around.

Once given the go-ahead to abandon Bone Zulu, we pulled our equipment in record time, blew everything else that we did not need but also did not want to fall into the enemies' hands, cut the sandbags open and dumped the contents and rolled up the concertina wire. Lastly we blew the claymore mines that were set out by Attack Company, as we did not want to run the risk of them being booby-trapped by the AIF. Blowing something up on your way out the door is much cooler anyway. Surely the AIF were watching, and they may have thought initially they had a small victory in their column—but they were in for a rude surprise.

Good-bye, Bone Zulu!

CHAPTER 14

THE AWAKENING

LET'S TURN THE CALENDAR back a couple of years before moving forward …

Ramadi, Iraq, 2005—Second Platoon (Hell-bent) C Co 1/9 IN 2nd ID: We were tasked to support the 1-503 IN "Air Assault" for a battalion-level mission. Our initial task was to set in a blocking position on the northern edge of Ramadi along the Euphrates River on a route called "Duster," while the 1-503rd conducted a clearing mission south in the main portion of eastern Ramadi. We also had a "be prepared" mission to reinforce as needed.

The 1-503rd had taken a few casualties and had one KIA, so the call was made to have us come down and reinforce the main effort. We were told to pull down into the south-central portion of the city and stand by for further instructions. The grid coordinates they had given us placed us smack in the middle of a traffic circle in the middle of no man's land. Traffic circles were target reference points for all the insurgents, and we knew to stay out of them. There were just too many directions that you had to try to protect against. After plotting our route carefully, we started our movement (on an important side note, I had just received a brand-new LT from the mortar platoon, and he had never been in a Bradley—and this was his first mission with his platoon).

We were heading east on Duster and then cut down a side road, when a thick block wall exploded onto the LT's track. It sent concrete and shrapnel flying, knocking down a telephone pole and dropping the power lines in the road. Luckily the insurgents' timing was off and the bulk of the blast missed the Bradley, so we kept rolling. As we turned and crossed over Route Michigan and headed toward our destination, we could feel the tension rise in our bellies. Once we pulled into the traffic circle and stopped our Bradleys, the few civilians present grabbed their belongings and scurried off. The open shops closed their steel doors, and the place turned into a ghost town within minutes—never a good sign.

While I was looking around to see how I wanted to position the Bradleys, LT Bramlette called me on the radio. Just as he started to talk, I could hear his gunner SGT Patel in the background yelling, "He's got an RPG!" Then came a fifteen- to twenty-round burst of machine-gun fire. SGT Patel had killed the guy in the street as he'd cut the corner with an RPG to engage their Bradley. Shortly after that, I opened my hatch to get a better view of where to position the platoon until we received further instructions. Seconds after I popped my hatch and surveyed the terrain, everything went black, followed by heat and a loud explosion. The next thing I knew, I was lying on the small turret floor, scrambling to figure out if I was dead or wounded. The one thing I knew for sure was that I was blind.

I crawled back up to my seat, and my gunner, SPC Forbes, was yelling, "Sergeant, you okay?" Staring at his blurred outline, I keyed my helmet's communication set and gave him an okay. Just as I started to get my wits back about me, the prayer speakers at a nearby mosque began booming out instructions in Arabic.

"That's no prayer!" I told the gunner. "Shoot the speakers off the mosque!"

So he started firing the 240C machine gun. My vision slowly started to return, and I strained to look through the sight to see my gunner's handiwork: he had been blazing the entire side of the mosque. I repeated that I only wanted him to silence the speakers; I guess he heard "Shoot the mosque." Just as we disabled the speakers, we saw three to four insurgents trying to flank our position about 400 meters to our west. We quickly killed them with a burst of 25mm high-explosive rounds. I knew we were in a bad situation that had the potential to get even worse. We needed to get out of the middle of the traffic circle ASAP.

Luckily for us, the UAV picked up seven to ten insurgents moving from a graveyard into a house a few blocks northwest from our location. Rock 6, the commander of 1-503rd, radioed the information and told us to go and cordon off the area until they could get some infantry over there to enter and clear the building. Not wanting to stay where we were, we happily moved north and then west as Rock 6 personally guided us onto the target house. After we drove down a side street, we made it to the cemetery and stopped until we could get another heading from the eyes in the sky. Only moments after we halted, an insurgent tossed a satchel charge over the cemetery wall. It harmlessly blew up on SSG Knight's track. His driver, PFC Maden, called it up but the wall was too close, we could not depress the gun enough to shoot.

With the UAV back on our position, Rock 6 talked us the rest of the way onto the target house. It was a two-story house with a balcony that had a red carpet hanging from it. We spotted it and planned our next move. I called the battalion commander and informed him that we were able to take down the house. We had two squads in the back of our Bradleys and they were ready to go. He gave us the go-ahead and off we went. SSG Knight rolled up, rammed the compound wall, then drove up to the house and dropped his ramp. SSG Tye's and SGT Donnelly's men came pouring out the back. Then LT Bramlette and his men did the same ... then my track ... and then my wingman, SSG Narron. It all flowed well, and SSGs Doherty and Tye had the house secured within a minute or two, with all the bad guys zip-tied. They started doing their search and they found a few thousand US dollars, plus weapons and propaganda. We tagged and bagged all AIF and the incriminating evidence, took pictures, then transported the enemy prisoners back to the Corregidor Base for further processing.

My time in Ramadi felt like the "Wild West"—and a place where killing Americans seemed to be a sport.

Now fast-forward back to our story ...

26 May 2007: One of our intelligence reports told us about a success story in Ramadi. It spoke about the "Sons of Iraq" and how they were working with the Americans. It went on to say that Ramadi hadn't had a major attack or any violence in weeks: no sectarian violence, no IEDs, no small-arms attacks, no nothing. Then the report showed a graphic about how the IA was planning a foot race in the city. As I looked at the graphics, I noticed all the places where they had water points set up, the exact same places where we used to have our Tier-1 IED hotspots plotted, along with major firefights, including the traffic circle where I'd had one of my near-death experiences.

The report sounded promising for Ramadi and the Al Anbar Province—certainly nothing so promising happened while I was there, and the Diyala Province, where we were now, was a different animal. Mainly I figured that all the AIF in Ramadi and Al Fallujah departed and headed into Diyala, which would give the impression that the surge was working and allowed the "Al Anbar Awakening"—to gain traction. I was skeptical about achieving Ramadi-type success in the Diyala Province. Intelligence reports indicated an estimated 2,000-2,500 fighters in the Diyala Province area, and I had no reason to think otherwise. I would remain hopeful, but we did not stand a chance until we cleared our area once and for all of hardcore al-Qaeda, then demonstrated to the population that we were going to be able to provide security side by side with the IA and IP forces.

After reading the Ramadi intelligence report, I settled into my daily grind out at the COP. I was planning on going out with one of the squads later that day on patrol. As time permitted, I'd try to go out on patrols with one squad or section from each platoon a few times a week, just to stay in touch with what was really going on outside the wire and stay in tune with their needs. It was easy for leaders to make up excuses for why they couldn't go out on patrols, but you had to make time to do it. If you were out of touch with what was going on, you couldn't effectively plan or manage your resources. Plus the soldiers would eventually start losing confidence in you as a leader because you were not sharing the same dangers and hardships as they were. The world was a lot different at 120 degrees while out on a foot patrol for three hours in a hostile environment.

Just as I was getting my kit squared away to go out on patrol, I heard a monstrous explosion. I froze in place and waited for a report to come over the radios. Naturally I thought about who was out of the wire, who was already back in, and the different contingencies I could come up with. I knew Shadow was out, and the tanks were out—and sure enough ...

Quiiisssh ...

"COP Adam, this is White 9. White 3 was just hit with an IED between 41st and C Avenue. Stand by for more information, over."

SFC Hudgins came back up on the radio and said they had a possible WIA, as the driver, SPC Trussel, was not responding inside his hatch. SGT Williams and his gunner were attempting to get to the driver, but the turret was out and they had to hand-crank it into position before the hatch was accessible either through the turret or the driver's hatch.

Naturally Shadow element moved to their location to secure the area while White 9 and his crew pulled security and helped try to evacuate SPC Trussel. SGT Williams and his gunner frantically cranked the manual turret traverse handles while yelling reassurance to their trapped comrade. But as the turret slowly spun to where they could get to the driver, they realized their cries of reassurance and comfort had fallen on deaf ears. At first, the report said that SPC Trussel was unconscious, but a quick check of his pulse told otherwise. The IED had detonated directly under the tank's driver position. It was so massive that it buckled the hull of the tank, crushing the driver in his compartment. The crew tried tugging on him to bring him through the turret, but it was no use; he was pinned inside. SGT Williams tried to get access to the driver from outside the tank but again was denied. The adrenaline started to wear off and they soon began to feel their own injuries. They made the decision to hook up to the tank and drag it up B Avenue and closer to the COP to work the extraction of the driver.

While SFC Hudgins and the crews worked on dragging the disabled track into the narrower street, I gathered some of the Shadow soldiers that were back at the COP to assist in getting the driver out. One of the Stryker sergeants told me they had a Jaws of Life and other rescue equipment that had been donated by a local fire department outside Fort Lewis before they left. I just looked at him in amazement; I could not believe that they had the Jaws of Life. The sergeant got the Jaws so we could test it inside the COP before we took it to the recovery site, and everything worked! Luckily the Strykers had external power outlets on their vehicles, so we were able to use the Jaws. We loaded everything up on one of the Strykers parked outside, then we rolled out the gate and went on standby until the tank was in the alley.

As the lead tank literally dragged the destroyed Abrams around the corner, the gun barrel of the destroyed tank jammed at the five o'clock position, caught a telephone pole, and slowly pulled it to the ground. Moments later, the tank itself clipped a cement wall and crushed it, as the hull was skipping and dragging across the ground trying to make the turn up B Avenue. Once the tank was on B Avenue, we pulled up next to it, trying to shield it between houses and the hull of the Stryker, reducing the angles from which we could be shot. The temperatures were at maximum levels for the day, with the sun directly overhead. The Stryker driver and I jumped out and started to get the Jaws of Life out of the box and into its operating mode, while the vehicle commander pulled security with the .50-caliber MG on top of the vehicle and the tank crews disconnected the tow cables from the lead tank. The turbine engine exhaust mixing with the 120-degree temperatures felt unbearable.

With the tank disconnected and pulled out, we quickly went to work to get the driver freed from his trap. I crawled on top of the tank and looked into the compartment to assess the situation. Fearing what my eyes were about to see, I peered over the edge down into the hatch to see Trussel smashed into his compartment. His arm was broken and bent in a peculiar unnatural angle, and his legs were smashed into the upper part of his instrument panel and pinned between the hull of the tank and the drivers T-handle (steering wheel). The explosion must have snapped his neck and broken his back instantly; without a doubt, he suffered little.

The M1 Abrams tank driver does not sit in his compartment like a regular driver. Due to the low profile of the tank hull, the driver basically lies back at a slight angle as if he is in a La-Z-Boy watching TV. The T-handle (steering wheel) is like a tricycle, and it has the throttle on the right side, like a motorcycle, to allow more room and better control in the confined space.

As I paused and looked at the situation, trying to figure out how we were going to get him out of the vehicle, the first thing I knew I had to do was take off all my gear so I could work without restriction in the confined space between the turret and the hull. I crawled down off the tank and stripped off my gear, then I crawled back up toward the driver's hatch and moved into position. I could feel the heat from the hull of the tank immediately start burning its way through the thin layer of my ACUs, cooking my skin. The Jaws of Life were awkwardly big and bulky, I strained as I tried to get them into the tight position to start working the steel T-bar, dashboard, and the driver's seat so it would loosen the grip on the driver's leg. As I tried to move Trussel's body, I noticed it was already starting to turn stiff from the heat; if we did not get him out of that hatch soon, it would turn the gut-wrenching task into an even worse situation.

The heat of the tank was too intense and it prevented me from being able to lay on it for an extended period without literally cooking my internal organs. At first, I attempted to fight it off by rolling from side to side, but it gave little relief. I attempted to pour water on it but that just soaked the area, so instead of baking me, it boiled me and eventually became unbearable. I had to crawl off the tank then take a knee and try to hydrate to prepare for another attempt.

As I knelt in the tiny slice of shade the Stryker provided, sipping on water, I noticed a suspicious person peeking around a corner from across 41st Street. I figured the next time he came around the corner, it would be with an RPG or AK-47, so I let a few warning shots rip down the street in his direction to scare him off. Anyone who was a non-combatant would not have still been around that area, so the guy was obviously trying to get a report on the IED's effects. I could not kill him because he wasn't doing anything to justify it within our rules of engagement. It was frustrating: sitting next to a destroyed vehicle that has your soldier's lifeless body trapped in it, and seeing the person that most likely did it or at least one of his associates, and there was nothing you could do. He was too far away to give chase, and even if I could catch him, it would do no good unless he was stupid enough to still be carrying something that would incriminate him. Triggermen were seldom armed, and with the exception of pushing a button or flipping a switch, it was hard to see them committing a "hostile act" that could give you the legal authorization to bust a cap in him. As a result, they got to simply walk away. They knew the game and played it to perfection.

After taking a few more minutes of rest, I climbed back on the tank and started working again. My endurance and ability to stay up there was fading each and every time I went up on the tank. I was fearing his body was going to lock up, so I was determined to get him out and not have to drag the vehicle all the way back to FOB Warhorse and take that chance. I was trying not to break any more bones, but it was going to be impossible to get him out without breaking his leg. I could not get a saw or a cutting torch in there without causing even more damage, so I hooked up the Jaws of Life

307

to get a good bite in the chain that was wrapped around the steel T-handle and went for it. Just as the Jaws were almost completely closed, I heard a pop and he was free. I apologized to Frank as we quickly guided his body through the turret and out the top hatch then down to a Stryker, where he was placed in a body bag and then transported back to FOB Warhorse. SGT Williams, the tank commander at the time, and his gunner were also evacuated. They all had been rocked pretty good, and concussions were almost a guarantee, plus they were suffering from smoke inhalation.

CPL Francis Trussel, Killed in Action, 26 May 2007, Tahrir, Iraq

The IED that had blown up the tank had been placed in a small choke point that was caused by two previous IED blast holes. The choke point forced our tanks and Bradleys to drive up on a sidewalk to avoid falling into the other blast holes. It was a mystery as to how the AIF had gotten the IED under the sidewalk without being detected and/or disturbing the area to the point that we did not notice it before. That same sidewalk had been walked on numerous times in the past.

A few days later, just down the road and east of the blast site, SFC Hunsecker of Shadow platoon found a cache of new Italian-style landmines in a small shed near the intersection of C Avenue and 41st. It was a good find, and they blew the landmines in place along with the shed. The concerns we had were that this wasn't the first time we had patrolled that area, and that this particular shed had been searched in the past on several occasions. The question remained: where were they getting the explosives and how were they getting them into the city? It stood to reason they had smaller caches throughout the city, and we just did not find them on our previous searches. It seemed as if every patrol that was sent out found some sort of IED or weapons cache. First platoon found a cache that had three empty propane tanks, one propane tank packed with HME, a suicide vest, surface-to-air rocket boosters,

Chinese military manuals, and various other items, almost all of which our soldiers stacked neatly into a pile and detonated—only saving the manuals and rocket boosters for further investigation.

The surface-to-air rocket boosters were an important find, since just a few days earlier Wolfpack 5 called in small-arms fire and a near miss from a surface-to-air missile. Normally the AIF would not keep all the components together for a system. If it was an RPG, they would separate the sight from the launcher body and keep the rounds separated from the boosters. If it was a sniper rifle, they would keep the rifle away from the sniper himself until the last minute, and then bring him the rifle since he was too valuable to get killed or captured. This trend continued with most weapons systems on the battlefield. So getting the SAM boosters off the streets would hopefully render the missiles useless and prevent them from downing one of Wolfpack's helicopters.

We had a connex back at the COP that was slowly getting filled with various weapons, ammunition, and propaganda from the caches the platoons and squads were finding. The patrols were now to the point they were carrying their own C-4 and other explosive materials to deal with the caches of various explosives. With the operation going on in the west, EOD and engineers would have been at least a three-hour wait. We had several people trained on explosives so we had them pre-rig a few C-4 packages to the point that a soldier just had to insert the blasting cap into the C-4 and pull the fuse igniters that were attached to a two-minute fuse connected to detonation cord. They were duel-primed just in case one was a dud. Pop and drop.

The reward of detonating the found items immediately far outweighed the risks of staying in a position for hours on end in the baking sun waiting for EOD to come and do something we could have done ourselves. The soldiers had seen enough explosives and various other scenarios to use their judgment on whether to blow it in place or call the professionals. Grunts will seldom ever tell someone "That's not in my job description" and they will adapt to virtually anything, as long as they are given the time and resources.

We were receiving steady intelligence reports that the AIF were staging and operating just north of Old Baqubah in a town called Chubianat. We figured they were infiltrating down through OB into Tahrir, conducting their attacks, and going back up north of OB once their missions were completed. Looking at the map, we could identify several areas where we had received enemy contact in the past, and also could identify several suspected infiltration routes and supply routes. A main road north called "Blue Babe" ran east to west, which allowed the AIF to use that road virtually unmolested by any US forces. One key piece of terrain on that route was "guarded" by an army unit of the coalition. Their loyalties were suspect so I will just call them "X" army.

The X army's services were needed elsewhere and eventually they rotated out of sector—but not before the AIF blew up one of the sections of the bridge while the X army was still guarding it. It was a miracle that not one X army soldier was injured by the massive explosion—absolutely amazing. The AIF somehow managed to park a VBIED (not a suicide VBIED) on top of the bridge and blew it up while under the watchful eye of at least a platoon of X soldiers. Fortunately for the X guys, that also happened to be their last day in sector before it was taken over by C Co 1-12.

With 5-73rd far north, C Co 1-12 Cav to our immediate north, and Bronco Troop 1/14 to our south, we had a pretty good in-depth presence in our area, and it was starting to prove its effectiveness, slowly strangling the AIF. The successes with the Sons of Iraq that were being achieved in Ramadi and other areas out west started to gain traction within Diyala. Over a week's time, we heard and witnessed the tracers and flashes of explosions lighting up the night's sky as major fighting raged in the south of our location down in Buhritz. Initially we would be on the radios waiting for Bronco Troop to report that they were in contact and needed some help, but the calls never came. We heard reports from Bronco OPs of "unknown units" fighting it out on the ground but no US elements were calling up "troops in contact." In the early stages of the unknown fighting, we thought it was our Special Forces conducting operations, but eventually we narrowed it down to insurgent-on-insurgent fighting between the 1920s Revolutionary Brigade and al-Qaeda.

The 1920s Brigade had been the main Iraqi insurgent group in that area since the war started, and they had aligned themselves with AIF when Al Zaqawi called for the Diyala Province to be the "New Islamic State." They initially placed their trust in the AIF, since the AIF came into Diyala with a grand vision and well-spoken words that convinced everyone to rise up against the "infidels." They (the AIF) would provide the means for a better future for the "New Islamic State." Naturally the local Muslim population would trust their fellow Muslims before they would trust the infidels. The initial relationship was what everyone had hoped for, but then the internal power struggles and sectarian violence erupted within the communities. The honeymoon phase wore off rather quickly and transitioned into radical Islam or Sharia Law. All the locals realized the direction that the city and AIF were heading in—and it wasn't what they'd signed up for. However, the deal was done, and the AIF had managed to gain a solid presence within the entire Baqubah area. So there wasn't much the people could do. The AIF instilled fear by torture, kidnapping, beheadings, religious police, and many other barbaric tactics that paralyzed the entire city.

The general population also had zero trust in the US since the US had so few troops in the area and did not own the cities. So the locals made a deal with the devil, and there wasn't much they could do about it until something changed. The change they had been looking for finally came with the troop surge in Diyala. We were able to take the offensive and sustain the pressure on the insurgents, and we managed to disrupt, kill, capture, and dissect many of the AIF's operational networks. The 1920s Revolutionary Brigade started taking notice, and they felt that if they could break away from the AIF and quickly work a deal out with the US, they would be on the winning side and be able to foster their own ideas of how they see the city being governed.

Once the fighting settled down in Buhritz, word spread that the leaders of the 1920s Revolutionary Brigade—also known as CLCs (concerned local citizens)—wanted to come and talk to the commander of Bronco Troop and work out a deal to join the US, as the others had out west. Bronco Troop was now laying the foundation with the CLCs that could possibly lead to another success story as it had in Ramadi.

This news was good to hear but also bitter at the same time. It was great to hear there was something promising as far as stopping the violence, but we also knew that the 1920s were the same people we had been fighting since we arrived in Buhritz—and now they would be working with US soldiers? It was hard to transition from being sworn enemies, determined to fight each other to the death, to allies working together. General Petraeus had said, "We can't kill our way out of this insurgency," which I agreed with to an extent. We had been trying to kill our way out since we'd arrived, and they just kept coming. In order for anything else to succeed, the insurgents/AIF and local fighters had to have limited options and know defeat was imminent, or they would never come to the table to begin with.

When dealing with the AIF, we earned respect through violence—not Beanie Babies. The population wanted security and wanted to trust that the people providing it were not going to leave in a week or two. It was our job to convince them that we could provide security alongside their Iraqi army and police and that they were competent.

We could build as many schools, police departments, fire stations, Government Centers, TV stations, medical facilities, and water treatment facilities as we wanted, but if we couldn't secure them and make the people feel safe enough to use what we'd built, we would be wasting our time. The conditions were now being set for all this to happen.

Shadow platoon was the first to find out how the AIF were

handling the CLCs and their partnership with the US Army. While conducting a patrol in southern Tahrir, Shadow spotted a body lying in a field just off Route Gold. They first set up a perimeter and got someone with a scope to check the body out to make sure it wasn't booby-trapped. Once they moved closer, they used a grappling hook to roll the body over to again ensure it wasn't booby-trapped. Once sure it was clear, they sent a small element to check it out. As the three-man team approached the body, they could tell he had been executed with a single shot to the head, then left out in the middle of the field for the entire city to see as a warning for others working with the US.

It turned out that the executed Iraqi man was a scout that worked with the 1920s and Bronco element in the south. He had somehow been captured (most likely at his house) and beaten, then executed, all for working with the US. This was a typical AIF way of trying to maintain fear and also intimidate the local fighters within the sector.

As the days slowly ticked by, the insurgents tried to figure out other ways to infiltrate back into Tahrir. Regular 3 radioed out to our COP and informed us that insurgents once again had moved the barriers blocking off C Avenue near the college campus. Hearing that news, we quickly dispatched the cargo truck with the crane and a squad of dismounts, supported by two Bradleys, to put the barriers back in place. We also called and put our BN snipers on notice that their services would be appreciated in deterring anyone else from moving the barriers.

The following day, the commander and I were both out at COP Adam going about our daily business when we got a call over the radio that our MTT Gorilla unit had been ambushed on Route Vanessa. They had several vehicles down, with a civilian vehicle on fire, and they needed some help. CPT Austin looked around the COP, and I looked at him. We were both thinking, *Let's roll.* I had gotten another Bradley just a few days earlier, and I had my crew and he had his crew. So it was an easy decision to send out the Bone 6 and Bone 9 crews to help out the Gorilla element.

The ambush had taken place just outside the southeastern edge of Old Baqubah, near the stadium and industrial area, and the college campus area on the north eastern side of Tahrir. As we pulled up to the area, the civilian vehicle, a truck, was totally engulfed in flames. I looked inside it as we pulled forward, but I could see that the driver had already been pulled out. The Gorilla element had "circled the wagons" around their downed vehicles and were waiting on us to show up before they attempted to do any recovery. Gorilla 9—SGM Devalle—was talking to us on the radio and had given us a general area on where all the direct fire had come from. So we oriented on the buildings and alleyways to our north, then crept back and forth looking for a target. We did not want to stay stationary and present an easy target for the AIF. Plus staying mobile allowed us to keep them guessing at our location if they tried to maneuver on us or egress from the area.

CPT Austin's crew took some small-arms fire from a large four-story industrial building and quickly returned fire with the 25mm high-explosive rounds. CPT Austin called for air support and it just happened that we had a fast-mover (F/A-18) on station and quickly got clearance to drop a Joint Direct Attack Munition (JDAM) on the building. CPT Austin went through all the friendly positions and verified with the pilot, also assessing the likelihood of collateral damage. Since this was an industrial area that had been vacant for quite some time, the drop was easily approved. The accuracy of the smart bombs was incredible, and we had total faith in the abilities of the Air Force to drop it on target once they got a good solid grid on the building. In anticipation of the shockwave and any flying debris, we closed our ballistic shield doors on our sights to prevent them from being cracked.

Soon we heard the calm voice of the pilot say, "Round is on the way."

Silence ... silence ... silence ... silence ...

Craaank!

A gigantic boom followed, then came a miniature mushroom cloud reminiscent of the atomic bomb blasts. However, it did not have the desired effect, so Bone 6 requested one more for good measure. After a repeat JDAM, the AIF in sector were effectively silenced through violence. The Gorilla element conducted their vehicle recovery and headed out of sector, and we returned back to COP Adam to finish the day's work that we had started an hour earlier.

Now that we had enough forces in sector, we could always count on someone coming to help us if we found ourselves in a jam. It didn't matter which unit you were from or what you were doing at the time; if you were in a pinch and needed help, someone was coming for you. When out at the COP, you never let your guard down and seldom took off your boots, with the exception of sleeping or airing them out after a long patrol. When that radio broke squelch and we had a TIC, it was all hands on deck. Bone Company just happened to be the biggest element in the area so we found ourselves helping out quite often, mostly the IA and IP, but we would have the occasional US element rolling through sector, including the "private security" people, and they would occasionally get in a bind.

One particular military police company working with the Iraqi police departments in our AO would always come through our sector. Sometimes they would call and ask for clearance and route suggestions; other times they would just roll into sector without our knowledge or permission then get themselves into a bind. It had gotten to the point that I had to go and talk to their 1SG. He needed to know how dangerous some of the areas were and how they needed better situational awareness (SA) before they got someone killed going somewhere they did not belong.

For example, they found themselves in a firefight in downtown Tahrir, in an area that we would not even venture into without a platoon of Bradleys and a few squads of infantry on the ground. It was a miracle that no one was killed that day. I think on that particular day, the AIF in sector were so dumbfounded by someone being there that it caught them off guard and the MPs got the better of them. Unfortunately their luck did not last. A few weeks later, they were heading up Route Gold and got hit with an IED that had been packed with some sort of accelerant. When the IED went off, it engulfed the entire HMMWV with everyone inside. SFC Reynolds and a few of his guys rolled up there to help with the security and evacuation but there was little they could do. The driver, a female, and the gunner had both been killed. The truck commander survived the blast but was burned over 90 percent of his body. I'm not sure what happened to him after that day.

In that type of environment, it was a professional and common courtesy to let people know you were in their sector. Such courtesy served many purposes, the number one being that we don't shoot you, and the number two being that we can plan to help you if need be. The Special Forces ODAs had a few close calls with our SKTs and snipers, and subsequently had gotten much better about telling us when and where they would be operating. We always maintained a good relationship with the Special Forces in our sector. Our BN snipers completed numerous operations with them. Plus our medics got some training from them, and we did a good bit of intelligence sharing. We were getting pretty good at our own human intelligence gathering and pattern analysis, and once we combined our thoughts, theories, and hard facts, we had a pretty good picture of what was going on in sector.

With the attacks and enemy activity picking up momentum in the north, CPT Austin decided we were going to do a company-level clearance operation. It would start from the southeastern corner of Old Baqubah and clear north through an industrial area using route Tora Tora as our western boundary and Trash Alley in the east. With C Co 1-12 to our north conducting their own independent operations and simultaneously acting as a blocking position for Bone, we would be able to contain the entire area rather easily. We could block off Tora Tora and Trash Alley with Bradleys or tanks and maximize the infantry inside our cordon.

15 June 2007: the mission started early in the morning around 0300 hours. The dismounts infiltrated into the city under the cover of darkness on foot, one squad at a time for maximum stealth. They

then moved into their assigned sectors and waited for all elements to be set. Once all the infantry squads were set, we sent our tanks and Bradleys to seal off the area, and then started our movement from south to north. CPT Austin was on the ground with first platoon, and I was in my Bradley with the task of controlling the cordon element with first platoon's mounted section. I was also there for logistical support and casualty evacuation.

The first major objective to be cleared was the building that CPT Austin had gotten the F/A-18 to drop two JDAMs on. The squads entered and cleared the first floor, finding little evidence that it had been used by the AIF, but as they entered and cleared the additional floors, it was apparent that the AIF had been using this building for multiple purposes, including observation and over-watch/support-by-fire as they moved into Tahrir and conducted attacks, just as we suspected. It also provided them an unobstructed view of the main supply route, Vanessa, and provided them a perfect position to fire onto the convoys as they passed, then easily withdraw back into the city under the cover of the urban jungle. The squads found numerous shell casings, medical equipment, sketches, propaganda, and other random equipment.

Once the building was secured and cleared, the squads moved through and funneled out numerous doors to continue their push north, deeper into the city. While the squads of infantry entered and cleared the sporadic residential houses and smaller commercial buildings along their routes, they were able to talk to or at least attempt to talk to the civilians along the way. Based on the unwillingness of the civilians to talk to the Americans from the safety of their homes, it was obvious the insurgents still had a major influence on them and were using this area as one of their last strongholds in the OB area.

The sun began to rise and the temperatures climbed close to 100 degrees, so it was imperative that our guys paced themselves and stayed on course, not outmaneuvering their supply chain. Once the platoons strong-pointed and secured an area, we planned to roll up with a section of Bradleys and drop off ice, water, and

IVs, and pick up any detainees that had been taken along the way. Route Tora Tora had not been completely cleared, and since we weren't able to keep continuous eyes on it after Attack Company left, it was likely that it had been rigged with more massive IEDs. We did not want to drive on it unless it was absolutely necessary, at least until we were able to have the route-clearance team come back into sector.

At about 1130 hours, the infantry squads had cleared three-fourths of their areas and had set up a strong point in several buildings, including a five-story building on the edge of Tora Tora overlooking the city and a major road intersection called Five Points. As the platoons were moving into position, I was getting ready to make a run to pick up ice and water to bring up to the designated resupply point.

Red 9—SFC Lane—had started to strong-point his platoon on the third floor of the building to wait for resupply. He had one soldier, SGT Graham, who was starting to dehydrate, so they were going to take a break and wait for ice and water. As the soldiers set up in their areas, SGT Graham's position ended up being in the sun, so he switched out with SPC Waldo. Just as they finished the switch, the building swarmed with a hornet's nest of automatic small-arms fire, followed by an intense explosion from an RPG. First platoon had a man down. SGT Graham was lying on the ground, curled up in pain and suffering from a gunshot wound to his abdomen.

Within seconds, the calm operation turned into a full-scale battle. More incoming RPGs and gunfire followed, then our infantry squads housed in that building returned fire. The numerous platoon and company radios crackled with reports of incoming fire.

Quiiisssh ...

"Bone 9, this is Bone 6. We're taking small-arms fire and RPG fire from the north and the west of our position. Red 9 is reporting they have one wounded in action, and we are moving to their location at this time with Doc to evacuate. Stand by for more information. Out."

Upon hearing that SGT Graham had been wounded, I started checking my map to try and pinpoint exactly where they were. I had a general idea of where first platoon had set up, but I was not 100 percent sure. I had my driver go back and forth on Route Vanessa so I could look up into the alleyways and various other openings to see if I could identify any movement and to find a route to drive up and help with the evacuation of the casualty. Without being able to identify a good route into the infantry's location, I decided to go back to Tora Tora and pull up a hundred meters and see if we could see them—but still no luck.

CPT Austin radioed that they were at first platoon's location and were going to ground-evacuate the casualty to Tora Tora. As CPT Austin and his security element moved to the building, they commandeered a vegetable cart and wheeled it to the opening of the building. Doc, SPC Cabreja, and SGT Sisson moved up the stairs to SGT Graham's location, and Doc immediately went to work. He found no major bleeding but there was a nice size bullet hole in SGT Graham's gut. So they stabilized him and hooked up an IV to pump some fluids back into his system before they attempted to move him out to the awaiting vegetable cart.

The evacuation down the narrow stairwells with 180 pounds of dead weight proved to be difficult and was slow going, as SGT Graham winced in pain every step of the way. Once down to the ground, they kicked the few remaining stacks of tomatoes off the cart then loaded the casualty and prepared to move. By this time, a 240B machine gun team led by SGT McGrath had linked up with SPC Cabreja and SGT Sission to provide covering fire and help with the evacuation.

I got the call that they were heading west on a side street and that they would link up with me on Tora Tora. Not sure what side street they were talking about, I inched my way forward up Tora Tora. I had one Bradley from Red's mounted section as my wingman, set off to one side of the street to provide covering fire in case we got into contact. As I moved forward, I was straining to see any sign of the dismounts. Finally I saw a tiny object get thrown out into the street, followed by another, and then came a spark and a puff of smoke. It was a White HC smoke grenade, followed by a yellow smoke, to conceal their movement down the street. As the smoke continued to billow, I saw the machine-gun team set up at the intersection, so we drove on. As the Bradley lurched forward, I saw the evacuation team cut the corner, running at full speed. SPC Cabreja pushed the cart, SGT Sisson and Doc provided security on the side, and the rear security was quickly picked up by SGT McGrath and PVT Cunningham with the 240B. It was an incredible sight to see: the sweat-soaked faces straining as they pushed the cart toward the Bradley that was closing to meet them.

When we pulled up, I told PVT Perry, the driver, to pivot-steer 180 degrees so they could load up SGT Graham without wasting any time. When PVT Perry started to pivot the Bradley, I realized I had made a mistake, as we would be exposing the Bradley to the enemy with the ramp down. The decision had been made so we rolled with it. The evacuation team was huddled along the sidewalk waiting for the ramp to come down. With a hollow clank, the ramp hit the blacktop and I looked out through the hatch to get the thumbs-up they were clear. I got the thumbs-up, so we raised the ramp and covered the evacuation team as they maneuvered back up Tora Tora and rejoined their platoon in the fight.

Once the evacuation team slipped out of sight, we took off for FOB Gabe. I radioed ahead, and they expected us in a few minutes. As we barreled through the gates, the guards stayed plenty clear of the vehicles when we rumbled past their barriers. We pulled up to the aid station, dropped the ramp, then carried SGT Graham into the emergency room and tossed him up on the table. Doc gave the physician's assistant a rundown on what happen and what we had done. As Doc was telling him about what happened, SGT Graham groaned every few seconds, so he was given a shot of morphine to take the edge off.

We hung out for a few minutes, then checked and made sure we had accountability of his sensitive items. Finally we got the word he was going to be flown out and that there wasn't much else we could do for him. So we mounted back up and continued mission. Once we rolled back into sector, it was like someone had turned a switch. It was back to the business of clearing the buildings. The rest of the operation went without incident, and the platoons moved back to COP Adam and prepared for the next operation.

The mission did confirm our theory that this was the major part of the AIF territory and that they had planned on making it very painful for us if we tried to occupy it. It was apparent they were ready for a fight in that specific location, or so they thought.

CHAPTER 15

KEEPING YOUR
ENEMIES CLOSER

BACK ON FOB WARHORSE, I took a group of soldiers from first platoon to the sterile yard. We needed to download the cargo truck that still had all the blown-up and mangled parts of the first-platoon Bradley in which SGT Martinez, Nash, and Romero had been killed. We initially parked the entire truck down in the sterile yard until we would have time to transfer the parts to another truck or flatbed trailer, but as usual, things got sidetracked and the truck ended up staying down there longer than expected. The sterile yard was a walled in compound enclosed with Texas barriers and double-stacked HESCO baskets, remaining hidden from the everyday passers-by. We would take all catastrophic-loss vehicles down there to keep them out of sight from the rubber-neckers and Fobbits that wanted to take pictures then post them on YouTube or a blog site and tell people about their narrow escape from death.

As I crawled on top of the pile of twisted steel that was flowing off the sides of the cargo truck, I paused and took a look around the yard. I was overwhelmed at the amount of destruction that surrounded me. The sterile yard was about 150 meters wide by about 100 meters deep, and it was packed full of destroyed vehicles (words can't describe what I saw). Apache Company's blown-up and burned M88 was down there and barely recognizable. Several M1 tanks sat where they had been dragged in and dropped in place. Some still had the tow bar hooked up to them. They sat on their belly armor because their road wheels and track were blown off. They rested in the dirt crooked and in awkward positions, their heavy steel track rolled up and placed on top of their turrets, which housed their once-proud 120mm gun tubes that now sagged and pointed down to the ground. I saw row after row of Bradleys, some sitting as the tanks were and others that were not even recognizable. The Bradleys burned so violently from the stored ammunition and the 175 gallons of fuel that they melted to the point where the turret collapsed in on itself and came to rest on the bottom of the vehicle's armored floor. The only thing truly recognizable was the heavy steel fluted gun barrel of the 25mm that protruded out of the melted rubble like a flag pole without a flag. I saw other Bradleys and M1 Abrams main battle tanks, the pride of the 1st Cavalry Division—vehicles that, if back at Fort Hood, would be parked meticulously on line, tarps tied tight, gun barrels lined up, track line spotless, not so much as a drop of oil on the white cement. What I saw that day was row after row of mangled tan steel as if in a junkyard that belonged to Satan himself.

The transferring of wreckage was a time-consuming task that took the better part of a morning. We had to stack piles of steel on pallets and try to band it all together so a forklift could come and pick it up to take it to its final destination. To make matters worse, at one point, one of my soldiers pulled me aside and handed me an unidentifiable part of a body that he'd found while moving metal around. It evidently was loaded up in the wreckage amid the chaos on the day the vehicle was destroyed. I looked at it for a moment, took it from him, then turned and jumped on a Polaris Ranger to drive over to mortuary affairs and drop it off. When I handed it to a young soldier, I think I caught him off guard, as he looked at me kind of crazy. Unfortunately that was just another day in Baqubah.

South in Buhritz, Bronco Troop was having success in their partnership with the Sons of Iraq—the CLCs. Word passed through the channels that the CLCs in Tahrir were willing to partner with us and work to stabilize the environment. The battalion and brigade were eager to replicate Bronco Troop's success in our sector, and CPT Austin was given the task of conducting linkup with the CLCs and starting negotiations. CPT Austin and I were both hesitant, talking in great detail about their real motives and we even war-gamed many scenarios. We had been unknowingly used in the past to eliminate someone's enemies in town by the insurgents, civilians, politicians, or police and army representatives. So we were trying to prevent a repeat of having this CLC mission blow up in our face, literally. CPT Austin started his plan with much skepticism and did as much as he could to get to the root of why they wanted to work with us and to confirm their core motives.

Within a few days, a meeting was arranged and CPT Austin went out to meet with the local CLC within Tahrir. There was no script or a hard-line agenda, with the exception of doing a face-to-face with the leader and some of his men to let them know we were open to talks and negotiations. Meetings and negotiations with Arabs were always a challenge within a challenge. The first major challenge was the language barrier, and then the nature of how they conducted business. When meeting with Arabs, it is customary to conduct all informalities up front, which include but are not limited to smoking cigarettes, drinking Chai tea with loads of sugar, eating fruits or vegetables, and consuming other mixtures that weren't so easily recognizable by the American eye or taste buds. While eating and drinking, we would make small talk that really didn't mean anything, but it put everyone somewhat at ease as we tried to find some sort of common ground.

After the informalities were over with, one major objective would be focused on, and after a few minutes of discussion, yet another meeting would be arranged to talk about it. Then the group would break up and go their separate ways. The major stumbling blocks that we tried to anticipate and prepare for were: Iraqis didn't want to admit they couldn't do something face-to-face and they would make commitments that they knew they couldn't follow through on, but they wouldn't admit it until it was usually too late, which led to major frustrations on both sides—ours, because we felt we couldn't trust them, and theirs, because they felt like they let us down. The other hurdles in this potential relationship would be their numbers. Whether it was personnel count, money, insurgent strength, or any other unit of measure, it tended to get exaggerated to the extremes, both to the plus and minus sides, depending on what was being discussed. Finally we were wary of the ever-present backdoor deals, bribery, and payoffs that were common place and sometimes even expected. Bribery had to be anticipated when locals were working with other locals. It was a delicate game of chess, and CPT Austin had his work cut out for him.

After a week or so of meetings with the CLC leadership, CPT Austin was able to pin down their motives and needs then find a common beneficial ground on which to start our relationship. The two most recognizable factors for their motives were to ensure they would get paid for their services and to get security for the town. If we paid them and pledged our support in eradicating the AIF from their cities, they would join sides with us.

Our conditions had to be met too. Our first condition was the amount of payment for services rendered (average was $37 per month per man). They had to agree with the set wages and they were not open for negotiating. In addition to the set wages, we had to be able to verify that each individual member of the CLC existed, and was in fact a CLC and not just a name on paper that would be drawing a paycheck to be split among the CLC leadership. It was made clear that we, the United States Army, would be making the payments to the individuals face-to-face and not the CLC leaders; they would not handle any money. Eventually, once the CLC leaders started to prove their loyalty and honesty, and expected to get paid on time, we would slowly put them in charge of payment of their security people, so that they would see the money coming from Iraqi locals and not the US Army, which

325

in turn would empower the CLC leadership (in theory). The wages were set nationally across the board to keep a balance. If we paid them too little, they could be forced to supplement their income by continuing their attacks and not severing ties with the AIF. However, if we paid them too much, they would have no incentive to move toward becoming a legitimate member of the country's security forces, either police or army.

Once the money part was agreed upon, the next challenge was the terms of how the CLCs would operate within the city. The CLC group's strength was around a hundred men, plus or minus ten to fifteen, depending on what day of the week it was. CPT Austin and I discussed this in great detail as to how we could best manage or contain them within sector until we built our relationship with them. We did not want the CLCs operating independently around town without the knowledge or support of the US. We wanted to be able to limit their authority and still be able to show the townspeople that we were ALL working together as one cohesive element: the US Army, Iraqi army, Iraqi police, and the CLCs. That way, it would be a tremendous victory for all parties involved.

Initially we decided that the CLCs would be limited to carrying only AK-47 rifles and only conducting defensive operations within a 150-meter radius in their assigned areas, which would be approved by CPT Austin and tracked by our command posts. In addition to their assigned "neighborhood watch" areas, they were to maintain communication with our CP by both walkie-talkies and cell phones. If they needed help, they were to call and wait for support from us and the Iraqi army unit that was co-located at COP Adam. Other finer details had to be sorted through as well, including how to tell the CLCs apart from the AIF forces. At first, we came up with brown army T-shirts (the only thing we had an abundance of) with numbers spray-painted on them to identify who they were and what sector they were in. Anyone armed and not wearing a T-shirt was subject to getting shot. Eventually we received enough florescent physical fitness belts to give to the CLCs so we could see them at night and during the day at greater distances.

With a lot of hard work and politics, CPT Austin constructed an agreement that both the CLCs and the IA/IP ALL agreed upon. The CLCs were put to work shortly after the deal had been struck and agreements signed. To begin with, we would do patrols through towns and check in on the CLCs to confirm locations and people that were there. We would sit, talk, and just try to get to know them and familiarize ourselves with their faces and various areas of operation. The CLC selected the areas that they wanted to protect and also selected the houses they would use as their "patrol bases." When all the locations were plotted on the map, it was blatantly obvious (now the writing was on the wall) that all the CLC-selected houses had been in use by them when they were conducting operations against us. I could connect the dots between the previous AIF patterns and attacks, and the locations of the houses—most disturbingly, the area where LT Pijpaert's and SSG Fili's squad were ambushed.

I went out on several patrols to confirm CLC locations and get a firsthand feel for what our guys were doing and how they were interacting with the CLCs. It was obvious in the beginning that neither side trusted each other and would always eye each other with suspicion. I know that I did when I went to the house that was only a few houses and streets away from the ambush site. I could not help but look at these guys and their weapons—and their trigger fingers—and think to myself, *Is this the guy that killed Doc? Is that the finger that pulled the trigger?*

Since the CLCs no longer operated in the shadows, and in fact did come out in the open, we did get a little comfort from the deal and the fact that we knew exactly who they were and where they and their families lived. If they decided to go sideways on us, it would be easy to track them down and finish what we started. Not surprisingly, the CLCs were well equipped and had all the insurgent kit items when they were out on their neighborhood watches. They had their well-maintained AK-47s, their ammo-pouch chest rig with their prescribed three magazines, and their brown US Army T-shirts. I have no doubt that somewhere locally they had some

RPGs and heavy machine guns stashed, just in case, but they were attempting to play by the rules and agreement. For now.

Unfortunately, within a week, the CLCs received a quick reminder of our agreement. First platoon was out doing a patrol. SGT Lunt led as the point man and turned a corner, identifying three military-aged males with a heavy machine gun in an area where no templated CLC outpost was supposed to be. When the CLCs saw the US patrol, they tried to run and get into a vehicle. That's when SGT Lunt opened up on them. They surrendered quickly but not before their car had been disabled and one of their guys was suffering from a gut wound. First platoon called it up, and I told them to confiscate the machine gun and get the names of the individuals involved. Within moments, the CLCs own boss was on the ground and evacuated their casualty to an unknown destination. Then he showed up at the COP demanding their machine gun back, plus he wanted answers about why we'd shot one of their guys.

I was never the political type of person. I left that stuff to CPT Austin. However, he was not there, so I did a pretty good job of explaining to this CLC guy that he was lucky that first platoon showed restraint and did not kill all three of his guys. Then I explained to him, through his own interpreter, that his men were in a place they were not supposed to be, doing things they weren't supposed to be doing, with weapons they were not supposed to have. I could see the frustration in his eyes, and he looked slightly perplexed as the interpreter explained this to him. I may have had the same look on my face, as I was perplexed at how he could sit there and question me on why his guy had gotten shot when they basically violated every single rule that we'd established.

The CLC leader asked one more time for his machine gun back, and I said "No" and that was that. He left with his interpreter and nothing else was ever mentioned about that incident. Two things came out of that incident from my perspective: one, I think the CLC leader was more worried about losing his RPK machine gun than getting a guy shot, and two, they were never out in the open again without someone in their group wearing a brown T-shirt—and they never had a heavy machine gun again. As for them being in a place where they were not supposed to be, they would again have to learn that the hard way in the future.

Within a few weeks, CPT Austin had integrated the dismounted and mounted patrols with CLCs and Iraqi police and army forces. It was truly a leadership challenge to get all these entities in one location, on time, and doing the same thing together. The most amazing part about it was the young US NCOs, officers, and soldiers making it happen. These weren't seasoned politicians or officers making this happen. It was the non-commissioned officers and young mid-twenty-year-old platoon leaders out coordinating with the local leadership and security forces, doing joint patrols and gathering intelligence, and planning for future stability operations. The soldiers of B Company, including the scouts from 5-20, were out planning the future of an entire city: future police stations, medical facilities, recruitment drives, schools, power grids, water and sewage services, and many other infrastructure initiatives.

The fighting within Tahrir started to fade away day by day. We were, however, still taking sporadic contact from the north in Old Baqubah. In order to combat this, we planned a clearance mission on the south side of Route Vanessa and the northernmost limit of Tahrir. The plan was to go to each and every house, talk to the people, and confirm that they were indeed the same families that had been living in those houses since we arrived a few months earlier. Then we would go clear a portion of the college campus and patrol our way back to the COP.

I placed myself in a squad from third platoon and appointed myself a rifleman with PFC Meyers as my battle buddy. I figured I could hang out in the rear of the formation and not get in the way of how the squads normally maneuvered, and also stay out of the way of the squad leader. He didn't need a first sergeant confusing his SOPs. First platoon would be conducting basically the same mission, but one city block to our south. Each platoon had a squad of IA soldiers with them and the maneuver plan had us leap-frogging from courtyard to courtyard as we moved to C Avenue and crossed into the college campus.

We made it to our first few houses, and, as normal, it was the typical family inside; nothing alarming, with the family for the most part friendly and talkative to the IA and US forces. As we left the secure compound walls, I felt a little uneasy since we were heading to the east, in the direction of the building that we had dropped a few JDAM missiles on earlier. Plus we were setting a pattern as we left the buildings. I wanted to alternate and jump a few of the courtyard walls instead of going out into the open each and every time we went to a new building, but I reluctantly did not say anything because I did not want to override the squad leader. I figured he was out there doing multiple patrols daily without me and my input, so I just let it go for an AAR (after action review) point in the debrief when we got back.

As we left the last building, we executed an extended movement until we made it to the next compound wall. The formation had just gotten its intervals and started to move east again when a burst of machine-gun fire erupted from our north. Everyone hit the ground within seconds and returned fire. Myers and I were stuck out in the open with zero cover. So we returned fire, then I checked the wind direction and tossed the HC smoke I had attached to my vest. Once the smoke billowed, Myers bounded behind me to an opening in a walled compound about fifteen meters away. He set up his SAW and I quickly joined him. Once inside the walled compound, I called up to the lead squad and got a SITREP. The only thing I heard over the firing was that they had one guy down. I reached for the map in my back pocket to call up Bradley support ... but the map wasn't there. I knew that I had my map at the last building we visited because I'd checked before we left. So I peeked around the corner and, lo and behold, there sat my unsecured map, lying right where I had hit the ground and rolled. For a split second, I thought about telling Myers to go out into the open under fire to get the map that I carelessly dropped, but I figured he would not think much of me after that. So I said a quick "Cover me while I move" then ran out and grabbed the map, turned, slipped, got back up on my feet again, and sprinted back to the walled compound, swearing to myself the entire time that none of us would ever carry a map in our back pockets without it being dummy-corded—EVER!

The lead squad from third platoon was unleashing a hailstorm of fire, including PFC Brothers launching multiple M203 grenade rounds into the buildings across the street. I had been able to call SFC Reynolds, and within minutes, he came with a section of Bradleys to lay down some fire. Once the Bradleys showed up, I moved over to the lead squad, who had the wounded soldier. It turned out to be a brand-new replacement who was out for his first patrol: PV2 Cunningham had been wounded in the arm. Luckily it had only grazed his upper forearm and cauterized the wound, as it neatly sliced his skin with the precision of a scalpel. With the Bradleys on station, the insurgents that opened up on us melted back into their cement jungle and lived to fight another day. PV2 Cunningham elected to continue the patrol after he was bandaged up by Doc.

The temperatures reached into the 120s, and we needed to keep moving before we found ourselves out of water and starting to take heat casualties. We maneuvered over to the college campus area, which was sprawling. It made your skin crawl in anticipation of being shot from any and every direction. No matter what wall you sought cover behind, you would be exposed in several other directions. It was a massive complex, so we decided that we would only go through the buildings that most likely had potential value to the AIF. As we darted from cover to cover, zigging and zagging, trying to avoid the sights of a sniper, we could feel the energy draining out of our bodies.

Once we got inside a building, I had to take a knee. I was exhausted and felt like I was on the verge of needing an IV. I did not want to be a heat casualty and become a liability, but I also did not want to slow down the momentum of the squads. I sucked it up the best I could and sipped on my water, reasoning within myself that if I drank all my water while stationary, that would be less water I would have to carry. It almost made sense, but we still had quite a ways to go, so I wisely conserved.

Once we finished our business in the college campus area, we moved back across C Avenue and worked our way to COP Adam. As usual, we did the bounding over-watch technique because enemy contact was likely. So one squad or fire team bounded forward while another sat over-watching their movement from a house or compound wall. It was effective, but time consuming.

About halfway back to the COP, I received a radio transmission that SGT McGrath had found a possible cache and was digging to confirm or deny its contents. I took a few guys and doubled back to the suspected cache. As I sprinted across the road and into the courtyard where SGT McGrath was, I got a nostril full of decomposing body. Unfortunately I was downwind from SGT McGrath as they broke through the protective layer of dirt and unleashed the dreadful odor in my direction, instantly making me start dry heaving. My body convulsed as it tried to expel the pungent odor from within, but nothing would come up from my empty stomach. Between dry heaves, I told SGT McGrath to leave it alone and move back to the COP. As I turned, I noticed a small child and an old broken-down, hunch-backed Iraqi woman peeking out her door, smiling at me. This country is crazy!

The exhaustion we felt that day seemed to be a constant daily companion for all soldiers throughout the summer: the 120- to 130-degree temperatures ... the sprinting from cover to cover ... the repetition of lifting your weapon up and down, time after time, to cover your buddies' movements, so much that it began to feel like it weighed a hundred pounds ... the stinging sweat running down your face and into your eyes ... the sweat-filled boots and soaked pants covered in perspiration and salt stains ... the chafing of your inner thighs ... and the sheer exhaustion you felt in every single muscle as your body carried the hundred pounds of gear and instruments of war. The human body and mind—combined with pride and the determination not to let your buddies down, and sometimes adrenaline—are amazing.

As the days and missions clicked by, we started integrating the CLCs into more patrols, to the point that CPT Austin felt comfortable taking them into Old Baqubah in a large-scale company operation. With the brigade-level operations going on in New Baqubah, CPT Austin figured he could catch the insurgents off guard in Old Baqubah, since the insurgents anticipated a major brigade-level operation in OB like those that happened in all other clearing operations. They likely figured that they still had time and did not expect any operations for at least a few more weeks. The CLC leader was adamant about knowing where all the AIF fighters were housed throughout the city, saying he could identify them if we would take them up there.

CPT Austin never agreed to the mission and did not let on to his thoughts with this newfound information. It was a major gamble since success or failure relied solely on the CLCs and secrecy, which, combined, would be a tough nut to crack. Having said that, the CLCs had steadily proven their loyalty to their community over the AIF, and we had everything to gain by trying to catch the AIF off guard in OB. CPT Austin worked nonstop for a week getting the approval and additional assets to conduct the operation. We needed everything we usually did, but on a smaller scale than what was being used for the operation in New Baqubah. The 1-12 and 3rd HBCT were a major help in getting us our resources. The 2nd ID could not afford to cut any of their resources from their operation on the west side, so we went about acquiring them from our 1st Cavalry brothers. CPT Jacobs hooked us up with some tactical air controllers from the Air Force, and brigade got us our human intelligence teams from the psychological operations unit, plus extra medical support, UAV support, and a few other resources that might come in handy.

We planned to divide the city up into four sections, one section each for first platoon, third platoon, Shadow platoon, and Gun Dog platoon (25th ID). We could plus-up the infantry platoons with their mounted crews by leaving the Bradleys parked, with the exception of two sections and my crew for reinforcement, resupply operations, and detainee and casualty evacuation. We would augment each platoon with a small section of CLCs and IA soldiers, and they would infiltrate into the city on foot late in the evening, around 2300 hours. The platoons would not clear the entire city; they would conduct targeted raids on several key buildings within their sectors, as led to the buildings by the CLCs. The Bradleys would stay back at COP Adam initially to maintain the business-as-usual posture and hopefully keep the enemy surprised. It was a bold plan, but if it worked, it would pay off in a major way. To add to the secrecy and complication of the plan, we could not tell the IA or the CLC exactly when, or even if, the plan was going to happen until it was the day of the operation—and even then, they did not get the full brief until they were at COP Adam and weren't going to leave.

Starting the operation at 2300 hours would have several benefits. One was that the heat of the day would be gone. It also would give our guys the ability to work through the evening under the cover of darkness and hit all of their objectives before daylight, then exfil before the city came alive with activity. We planned for ten to fifteen high-value targets and a few other random detainees throughout the operation, figuring we would need the entire eight hours of darkness to complete the operation.

The CLCs showed up at the COP around 1800 hours, many of them with full combat gear, body armor, AK-47s, and miscellaneous head gear, including my all-time favorite: the black ski mask. These guys were not the average CLCs that we talked to in the neighborhood-watch program; these guys had the hardened fighter look and posture. Their equipment was well maintained, their physical fitness levels were obvious, and they just appeared to be professional fighters that were all about business. They all knew a big mission lay ahead, and they had a good idea of what was going to happen, so they were "switched on." Once they found out exactly what the mission was, they knew that if we were successful in eliminating their opposition that evening in one massive operation, they would be able to secure power in the Old Baqubah area and be an influential part of the future development of all the cities on the east side of the Diyala River.

The COP was a flurry of activity all through the evening, as everyone conducted the basic-movement rehearsals with their newly formed groups. As the hours turned to minutes and departure time grew closer, the excitement and nervousness settled into pure concentration on the task at hand. Everyone was lined up outside the building but inside the compound walls, smoking cigarettes and doing last-minute weapon checks—until they finally got the word to push out. The platoons staggered their movement, with the platoons that had the farthest to move leaving first. I stood there watching each soldier disappear into the darkness. Within an hour, the COP was nearly empty and silent, with the exception of the tank platoon manning the OPs and other security positions—and my small contingent manning the radios and ready to roll out at a moment's notice.

I tracked the movements of each platoon by moving their magnetic icons along the map as they called up their various phase lines and checkpoints. A third-platoon squad, with SFC Reynolds, was first to reach their initial target house. They called up and reported their location, then had to wait for their other squad to get into position. Since the houses were so close to each other, they wanted to take them down at the same time to avoid spooking the other house. They had some initial confusion with the CLCs on which houses were which, but they worked it out on the ground in rather short order and were ready to do a simultaneous takedown of the first two buildings of the evening. The radios went silent, and my nerves went into overdrive as I anxiously awaited the radio call saying they had gained a foothold in the buildings.

Quiiisssh ...

"COP Adam, this is Blue 9. We are in objective one. We have three detainees, four AK-47s, one RPG site, one RPG propellant round, and three cell phones. Break. We will maintain control of our detainees until we are complete on objective three, over."

That was a good decision by SFC Reynolds. If they could walk the detainees to the next target area and maintain their stealth, the better it was for everyone. If we started running Bradleys up and down the streets, the insurgents would be on alert and calling their buddies. By the time Blue made it to their third objective, the other platoons had gained entry in their first and second objectives as well. They, too, had taken at least one or two detainees per objective house and escorted their detainees to their next objectives.

CPT Austin's plan was going better than we could have hoped for. The only glitch in it now was that, in the first few target houses, we had already managed to accumulate a nice collection of contraband and detainees. The platoons had picked up twelve AIF between the four elements. My concern was that we would have to deal with a mass influx of detainees and contraband rather than a slow trickle per objective area.

In order to avoid a massive cluster of chaos, I started trying to organize the areas and assign available guys to specific tasks. I did not want to drop the ball on the processing of the detainees. Once they had been detained, it was imperative that all the paperwork be filled out properly, with anything that helped build the case against them logged and documented if we had any hope of keeping these guys locked up. I did not want them back on the streets once they had been put away, and the best way to do that was fill out the detainee packets properly. That meant we had to have sworn statements filled out by at least three soldiers, and in this case, we would have the CLCs fill out at least one. We had to take pictures of them, register their retinas in BATS (Biometrics Automated Toolset System), so that, just in case they were picked up again, we could track them. We would also have to draw sketches, take pictures of the contraband, and handle many other small details that helped build the case. My biggest concern was being able to conduct our questioning of the detainees. It was a must-do task before the detainees left our outpost. If we released them to another component of the coalition, by the time we got back any information, it would be outdated by weeks if not months. So this would be a great opportunity to get some answers on past events and to start building intelligence packets for future operations.

At about 0330 hours, the platoons had held onto their detainees long enough, and it was time to start bringing them back to the COP so that the platoons could finish their movements before the night turned into day. My crew and another Bradley crew, with two additional guards in the back of the Bradleys, rolled out and headed north to conduct linkup with SFC Reynolds and pick up their six detainees. On the way north, we got the call that first platoon had also moved over to SFC Reynolds' position to drop off their detainees, which would cut down on our movement through the city. However, no one told me that they, too, had six additional detainees. The old saying in the Army is "There is always room for one more." We tested that theory on the first load of detainees. According to the technical books, the Bradley could hold seven people in the back, but that really wasn't the case—especially when the vehicle was an older version like the one I had, with the "over-engineered" seat design instead of the bench setting. And the other Bradley just happened to be a BFIST, a fire-support officer version that had hardly any room for personnel in the back since it had radios and oversized seats that took up most of the space in the rear.

When we pulled up and dropped ramps to load the detainees, it was a sight to see. We crammed the detainees in one by one. We had one in the "hell hole" (the small passageway that led to the driver's compartment), one in the turret with us, and the rest sitting like they were part of the Jamaican bobsled team. We had them all crammed in and were ready to raise the ramp until an unidentified soldier yelled, "Wait! You forgot the sacks of contraband!" So I reluctantly crawled out the top hatch and down the front of the vehicle, then tossed the bags of contraband onto the top cargo deck of the Bradley for the ride back, because it sure as hell wasn't fitting in the back.

As we pulled into the COP and backed up to the entrance to download the detainees, I noticed some commotion going on and saw that some detainees had already made it back to the COP. Totally dumbfounded, I walked into the COP and asked where the hell the detainees had come from. One of my guys said that Gun Dog had brought them in, then the RTO proceeded to tell me that they'd commandeered a truck then loaded up the detainees and sent a small patrol back to drop them off. Nice! I was impressed by their initiative and willingness to adapt to a fluid situation. They were going to do okay working with Bone.

We no sooner established some order than we got a call that other detainees were ready to be picked up from the Shadow element—and more from first platoon. Upon hearing that, we mounted up and rolled back out. We picked up eight more detainees and quickly rolled back to COP Adam to start processing them. On the way back, I added up the number of detainees in my head, as well as how many soldiers we had at the COP—and quickly came to the conclusion we were even: twenty and twenty. But most of my twenty were on OPs and radio guard, or pulling some other critical duty. No worries, though, as the detainees were all blindfolded and zip-tied. It would just take awhile to process them, and it just so happened that I had about three months left on my tour, so I was in no hurry.

Around 0500 hours, the morning prayer kicked off, which was our cue to pick things up and finish the last few targeted houses within the sector then start working our way back to the COP. It had been a long night for everyone, and with the massive lineup of detainees that we had to process, it would be an even longer day until the mission was completed. I grabbed Doc and had him start doing some quick medical screening on the detainees—and checking the zip-ties to make sure they were not too tight. Sometimes in the heat of "tagging and bagging" the AIF, their flex-cuffs got put on too tight then had to be cut before putting on new ones. The one thing I did not need was for some AIF prisoner to claim abuse against some of my guys. We did not need any distraction or investigation, so I always made it very clear that we took care of our detainees and didn't need any scandals.

About thirty minutes into the screening process, I got a call: "We need a detainee pickup at grid AB12345678." The platoons were on a roll, and by that point, I figured they were just detaining the entire city, which was fine by me. We rolled up just as the sun was rising, picked up a group of seven, then headed back to the COP. Once back, we organized everyone, broke them down by detaining platoons, and gathered all their contraband. Then we started to lay all the contraband out for the photos and further investigation of the written documents—once the interpreters got back.

The Gun Dog platoon came back first. They wheeled into the compound with the commandeered truck, now loaded with another five detainees. That gave us a grand total of thirty-two detainees. Yeah, we had our work cut out for us. I had the majority of the detainees outside the COP in the rear area. They were all segregated and blindfolded, and we shifted their flex-cuffs to the front so they could drink water from a bottle and use the bathroom. A few soldiers and I organized them into their groups, then I told one of the privates to keep an eye on them, saying that I would be right back, as I had to go in and check on the rest of the platoons and find out about getting some chow for the detainees.

I went into the company command post and got SITREPs (situation reports) from the platoons. Then I organized the detainee processing with the THT (tactical human-intelligence team) units. So I was gone way longer than expected. When I went back outside to check on the private and the detainees, I about fell over. The Iraqi army guys had come back with the Gun Dog element and had grabbed a detainee. They'd set him on a chair, taken off his blindfold, and were getting ready to start beating on him. About three to four Iraqi army guys surrounded him. As I walked out and saw the situation, it registered in my brain what was happening. I yelled just as one IA soldier was preparing to tee off on the guy. Thankfully he stopped in mid motion.

"What the hell are you doing?" I said, looking at the private. "Why didn't you stop them?

"I figured since they were Iraqis that they could do it to their own countryman," the private said.

I explained to him that if they wanted to beat their own countryman, they would have to do it on their own time and not on our watch, then reiterated that we did not need any scandals or investigations. After my discussion with the young private, I tripled the guards, since we had more people on hand to deal with the detainees.

The detainee that nearly got pimp-slapped by his countryman looked about ready to talk, seeming to be scared to death of the Iraqi soldiers. I decided to use this to my advantage when doing the questioning. I told him and the other detainees that we were in earshot of the IA guys, but that if they talked and cooperated with us, we would ensure they got detained by the US Army. If they did not cooperate, then we would turn them over to the IA soldiers to be "further processed." It worked pretty darn good—with the exception that we did have to let the IA process them, so I kind of told a fib.

As the platoons rolled in, I was able to grab the detaining squad leaders and the CLCs that indentified them to start getting information on why these guys were being detained. All the guys we had detained were military-aged males between the ages of eighteen and fifty-five, with the exception of two young kids, one of which intelligence pictures showed carrying an AK-47. He was fourteen years old and known in the AIF world as a "scout." Another detainee had been known as "The Butcher" and another as "The Scientist." One guy really got my attention: the CLCs said he was the one responsible for the IED that had blown up the Stryker and killed the seven soldiers and the reporter. Hearing that come out of the mouth of one of the CLCs, then looking at the guy sitting there in front of me, and knowing that he was most likely the guy responsible for directly killing Americans, I wanted to ...

Anyway, CPT Austin came back and I gave him a thumbs-up on the mission and a job well done. The plan was awesome, and with the exception of a few door breeches, not a shot had been fired. Bone, along with the Iraqi army and a handful of CLCs, managed to go through the entire town of Old Baqubah in one long evening and deliver a significant blow to the AIF within sector. The intelligence we gathered from the houses left no doubt that we had gotten the right people and that they were indeed AIF supporters. The names and call logs from the cell phones also confirmed that we had the right people, with the final evidence being some of the text messages we pulled off of the cell phones.

As the sun came up and we sorted the equipment, various cell phones in the piles started ringing. I could not resist, so I picked one up and answered it: "Hello. Sorry, but Haji isn't able to come to the phone right now. He's a little tied up at the moment. Can I take a message?"

CHAPTER 16

GUT CHECK

NEARING THE BEGINNING OF August 2007, we had delivered a significant blow to the AIF with our raids into Old Baqubah, and the brigade-level clearing operations on the west side of the Diyala River applied plenty of pressure on the insurgents' networks. The clearance operations on the west side of the Diyala River were steady but at a much slower pace, due to the fact that the fleeing insurgents had booby-trapped everything they possibly could to slow the advancing coalition troops. It got so bad that the only way to counter the booby-trapped houses was to blow them in place by dropping smart bombs on them. It was not worth the risk to send in EOD or other elements to deactivate the massive amounts of ordinance. Some of the houses had been packed with so many explosives that the secondary explosions leveled the surrounding houses.

With the clearance of the cities in the west completed, COL Townsend's 3-2 SBCT and 1-12's Apache Company were able to secure multiple areas and start to build up their combat outposts and plan for the subsequent operation back into Old Baqubah and then north into Chabranot to deliver the final blow to the insurgents within the Diyala River Valley. LTC Antonia and his staff from 5-20 IN came down to COP Adam to get a debriefing of Bone's previous mission in Old Baqubah and to get our take on the enemy situation that remained in our AO. CPT Austin started his brief with the background on how the mission originated and then went into the different phases of the operation, discussing each phase of the operation in detail. LTC Antonia and members of his staff listened to everything that was said, and at the end of the briefing, LTC Antonia looked at CPT Austin with a look of approval and said, "I'll tell you what: you sure did more than disrupt the AIF's activities in sector." With that, the commander and his staff mounted up and headed back to FOB Warhorse to finalize their plan for the operation into OB.

With the absence of the US or CLCs in Old Baqubah, we still had to continue conducting operations up in Old Baqubah to keep pressure on the remaining AIF and deny them the ability to establish any more networks in that area. CPT Austin had a mission planned for the very next day: a "movement to contact" mission, or "joint presence patrol," in order to show the townspeople that we were working together with the CLCs and the IA and that no one was going anywhere, anytime soon.

The missions in Tahrir started to be geared more toward stability operations than combat operations. Each platoon was assigned sectors and were out identifying key leaders and representatives for various projects to be conducted in the future. We had a long list of projects that had been on the back burner for almost a year, simply because the environment was not conducive enough to allow the projects to move forward. We started out with small projects within our own outpost to try and foster a relationship with the local "contractors." We needed to get air conditioners for the COP, and we needed various carpentry, electrical, and plumbing work done. We were authorized to purchase furniture and other living comforts, such as satellite TV, for our outpost. So the platoons went from trying to find "Butchers" and "Scientists" to finding plumbers, electricians, and carpenters.

The outpost got more comfortable as the weeks went by,

especially because people were not trying to kill us 24/7. I still had my concerns. I was worried about the CLCs turning on us, or at least someone within the CLCs. I also worried a lot about the soldiers letting their guard down. We had been in country for almost a year and did not want anyone getting busted up in the home stretch. When you've been in a hostile environment, it was easy to stay switched on 24/7. But as things started to calm down, I worried about soldiers letting complacency set in. We did everything we could to keep them actively engaged. Most of them knew the war was not over and that a serious threat still existed—and that it would only take one time for someone to let their guard down and get someone killed.

One serious threat was the chance of a suicide bomber making his way within the walls of the compound disguised as a CLC or an Iraqi police or army officer. An even greater threat would have been a direct assault with the CLCs, or someone acting as the CLCs and trying to come in under the disguise of them. That would have severely fractured our trust with the CLCs and made it difficult to work with them afterward. I did not want to take any chances so I tasked a platoon to set up a machine-gun position that covered the front-door entrance area and also posted a guard. It may not have been the most politically correct answer, since the machine gun also pointed directly down the hall to where the IA lived, but I did not want to take any chances. We had too many CLCs and contractors coming in and out of the building.

The COP began to get more comfortable, at least to us, with the air conditioners getting installed ... the plumbing working to the point that you could at least take a leak and a shower inside the building ... the barber shop ... Armed Forces Network on a big-screen TV ... the kitchen unit ... and a small patio area where soldiers could hang out and play cards or dominoes, smoke cigarettes, and just relax with only a small threat of getting killed lingering.

We had a female major come out to the COP to conduct a pre-site survey on the electrical situation and to formulate a plan for a team of real Army electricians to come out and set in outlets and a new breaker box. No matter how much we tried to get locals to run electricity, it was never to a safe standard and a lot of soldiers in country were getting killed by electrocution while on FOBs and outposts. When I walked the major through, I felt proud of how well we'd set up the COP. It was a thousand times better than when we had lived in Buhritz (hence, why we initially called this place "Bone Disney"). But during my discussion with the major, she walked into one of the rooms and came to an abrupt halt, stopping in mid-sentence and saying, "These living conditions are abysmal." I wasn't sure if she realized she just insulted the hell out of me, but she started telling me how much she was going to help us, promising that she would send someone out to get us squared away. I really did not give it much thought and figured she would just disappear like the many others that pledged some sort of help in the past before it all got caught up in the system. But one day shortly after her visit, we got the call that we had an entire section of Army electricians waiting to come out to the COP. Those guys came out and went nonstop for three straight days. They did a great job, and I was glad to say that we did not pop any more breakers or electrocute any soldiers!

Things were getting a little too comfortable, so I guess HQ figured it was time to get Bone out and about. We had lost the 5-20 scout platoon back to their battalion to support the west-side operations, and Bone had been given back to 1-12 Cavalry and fell back under LTC Goins, so it was business as usual, kind of. The task organization was a bit robust to say the least. The 1-12 Cav had been given operational control of a Stryker company in the north in Old Baqubah, but 1-12 Battalion was still assigned to 3-2 SBCT under COL Townsend and not COL Sutherland. It was confusing and amazing all in one, and it somehow all came together and worked great.

We received word that we had been tapped for a company-plus-attachments-sized mission south of Buhritz. The intelligence reports said that the town was still untouched by coalition troops and was the last and final stronghold of the insurgents in the south. The mission had Bone as the major component plus another US infantry platoon, IA platoon, and a few CLCs. The unit would go in light and kill or capture any remaining insurgents in the small village. Previous missions against this town in the past had been completed by helicopter, and they were successful. However, we had intelligence that the prospective landing zones were booby-trapped with IEDs. Not wanting to risk getting helicopters blown up on the LZs, CPT Austin opted to walk the company in.

We were once again going to park all the Bradleys and have all mounted crew become heavy weapons squads for their respective platoons. We also coordinated for a company of Strykers to come down and pick up the company to drive us to the southernmost part of Buhritz then drop us off under the cover of darkness. We would then infiltrate through a series of palm groves into the town about two and half kilometers away from our drop-off point. We figured we could maintain the element of surprise and be on top of them before they knew what was happening.

The mission was planned to last two days. While we would conduct the town-clearing mission, War Dog would clear Route Lime south and push their way to our location. The route had been reported to have multiple deep-buried IEDs on it, so it had to be cleared before we sent any vehicle traffic down it. Once they cleared the route, the Strykers would be able to resupply us, and once the mission was completed, they could pick us up and drive us back to our COP. It was a solid plan, and once again, CPT Austin jumped in with both feet and went on a personal planning jihad.

Within a few days, CPT Austin had the overall support plan and scheme of maneuver 99 percent completed. He asked for my input and perspective on it, so we war-gamed it and asked "what if" about the plan on multiple levels. We ended up building some solid contingency plans and felt pretty comfortable with the overall plan. The one biggest "what if" was, what if the road didn't get cleared in time and we couldn't get supplies in or soldiers out? We came up with a simple solution. We would carry at least one day's worth of supplies on us since it was only a two-and-half-kilometer march to the objective area. If things went well, we would be able to be resupplied by vehicles, or worst case, clear an LZ, then Blackhawks could drop resupplies. As for getting off of the objective area, we could walk back out to a pre-designated pickup point when the mission was over.

The plan had a lot of moving pieces, including another platoon coming in to help out SFC Hudgins and his platoon in manning the COP and conducting patrols in our absence. Plus the BN snipers needed to be inserted before us, and we needed air strikes on a few targets just prior to our infiltration (air strikes were a normal occurrence and were not always a precursor to a ground assault). After a few adjustments, we felt pretty comfortable with the plan, and we set off to brief LTC Goins and his staff, and to gather the last few resources for the operation. The briefing went well, and support for the mission, as usual, was not an issue. So we headed back out to COP Adam and started to prepare for the company operations order to the platoons. We would be able to get SFC Davenport's platoon rather quickly since the mission was to kick off in less than seventy-two hours.

The platoons spent the next several days planning and rehearsing their parts in the operation. We were given an Associated Press reporter who would be embedded with us from that point until the time we got back to Fort Hood. We also got an Army photographer and Army journalist for this operation. All of them were distractions that I really did not need at the moment. The AP journalist seemed pretty good. He had an easy-going attitude and seemed low maintenance from the start. I gave him the same brief that I had given the other reporters in the past about how our guys did not need any bad press, and that they were out doing a difficult job in a difficult environment, so we really would appreciate it if the press had no hidden agendas when it came time to print articles. I knew they would print what they felt, but I also hoped that they had some sort of decency and respect for the guys doing the hard job on the ground and that they did not want to use them in some slanted way. About 99 percent of our experiences with the press were positive, and we wanted to keep it that way.

In preparation for the operation, I anticipated a goat rope with the loading of the soldiers onto the Strykers. We were totally unfamiliar with this, so I gave it extra attention and figured if we could get everyone loaded in order, the rest of the movement would be good to go. Trying to get specific squads, CLCs, and IA soldiers onto vehicles in the dark, in the right order—so that when they hit the ground, they knew who was in front and in back of them—would be a challenge. I made it like a regular manifest site back at Fort Hood. I got orange traffic cones, printed out rosters of who was on what vehicle and what order they were to go into the objective on, then posted the rosters on the cones that were placed in a makeshift holding area. Then the Stryker commanders would come into the COP in the order of movement they were in and personally grab the squads that were lined up behind the cone that had their Stryker number on it. The procedure may have been a little overkill, but I wanted the operation to start out on a good note with no problems. It did, then continued well—all the way up to our infiltration into the objective area.

We were dropped off at our designated areas and put in a holding pattern until the air strikes were finished. Once the bombs were dropped, that would be our signal to initiate movement. We liked being attached to 5-20 IN, but it was nice to be back under the control of our people and have our leaders back on the ground. As we waited for the bombs to drop, we did the rucksack flop on the sides of the roads and pulled security. The illumination was less than 20 percent, so it was pitch dark. I heard a HMMWV's diesel engine idling in the shadows, so I walked back to see who was in it and found out it was CSM Harris. I was pleasantly surprised to see him there (you never knew where he would show up). He was there to support as needed with the 1-12 snipers and the 1-12 Tactical Operations Center setup since we were pushing the limits of our conventional communications equipment.

I chatted with him for a minute, then the radios broke squelch with traffic from the BN snipers, reporting that they had a team member down. They had come across some really rough terrain on their infil into the target area, and one of their guys fell into a ravine and busted up his ankle pretty bad, so they could not continue and would be heading back to the rendezvous site.

Moments later, we got the call that the fast-movers were on station and ready to drop their payloads on target. We quietly passed the word down the line that bombs were inbound, then we waited for the fireworks. They soon dropped a series of BIG bombs, explosions that rocked your internal organs to the core. With the bombing run over, we all shouldered the heavy burden of our packs, did one last equipment check, and started our movement into the palm groves. Third platoon led the company, with CPT Austin's element behind them and then first platoon. After first platoon came my element, which consisted of the company forward observers, SGT Matthews and PFC Hendrix—each carrying their own radio set on the BN fires net and a dismounted laser to guide bombs in if needed—and then the company communications specialist, CPL Pester—carrying a long-range antenna so we could reach our BN tactical operations center—followed by CPL Sieng as the battalion RTO. I was next in line, carrying a radio on the company net with the Army journalist tucked up close to me. In the rear of the formation was SFC Davenport's platoon. Everyone was loaded down pretty good with extra water, batteries, IVs, ammunition, tripods, communication equipment, breeching equipment, and explosives. No one had been afforded the luxury of traveling light—no one.

The movement started out, purposeful and steady, as we melted into the palm groves toward the distant orange glow of the palm groves that now burned up ahead, thanks to the bomb drops. As we started to maneuver through the sporadic farm fields, we noticed this terrain was not what we were used to seeing. The farm fields and palm groves were littered with massive wadis and irrigation ditches, along with smaller canals and thick underbrush laced with small strands of barbed wire. It made our movement miserably difficult. We found ourselves sliding down into these massive ravines and then having to push and pull our battle buddies up the other side—only to hit another ravine within a few more paces. It was a grueling hump that already managed to break the Army journalist's camera lens within the first few hundred meters. As we steadied under our loads and our shoulders went numb, we began to expect that the difficult terrain would be our companion for the near future and that we would just have to deal with it. We had managed to move a kilometer when we got a call from the Apaches that were over-watching our movement. They reported that our intended axis of advance was now blocked by a huge wall of fire and that we would have to come up with an alternate route, because even our planned alternate route was engulfed in flames. We did a company halt, then I linked up with CPT Austin and we called in all the PLs and PSGs for a quick huddle to adjust the route and the plan.

We decided to send a reconnaissance element forward to indentify another route into the objective area while the rest of the company did a security halt. The route recon would add another thirty to sixty minutes to our time line but it was better than the entire company walking aimlessly through the woods. Third platoon was tasked to send the recon element out, so they stripped down to just their basic equipment and moved their radio to the company frequency so they could talk directly to the Apache pilots flying above. This worked out pretty good, as the pilots identified a tentative route from the air, but we had to confirm it on the ground. It took awhile for the recon element to work its way through the woods and over the rough terrain, but they returned an hour later with the thumbs-up that they had a good route into the objective area. The bad news was that it would add an additional three kilometers, which might not seem like a lot, but considering the terrain, we would be walking the majority of the evening and it would take every ounce of energy we had.

The platoons picked up one at a time and started their movements along the new route. My element fell in and started to move quietly down a trail, keeping our intervals so we could just see the man in front of us. We moved about a hundred meters in a stop-and-go fashion for the majority of the distance—and then I realized why. We were walking up to a ravine that was at least ten feet deep and almost a straight drop down. We had to sit on the edge and inch our way off the ledge, then let gravity take care of the rest. Once at the bottom, you had to first help the man in front of you by pushing him up the other side of the ravine wall, or letting him use you as a step stool to shorten the distance of his climb as another man topside reached down and grabbed hold of the climber's hand to drag him up the steep wall. This would have been a chore during the day with no gear, and it was only the start of a long movement in.

The interval between ditches varied. It seemed that just when you got settled into flat terrain, we'd hit another ditch or ravine. About an hour in, we came across a ravine that was really deep. Luckily someone found a crossing that the Haj had made with fallen trees, mud, and grass. As I walked across it, I could feel it strain under my weight and bounce with each step. I thought, *I hope it holds.* Then I reassured myself that it had probably been there for a hundred years and three-quarters of the company had already walked over it, so why would it have broken for me? My self-reassurances ended up being correct: it did not break and safely carried me across to the other side. However, as the very next guy behind me (I think it was one of the forward observers) came across, I heard a loud snap and then a thud, and I knew exactly what had happened. The bridge had finally broken. I figured for sure that someone was hurt, so I turned around and strained to look down into the darkness. To my relief, I heard, "I'm okay. Help me out of here." I reached into the shadows until I felt someone grab hold of my hand and then I pulled him out. So the rest of the company had to make it through one at a time, down one side and up the other.

We finally hit a trail on flat ground and were able to make up for lost time. This was where the physical conditioning and long forced marches over the past seventeen years paid off. We were trying to beat the clock and get to our objective rally point before sun up, so we started stepping it out. The difference between this movement and the road marches back in the States was that here we had no truck to pick us up if we couldn't hang. And there was no finish line to cross then drop our equipment and forget about the pain. Our finish line was called the objective rally point (ORP), and it was a few demolished houses about 300 meters away on the outskirts of the town. So we did it just like the Army had trained its men since World War II. We sent our lead recon in to check it out and clear it. We had our guides for each of the platoons and we silently crept in and set up our company-size ORP and platoon sectors of fire.

It was about 0300 hours, and we had about two and half hours before the sun would start to rise. We set up 50 percent security so some guys could try and get some rest—for the few gifted soldiers that had the ability to fall asleep at the drop of a hat. I dropped my rucksack next to a building that my small HQ element had selected away from the commander's element and figured I would walk the perimeter and familiarize myself with what was out there and who was where, just in case we were attacked. I walked the lines looking through my PVS-14's (night vision) and made sure we had no gaps in our perimeter. I stopped at a few positions and checked on the soldiers to see how their feet were and just to let them know that I was out and about.

About that time, the commander checked his map and thought through the adjustments of the plan, now that we were actually on the ground. He gathered up the PLs and PSGs, then gave them the final plan and set a time for our attack in the morning.

The plan had third platoon establishing a local support-by-fire position on the edge of the palm grove with their heavy weapons squad. Their other three squads would simultaneously enter and clear the three closest buildings, one being the tallest in the village, which would give us good eyes on the rest of the village for command and control. Once a foothold had been established and an over-watch set, the rest of the platoons would move into their designated sectors and basically do the same thing.

I moved with third platoon since that was where I would set up the company command post and track progress as the platoons moved through their sectors. CPT Austin would remain fluid throughout the entire clearance operation and retain the ability to flex from one area to another without interrupting the platoons. Everything went smoothly and as planned, and we were soon inside the first three buildings, nice and quiet. We caught three suspected AIF sleeping on top of the tallest building. We initially did not find anything suspicious in their possession but knew they were fighters just by the way they looked and acted. As the sun came up, the squads found three AK-47s, hand grenades, and ammo pouches filled with AK-47 magazines and ammunition, all stashed on the rooftop under some rubble.

The rest of the platoons moved into their assigned sectors quickly and quietly. The entire village had no idea we were there. So, to their astonishment, as the sun came up, 150 soldiers were moving through their village, house by house. Everything was still on track and we had not encountered any enemy resistance throughout the day. The platoons had discovered various caches and weapons within the village, but as the day wore on, the prospects of catching people red-handed diminished.

The townspeople were not used to seeing Americans—and to further their discomfort, they saw Americans working with Iraqi army and CLCs. The family that lived in the house that we took over as our company command post consisted of three older females. I determined the oldest to be the grandmother, and the other two middle-aged women, one being a wife to a guy we found sleeping in a different section of the house. The other female was her sister, and both of them had several kids ranging from three to eight along with a young teen. We detained the man of the house for questioning since it would have been impossible for him not to know those guys sleeping on the roof. Once we detained the male, the entire family started sobbing. They all cried and screamed and slapped themselves and cried some more when they saw us pull the guy aside for questioning. No matter what we said or did, they just kept the tears and drama going. The kids eventually warmed up to us, as we bribed them with various goodies from the MREs—but the adults were not so easily had.

By 1100 hours, the temperatures climbed well into the hundreds, and the platoons were reporting they were Amber on water (50 percent of their water was used). We would need a resupply if we were going to be able to keep moving. The engineers, meanwhile, found more IEDs than had been anticipated, and the route was nowhere near being cleared, so our supply route was not open for business yet—and would not be for the unforeseen future. We decided that we would call in an aerial resupply. SFC Lane and his guys secured a school with a good-sized clearing that a Blackhawk could land in, then drop the water and take off quickly. The school was located on the far section of town, so we would "borrow" a local vehicle then load up the water and drive it to a central location for the other platoons to rotate by and conduct their resupply. Luckily we'd had every soldier pack a minimum of one extra bottle of water before we'd left for the mission. With the extra distances we had to walk due to the palm grove fire, and now with the resupply road still blocked, we could have been at a standstill.

I made a call to the BN TOC and they relayed our water request back to FOB Warhorse. I was pretty sure they had already anticipated our needs upon hearing the reports from War Dog and their slow progress on clearing the route into our objective area. Within an hour, we had the Blackhawk pilots drop down to our frequency and get further guidance from SFC Lane on the LZ. Shortly after they popped smoke, we heard the rotor blades whopping as they touched down, leaving the engines at a high RPM to take off at a moment's notice. They kicked the seventy-five cases of water off each side of the bird and were gone in minutes.

First platoon had borrowed a beat up Toyota mini truck and loaded all seventy-five cases of water onto it. As the grossly overloaded vehicle came pulling into our compound, led by a fire team of soldiers, I couldn't help but smile at the odd sight.

Amazingly enough, the water was ice cold! I don't know what our battalion or brigade did to make that many cases of water ice cold, but they did—and, damn, it was nice to have something cold. We expected the typical 100-degree water that had been sitting on the tarmac getting roasted for weeks on end. The cool water was certainly a huge morale booster for everyone!

I checked each one of the houses off of my map one by one as the platoon leaders and sergeants called them up on the radio. Our hopes of the vehicles coming down to link up with us were suddenly shattered when we heard a gigantic explosion in the distance, in the direction of War Dog. Typically, if it was a friendly explosion—also known as a "controlled detonation"—we would have been notified over the radio, but we did not get any advance warning, leading us to believe that the route-clearance team had just gotten engaged with an IED. Shortly after the explosion, our fears were confirmed. We got a report that said the Buffalo that War Dog had been using was completely destroyed, and they would thus not be able to finish the route-clearance mission on Route Lime. (CSM Harris was rolling with War Dog and later told me he was amazed that anyone even survived that explosion.)

We would have to walk our way back out, an additional four to five kilometers. With the FRAGO[52] to our plan, CPT Austin had all the platoons work their way back toward the company command post then assigned them sectors surrounding it to strong-point for the evening. The plan for the rest of the evening was to have the EOD team blow all the contraband we'd found throughout the day so we did not have to hump it out with us. We would also send out a few security patrols throughout the night. Then in the morning, we'd start working our way into the surrounding farm fields and look for caches and other AIF hiding areas, clearing our

---

52 Fragmentary order: change of plan

way out to the main MSR, where we could then be picked up by the Strykers.

By the time night fell, the platoons were ready for some well-deserved rest. They had been going nonstop for the past thirty-six hours straight. The 120-degree temperatures mixed with the heavy loads and terrain were testing the endurance levels of even the fittest soldiers. CPT Austin called the PLs in for a huddle and went over the final phases of the operation, then we settled into the tasks of getting ready for the night missions and morning movement.

The evening went by quickly, and we were soon all up and ready to move out before the sun rose. The platoons took off in staggered intervals and pushed into their assigned sectors. My HQ element—along with our three detainees and two guards from first platoon—were going to move on the tail end of first platoon's squads. We got a good start on the day, and everyone was happy to be heading back to the vehicles that awaited us after we cleared the fields.

Our enthusiasm did not last long, though. Within the first few hundred meters of getting into the fields, we were physically drained of the little energy we'd recovered overnight. Unbeknownst to me and everyone else, the fields were actually vineyards. We encountered a maze of wire about shoulder height, and the ground was rippled with long dirt mounds in which the farmers planted their seeds. The wire forced us to spend 75 percent of our time duck-walking, with only brief periods of relief between rows in the vineyard. What appeared to be an easy four-kilometer patrol turned into a nightmare of obstacles for the soldiers on the ground. The movements were slow and painful as we picked our way north to the linkup point.

After we finally cleared the vineyards, we had to stop and wait for the other platoons to get online, as some platoons were in even worse terrain. While we remained at a short halt, first platoon sent out a small recon team to scout ahead and see if we would have to deal with any more surprises. When the fire team pushed forward, they found a hide position that the AIF used for an observation post and an IED trigger position. They found the ends of a command wire and traced it 300 meters to Route Lime, confirming that it was still hooked up to an IED. We tried to detonate it with a radio battery but it did not want to blow, so we had to call the EOD team we had attached to us to come forward and place a charge on the IED.

The attached EOD team was pretty good. They were Johnny-on-the-spot the evening prior, blowing the items the platoons had found throughout the day—and they did not whine or snivel about all the walking they had to do. Typically the EOD teams were mounted in their vehicles but we were able to get these guys the entire time with us on the ground, which was a major perk. So the EOD team carefully worked its way up to the IED. One guy crawled up to the mound of explosives dug into the side of the road and placed a charge on it, then carefully worked his way back to the initiator. We got the word: thirty seconds until controlled detonation—and then a "Five, four, three, two, one ..." *BOOM!* We all watched and PVT Hendrix videotaped the massive explosion. That particular IED was huge, and if that was the size that War Dog had hit the day before, it was no wonder CSM Harris said it was a miracle that anyone had survived.

With the controlled detonation complete, we moved out once again in the direction of the vehicles, up and over Route Lime and down into some more palm groves and farm fields. Everyone was running on fumes by then. The temperatures again climbed into the 100s, and the terrain presented one obstacle after another. It took every ounce of energy I had to hurdle a small drainage canal. The muscles in my legs and back felt like they were on fire. My legs were moving on pure reflex and muscle memory as we continued to move toward the vehicles. Every time we stopped to pull security for crossing a road or a trail, it was a major effort to get back up from the kneeling position. We took a final security halt a few hundred meters out and called the Strykers so they would not shoot us as we entered the clearing. I could hear the slight sound of the engines running in the distance, and it got louder as we worked our way to the awaiting vehicles. Finally we saw the lead Stryker and then the others lined up behind it. What a great sight! I posted myself up at the lead vehicle, and as the platoons flowed through, I got the up on sensitive items and personnel and watched everyone load up on the vehicles. Once I was sure we had everyone on the Strykers, I told CPT Austin we were good to go. Then the two of us loaded up on separate vehicles and off we went, back to our COP.

Once back, the guys were fired up and full of energy, knowing the mission was over and that we were only about forty-five days away from getting out of the Diyala Province and heading home. The cooks were out in the kitchen mixing up some omelets and French toast sticks for the boys, so I went out and gave them a hand. NCOs don't eat before the soldiers, so I figured I would show off my cooking skills and help the cooks make the omelets as the guys filed by with their plates in hand. After the last guys filed past, I made myself an omelet and went into the COP to sit down and eat. Looking around, I saw that the guys' previous adrenaline had been overtaken by the cool air of the COP and their full bellies. Everyone was slowly fading off into a well-deserved sleep.

CHAPTER 17

MOVE THAT BUS!

IN EARLY NOVEMBER, NO one wanted to talk about going home, especially when they were still in an extremely dangerous environment. The past month and a half had come and gone with a drastic reduction in violence. Tahrir and Old Baqubah had almost returned to normal with the traffic jams and pedestrian foot traffic. The vendors and storekeepers had their shops open on a daily basis and had tripled their inventories, which in my opinion was a good sign that they were willing to invest in their future.

The CLCs had been working out okay for the most part, with the exception of two specific incidents. One incident involved Gun Dog getting into a firefight with them in the middle of the night as they occupied an over-watch position. Once again, the CLCs were in a place they did not belong. So when Gun Dog occupied a building right next to them, they thought Gun Dog element was a group of insurgents moving in on them and started shooting. Of course, Gun Dog returned fire and tossed hand grenades over the walls, driving them out of the building, on which we then had our mortars drop some 120mm love. The most interesting part of that evening was that we had air weapons teams on station shortly after the initial fighting took place, so we got an alarming play-by-play from the Apache pilot as he described the action to us from the air. It was disturbing to see how efficient the CLCs were at reinforcing and withdrawing fighters from an area. The CLCs dispatched two vehicles—one an ambulance and the other a larger passenger car with an additional six fighters to the area—within minutes. They beat our own QRF to the location.

After a heated debate and arguing on the ground, the elements departed from one another and went back to their posts, since no one in their right mind was going to go near that location after all the shooting and fireworks that had just taken place. We had the pilot track the ambulance and the car back to their hideout so we would know the location for any future contingencies—and it would be a good piece of intelligence to know where they had a so-called safe house. It was all part of the game, and we were more than willing to play.

The other incident involved CPT Austin and me directly—well, more so CPT Austin. I was just there for moral support. We were asked by the CLC leaders to have a meeting, so, as usual, we obliged and arranged a meeting to take place at COP Adam. The meeting started out as a friendly get-together, with the head of the CLCs. The guy's name was Haji (seriously, you can't make this stuff up!). The meeting started with the typical greetings, hand-shaking, and chest-tapping, then settled down into the small talk. We could tell something was not right, and Haji seemed a little nervous and kept beating around the bush about his reason for the meeting. We figured he wanted more money, and our suspicions were soon proven correct when Haji admitted that was what he'd come to talk about. CPT Austin tried to be as diplomatic as possible, staying firm with the previously agreed-upon amount. As the conversation dragged on, I sat a little away from the table going over in my head how I would draw my 9mm from my holster and deciding whom I would shoot first if I had to. Probably not someone's everyday thoughts during a meeting, but this wasn't your everyday meeting.

Out of nowhere, Haji abruptly told CPT Austin that he and his CLCs were going to break the agreement if they did not get more money and that we would have to deal with the consequences. Suddenly CPT Austin's voice rose higher than I had ever heard it in that type of setting. He leaned forward at the table and told Haji: "That's fine. You want to leave because you're not getting paid enough, then go! But ... if one IED goes off, or one shot is fired at my men, I will come and hunt you down. I will drop a bomb right on your house.!"

When CPT Austin said that, I was all fired up and gave every single one of them my best "Yeah, what he said" look, with my hand resting non-threateningly on my 9mm. CPT Austin had called his bluff, and we soon sent them on their way. Within twelve hours of their departure, we had another meeting to rectify the situation. If anything, after that first meeting, the productivity of the CLCs increased over the remainder of our time in Tahrir. We did, however, initiate an incentive program in which they could get paid for weapons and IEDs that they turned in and reported to us. The program worked so well that we had to tell them to stop bringing IEDs to us and instead to leave them in position and just call us, as the last thing we needed was a bunch of Middle Eastern dudes running around Tahrir with IEDs in carts and cars. We'd had enough of that over the past fourteen months.

In the final days of our rotation out at COP Adam, one specific event really caught my attention. One of the squads was out conducting its daily patrol in the community when an elderly gentleman that lived on C (or Chuck) Avenue stopped the squad and warned them about an IED that had been put in the road several months ago. It was hidden so well that when the citizen showed the squad leader exactly where it was, it took every bit of the squad leader's imagination to find the outline of the IED within the blacktop road. When I heard that report come over the radio, it cemented my personal thoughts and made me feel pretty confident that we had finally beaten the insurgency in our sector. We had been trying to gain the community's support in defeating the insurgency for the past fourteen months. So with that one old man's act of telling a patrol about the IED, we had hard evidence on the ground that all our fighting and sacrifices were finally paying off.

Soon 2 ID departed the area for its journey home, back to Fort Lewis. The unit that would relieve us began trickling into FOB Warhorse and building up their combat power. The atmosphere was still intense, but we were not used to having so much quiet time, so we were waiting each and every day for something bad to happen. We continued our patrols, and if anything, we were even more vigilant, trying to counter the "smelling the barn" syndrome.

We did, however, have a warm feeling inside us as the many projects we'd set on the back burner were actually starting to gain traction and become realities, including having the school right outside COP Adam's walls get funding to be rebuilt. We also did community medical and dental missions, supported by both the IA and CLCs. Locals for the first time in years, or maybe even their lifetime, were actually seen by a doctor. We had multiple police stations manned and operating 24/7. We turned the COP in the south of Buhritz completely over to Iraqi army units. We reopened a gas station that had been closed for years under the Saddam regime. The electricity ran more consistently and all the power lines that were destroyed in the fighting were now getting repaired. We paid local construction companies to clear and repair the roads and fill the hundreds of IED craters so that traffic could flow more freely. We paid other residents to remove the abandoned cars that littered the roads and side streets. We were pumping thousands of dollars into the community each day and giving the economy a jump start. It was truly an amazing site to witness, as the city transitioned from being a ghost town that had death looming in the air to being a thriving city eager to get back to some sort of normality.

With things cooling down in sector, I started shifting my focus to redeployment and making sure that we got caught up on all the administrative issues that would quickly overwhelm me if I did not get on them. The end-of-tour awards were due. Non-commissioned officers' evaluation reports had to be up to date, and with the turbulence of our battalion S-1 shop shutting down to prepare for the redeployment, we had to make sure we were a month or two ahead. I also had a few other battles that I had to fight administratively, including Purple Heart awards for two soldiers. The awards had been submitted earlier but were kicked back to me, denied. The first wounded soldier in question (at least in someone's mind it was a question) was PVT Cunningham, who had been shot in the arm. Although it was a grazing gunshot wound, I figured being shot was being shot. The other soldier had been hit with shrapnel during a mortar attack on the FOB and had to go to the aid station and have it removed from his forearm. The criteria for a Purple Heart are somewhere along the lines of "wounds inflicted by the enemy," and I thought that was pretty clear. But apparently it hadn't been clear, and the awards were kicked back. The frustrating part was that there are no measurements of how many ounces of blood must be leaked, or what dimensions of a wound a soldier must suffer to be awarded the Purple Heart. So it's left as a judgment call by a staff person. In this case, he or she for whatever reason declined them. I knew it was a lost cause to fight it, and it is a sore subject for me to this day.

To add fuel to the administrative fire, CSM Harris gave me a printed list of who was on orders to leave the unit when we got back to Fort Hood. It appeared to be almost all the upper leadership, including me. Knowing this, I had to make sure the PSGs, PLs, and squad leaders were getting on the awards and NCO evaluation-writing bandwagon, or we would be way behind the curve. Awards had to be submitted up to 120 days out, depending on what chain of command they had to go through for approval.

Unfortunately administrative duties didn't stop just because there was a war going on, and that included the retention and reenlistment program. I assigned SSG Johnson as our retention and re-up NCO, and he did an excellent job finding out all the different options available for our troopers. If an incentive existed, we wanted our soldiers to know about it: bonuses, MOS change, stability, Ranger School, Jump School, college, etc. The truly amazing piece of the retention mission was that, despite all the madness that Bone Company witnessed in and had partaken in over the past fourteen months, our reenlistment numbers were through the roof. Our company surpassed FY06 (fiscal year 2006) numbers, and we were on track to meet FY07 yearly reenlistment numbers by the second quarter. Bone was leading the brigade in reenlistments! I credited those results to leadership on all levels and to truly caring about a soldier's future, both personally and professionally.

We were scheduled to start "right-seat riding" with the incoming unit in a few days, and we had a ton of stuff to get ready. I had also been given the heads-up that we were going to be doing a battalion awards ceremony out at COP Adam. The awards would be for all the personnel being awarded the Purple Heart or a Valor award. So it was decided that it would be appropriate to do it out at COP Adam since Bone was unfortunately leading the BN in Purple Hearts and Valor awards. The reason why I say "unfortunately" about the Valor awards is that usually if someone gets a Valor award, it means that someone else was killed or wounded.

The award ceremony went without incident and it was nice to see all the soldiers get recognized for their heroics. GEN Odierno had come out to pin on some of the awards and talk to the men and praise 1-12 Cavalry for their dedication to the mission and sacrifices. It was great to see the top leadership come out and give us an "Atta boy."

Amongst some of the Bonecrusher awardees out at COP Adam that day were: SSG Fili (Bronze Star with Valor), SGT McGrath (Bronze Star with Valor), SSG Embry (ARCOM with Valor), PFC Myers (ARCOM with Valor), Doc Devries (ARCOM with Valor), SSG Wallat (ARCOM with Valor), LT Pijpaert (Purple Heart), PFC Russell (Purple Heart), and PFC Davis (Purple Heart). The BN snipers received several valorous awards that day as well. The most senior person to receive a medal that day was CSM Harris; he received the Bronze Star medal with Valor for his actions at the BIP in December. Many of Bone's soldiers and leadership received awards from 2 ID prior to their departure from Iraq. Several other soldiers were recognized for their bravery and achievements once back at the States.

Now that the inbound unit was on the ground, I conducted linkup with their company first sergeant. We did a few sit-downs together and then we went out to the COP, where I gave him the tour of his new home. I don't think he was as enthusiastic about getting the COP as I was about giving it to him. I told him some of the do's and do not's that would make his life easier, and I also introduced him to the Iraqi 1SG that lived on the other side of the COP. Later I took him out on a few patrols to show him the area and let him get a feel for the environment. To an outsider coming into our city and seeing the aftermath of the fighting and trying to comprehend exactly how this much destruction occurred, I think it could be overwhelming. He, like most first sergeants, once shown the big picture, had his mind set on how he wanted to do things and told me he appreciated the help and insight. Then he said he was ready to get to work and that if he had any questions, he would come find me, so I left it at that and focused on my company (by the way, I never saw him again).

At that point, I was 100 percent focused on redeployment and getting everyone home as fast and smoothly as possible. The major issue back at Fort Hood would be housing for the single soldiers and the soldiers who were geographical bachelors (wives still living in another state). Bone left Fort Hood from one barracks area and would be moving back into another completely different barracks area, so everything had to be restructured from scratch. It was a daunting task but between me, the XO—now CPT Branford—and SSG Morales, we got a solid plan together and made the best of it. In preparation for the entire company coming in, SSG Morales was sent back in advance to Fort Hood. I was confident that he would do everything he could to make sure Bone got the best that was available, or at least what was expected.

The next few days were a flurry of activity: trying to get things loaded, cleaned, inventoried, packed, signed over to the new unit, plus damage statements, battle-loss statements, and more miscellaneous paperwork than anyone could imagine. Someone brought up that we should load up our Bradleys and take them back to Kuwait to be sent to the United States to be restored/refitted. As we went down the list of vehicles to be loaded, we realized that with all the destruction that had happened to our vehicles, only one of our original fourteen Bradleys would be loaded up. The rest of what we had were loaners throughout the BN and theater-provided equipment (TPE), and would be sent back to their original owners. SSG Williams, SPC Osbourne, and SPC Aparicio were the only crew that had made it through the entire rotation without losing a Bradley (hit multiple times by IEDs, but repaired). The amazing part of that equation: they were the lead Bradley in every movement for their platoon the entire rotation. In total, our company had lost eighteen out of fourteen assigned Bradley's (three replacements were destroyed), and three of four M1 tanks had also been destroyed.

Another sobering event occurred when I scrubbed the platoon rosters in order to get the barracks rosters and the flight manifests completed. As I went down the list of names, I realized just how many replacement soldiers we had received and how many soldiers had left the company throughout the tour, one way or another. Out of the 140 soldiers now on the roster, 30 percent of those (42) were replacements. In total, Bone had thirty-two wounded in action, and eight killed in action, including the two Dealer Company soldiers—CPL Barta and Trussel—the three HHC soldiers—Doc Nguyen, SPC Nash, and SGT Schaffer—and CPT Jensen (Thunder 6) from 5-20 IN, 2nd ID, who'd lost his fight and died of his wounds back at Fort Lewis in Washington state. That brought the total to fourteen KIA soldiers that had been part of Bravo Company during Operation Iraqi Freedom 06-07.

I quickly stashed those thoughts away into the "deal with later" file in my brain and shifted focus back on the task at hand, which was getting everyone home. It was a long-awaited and welcome task that everyone took on with pleasure. Though we still had some complaining and griping, everyone could finally see the light at the end of the tunnel.

The Dumpsters were overflowing with various items that the soldiers had decided weren't worth the hassle of trying to get through customs inspections. The amount of junk that had been acquired and later discarded from the rooms was staggering to say the least. Other enterprising young soldiers were out trying to make deals with the incoming units, selling anything from power converters, TVs, guitars, and PlayStations to refrigerators and probably many other items I did not want to know about. It was getting closer and we were ready.

I decided that I could best serve the company by being on one of the first main-body flights out of country. The XO already returned with the advance party with the arms room NCO and a supply specialist, and the commander had to stay and finish up the property books with the incoming unit. So that left me to take the first main-body back for the company. I was not complaining.

The movement plan was for us to fly out of FOB Warhorse on Chinooks. They would be running shuttles all night to get everyone to Balad Airbase. Once at Balad, we would stay at least a day or two and then take a C-17 to Kuwait, which is where we would wait for a commercial flight into Fort Hood, with a refueling stop in Germany or Ireland.

We were slated for a 20 November flight out of Kuwait, so we started our movement from FOB Warhorse on the eighteenth. We turned in all our ammunition, packed our bags, stacked the bags outside to be loaded onto a truck, then cleaned our rooms and headed down to the helipad to manifest for our flights. The flights would not start until evening to reduce the risk of getting shot at, so we still had a little bit of time to kill. We hung out in the gravel parking lot, and some guys put on headphones and stared off into space, while some thought about their families or girlfriends, and others thought about that new shiny car or motorcycle they were going to buy with the money they'd saved while in Iraq. Others talked openly about their reunions with their families and loved ones. The most entertaining stories to listen to were from the single guys that were teaming up and hatching plans to go out on the town and party. I thought to myself that Dallas/Fort Worth, Austin, and San Antonio were in for some trouble if those guys followed through with their plans.

I, too, finally gave in and let my mind drift off to a happy place—the thoughts that I had deprived myself of since I first came over to Iraq, the thoughts and dreams that I had locked away because they were so far off and at times just that: dreams. I had thoughts of Jen and Abby, and what our reunion would be like, about how nice it would be to walk on carpet in my bare feet, to smell clean sheets on a comfortable bed, to go to the bathroom in the middle of the night without having to walk fifty meters, to not have a weapon everywhere I went, to eat real food, to see no sand or dust, and to not worry about getting shot when I went outside. I was getting excited.

Then my excitement turned to worry. I had missed another birthday for Abby. By that point in her life, I had not really been a part of it, and she was already four years old. I knew Jen was also more independent, having totally turned her life over to God and becoming a devoted follower of Christ, and really getting involved with North Pointe Church in Copperas Cove. They had become her family in my absence, and I started to wonder how all this was going to work out. I was by no means a "born again" Christian and I had every intention of going back to my normal life, which, when away from the Army, involved drinking beer, partying, and wrenching on and riding motorcycles. Since I'd left for Korea in 2004, I spent thirty-four months away from the family, so naturally I wondered if we were still going to be compatible, and if we would make it. Then, though, I decided to just enjoy the pleasant thoughts of a happy homecoming.

I was quickly brought out of my happy place at the sound of incoming choppers. I grabbed my kit and started strapping it on. Everyone was ready to load up and get the hell out of there. It was safe to say that no one would be missing this place. The Chinooks touched down, and the crew chief came out and guided us up the back ramp and into the hollow body. I was the last to get on and sat down in the seat closest to the rear ramp. I always liked that seat, as it gave me a chance to see outside as the earth and the sparsely lit towns zipped by en route to our new destination—one step closer to home.

The flight to Balad was short and uneventful. After landing, we got on awaiting buses and were shuttled to a holding area where we signed in and waited for our bigger plane to carry us into Kuwait. We spent a day in Balad then flew out that evening on a C-17 and landed in Kuwait. We got on buses again and went to Camp Virginia, where we would hopefully jump on flights the very next day and be on our final leg home. Once in Kuwait, everyone was pretty fired up. It was really real: we'd made it out of Iraq! An unusual easiness hung in the air, one that had not been felt up to that point. The farther we distanced ourselves from Iraq, the easier it became to let our guard down.

I was given the word that we would be flying out the evening of the twentieth and that I needed to have everyone ready to manifest at 1700 hours. I went back and gave the platoon representatives the timeline and told them to make sure everyone had good haircuts and a shiny uniform for the flight home. I did not want any rag bags getting snatched up by some sergeants major and ruining our homecoming. This was it: we were on our way home. Everyone took their final showers and tossed their toiletries and everything else they did not absolutely need for the flight home. We cleaned and swept the tent, organized the cots, and went out into formation.

I went over to the head shed to get an update and final instructions, and was quickly notified that the flight had been cancelled. We would not be leaving that night. So I had to go back to the same tent and stand by for further instructions. At that point, I was glad they had taken all our ammunition away from us, since I had to go back and tell the entire group that we would not be flying out that night. I walked back, gathered the entire group around me in a horseshoe formation, and reluctantly told them,

"There has been a slight change of plans." I figured that would soften the blow a little bit—and it did, but not much. I finished up with a, "We'll try it again tomorrow, but don't get your hopes up."

The next day was an exact repeat of the previous, with the exception of the mass disappointment, as the guys kind of expected it. The thing that really pissed everyone off was that they had to go buy new toiletries. The other big one was that the families back home had expected us two days ago. They were spending extra vacation days, or just flat-out missing workdays. In addition to the idle time at the Fort Hood/Killeen area, they were spending extra money on hotels and food. I knew there had to be some disappointed families and kids. I knew one soldier's family was on a tight timeline because of their business, and they ended up having to fly back before ever even seeing their son. I hate to say it, but you can never bank on flights and a redeployment timeline, and we warned everyone many times in the past—nothing is 100 percent.

Finally 22 November rolled around, and we were given the green light and told the buses were en route. No one believed it, including me, and I would not allow myself to get one bit excited until I was actually sitting on an airplane. Well, sure enough, the buses came rolling in and loaded everyone up, then we were off to the airport. Unlike the bus rides in, everyone was wide awake and ready to go. We went right from the buses onto a plane and settled in for our flight home. After what seemed like forever, the plane finally cranked up and started to taxi down the runway. I could feel the excitement building in the pit of my stomach as the plane picked up speed. Then the nose of the plane lifted off the ground and I finally felt the thud of the wheels lifting off of Middle Eastern soil. A slight cheer came from the inside of the plane, and like a switch had been thrown, everyone went to sleep in hope of waking up one stop away from the US.

The flight home was long and uneventful, and I do not even recall the country where we stopped to refuel. I do remember watching the digital readout and the plane icon moving closer to the glowing outline of the United States on the TV screen. As the icon got closer, I got more fired up and started mentally going through what all had to be done before I left with my family. I knew we had to turn in weapons and a few sensitives, and that task alone had the potential to be a total goat screw if things went wrong. I also needed to take care of billeting for the soldiers. Then paperwork: there was always paperwork that needed to be finished, and my mind kept racing from one task to another, all of which had to be completed before we could be released to our families. Oh, then there was the final formation. I dreaded the days of when some general got out in front of the returning troops and unleashed a verbal assault, torturing the soldiers and their families with a forty-five-minute speech to display how great his public speaking skills were. I hoped that the welcome-home speech would be short and sweet. I also hoped that someone had taken time and put some effort into the baggage pickup, as there was nothing like losing your bag or spending an hour looking for it while your family waited for you. The soldiers already been safety-briefed to death, so if things were as squared away as I hoped, I would be back at my house within three hours of touching down at Robert Gray Army Airfield.

As the plane's flight crew readied the cabin for our final approach, I could feel the tension build inside the plane. Everyone opened the shades and strained to look through the clouds for their first glimpse of the United States in a long time—and for some, a sight they thought they would never see again. I was looking out and trying to identify where we were. I saw the 4th ID water tower and the rows of empty motor pools. I knew it wasn't long now. The plane banked, and my view turned to sky and then back down to a ground view. Then the plane leveled off and we were on our way down.

I felt the wheels come out of the belly of the plane, then the wings tilted to create drag and reduce airspeed. It was getting real close. Then back wheels thudded on the ground, and a roar went up inside the plane. Everyone started hooting and hollering. They made it. We made it. I made it.

An Air Force sergeant and some Army officer came on and briefed us about the procedures of deplaning and the processing scheme of maneuver, and then we quickly deplaned. As we walked down the steps, the 1st Cavalry band was playing, and a general officer and a string of other high-ranking officials were there to shake the hands of every returning soldier. We were ushered over to a hangar where they had all the companies broken down, and supply representatives and arms room personnel waiting to take our weapon and sensitive items—and the single soldiers signed for their room keys on the spot. Everyone was then handed a small instruction booklet that had a time line and instructions to follow once our four-day pass was over. Then we were ushered to awaiting buses and loaded up for our trip back to 1st Cavalry Division Headquarters, where our families were supposed to meet us and we were to get our bags.

When the buses drove off from Robert Gray Airfield, we had an MP escort with the lights flashing and the sirens going. They blocked off all the intersections so we could go straight to division HQ without delay. On the route through garrison, we saw signs and "welcome home" banners strung all over the place. It was apparent that the family readiness groups were working overtime in anticipation of our homecoming. As the buses looped around the division HQ building, we came to a stop on the main road in front of the parade field, where they had road guards and police cars everywhere. It was quite the production they had going on, but then again, it was the cavalry—and they tend to do things big!

The road guards pulled the buses up close, so close that we thought the buses were going to hit each other. I did not know what was going on, but it seemed organized and well planned. Once all the buses were parked tight up against each other, we were instructed to get off the buses and line up in one mass formation. As I jockeyed my way to the rear of the formation, I could hear some chanting. It was ALL the family members in the bleachers, yelling, "MOVE THAT BUS! MOVE THAT BUS!" Just as we got organized, the buses pulled forward and we marched across the parade field. WOW!

The general that gave the speech must have been on the parade field at one time himself, as his speech took less than three minutes. Then we were released to find our families in the crowd. Some families had prearranged signals with balloons or colored clothing. Not mine. I can always sense when they are around— or so I thought. I stood there as the crowds started to disperse and just watched in amazement that such a production was going on. The people in charge of making sure our homecoming was unforgettable (in a positive way) did an awesome job!

I stood all alone for a minute, just enjoying the moment, as I watched various soldiers reunite with their families. I had some soldiers walk their wives and parents over and introduce them to me. I'd shake their hands, and it made me well up inside with pride, knowing that the soldiers would take time to introduce me to their parents. The loved ones in turn thanked me for looking after their husband/son while he was away from them.

The crowds began to thin out, and everyone was walking toward the massive tents the cavalry had put up to stow our baggage. I figured that I would find Jen and Abby there. As I turned and started to head in that direction, I felt a little hand slap me on my butt. Knowing that could be only one person, I turned around to be hugged by my wife and daughter.

Home at last!

AUTHOR'S NOTES

SHORTLY AFTER MY TOUR in Baqubah, Iraq, I received orders to report to the University of Central Florida, where I had the distinct honor and pleasure of being the Senior Military Instructor and MS III Instructor my final years in the Army. I tell everyone I can that I could not have asked for a better assignment to retire from. To be given an opportunity to share not only my real-world combat experiences with the Army's future leaders but also to be able to share some of my personal and lifelong experiences was a true blessing from God.

I would like to think of my Author's Notes as a counseling statement to anyone who is willing to listen. In my older and wiser years, I have been able to see a small portion of the future based on the past and would like to share a few points with the young and upcoming leaders.

Civilian and Military Education

Education is the key to everything in life, no matter if you're a soldier, NCO, officer, or civilian. It will help you be a wiser person and help you throughout life. If you do not take the time to learn and to better yourself, you have no one to blame but yourself when the world passes you by—and it will. If you are not challenging the way you think and the way others think, you will be doing yourself, your family, and the people around you an injustice. Challenge yourself to be a better person both personally and professionally—to go from good to great. Remember, you don't know what you don't know.

The military services all have excellent educational benefits for enlisted soldiers. If both officers and senior NCOs take the time and really put an effort into motivating and mentoring our younger enlisted troopers, we will be a better Army for it. The soldiers can get a good education, and everyone involved can benefit from it now and in the future. There is life after the Army, and you have to take time and prepare for it now.

For the high school graduate who wants to go to college first and be an officer later, you have many ways to go about it. You can go to any major state university, like the University of Central Florida, that offers an ROTC program and join—or just sign up for the classes and feel it out to see if it is what you like, and then make your decision to join or to go onto other ventures in life. No commitment up front—and if nothing else, you'll have fun, meet people, and learn something about leadership. Or you can go off to one of the many academies, like West Point, Virginia Military Institute, Georgia Military College, etc. Chances are there is something out there that fits what you're after. I think all the programs have pros and cons, but when it comes to instruction, they all have one thing in common to offer and that is LEADERSHIP. It is up to the individual person to take it from there and apply it.

Leadership

You can argue the fact that "leaders aren't born they are made" all day long until you're blue in the face. My opinion is you have to be born with the desire to be a leader. I have seen people throughout my career that had no business being in front of soldiers because they lacked the desire and I had to ask myself "Why?" So I am going to tell you why: someone failed along the line and did not want to hurt someone's feelings. I have heard the "We have to give him/her a chance to succeed or fail, first," when it was obvious what the outcome was going to be (I am not talking about people with potential or in training environments). The most unfortunate part about the "let them try first" theory is that the soldiers, NCOs, and officers around them suffer in many ways, just for the sake of not wanting to tell someone "You may want to find another career field, because you're just not cut out for this type of work." The soldiers deserve the best and we owe it to them!

Leaders MUST share in the hardships and dangers with their soldiers. If they stay detached from the soldiers' reality and the reality of what is actually happening in real time, they can't effectively plan and execute accordingly. A leader who does not share in the hardships of his soldiers will never gain the respect of their troopers. I am not saying they have to be there 24/7. As a matter of fact, the soldiers don't want them around 24/7, but there needs to be a balance. Leadership is not a right; it is a privilege and an honor to be trusted with America's sons and daughters, now including my own daughter. So get out and lead!

Lead by example: always, and in everything you do. Soldiers and subordinates are watching everything you do. They will take notes on your personal appearance, personal habits, personal relationships, work ethics, self-discipline, physical fitness, overall health, and everything else that you expect them to excel in. They will look to you as the standard bearer and then try to emulate you. NCOs are the official standard bearers and enforcers, but there is nothing more detrimental to an NCO's authority than when someone says, "Oh, that. Well, they can do that because they are an officer or a senior NCO." Wrong! Everyone must be on the same sheet of music.

Training

Training needs to be taken seriously all the time. I have heard too many people say, "This is just training; we'll do it right when it is for real." Are you kidding me? If you're not doing it right, how are you going to make improvements on it and refine the technique?

Train as you would fight! Never say, "This won't happen in real life." Soldiers and officers are finding themselves coming straight out of training and going right into a real-world situation where people's lives depend on them to do what they were trained and taught to do. If they fell asleep in a class, cheated on an exam, or skipped out on a training event, they cut a corner—and that may have been the one class or training event that might have saved them or their buddies' lives.

Cross Training

Everyone in a company needs to be trained/familiarized on everything within its mission essential task list, and more. Soldiers go on leave, get wounded, killed, sick, and relieved. Equipment that works well in one situation may not work well in others, and equipment breaks. You have to remain flexible in how you fight and not become solely depend on the status quo.

Resources

You will never have ALL the time, troops, and equipment when fighting a war. Just read the history books: I don't think there has ever been a commander or a soldier that wrote a book and said they had too much time, too many soldiers, or an overly efficient supply system that pushed too many supplies to them. Get over it! You don't have what you don't have, so make the best out of a bad situation. That's what leaders do.

What I have written in my Author's Notes is really nothing new. I just felt like I had an opportunity to maybe influence a few more people before this book was over with. If I have spurred just one person's thoughts, I have accomplished my mission. Thanks for listening.

TESTIMONY

GOD HAS A PLAN for everyone, and I am a firm believer that everything is happening to us for a reason. It is up to us to figure out why. The closer you are to God, the easier it is to identify what the true motives are. For myself, I like to call it "connecting the dots." As I have ventured through life, I have had some significant events happen to me and some not so significant (at the time), but as I look back on things, I can begin to draw the lines from dot to dot. I can answer why things happened the way they did.

Well, I have come to the conclusion that it is God's way of making a lasting impact. Just like some of the hardheads out there (like me), I probably would have chalked up one big event to a coincidence and never thought about it again. But the constant steady thumping upside my skull has finally made me come around.

When Jennifer turned her life over to God in Copperas Cove, Texas, in that tiny little congregation, I remember sitting there asking myself, "When am I going to have my defining moment with God?" I always waited for "the moment" that would turn me around like I had read about in so many books of people's "born again" moment. That never really came—even as I sat in my room in Baqubah, Iraq, after we had lost SSG Ross, SGT Shaw, and PFC Camacho, and I was on the verge of a breakdown until I had the Bible verse come into my head: God will only give you what you can handle. Yes, that verse helped me get through that evening and many other difficult times since then. And it still helps me, and I tend to share it with people when the opportunity presents itself. But it wasn't like it all came together in that one moment.

So I am still connecting dots, and every time I do, it just reassures me that God is in control and not me. I would like to share some of my dots with you.

Ramadi, Iraq, 2004-2005

I was a platoon sergeant for thirty-five soldiers for 2nd Platoon (Hell-bent) C Co 1-9 IN, 2nd ID, and was doing my regular duties, just feeling my way through my first combat tour. About every month or so, I would get a care package in the mail from some strange church in Florida. I had no idea who they were and I really did not care. The package was addressed to me, and it had goodies in it—that's all that mattered. I'm talking good stuff, too: CDs, movies, batteries, candy, and various other items—even a CD of a church service, which I would look at and say, "Sneaky church people trying to buy me with their gifts," then toss it back into the box. After I had taken what I wanted, I would toss the package aside for my soldiers to root through. An entire year went by, and I kept getting these packages. It was always the same routine: open, raid, give leftovers to soldiers. I never thought anything of it. The end of my tour came around, and I rotated back to the States and carried on with life.

When I had come back from that tour, I stayed home for a few days to see the family, then took a road trip on my motorcycle to Florida by myself to unwind and see some family, including my daughter, Brianna, who was fourteen at the time. She had come down from Pennsylvania, and I was pretty excited—and nervous—about seeing her. I really had not spent any time with Brianna since her mother and I divorced in 1994, and she really did not know who I was. I had always wanted custody of her, but being in the Army and away and single for the better part of my adult life, it was not in the cards. When I made it to Florida, the visit went great. I got to hang out with the folks, see Brianna, and ease myself back into the real world. Then it was back to Texas to hang out with the family for the remainder of my leave.

Nothing out of the ordinary really happened while I was back in Texas between tours, with the exception that Jen and Abby were going to church every Sunday. Sundays were our family day, and I was starting to get a bit suspicious of all this church stuff, so I told Jen I was going to go to church and see what was going on—especially since this was the "Christian church stuff." I didn't want her getting "healed" and then drain our bank account because of some slick-talking preacher. So I went to see what was going on. We went in separate vehicles because she did volunteer work and needed to be there early. So I rode my chopper, and I did not bother to dress up. I went in my riding clothes since my Shovelhead tended to sling oil off the chain and put a stripe up my back. Besides, I really wasn't there to impress anyone. I rolled in and gave everyone the "What are you looking at?" stare as I gunned my straight pipes through the parking lot and parked out front away from the few other shiny bikes. I kicked my kickstand down with a little extra authority and slid of my bike to be greeted by a man who introduced himself as Pastor Billy.

"Wow, that sure is a neat ride!" he said with genuine enthusiasm.

I was like, "Yeah, I know. Whatever, Pops." Then I walked away.

I went inside to listen to what they had to say and was extremely critical of the people and the words that came out of their mouths. I was a Catholic, and anything different was just malarkey. So I went about my business of exposing their true motives and listened extra carefully so that I had a good argument for Jen on why we should not bother with the church stuff. As I was listening, I almost got up and walked out in the middle of the service, just because I could, but Pastor Billy was a pretty entertaining guy and somewhat funny, so I figured I would stay and listen to what he had to say. Besides, it meant a lot to Jen and I did not want to embarrass her. When the service was over, Jen introduced me to Pastor Billy's two sons, both of whom rode bikes, so we all talked for a minute as I walked outside to my bike. They followed me over to my bike and checked it out, then asked some questions and made small talk. I felt a little uncomfortable, so I excused myself, jumped on my bike, gave her a quick kick, slapped it into gear, and rolled out.

Jen never said anything to me and never forced me to go to church, or gave me an ultimatum to go to church or else. I guess she figured that would not work too well. However, in the meantime, little did I know that she was doing some covert operations and praying for me every day and every time she went to that church—and had been doing so since she first went to that church when I was in Iraq. Sneaky and unfair, I know. After the first time I set foot in Trinity Living Center (now known as North Pointe), I made it to church more often than not. They seemed like good people, and I liked hearing Pastor Billy and the message he was sending out to the people. It was not a big church—about fifty or so people in the services—so it felt pretty personal.

I also felt good about the company Jen was keeping, especially since I was staring at another tour in Iraq in less than six months. The months came and went pretty quick. I focused more on my job and the upcoming deployment than I was on church and God, so I started to slip on my trips to church, trying to catch up on sleep and things around the house, but really it turned out to be any excuse I could think of not to go to church. I was still running hard with my friends and trying to catch up on the good times I missed on the last deployment—and trying to stock up on the good times before the upcoming deployment. I have always worked hard and played even harder. Always ready for a good time, I did not need an excuse for a ride; I would roll out on the drop of a dime.

Deployment time rolled around on 11 September 2006. I was on my way to Iraq again. The deployment was quite the zinger. On occasion I tried to pray to God in my own way. It went something like, "Lord, please keep me and my men safe and don't let us get blown up today. Amen." I did read a few books Jen had sent out to me. One was about an NCO in the Rangers during the "Blackhawk Down" saga in Somalia and his story of how he turned his life over to God. Stephen Baldwin, the actor, and Brian Welch, the bassist and song writer for the band Korn, also had written books and I read them both. All these books were about dudes that were rough around the edges and somehow had managed to seek God as their savior. I read them, but did the "Good for them, that's nice" and left it at that.

During that deployment, my God-related experience really only consisted of that one time when we had lost SSG Ross, SGT Shaw, and PFC Camacho. But ever since that moment, I had an unusual calm about everything and felt like God had me out there doing his work—and maybe needed someone a little rough around the edges at that specific place and time.

Remember the packages I got while I was away on my first deployment? Well, they started back up again, and this time I was getting even more. I remember opening one up and looking on the inside extra careful to find a name or a card, but it was still just full of cool stuff—and church CDs. So I went into my routine of pulling out things that I wanted and taking the rest out to COP Adam or setting it outside my door (there was a collection spot there for people who had received care packages and wanted to share).

Next thing you know, I was back in the United States and celebrating my return every day. I was twice as bad with my drinking and partying. I just kept going and really didn't care about anything. I was working out in the garage on my friend Bill's Panhead every chance I got. When we were done working on it for the day, we would sit in the garage and drink beer and talk about everything under the sun until the wee hours of the morning. Jen never said a word and just let me go about my business. I knew I was going down a slippery slope. I felt so guilty on the inside that I started going to church on a regular basis. I figured if I was going to act like a fool on Friday and Saturday, the least I could do was make her happy and go to church. The thing was, I liked going to that church. Pastor Billy and his boys were good solid people, and the members of the church were real nice and took good care of Jen and Abby while I was gone—and that deployment was just as rough on her as it was me.

Within a few months of being back, I received an e-mail out of the clear blue from the Department of Army, assigning me to University of Central Florida in Orlando. I almost fell over. I'd never gotten assignment like that, so I wondered how in the hell I lucked up. My parents lived down there, and I had always wanted to live in Florida. I figured eventually, when I retired, I would head down there and at least go to one of their motorcycle mechanics schools and then head back to Texas or wherever I decided to retire. So this was a great opportunity for the entire family to go down and feel things out, without making anything permanent.

Jen was a little less thrilled than I was. She was happy with the way things were: we had a nice house in a nice neighborhood, and she spent her free time making our home how she wanted it. We were going to a good church, and I had a good opportunity to get a job around Fort Hood when I retired. She had also started up her small church ministry and had invested a lot of time and energy into it, and thus did not want to leave it behind. That was all way too safe for me. I was ready to head off to Florida and not look back. We decided to feel it out and see what happened, but Jen made it very clear that it would take a miracle for us to live down in Florida forever.

We went down on a visit to my parents to scout out a neighborhood or an area that we might want to live in, so that when we went back to Texas, we could house hunt online. During our visit to Florida, Jen had a less than exciting time. We did do Disney and some other attractions, but we never did really find a "great neighborhood" that fit our criteria. My parents kept asking, "Why don't you just live in Daytona?" I told them I would love to, but the commute and gas money on top of rent would have been too much. I would have to find a place pretty cheap and I did not see that happening in Daytona.

We went back to Texas and went about our business. I was still busy being a 1SG and working on Bill's bike. Now, though, we had a deadline, as I had to have his bike built before the end of May 2008, the month we planned to leave for Florida. So the two of us went into high gear on the weekends. With the tight timeline and only working with Bill on the weekends, I had skipped church a few times to get ahead. It seemed like every time I skipped church to get ahead, things would go wrong and I was in worse shape than if I would have not worked on the bike at all.

Jen and Abby would come back from church, and I'd be working in the garage. Jen could always tell when things weren't going right, and she would tell me, "That's God's way of telling you to go to church."

Fast-forward a few months: I had turned in my first sergeant diamond for some master sergeant rank and really did not have a job, so that provided me a little extra time to out-process and work on Bill's bike. As it was getting down to the wire, my mother called and told me that the guy next door to them called and said he wanted to sell his house and wanted to know if my parents were interested. My parents had wanted to buy the house for the past sixteen years but the guy never wanted to sell it. But he always said, "If I ever do decide to sell it, you guys will have first offer on it." Well, needless to say, they made an offer on it, and soon it was a done deal, which meant that my parents then offered to rent us their newly purchased house at a reasonable rate.

I was pretty excited about living next door to my parents. I had missed out on having parents locally over the past eighteen years, so it would be nice, plus they could have a grandchild running around too. I figured we would be able to make up for lost time and then some.

About this time, Abigail was continuously getting sick (bad belly aches and coughing all the time) at school and at home for some unknown reason. Both Jen and I knew something was not right and made multiple doctor's appointments to try to find out what was wrong with her. We kept getting random diagnoses and treatments/medications, but nothing was working. It was to the point we were getting upset with the medical provider and were going to switch, but since we would be leaving town in a few weeks, we decided to wait until we got to Florida and start fresh.

Well, Bill's bike went down to the wire. The movers were moving things and loading the truck as we were doing the final assembly on his bike. My father had come to Texas to help get the house squared away to rent and also help with the move.

The move went great and we found ourselves living in Daytona Beach, Florida. I was not too thrilled about the commute to work, but it was a sacrifice I was willing to make for my parents to be around us and for Abby to have her grandparents around. One of the first things on the "to do" list was to find a doctor for Abby—and Jen wanted to find a church to go to. So we went out church-hopping for a few weeks.

The church-hunting expedition felt kind of like being Goldilocks. Some were too big, some were too small, and one was just right. The day we found our church, we had gotten lost and showed up with only twenty minutes of the service remaining. But we walked in, slid into a row, and listened to what was being said and how it was being said. I looked around at the people and felt pretty good about what I was experiencing. I leaned over to Jen and told her, "I like this church." She looked at me and said, "Me, too. We'll have to come back for a full service." I gave her a head nod and we continued to take in our surroundings.

As the service was ending, the praise and worship team started to play. They were high-energy, and I really liked it and so did Jen, so that was another major plus. Before we walked out, I looked up on the screen and I saw something that almost knocked me over. It was the church logo—the same logo that had been on all those packages and church CDs I received on both my tours in Iraq, dating back to 2004. I froze in place and told Jen—and we were both in shock!

Well, we had found our church: Tomoka Christian Church, and Pastor Joe Putting was the man. He reminded us a lot of Pastor

Billy. The congregation was a little bigger but it still had a personal feel to it. So that was a major dot connected for me.

As we continued to get settled into our new home and I got settled into my new job, things seemed great. I was spending more time with the family (both my parents, and Jen and Abby). My job was great and I had a great boss: LTC Christiansen. He was laid back, but all business when he needed to be and had a good way of putting people at ease. And I needed someone like that at the time, since I was making one hell of a transition from a combat infantry first sergeant of 135 soldiers to a college environment with young students. It was interesting, to say the least. LTC Christiansen only had to put me in the proverbial headlock a few times.

One day at the office, I got a call on my cell phone and it was Abby's doctor's office. The nurse told me she could not get in touch with Jen so she decided to try me since I was listed as the alternate. With very little warning, the nurse went on to say that they had done some preliminary tests on why Abby was having a bad cough and belly aches all the time—and the results came back positive for cystic fibrosis. My world stopped, and it felt like someone had just hit me with a baseball bat. I paused, gathered my thoughts, and asked, "Exactly what is cystic fibrosis?" She could or would not tell me a lot over the phone, saying that I should come and talk directly with the doctor. Then she told me that she would still attempt to call Jen since she was the primary point of contact on the registration form. I asked her to let me tell her, but she insisted that she had to notify the primary contact.

After my phone call with the nurse, I went in to talk to LTC Christiansen and told him about my situation, and that I wanted to leave work early and try to be the one to tell Jen, plus I wanted to sort through exactly what cystic fibrosis (CF) was and what we were going to do about it. LTC Christiansen told me two things that really stuck out. The first was that with ROTC, we actually had time to be there for our families in tough times like the one I was experiencing at the moment. And the other: there were two other members of the cadre team—a husband and wife—that had a child with CF, so he gave me a telephone number in case Jen or I wanted to call them to talk about it.

With the talk complete with LTC Christiansen, I jumped in my truck and headed back to Daytona Beach to be with my wife. The ride from UCF in Orlando to the house in Daytona was exactly one hour. That gave me some time to sort things out on the way back. The first thing that struck me was how fast we got a diagnosis since we had been in Florida and how nice it was to just be able to leave work without worrying a whole lot about leaving the soldiers (school had not started yet).

I made it to the house in the one hour as usual, but it was too late: Jen had already gotten the call and been informed. She was handling it better than I was; maybe I subconsciously wanted her to be there for me? Or maybe we were there for each other. Naturally we went straight to the Internet to look up CF and read everything we could about it. And that confused and scared me even more. After the Internet scare, I decided I would call the number the LTC had given for the Nelsons (whom I had never met). Within a few minutes of talking to Jovanna, I felt okay. She reassured me that one of the best CF medical treatment facilities in the country was right there in Orlando!

Another dot had been connected.

Jen and I talked at great length about this. Here we thought that God had made it possible for us to go to Florida so I could be with my parents and pursue schooling for a career after the Army in motorcycles. We could not have even imagined in the slightest that he had sent us to Florida so we could have the best care for our daughter! Wow ... God is great.

The thing is, God wasn't even close to being finished. The verse that I always remembered was that he will only give you what you can handle. So we eased our way into our new situation pretty good. Abby, like always, was a trooper and went with the flow of things and settled into a routine as a young child with CF does. The school year had started, and I loved being an ROTC instructor. I enjoyed teaching and telling my Army stories and philosophy to the young leaders. They were like sponges and soaked up everything I told them. I had also been working on the side building motorcycles and fixing them on the weekends with whatever free time I had. It was a great opportunity for me to get a feel for the motorcycle world in Daytona Beach, and seeing if it was something I was willing to continue doing when I retired from the Army.

The school year flew by and we were heading into summer. I was getting further into the motorcycle customizing and repair, and had even opened a part-time shop that I ran on the weekends, working on friends' and friends of friends' bikes and selling parts both from the store and swap meets. Things were looking okay, but I was killing myself and barely paying the bills for the shop. Every spare moment I had was invested into the bike shop, and it seemed like even when I was not at the shop, I was doing something for the shop. I never let it interfere with my Army work, but my family sure did take a backseat. I justified it in my mind, figuring that it was an investment for the future.

As summer started to wind down, I got a call from my ex-wife in Pennsylvania. Things were not going well with her and my daughter, so she asked if I could take care of her. Without any hesitation, I said, "Yes, let me go talk to my boss and see when I can come up to get her." LTC Christiansen had retired at the end of the school year and had been replaced by LTC Morgan. So I went into LTC Morgan's office and explained to him what was going on. I asked if I could leave on a four-day pass and drive up to Pennsylvania to pick my daughter up. Again, it was summer, and school was not in session—and was not scheduled to start for another week or so. He gave me the go-ahead, and I was in Pennsylvania late the next evening. I picked up Brianna and was on my way back to Florida with her shortly thereafter.

Yet another dot had been connected. I had always known, deep down inside, that I would get custody of my daughter. I just did not know when or how. Well, it turned out I got her a week before she started her senior year in high school. The great part about her coming to Florida (other than her hanging out with me and my family) was, with her high GPA and love for academics, I knew she would be a shoe-in for the Florida Bright Futures Scholarship and college, if she stayed on track. And with the help and love of our family, I knew she would make it, no doubt.

Within six months of Brianna being in Florida, she came to know Jesus, who up until that point had been a complete stranger. She turned her life over to God at Tomoka Christian Church and became an active member in the youth ministry and church choir. Wow again!

As of this writing, I have retired from the Army. My family and I have settled down in Ormond Beach, close to Tomoka Christian Church. I closed the bike shop and decided to keep motorcycles as a hobby, not a career.

Jen leads her ministry at church, and it is bigger than she ever could have imagined. Abby is doing great and we continue with her treatments and pray for a miracle each and every day. Brianna graduated with honors from high school and is now enrolled in the University of Central Florida's US Army ROTC Program, and going to college full-time in Orlando.

My life with God is just beginning, and I struggle every day with trying to break free from my way and instead doing things his way. I know he is in charge of my life and has a purpose for me. So I will take it as it comes. I have faith.

I would like to close by saying that once my life is done on this earth, if someone were to connect all the dots that God created in my life to see the final picture—which up until that point was just a canvas with random dots—it would be a picture of Jesus on the cross, dying for my sins.

May God bless you, the US Armed Forces, and the United States of America!

Quiiisssh ...

This is Bone 9, out!

ACKNOWLEDGMENTS

I would like to give special thanks to the following people:

God: Thank you for your guidance and strength in my darkest hours. Thank you for putting all these great people in my life and keeping me on the right path. Thank you for giving me the wisdom and knowledge to make the decisions I made in both my personal and professional life. I look forward to each and every day and having a small piece of your plan revealed to me.

Military Contributors: LT Ebarb, LT Pijpaert, SSG Embry, SGT Demuth, SPC Waldo, SPC Cabreja, SFC Malaki (Fili), SFC McGrath, SSG Heinz, SGT Sisson, CPT Conely, 1SG Davenport, and SSG Wallat. Thank you for bringing up some of the hard memories and helping make this book a reality.

Stacy and Ben Shawiak, John David Kudrick, Greg Colella, Brett Swanke: I want to thank you for your counsel, expertise in writing, insight, and opinion. If it was not for each of you, this book would still be a thought.

Chain of Command: COL Sutherland / CSM Felt and LTC Goins / CSM Harris and MAJ Poznick for allowing me to be part of the team.

Soldiers of Bonecrusher: For your daily sacrifice, heroics, compassion, and inspiration.

To the wives, children, and parents of Bone: For your long long days and nights of worry, unwavering support, letters and packages, and taking care of each other.

The Iraqi soldiers and citizens who were willing to stand up and fight for their freedoms side by side with the Soldiers of B Co 1-12 CAV.

Thanks to all the soldiers and units that fought side by side with Team Bone, and a special thanks to 5-20 Infantry and the Wolfpack AWTs.

Call Sign "Sidewinder 25" and "Sidewinder 26" Blackhawk crews that came into a hot LZ to extract our scouts from a catastrophic event.

MAJ William Gibbons (USMC) for his insight and counsel during the final stages of the book.

President George W. Bush for having the guts to go against the popular opinion and do what was right.

To Pete Chapman and Marc Austin: Thank you for your friendship and most of all your leadership.

Mom and Dad, thanks for instilling in me the values and discipline that made me who I am today.

Jennifer, Brianna, and Abigail: Thank you for your personal sacrifices in supporting me and the team without complaint or question. Your support and dedication to me and my job contributed greatly to my success. Your support allowed me to focus on the troops and the fight, and for that I cannot thank you enough. You guys are my motivation for everything I do.

Helping Our Warriors

In closing, I would like to take a few moments to help bring awareness and support to a few veteran programs that I have witnessed firsthand as they have made a difference in the lives of *our* veterans and their families.

With the war in Iraq ended and the war in Afghanistan drawing to a close over the next year or so as I write these words, I have no doubt that the discussions of the news anchors and newspaper headlines will have long shifted to other domestic and worldly events. American citizens will turn their focus to the current state of affairs and the future of an America not at war, as both conflicts will have slowly slipped away into the history books.

Unfortunately for the wounded service members and their families, they will have a constant daily reminder of the price paid for our freedoms and security that we as Americans enjoy each and every day. Some service members will be reminded as they strap on their prosthetic legs and arms before starting their day. Other wounded service members will have the reminders of war as they negotiate the day's trials and tribulations in their wheelchair, while still others will be reminded by simply looking into a mirror or closing their eyes at night.

In order to help the veterans of our great nation meet these daily struggles head on and be victorious, they need our help now—and for many years to come. I don't *ever* want the wounded service members or families to think that America has forgotten about them.

I want to ask you, the reader, to take a moment and go to the websites listed for the following programs and to read their mission statements, success stories, and how the programs are making a difference in the lives of *our* veterans and their families. I respectfully challenge each and every reader to reach out and help one of these organizations.

WOUNDED WARRIOR PROJECT

The mission of Wounded Warrior Project™ (WWP) is to honor and empower wounded warriors. The purpose of WWP is to raise awareness and to enlist the public's aid for the needs of injured service members, to help injured servicemen and women aid and assist each other, and to provide unique, direct programs and services to meet their needs. To get involved and learn more, visit **www.woundedwarriorproject.org.**

http://teamrwb.com

Vision and Mission

Team Red, White & Blue's (Team RWB) vision is to transform the way wounded veterans are reintegrated into society when they return from combat and exit their position.

While much has improved since the post-Vietnam era, some polarization between veterans and our society still exists today. Strong relationships between wounded veterans and their fellow Americans are critical to veterans' reintegration into civilian life as well as our nation's success. That's why Team RWB's mission is to enrich the lives of wounded veterans and their families.

Team RWB works toward this mission by focusing on three key areas:

1. ENDURANCE EVENTS

Endurance events (e.g., half-marathons, marathons, ultra-marathons, triathlons or even hikes) allow the Team RWB community to come together and honor the commitment and dedication of our veterans – both in service and now during their struggle for reintegration. More specifically, these events help raise awareness and funding, and connect Team RWB members with other like-minded individuals to inspire our movement of personal appreciation and caring for war service veterans and their families. Team RWB sponsors its own events and organizes Team RWB participation in existing events throughout the country. However, our movement would not be possible through Team RWB-sponsored or organized events only. Athletes are encouraged to represent Team RWB in any event that is of interest to them and/or host their own events in support of Team RWB. Examples include 1 mile fun-runs or 5k races for family and friends, long-distance hikes or walks and community bike rides.

2. SOCIAL LEADERSHIP-BASED NETWORK

During a June 2010 study of Iraq and Afghanistan combat veterans, almost all veterans surveyed expressed interest in services to help adjust to civilian life. Additional research has shown that 90 percent of today's war service veterans actively search for information and connections online. Team RWB will launch a social leadership-based network using social media and other interactive tools to meet both of these needs, achieving local impact on a national scale. Once complete, teamrwb.com will enable all interested team members to create relationships within and outside their local communities. This network/community will serve as the backbone for raising awareness and funds, and connecting wounded veteran families with athletes, advocates and others.

3. ONE-ON-ONE RELATIONSHIPS

Today's veterans face many challenges to successful reintegration into society following their experiences in a combat zone. Short-term solutions can include medical prescription drugs or counseling; however, research has shown that veterans' reintegration challenges can be compounded by feelings of isolation from no longer being part of a "unit" or team. Team RWB aims to combat these challenges by connecting veterans and their families with others (known as "advocates") through meaningful, friendship-based relationships. Wounded veterans and advocates define the exact nature of their relationship, ensuring each relationship is mutually beneficial and unique. To better meet veterans' needs, advocates will focus on the "everyday" – not the spectacular: being a friend, spending time together and performing small acts of kindness on a personal level.

http://teamrwb.com

ISG Robert S. Colella, Retired

Association of the United States Army

www.AUSA.org

Since 1950, the Association of the United States Army has worked to support all aspects of national security while advancing the interests of America's Army and the men and women who serve.

AUSA is a private, non-profit educational organization that supports America's Army - Active, National Guard, Reserve, Civilians, Retirees, Government Civilians, Wounded Warriors, Veterans, and family members. AUSA provides numerous Professional Development Opportunities at a variety of events both local and national.

THEIR MISSION

AUSA represents every American Soldier by:

- Being the voice for all components of America's Army
- Fostering public support of the Army's role in national security
- Providing professional education and information programs

THEIR VISION

As the premier voice for America's Soldiers, we are a dedicated team committed to building the best professional and representative association for the world's best Army.

THEIR VALUES

- Excellence
- Innovation
- Professionalism
- Inclusiveness
- Integrity
- Responsiveness

ADVOCACY

AUSA speaks out for the men and women of the United States Army who proudly serve our country.

This is a great organization that gives soldiers and veterans a peace of mind.

Please help support.

ABOUT THE AUTHOR

ROBERT S. COLELLA WAS born and raised in Levittown, Pennsylvania. He graduated from Harry S. Truman High School before joining the US Army and serving throughout the world, including multiple tours of duty in Iraq. He retired as a senior military instructor with the University of Central Florida's ROTC program. He lives in Florida with his wife, Jennifer, and two daughters.